Broadway on Record

Recent Titles in Discographies
Series Editor: Michael Gray

International Discography of Women Composers
Aaron I. Cohen, compiler

Walter Legge: A Discography
Alan Sanders, compiler

The Rudy Vallee Discography
Larry F. Kiner, compiler

Rockin' the Classics and Classicizin' the Rock:
A Selectively Annotated Discography
Janell R. Duxbury

The American 45 and 78 RPM Record Dating Guide, 1940-1959
William R. Daniels

The Johnny Cash Discography
John L. Smith, compiler

A Discography of Hindustani and Karnatic Music
Michael S. Kinnear, compiler

Women in Jazz
Jan Leder, compiler

The King Labels: A Discography
Michel Ruppli, compiler

Thank You Music Lovers:
A Bio-Discography of Spike Jones and His City Slickers, 1941-1965
Jack Mirtle, compiler

John McCormack: A Comprehensive Discography
Paul W. Worth and Jim Cartwright, compilers

Count Basie: A Bio-Discography
Chris Sheridan, compiler

The Symphonies of Gustav Mahler
Lewis M. Smoley, compiler

V-Discs: First Supplement
Richard S. Sears, compiler

French Horn Discography
Michael Hernon, compiler

The Clef/Verve Labels: A Discography
Michel Ruppli, compiler

The Cliff Edwards Discography
Larry F. Kiner, compiler

BROADWAY ON RECORD

A Directory of New York Cast Recordings of Musical Shows, 1931-1986

Compiled by
Richard Chigley Lynch

Discographies, Number 28

Greenwood Press
New York • Westport, Connecticut • London

Library of Congress Cataloging-in-Publication Data

Lynch, Richard Chigley, 1932-
Broadway on record.

(Discographies, ISSN 0192-334X ; no. 28)
Includes index.
1. Musical revues, comedies, etc.—Discography.
I. Title. II. Series.
MLL56.4.046L9 1987 016.7899'12281'097471 87-11822
ISBN 0-313-25523-7 (lib. bdg. : alk. paper)

Library of Congress Catalog Card Number: 87-11822
ISBN: 0-313-25523-7
ISSN: 0192-334X

First published in 1987

Greenwood Press, Inc.
88 Post Road West, Westport, Connecticut 06881

Printed in the United States of America

The paper used in this book complies with the Permanent Paper Standard issued by the National Information Standards Organization (Z39.48-1984).

10 9 8 7 6 5 4 3 2 1

For my parents, who introduced me to
records and record collecting

Contents

Introduction

The purpose of this discography is to provide a listing of the songs and the singers who performed them as recorded on commercially available original cast albums of the popular Broadway and Off-Broadway New York musical theatre. Chronologically, it covers the period from the opening of The Band Wagon on June 3, 1931, to that of Me and My Girl on August 10, 1986, fifty-five years later. There are 459 recordings listed, with some 6000 song titles represented.

The term original cast means that the performers on the recording actually appeared on stage in the show. Also included are recordings by casts of revival productions. However, this discography only lists those cast members who actually performed songs on stage and then recorded them for the original cast albums; it does not include actors who did not sing either on stage or on the recording, nor does it include the titles of songs performed on stage but not included on the recording. There are also the occasional instances where the stage performer was replaced on the recording, because of illness or contractual problems, by someone else. Therefore, the show recordings listed sometimes differ from the stage productions both in cast and song. I did not include recordings of scores by casts assembled only for the purpose of making the recording, or what are known as studio cast recordings. Operas, children's shows, radio broadcasts, archival recreations, one-person shows, folk revues, and recorded plays that may have included a song or two also were excluded in the compilation of this discography.

The entries are arranged alphabetically by show title and each contains the show's opening date and the name of the theatre in which it opened. Revival productions are identified and any multiple recordings of the same show are arranged chronologically. The original record label and number are given, as is information on the most recent reissue. Whether the recording is in mono or stereo or available as a compact disc (CD) is also indicated. Composer, lyricist, and conductor credits are given, along with source material for the book if this appears in the original show credits. Cast members who sing on the recording are listed alphabetically.

All the songs included on the album are then listed in the order they are performed on the recording, followed by the name of the artist(s) who performed them. The broken lines (---) separate the different sides of the record. Additional composers and lyricists are also listed when, as in the case of revues, different persons contributed to the score of a show. All of this information is occasionally followed by a note of interest to the reader.

Following the alphabetical discography is a chronological listing of the productions. There are two separate indexes. The first lists performers in alphabetical order, each performer followed by the titles of all the albums he or she sings on which are also listed alphabetically. The second, the Technical Index, is a listing of composers, lyricists, and musical directors, again in alphabetical order with the show titles following. A song title index having proved unwieldly, the researcher is referred to two detailed song indexes: Bloom, Ken, _American Song_ (Facts on File, 1985) and Hodgins, Gordon W., _The Broadway Musical: A Complete LP Discography_ (Scarecrow, 1980).

There are many individuals I would like to thank for their assistance in the preparation of this discography, including the staff of the Rodgers and Hammerstein Archives of Recorded Sound, The New York Public Library at Lincoln Center; and all of the dedicated individual collectors who donated their time and thoughts to this project. I would also like to acknowledge the help the following two volumes provided me: _The Collector's Guide to the American Musical Theatre_ by David Hummel (Scarecrow, 1984), and Jack Raymond's _Show Music on Record_ (Ungar, 1982).

In addition to the four reference sources noted above, the following titles will be of interest:

Bordman, Gerald. _American Musical Theatre_. Oxford, 1978.
Craig, Warren. _Sweet and Lowdown: America's Popular Song Writers_. Scarecrow, 1978.
Gottfried, Martin. _Broadway Musicals_. Abrams, 1979.
Green, Stanley. _Broadway Musicals Show by Show_. Hal Leonard, 1985.
Jackson, Arthur. _The Best Musicals_. Crown, rev. ed., 1979.
Lewine, Richard and Alfred Simon. _Songs of the American Theatre_. Wilson, 1985.
The New Grove Dictionary of American Music. Macmillan, 1986.
Rust, Brian. _London Musical Shows on Record_. Gramophone, 1977.
Show Music. A Quarterly Journal. Preeo, Max O., editor. 5800 Pebble Beach Blvd., Las Vegas, NV 89108
Wildbihler, Hubert and Sonja Volklein. _The Musical: An International Annotated Bibliography_. Saur, 1986.

Broadway on Record

Discography

THE ACT (October 29, 1977, Majestic Theatre)

DRG Records 6101 stereo CD

Music: John Kander; lyrics: Fred Ebb; musical direction: Stanley Lebowsky

Cast: Gayle Crofoot, Roger Minami, Liza Minnelli

Songs: Shine It On (Minnelli, chorus)
It's the Strangest Thing (Minnelli)
Bobo's (Minnelli)
Turning (Shaker Hymn) (Minnelli, chorus)
Little Do They Know (Minami, Crofoot, chorus)
Arthur in the Afternoon (Minnelli)
The Money Tree (Minnelli)
City Lights (Minnelli, chorus)
There When I Need Him (Minnelli)
Hot Enough for You? (Minnelli, chorus)
Little Do They Know (reprise) (chorus)
My Own Space (Minnelli; John Kander, piano)
Walking Papers (Minnelli, chorus)

AIN'T MISBEHAVIN' (May 9, 1978, Longacre Theatre)

RCA CBL 2-2965 (two records) stereo

Music: Fred E. Ahlert, Herman Autrey, Ada Benson, Harry Brooks, Hoagy Carmichael, Nat 'King' Cole, Fred Fisher, Porter Grainger, Charlie Johnson, Harry Link, Frank McHugh, Billy Mayhew, Everett Robbins, Roy Turk, Thomas Waller; lyrics: Fred A. Ahlert, Ada Benson, Nat 'King' Cole, Dorothy Fields, Fred Fisher, Porter Grainger, Murray Horwitz, Charlie Johnson, J.C. Johnson, Ed Kirkeby, Ted Koehler, Frank Loesser, Richard Maltby, Jr., George Marion, Jr., Billy Mayhew, Andy Razaf, Billy Rose, Lester A. Santly, Roy Turk, Clarence Williams, Joe Young; musical direction: Luther Henderson

Cast: Nell Carter, Andre DeShields, Armelia McQueen, Ken Page, Charlaine Woodard

Songs: Ain't Misbehavin' (cast) music: Waller, Brooks; lyrics: Razaf
Lookin' Good but Feelin' Bad (cast) music: Waller; lyrics: Santly
'T Ain't Nobody's Biz-ness If I Do (DeShields, cast) music, lyrics: Grainger, Robbins, Maltby, Horwitz
Honeysuckle Rose (Page, Carter) music: Waller; lyrics: Razaf
Squeeze Me (McQueen) music: Waller; lyrics: Williams
Handful of Keys (cast) music: Waller; lyrics: Maltby, Horwitz
I've Got a Feeling I'm Falling (Carter, cast) music: Waller, Link; lyrics: Rose
---
How Ya Baby (DeShields, Woodard, cast) music: Waller; lyrics: J.C. Johnson
The Jitterbug Waltz (cast) music: Waller; lyrics: Maltby
The Ladies Who Sing with the Band (DeShields, Page) music: Waller; lyrics: Marion
Yacht Club Swing (Woodard) music: Waller, Autrey; lyrics: J.C. Johnson
When the Nylons Bloom Again (McQueen, Woodard, Carter) music: Waller; lyrics: Marion
Cash for Your Trash (Carter) music: Waller; lyrics: Kirkeby
Off-Time (cast) music: Waller, Brooks; lyrics: Razaf
The Joint Is Jumpin' (cast) music: McHugh; lyrics: Razaf, J.C. Johnson
---
Entr'acte (orchestra)
Spreadin' Rhythm Around (cast) music: McHugh; lyrics: Koehler, Maltby
Lounging at the Waldorf (McQueen, Woodard, Page, Carter) music: Waller; lyrics: Maltby
The Viper's Drag (The Reefer's Song) (DeShields, cast) traditional
Mean to Me (Carter) music, lyrics: Turk, Ahlert
Your Feet's Too Big (Page) music, lyrics: Benson, Fisher
That Ain't Right (DeShields, McQueen, cast) music, lyrics: Cole, Maltby, Horwitz
---
Keepin' Out of Mischief Now (Woodard) music: Waller; lyrics: Razaf
Find Out What They Like (McQueen, Carter) music: Waller; lyrics: Razaf
Fat and Greasy (DeShields, Page) music, lyrics: Grainger, Charlie Johnson
Black and Blue (cast) music: Waller, Brooks; lyrics: Razaf
Finale:
I'm Gonna Sit Right Down and Write Myself a Letter (Page) music: Ahlert; lyrics: Young
Two Sleepy People (McQueen, Page) music: Carmichael; lyrics: Loesser
I've Got My Fingers Crossed (Woodard, McQueen, Page) music: McHugh; lyrics: Koehler
I Can't Give You Anything but Love (DeShields, Woodard) music: McHugh; lyrics: Fields
It's a Sin to Tell a Lie (Carter, cast) music, lyrics:

Mayhew
Honeysuckle Rose (reprise) (cast) music: Waller; lyrics: Razaf

AIN'T SUPPOSED TO DIE A NATURAL DEATH (October 20, 1971, Ethel Barrymore Theatre)

A and M Records SP 3510 (two records) stereo

Music, lyrics: Melvin Van Peebles; musical direction: Harold Wheeler

Cast: Barbara Alston, Toney Brealond, Marilyn B. Coleman, Bill Duke, Gloria Edwards, Joe Fields, Clebert Ford, Arthur French, Minnie Gentry, Carl Gordon, Albert Hall, Jimmy Hayeson, Sati Jamal, Lauren Jones, Garrett Morris, Madge Wells, Ralph Wilcox, Dick Williams, Beatrice Winde

Songs: Just Don't Make No Sense (French)
The Coolest Place in Town (Edwards)
You Can Get Up Before Noon Without Being a Square (Wilcox)
Mirror Mirror on the Wall (Fields)
--- Come Raisin Your Leg on Me (Coleman)
You Gotta Be Holdin Out Five Dollars on Me (Gordon, Wells)
Sera Sera Jim (Jones)
Catch That on the Corner (Ford)
The Dozens (Hayeson)
--- Funky Girl on Motherless Broadway (Brealond)
Tenth and Greenwich (Winde)
Heh Heh (Chuckle) Good Mornin Sunshine (French)
You Ain't No Astronaut (Hayeson)
Three Boxes of Longs Please (Hall)
Lilly Done the Zampoughi Everytime I Pulled Her Coattail (Morris, Alston)
--- I Got the Blood (Duke)
Riot (orchestra)
Salmaggi's Birthday (Williams)
Come on Feet Do Your Thing (Jamal)
Put a Curse on You (Gentry)
Just Don't Make No Sense (finale) (cast)

ALL AMERICAN (March 19, 1962, Winter Garden Theatre)

Columbia KOS 2160 stereo reissued: CSP AKOS 2160

Music: Charles Strouse;lyrics: Lee Adams; musical direction: John Morris

Cast: Ray Bolger, Anita Gillette, Eileen Herlie, Ron Husmann, Fritz Weaver

Songs: Overture (orchestra)
Melt Us (Bolger, chorus)

What a Country! (Bolger, chorus)
Our Children (Bolger, Herlie)
We Speak the Same Language (Husmann)
It's Fun to Think (chorus)
Once Upon a Time (Bolger, Herlie)
Nightlife (Gillette, chorus)
I've Just Seen Her (Husmann)

Physical Fitness (chorus)
The Fight Song (chorus)
I Couldn't Have Done It Alone (Husmann)
If I Were You (Bolger, Herlie)
Have a Dream (Weaver)
I'm Fascinating (Bolger)
The Real Me (Herlie, Husmann)
Which Way? (Bolger)
Finale (chorus)

ALL IN LOVE (November 10, 1961, Off Broadway, Martinique Theatre)

Mercury OCS 6204 stereo

Music: Jacques Urbont; lyrics: Bruce Geller; based on Sheridan's The Rivals; musical direction: Jacques Urbont

Cast: David Atkinson, Gaylea Byrne, Lee Case, Michael Davis, Dom de Luise, Christina Gillespie, Mimi Randolph

Songs: Overture (orchestra)
Poor (Byrne, Atkinson)
What Can It Be? (Gillespie, chorus)
Odds (de Luise, Atkinson)
I Love a Fool (Atkinson)
A More Than Ordinary Glorious Vocabulary (Randolph, Cass)

The Lady Was Made to Be Loved (Cass, Atkinson)
Honour (Davis, de Luise)
I Found Him (Gillispie)
Day Dreams (chorus)
Don't Ask Me (Atkinson)
Why Wives? (Davis, men)
All in Love - Finale (Cass, Atkinson, chorus)

ALLEGRO (October 10, 1947, Majestic Theatre)

RCA LOC 1099 mono

Music: Richard Rodgers; lyrics: Oscar Hammerstein II; musical direction: Salvatore Dell'Isola

Cast: John Battles, Patricia Bybell, William Ching, Annamary Dickey, Julia Humphries, Roberta Jonay, Sylvia Karlton, Lisa Kirk, Kathryn Lee, Muriel O'Malley, Robert Reeves, Gloria Wills

Songs: Joseph Taylor, Jr. (chorus)

I Know It Can Happen Again (O'Malley)
One Foot, Other Foot (chorus)
A Fellow Needs a Girl (Dickey, Ching)
So Far (Wills)
You Are Never Away (Battles, chorus)

To Have and to Hold (chorus)
Wish Them Well (chorus)
Money Isn't Everything (Jonay, Lee, Humphries, Karlton, Bybell)
The Gentleman Is a Dope (Kirk)
Allegro (Battles, Kirk, Reeves, chorus)
Come Home (Dickey, chorus)

AMBASSADOR (November 19, 1972, Lunt-Fontanne Theatre)

RCA SER 5618 (British) stereo

Music: Don Gohman; lyrics: Hal Hackady; based on Henry James' novel, The Ambassadors; musical direction: Gareth Davies

Cast: Toni-Sue Burley, Margaret Courtenay, Danielle Darrieux, Blain Fairman, Neville Jason, Howard Keel, Judith Paris, Isobel Stuart, Nevil Whiting

Songs: Overture (orchestra)
A Man You Can Set Your Watch By (Keel, chorus, Courtenay, Paris)
It's a Woman (Courtenay, Keel, Paris, Whiting)
Lambert's Quandary (Keel)
Lilas (Burley)
The Right Time - The Right Place (chorus)
Suprise (Darrieux)
Charming (Keel, Darrieux)
All of My Life (Keel)
What Can You Do With a Nude? (Fairman, chorus)
Love Finds the Lonely (Stuart)

Tell Her (Keel)
Young With Him (Darrieux)
I Thought I Knew You (Keel, Darrieux)
Lilas (reprise) (Burley)
What Happened to Paris (Keel)
Too Much to Forgive (Keel)
That's What I Need Tonight (Darrieux, Keel, chorus)
You Can Tell a Lady by Her Hat (Jason)
This Utterly Ridiculous Affair (Darrieux, Keel)
Gossip (female chorus)
Not Tomorrow (Darrieux)
Thank You, No! (Keel)
All of My Life (reprise) (Keel)

Note: London cast recording; Darrieux and Keel only cast members appearing on Broadway.

ANKLES AWEIGH (April 18, 1955, Mark Hellinger Theatre)

Decca DL 9025 mono reissued: AEI 1104

Music: Sammy Fain; lyrics: Dan Shapiro; musical direction: Salvatore Dell'Isola

Cast: Mark Dawson, Gabriel Dell, Betty George, Betty Kean, Jane Kean, Ray Mason, Lew Parker

Songs: Overture (orchestra)
Italy (chorus)
Skip the Build Up (B. Kean, Parker)
Nothing at All (J. Kean, Dawson, chorus)
Walk Like a Sailor (J. Kean, Parker, Dell, chorus)
Headin' for the Bottom Blues (George, chorus)
Here's to Dear Old Us (B. Kean, Parker, Dell)

His and Hers (J. Kean, Dawson)
La Festa (Mason, chorus)
Ready Cash (chorus)
Nothing Can Replace a Man (J. Kean)
Kiss Me and Kill Me With Love (J. Kean, Dawson)
Honeymoon (B. Kean, chorus)
An Eleven O'Clock Song (B. and J. Kean)
Finale (company)

Note: Betty George replaced Thelma Carpenter for this recording, due to contractual problems.

ANNIE (April 21, 1977, Alvin Theatre)

Columbia PS 34712 stereo CD

Music: Charles Strouse; lyrics: Martin Charnin; based on Little Orphan Annie; musical direction: Peter Howard

Cast: Laurie Beechman, Edie Cowan, Donald Craig, Barbara Erwin, Sandy Faison, Robert Fitch, Dorothy Loudon, Andrea McArdle, Reid Shelton, Raymond Thorne, Penny Worth

Songs: Overture (orchestra)
Maybe (McArdle, girls)
It's the Hard-Knock Life (McArdle, girls)
Tomorrow (McArdle)
We'd Like to Thank You (chorus)
Little Girls (Loudon)
I Think I'm Gonna Like It Here (Faison, McArdle, chorus)
N.Y.C. (Shelton, Faison, McArdle, girls)

Easy Street (Loudon, Fitch, Erwin)
You Won't Be an Orphan for Long (Faison, chorus)
You're Never Fully Dressed Without a Smile (Craig, Beechman, Cowan, Worth, girls)
Tomorrow (reprise) (McArdle, Thorne, Shelton, men)
Something Was Missing (Shelton)
I Don't Need Anything but You (Shelton, McArdle, Faison, chorus)
Annie (Faison, chorus)
A New Deal for Christmas (McArdle, Shelton, Faison, Thorne, chorus)

ANNIE GET YOUR GUN (May 17, 1946, Imperial Theatre)

Decca 8001 mono reissued: MCA 1626

Music, lyrics: Irving Berlin; musical direction: Jay Blackton

Cast: Leon Bibb, Kathleen Carnes, John Garth, Robert Lenn, Ethel Merman, Ray Middleton, Clyde Turner

Songs: Doin' What Comes Natur'lly (Merman)
Moonshine Lullaby (Merman, Bibb, Garth, Turner)
You Can't Get a Man With a Gun (Merman)
I'm an Indian Too (Merman, chorus)
They Say It's Wonderful (Merman, Middleton)
Anything You Can Do (Merman, Middleton)

I Got Lost in His Arms (Merman, chorus)
I Got the Sun in the Morning (Merman, chorus)
The Girl That I Marry (Middleton)
My Defenses Are Down (Middleton, male chorus)
Who Do You Love I Hope (Lenn, chorus)
There's No Business Like Show Business (chorus)

ANNIE GET YOUR GUN (Revival, May 31, 1966, New York State Theatre)

RCA LSO 1124 stereo

Musical direction: Franz Allers

Cast: Ronn Carroll, Ethel Merman, Jerry Orbach, Rufus Smith, Benay Venuta, Bruce Yarnell

Songs: Overture (orchestra)
Colonel Buffalo Bill (Orbach, Venuta, chorus)
I'm a Bad, Bad Man (Yarnell, girls)
Doin' What Comes Natur'lly (Merman, Carroll, children)
The Girl That I Marry (Yarnell)
You Can't Get a Man With a Gun (Merman)
There's No Business Like Show Business (Merman, Yarnell, Smith, Orbach)
They Say It's Wonderful (Merman, Yarnell)

Moonshine Lullaby (Merman, children)
There's No Business Like Show Business (reprise) (Merman)
My Defenses Are Down (Yarnell, boys)
I'm an Indian Too (Merman)
I Got Lost in His Arms (Merman, chorus)
I Got the Sun in the Morning (Merman, chorus)
An Old Fashioned Wedding (Merman, Yarnell)
Anything You Can Do (Merman, Yarnell)
Finale:
There's No Business Like Show Business (chorus)
They Say It's Wonderful (chorus)

ANYA (November 29, 1965, Ziegfeld Theatre)

United Artists UAS 5133 stereo

Music: Sergei Rachmaninoff; lyrics: Robert Wright, George Forrest; based on Anastasia by Marcelle Maurette, Guy Bolton; musical direction: Harold Hastings

Cast: Barbara Alexander, Boris Aplon, Lillian Gish, George S. Irving, Michael Kermoyan, John Michael King, Irra Petina, Michael Quinn, Karen Shepard, Ed Steffe, Constance Towers

Songs: Choral Prelude: Anya (chorus)
A Song from Somewhere (Towers)
Now Is My Moment (Kermoyan)
Vodka, Vodka! (Petina, Aplon, chorus)
So Proud (Kermoyan, Irving, Steffe, Aplon)
Homeward (Petina, chorus)
Snowflakes and Sweethearts: The Snowbird Song (Alexander, Towers, Quinn, chorus)
Six Palaces (Towers, Kermoyan, Irving, Steffe)
Hand in Hand (Towers, King)

On That Day (Irving, Steffe, Aplon, Petina)
This Is My Kind of Love (Towers, Kermoyan)
A Sense of Love and Humor (Shepard)
On That Day (reprise) (King, chorus)
That Prelude! (Kermoyan, Petina, Steffe, Aplon, Irving, chorus)
A Quiet Land (Towers)
Here Tonight, Tomorrow Where? (Irving, Steffe, Aplon)
Leben Sie Wohl (Petina, men)
If This Is Goodbye (Towers, Kermoyan)
Little Hands (Gish, chorus)
All Hail the Empress (chorus)
Choral Finale: Anya (chorus)

ANYONE CAN WHISTLE (April 4, 1964, Majestic Theatre)

Columbia KOS 2480 stereo reissued: CSP AS 32608

Music, lyrics: Stephen Sondheim; musical direction: Herbert Greene

Cast: Sterling Clark, Gabriel Dell, Harvey Evans, James Frawley, Harry Guardino, Angela Lansbury, Lee Remick, Larry Roquemore, Arnold Soboloff, Tucker Smith

Songs: Prelude (orchestra)
Me and My Town (Lansbury, Clark, Evans, Roquemore, Smith)
Miracle Song (Lansbury, Soboloff, chorus)
Simple (Lansbury, Guardino, chorus)
Come Play Wiz Me (Lansbury, Guardino)

Anyone Can Whistle (Remick)
A Parade in Town (Lansbury, chorus)
Everyone Says Don't (Guardino)
I've Got You to Lean On (Lansbury, Dell, Soboloff, Frawley)
See What It Gets You (Remick)
The Cookie Chase (Lansbury, Remick, chorus)

With So Little to be Sure Of (Remick, Guardino)

Note: An additional selection (cut from show) is included on A Collector's Sondheim, RCA CRL4-5359:

There Won't Be Trumpets (Remick)

ANYTHING GOES (Revival, May 15, 1962, Off Broadway, Orpheum Theatre)

Epic FLS 15100 stereo CD

Music, lyrics: Cole Porter; musical direction: Ted Simons

Cast: Mickey Deems, Margery Gray, Barbara Lang, Hal Linden, Kenneth Mars, Kay Norman, Eileen Rodgers

Songs: Overture (orchestra)
You're the Top (Rodgers, Linden)
Bon Voyage (Deems, Lang, Linden, Mars, Norman, chorus)
It's Delovely (Linden, Lang, chorus)
Heaven Hop (Gray, girls)
Friendship (Deems, Linden, Rodgers)
I Get a Kick Out of You (Rodgers)
Anything Goes (Rodgers, ensemble)

Public Enemy Number One (chorus)
Let's Step Out (Gray, chorus)
Let's Misbehave (Rodgers, Mars)
Blow, Gabriel, Blow (Rodgers, chorus)
All Through the Night (Linden, Lang)
Be Like the Bluebird (Deems)
Take Me Back to Manhattan (Rodgers, girls)

APPLAUSE (March 30, 1970, Palace Theatre)

ABC Records OCS 11 stereo reissued: MCA 1632

Music: Charles Strouse; lyrics: Lee Adams; based on the film All About Eve; musical direction: Donald Pippin

Cast: Lauren Bacall, Len Cariou, Bennie Franklin, Penny Fuller, Brandon Maggart, Robert Mandan, Lee Roy Reams, Ann Williams

Songs: Overture (orchestra)
Backstage Babble (chorus)
Think How It's Gonna Be (Cariou)
But Alive (Bacall, boys)
The Best Night of My Life (Fuller)
Who's That Girl? (Bacall, Fuller)
Applause (Franklin, chorus)
Hurry Back (Bacall)
Fasten Your Seat Belts (Bacall, Williams, Cariou, Mandan, Reams, chorus)

Welcome to the Theatre (Bacall)
Good Friends (Bacall, Williams, Maggart)
She's No Longer a Gypsy (Franklin, Reams, chorus)

One of a Kind (Bacall, Cariou)
One Hallowe'en (Fuller)
Something Greater (Bacall, Cariou)
Finale (chorus)

THE APPLE TREE (October 18, 1966, Shubert Theatre)

Columbia KOS 3020 stereo

Music: Jerry Bock; lyrics: Sheldon Harnick; based on stories by Mark Twain, Frank R. Stockton, Jules Feiffer; musical direction: Elliot Lawrence

Cast: Alan Alda, Larry Blyden, Barbara Harris, Marc Jordan

<u>The Diary of Adam and Eve</u>
Songs: Eden Prelude (orchestra)
Here in Eden (Harris)
Feelings (Harris)
Eve (Alda)
Friends (Harris)
The Apple Tree - Forbidden Fruit (Blyden)
Beautiful, Beautiful World (Alda)
Go to Sleep, Whatever You Are (Harris)
It's a Fish (Alda)
What Makes Me Love Him (Harris)
<u>The Lady or the Tiger</u>?
Songs: Prelude (orchestra)
I'll Tell You a Truth (Blyden)
Make Way (chorus)

Forbidden Love - In Gaul (Harris, Alda)
I've Got What You Want (Harris, Blyden)
Tiger, Tiger (Harris)
Make Way (reprise) (chorus)
Which Door (Jordan, Alda, Harris, chorus)
The Lady or the Tiger (Blyden)
<u>Passionella</u>
Songs: Prelude (orchestra)
Oh to be a Movie Star (Harris)
Gorgeous (Harris)
Who Is She? (Harris, chorus)
I Know (Harris, chorus)
Wealth (Harris)
You Are Not Real (Alda, chorus)
Finale (Harris, Alda, chorus)

ARABIAN NIGHTS (June 24, 1954, Off Broadway, Jones Beach Marine Theatre)

Decca DL 9013 mono

Music, lyrics: Carmen Lombardo, John Jacob Loeb; musical direction: Pembroke Davenport

Cast: William Chapman, Ralph Herbert, Hope Holiday, James

McCracken, Lauritz Melchior, Helena Scott, Gloria van Dorp

Songs: Overture (orchestra)
What a Pity (Herbert, male chorus)
It's Great to Be Alive (Holiday, girls chorus)
A Thousand and One Nights (Chapman, Scott)
The Grand Vizier's Lament (Herbert, chorus)
Hail to the Sultan (Melchior, Herbert, chorus)

The Hero of All My Dreams (Scott)
A Whale of a Story (Chapman, McCracken)
The Bath Parade (van Dorp)
How Long Has It Been? (Chapman, Scott)
Teenie Weenie Genie (Holiday, male chorus)
A Long Time Ago (Melchior)
Marry the One You Love (Melchior)
Finale (chorus)

ARMS AND THE GIRL - see page 259

ATHENIAN TOUCH (January 14, 1964, Off Broadway, Jan Hus Auditorium)

Broadway East Records OCS 101 stereo

Music: William Straight; lyrics: David Eddy; musical direction: Glen Clugston

Cast: Alice Cannon, Ken Cantril, Robert Cosdon, Ronn Hansen, James Harder, Mark Holliday, Richard Ianni, Janet McCall, Butterfly McQueen, Marion Marlowe, Peter Sands

Songs: No Garlic Tonight (McQueen)
The Contract (Marlowe, Cantril, Ianni, McCall)
The Singer and the Song (Sands, Cannon)
Greek Comedy (Cosden)
What Is a Woman (Marlowe)
Eleleu! (Cosden, chorus)
Look Away (McQueen)

There Goes Time (Cosden)
Love, You Are So Difficult (Marlowe)
A Lady of Leisure (Marlowe, McQueen)
Awkward Little Boy (Sands)
Lysistrata (Harder, Ianni, Hansen, Holliday)
All We Need to Know (Marlowe, Cosden)

BABY (December 4, 1983, Ethel Barrymore Theatre)

Polydor 821 593-1 Y-1 stereo CD

Music: David Shire; lyrics: Richard Maltby, Jr.; musical direction: Peter Howard

Cast: Liz Callaway, James Congdon, Catherine Cox, Kim Criswell, Beth Fowler, Todd Graff, Philip Hoffman, Martin Vidnovic, Dennis Warning

Songs: Opening (Criswell, ensemble)

We Start Today (Graff, Congdon, Callaway, Fowler, Vidnovic, Cox, chorus)
What Could Be Better? (Callaway, Graff)
The Plaza Song (Congdon, Fowler)
Baby, Baby, Baby (Vidnovic, Cox, Fowler, Congdon, Callaway, Graff)
I Want It All (Cox, Callaway, Fowler)
At Night She Comes Home to Me (Vidnovic, Graff)
Fatherhood Blues (Graff, Congdon, Vidnovic, Hoffman, Warning)
Romance (Vidnovic, Cox)
I Choose Right (Graff)

The Story Goes On (Callaway)
The Ladies Singing Their Song (Callaway, female chorus)
Patterns (Fowler)
Romance II (Vidnovic, Cox)
Easier to Love (Congdon)
Romance III (Cox)
Two People in Love (Callaway, Graff)
With You (Cox, Vidnovic)
And What If We Had Loved Like That? (Congdon, Fowler)
The Birth - Finale (Graff, Callaway, Vidnovic, Cox, Congdon, Fowler, company)

BAJOUR (November 23, 1964, Shubert Theatre)

Columbia KOS 2700 stereo

Music, lyrics: Walter Marks; musical direction: Lehman Engel

Cast: Herschel Bernardi, Robert Burr, Nancy Dussault, Herbert Edelman, Mae Questel, Chita Rivera, Gus Trikonis

Songs: Overture (orchestra)
Move Over, New York (Bernardi, chorus)
Where Is the Tribe for Me? (Dussault)
The Haggle (Bernardi, Edelman, male chorus)
Love-Line (Rivera)
Words, Words, Words (Dussault, Bernardi)
Mean (Rivera, female chorus)

Bajour (Bernardi, chorus)
Must It Be Love? (Dussault)
Soon (Rivera, Trikonis, chorus)
I Can (Rivera, Dussault)
Living Simply (Burr, Dussault, trio)
Honest Man (Bernardi, Edelman)
Guarantees (Questel)
Love Is a Chance (Dussault)
Move Over, America (Bernardi, chorus)

BAKER STREET (February 16, 1965, Broadway Theatre)

MGM Records SE 7000 OC stereo

Music, lyrics: Marian Grudeff, Raymond Jessel; adapted from

the Sherlock Holmes stories of Sir Arthur Conan Doyle; musical direction: Harold Hastings

Cast: Martin Gabel, Teddy Green, Patrick Horgen, Daniel Keyes, Peter Sallis, Inga Swenson, Virginia Vestoff, Fritz Weaver, Martin Wolfson

Songs: Overture (orchestra)
It's So Simple (Weaver, Sallis, Horgan, Keyes)
I'm In London Again (Swenson, chorus)
Leave It to Us, Gov (Green, boys)
Letters (Swenson)
Cold Clear World (Weaver)
Finding Words for Spring (Swenson)

What a Night This Is Going to Be (Weaver, Swenson, Sallis, Vestoff)
I Shall Miss You (Gabel)
Roof Space (Green, boys)
A Married Man (Sallis)
I'd Do It Again (Swenson)
Pursuit (Weaver)
Jewelry (Wolfson, chorus)

BALLAD FOR BIMSHIRE (October 15, 1963, Off Broadway, Mayfair Theatre)

London Records AMS 78002 stereo

Music, lyrics: Irving (Lord Burgess) Burgie; musical direction: Sammy Benskin

Cast: Ossie Davis, Robert Dolphin, Eugene Edwards, Clebert Ford, Frederick O'Neal, Jimmy Randolph, Christine Spencer, Alyce Webb

Songs: Ballad for Bimshire (Webb, Edwards, Ford)
Street Cries (Webb)
Lately I've Been Feeling So Strange (Spencer, Webb)
'Fore Day Noon in the Mornin' (O'Neal, chorus)
Deep in My Heart (Spencer)
Have You Got Charm? (Spencer, O'Neal)
Hail Britannia (Davis, chorus)
Welcome Song (female chorus)
Belle Plain - I'm a Dandy (chorus)
Silver Earring (Randolph)

My Love Will Come By (Spencer, Randolph)
Chicken's a Popular Bird (Dolphin)
Pardon Me, Sir (Ford)
Yesterday Was Such a Lovely Day (Randolph, Spencer)
My Master Plan (Spencer)
Chant (Webb)
Finale - We Gon' Jump Up (chorus)

Note: Includes narration by Davis.

BALLROOM (December 14, 1978, Majestic Theatre)

Columbia JS 35762 stereo

Music: Billy Goldenberg; lyrics: Alan, Marilyn Bergman; musical direction: Don Jennings

Cast: Vincent Gardenia, Bernie Knee, Dorothy Loudon, Lynn Roberts

Songs: Overture - The Stardust Waltz (orchestra)
A Terrific Band and a Real Nice Crowd (Loudon)
A Song for Dancin' (Roberts, Knee)
One by One (Knee, Roberts)
The Ballroom Montage (orchestra)
Dreams (Roberts)
Somebody Did All Right for Herself (Loudon, Roberts)

I've Been Waiting All My Life (Knee)
The Tango (orchestra)
I Love to Dance (Loudon, Gardenia)
Good Night (Is Not Goodbye) (Roberts, Knee)
More of the Same (Roberts, Knee)
Fifty Percent (Loudon)
I Wish You a Waltz (Loudon)

THE BAND WAGON (June 3, 1931, New Amsterdam Theatre)

RCA L-24003 mono reissued: Smithsonian R 021

Music: Arthur Schwartz; lyrics: Howard Dietz; musical direction: Leo Reisman

Cast: Adele Astaire, Fred Astaire

Songs: Overture (orchestra)
Sweet Music (Fred and Adele Astaire)
High and Low (orchestra)
Hoops (Fred and Adele Astaire)
Confession (orchestra)
New Sun in the Sky (orchestra)
I Love Louisa (Fred Astaire, chorus)
Ballet Music (orchestra)
Beggar's Waltz (orchestra)
White Heat (Fred Astaire; Arthur Schwartz, piano)
Dancing in the Dark (orchestra)

Note: Includes narration by Reisman.

BARNUM (April 30, 1980, St. James Theatre)

Columbia JS 36576 stereo CD

Music: Cy Coleman; lyrics: Michael Stewart; musical direction: Peter Howard

Cast: Glenn Close, Leonard John Crofoot, Jim Dale, Marianne Tatum, Terri White, William C. Witter

Songs: Overture Chase (orchestra)
There Is a Sucker Born Ev'ry Minute (Dale)
Humble Beginnings Chase (Witter)
Thank God I'm Old (White)
The Colors of My Life, Part I (Dale)
The Colors of My Life, Part II (Close)
One Brick at a Time (Close, chorus)
Museum Song (Dale)
Female of the Species Chase (Witter)
I Like Your Style (Dale, Close)
Bigger Isn't Better (Crofoot)
Love Makes Such Fools of Us All (Tatum)

Midway Chase (Witter)
Out There (Dale)
Come Follow the Band (Dale, chorus)
Black and White (Close, Dale, White, chorus)
The Colors of My Life (reprise) (Dale, Close)
The Prince of Humbug (Dale)
Join the Circus (Witter, Dale, chorus)
Finale Chase (Witter)
The Finale Event - There Is a Sucker Born Ev'ry Minute (reprise) (Dale)

BEI MIR BISTU SCHOEN (October 21, 1961, Off Broadway, Anderson Theatre)

Decca DL 79115 stereo

Music: Sholem Secunda; lyrics: Jacob Jacobs; musical direction: Sholom Secunda

Cast: Charlotte Cooper, Leo Fuchs, Jacob Jacobs, Miriam Kressyn, Leon Liebgold, Seymour Rexite, Rebecca Richman

Songs: Overture (orchestra)
Nachas fun Kinder (Joys from Children) (Liebgold)
Social Security (Jacobs, Cooper)
Folgen A Tatten (Obeying Father) (Jacobs, Liebgold, Rexite)
Hob Mich Lieb (Love Me) (Fuchs, Kressyn)
Bei Mir Bistu Schoen (Fuchs)
Machst Mich Feelen Yinger (You Make Me Feel Younger) (Fuchs, Richman)
Hora (Fuchs, ensemble)

B'Rochos L'Havdoloh (Blessings of the Havdoloh) (Liebgold, ensemble)
Itsche (Jacobs)
Mein Hartz Flegt Zogen Mir (My Heart Told Me) (Kressyn, Richman)
T'Ain't Kosher (Fuchs, chorus)
Finale: Hob Mich Lieb; Machst Mich Feelen Yinger; T'Ain't Kosher; Hora (company)

THE BELIEVERS (May 9, 1968, Off Broadway, Garrick Theatre)

RCA LSO 1151 stereo

Music, lyrics: Benjamin Carter, Dorothy Dinroe, Josephine Jackson, Anje Ray, Ron Steward, Joseph A. Walker; musical direction: Brooks Alexander

Cast: Ladji Camara, Jesse DeVore, Barry Hemphill, Jo Jackson, Shirley McKie, Don Oliver, Anje Ray, Veronica Redd, Ron Steward, Joseph A. Walker

Songs: African Sequence (chorus)
Believers' Chants (Hemphill, McKie)
Believers' Lament (chorus)
Drum Solo (Camara)
This Old Ship (chorus)
Where Shall I Go? (chorus)
What Shall I Believe in Now? (chorus)
Field Hollers and Work Songs (chorus)
He's Got the Whole World in His Hands (Jackson, chorus)
Jesus, the Light of the World (Oliver, chorus)
Sermon: The Life of Peter (DeVore) spoken
I Turn to Jesus (Ray, chorus)
I'm So Glad (chorus)

I Just Got in the City (Hemphill)
City Blues (Steward)
You Never Really Know (chorus)
Naked Foot (chorus)
Early One Morning Blues (Ray, chorus)
Daily Buzz (Walker)
Children's Games (chorus)
School Don't Mean a Damn Thing (chorus)
I'm Gonna Do My Thing (Steward, chorus)
Where Do I Go from Here (Redd, chorus)
Burn This Town (Steward)
Learn to Love (Ray, Oliver)
Finale (chorus)

BELLS ARE RINGING (November 29, 1956, Shubert Theatre)

Columbia OS 2006 stereo reissued: CSP AOS 2006

Music: Jule Styne; lyrics: Betty Comden, Adolf Green; musical direction: Milton Rosenstock

Cast: Sydney Chaplin, Peter Gennaro, Judy Holliday, Eddie Lawrence, Jean Stapleton

Songs: Overture (orchestra)
Bells Are Ringing (girls chorus)
It's a Perfect Relationship (Holliday, boys)
On My Own (Chaplin)
It's a Simple Little System (Lawrence, chorus)
Is It a Crime? (Holliday)
Hello, Hello There (Holliday, Chaplin, chorus)

I Met a Girl (Chaplin, chorus)
Long Before I Knew You (Holliday, Chaplin)
Mu-Cha-Cha (Holliday, Gennaro, chorus)
Just in Time (Holliday, Chaplin, chorus)
Drop That Name (Holliday, chorus)
The Party's Over (Holliday)

Salzburg (Stapleton, chorus)
The Midas Touch (chorus)
I'm Going Back (Holliday)

BELOW THE BELT (June 21, 1966, Off Broadway, Downstairs at the Upstairs)

Upstairs Downstairs UD-37W56-Vol 2 (two records, with MIXED DOUBLES) stereo

Music: Jerry Powell, Rod Warren; lyrics: Michael McWhinney, Rod Warren; musical direction: Michael Cohen

Cast: Richard Blair, Genna Carter, Judy Graubart, Madeline Kahn, Larry Moss, Robert Rovin, Janie Sell, Gary Sneed, Lily Tomlin

Songs: The Great Society Waltz (Carter, Graubart, Kahn, Sell, Tomlin, Blair, Moss, Rovin, Sneed) music, lyrics: Warren
Love's Labour Lost (Carter) music: Powell; lyrics: McWhinney
Camp (Carter, Kahn, Tomlin) music, lyrics: Warren
Suburbia Square Dance (Carter, Kahn, Tomlin, Blair, Rovin) music: Warren; lyrics: McWhinney
International Monopoly (Carter, Kahn, Tomlin, Blair, Rovin) spoken

BEN FRANKLIN IN PARIS (October 27, 1964, Lunt-Fontanne Theatre)

Capitol SVAS 2191 stereo

Music: Mark Sandrich, Jr.; lyrics: Sidney Michaels; musical direction: Donald Pippin

Cast: Jack Fletcher, Sam Greene, Bob Kaliban, Franklin Kiser, Robert Preston, Ulla Sallert, Jerry Schaefer, Susan Watson

Songs: Overture (orchestra)
We Sail the Seas (male chorus)
I Invented Myself (Preston, chorus)
Too Charming (Sallert, Preston)
Whatever Became of Old Temple? (Kiser)
Half the Battle (Preston, Schaefer, Kiser, Kaliban)
A Balloon Is Ascending (chorus)
To Be Alone with You (Preston, Sallert)
--- You're in Paris (Watson, Kiser, chorus)
How Laughable It Is (Sallert)
Hic Haec Hoc (male chorus)
God Bless the Human Elbow (Preston, Fletcher, Kaliban, men)
When I Dance with the Person I Love (Watson)
Diane is Looking for Small Pleasures (Preston, Sallert)
I Love the Ladies (Preston, Greene, Kaliban, Kiser, men)
Finale (Preston, chorus)

BERLIN TO BROADWAY WITH KURT WEILL (October 1, 1972, Off Broadway, Theatre de Lys)

Paramount Records PAS 4000 (two records) stereo

Music: Kurt Weill; lyrics: Maxwell Anderson, Alice Baker, Marc Blitzstein, Bertolt Brecht, Jacques Deval, Michael Feingold, Ira Gershwin, Paul Green, Langston Hughes, Alan Jay Lerner, Gene Lerner, Ogden Nash, George Tabori, Arnold Weinstein; musical direction: Newton Wayland

Cast: Margery Cohen, Ken Kercheval, Judy Lander, Jerry Lanning, Hal Watters

Songs: Introduction (Kercheval) spoken
How to Survive (Cohen, Lander, Lanning, Watters) lyrics: Brecht, Blitzstein
Barbara Song (Lander) lyrics: Brecht, Blitzstein
Useless Song (Watters) lyrics: Brecht, Blitzstein
Jealousy Duet (Cohen, Lander) lyrics: Brecht, Blitzstein
Useless Song (reprise) (Watters)
Mack the Knife (Lanning, Cohen, Lander, Watters) lyrics: Brecht, Blitzstein
How to Survive (Cohen, Lander, Lanning, Watters) lyrics: Brecht, Blitzstein
March Ahead to the Fight (Cohen) lyrics: Brecht, Feingold
Don't Be Afraid (Cohen) lyrics: Brecht, Feingold
Bilbao Song (Lanning Watters) lyrics: Brecht, Feingold
Surabaya Johnny (Lander) lyrics: Brecht, Tabori
Childhood's Bright Endeavor (Cohen) lyrics: Brecht, Feingold
Mandalay Song (Kercheval, Lanning, Watters) lyrics: Brecht, Feingold

---

Alabama Song (Cohen, Lander, Lanning, Watters) lyrics: Brecht, Weinstein
Deep in Alaska (Watters) lyrics: Brecht, Weinstein
Oh, Heavenly Salvation (Cohen, Lander, Watters, Lanning) lyrics: Brecht, Weinstein
As You Make Your Bed (Kercheval, Cohen, Lander, Lanning, Watters) lyrics: Brecht, Weinstein
Pirate Jenny (Lander) lyrics: Brecht, Blitzstein
I Wait for a Ship (Cohen) lyrics: Deval, Baker, G. Lerner
Sailor Tango (Lanning, Cohen, Lander, Watters) lyrics: Brecht, Feingold
Songs of Peace and War (Lanning, Cohen, Lander) lyrics: Green
A Hymn to Peace (Watters) lyrics: Green
Listen to My Song (Watters) lyrics: Green

How Can You Tell an American? (Cohen, Lander, Lanning, Watters) lyrics: Anderson
September Song (Lanning) lyrics: Anderson
Girl of the Moment (Lanning, Watters) lyrics: Gershwin
Saga of Jenny (Lander, Lanning, Watters) lyrics: Gershwin
My Ship (Cohen) lyrics: Gershwin
Speak Low (Cohen, Lander, Lanning, Watters) lyrics: Nash

That's Him (Cohen) lyrics: Nash
--- Progress (Lanning, Watters) lyrics: A. Lerner
Ain't It Awful the Heat (Cohen, Lander, Lanning, Watters) lyrics: Hughes
Lonely House (Watters) lyrics: Hughes
Trouble Man (Lander) lyrics: Anderson
Train to Johannesburg (Watters, Cohen, Lander, Lanning) lyrics: Anderson
Cry, the Beloved Country (Cohen, Lander, Lanning, Watters) lyrics: Anderson
Lost in the Stars (Lanning) lyrics: Anderson
Love Song (Watters, Cohen, Lander, Lanning) lyrics: A. Lerner
Moritat (reprise) Happy End (Kercheval, Cohen, Lander, Lanning, Watters)

BEST FOOT FORWARD (Revival, April 2, 1963, Off Broadway, Stage 73)

Cadence CLP 24012 stereo reissued: Stet DS 15003, Piccadilly 3484

Music, lyrics: Hugh Martin, Ralph Blane; musical direction: Buster Davis

Cast: Gene Castle, Paul Charles, Kay Cole, Edmund Gaynes, Jack Irwin, Liza Minnelli, Don Slaton, Grant Walden, Glenn Walken, Ronald Walken, Paula Wayne, Renee Winters, Karin Wolfe

Songs: Wish I May (chorus)
Three Men on a Date (G. Walken, R. Walken, Gaynes)
Hollywood Story (Wayne, Walden)
The Three B's (Minnelli, Cole, Winters)
Ev'ry Time (Wolfe)
Alive and Kicking (Wayne)
The Guy Who Brought Me (Wayne, Walden, Gaynes, G. Walken, R. Walken)
--- Shady Lady Bird (Wolfe, Gaynes, Castle, Slaton, Charles)
Buckle Down Winsocki (Irwin, Gaynes, Charles, chorus)
You're Lucky (Wayne)
What Do You Think I Am? (Gaynes, Minnelli, Cole, R. Walken, chorus)
Raving Beauty (R. Walken, Cole)
Just a Little Joint with a Juke Box (Minnelli, Castle, Slaton, Charles)
You Are For Loving (Minnelli)
Buckle Down Winsocki (chorus)

Note: Ronald Walken later became Christopher Walken.

THE BEST LITTLE WHOREHOUSE IN TEXAS (April 17, 1978, Off Broadway, Entermedia Theatre; June 19, 1978, 46th Street Theatre)

MCA Records 3049 stereo

Music, lyrics: Carol Hall; musical direction: Robert Billig

Cast: Clint Allmon, Lisa Brown, Gerry Burkhardt, Jay Bursky, Henderson Forsythe, Jay Garner, Carlin Glynn, Delores Hall, Susan Mansur, Michael Scott, Paul Ukena, Jr.

Songs: 20 Fans (company)
A Lil'ole Bitty Pissant Country Place (Glynn, girls)
Girl, You're a Woman (Glynn, girls)
Watch Dog Theme (Burkhardt, Bursky, Scott, Ukena)
Texas Has a Whorehouse in It (Allmon, company)
Twenty Four Hours of Lovin' (Hall, company)
Doatsy Mae (Mansur)
The Angelette March (Garner, Brown)

The Aggie Song (Ukena, Scott, Bursky, company)
The Bus from Amarillo (Glynn)
The Sidestep (Garner, company)
No Lies (Glynn, Hall, company)
Good Old Girl (Forsythe, company)
Hard Candy Christmas (girls)
Finale (company)

THE BEST OF BURLESQUE (September 29, 1957, Off Broadway, Carnegie Hall Playhouse)

MGM Records SE 3644 stereo

Narrative, dramatic, musical continuity: Jack Vaughan, musical direction: Herb Harris

Cast: Sherry Britton, Vini Faye, Sugar Glaze, Tom Poston, Emmett Rose, Nancee Ward, Lilly White, and Nelle's Belles

Songs: Prologue - narration (Sentimental Journey) (Rose)
Overture: Fine and Dandy, Toot Toot Tootsie, Diane, Limehouse Blues (orchestra)
Hello Everybody (Nelle's Belles)
Autumn Salutation (Nelle's Belles)
Higher Education (Posten, Faye, Ward, Glaze, White, Rose) spoken
Pagan Love Song (Faye, Nelle's Belles)
Dagger Dance (Faye, Nelle's Belles)
Fan Dance (orchestra)
I'm Forever Blowing Bubbles (Nelle's Belles)
Candy Butcher (Rose) spoken

Prelude: Three Little Words, Pagan Love Song, Should I (orchestra)
Floogel Street (Posten, Rose, Ward, Glaze, White, Faye) spoken
Pagan Love Song (Nelle's Belles)
Strip Tease: A Pretty Girl is Like a Melody (Britton)
Finale: Sophisticated Lady (Faye, Nelle's Belles)

BIG RIVER (April 25, 1985, Eugene O'Neill Theatre)

MCA 6147 stereo CD

Music, lyrics: Roger Miller; adapted from The Adventures of Huckleberry Finn by Mark Twain; musical direction: Linda Twine

Cast: Rene Auberjonois, Patti Cohenour, John Goodman, Bob Gunton, Peggy Harmon, Andi Henig, Daniel Jenkins, Ron Richardson, John Short, Jennifer Leigh Warren, William Youmans

Songs: Overture (orchestra)
Do Ya Wanna Go to Heaven? (company)
The Boys (Short, boys)
Waitin' for the Light to Shine (Jenkins)
Guv'ment (Goodman)
Hand for the Hog (Short)
I, Huckleberry, Me (Jenkins)
Muddy Water (Richardson, Jenkins)
The Crossing (chorus)
River in the Rain (Jenkins, Richardson)
When the Sun Goes Down in the South (Auberjonois, Gunton, Jenkins, Richardson)

Entracte (orchestra)
The Royal Nonesuch (Auberjonois, company)
Worlds Apart (Richardson, Jenkins)
Arkansas (Youmans)
How Blest We Are (Warren, company)
You Oughta Be Here with Me (Cohenour, Harmon, Henig)
Leavin's Not the Only Way to Go (Jenkins, Cohenour, Richardson)
Waitin' for the Light to Shine (Jenkins, chorus)
Free At Last (Richardson, chorus)
Muddy Water (reprise) (company)

THE BILLY BARNES REVUE (June 9, 1959, Off Broadway, York Playhouse)

Decca DL 79076 stereo

Music, lyrics, musical direction: Billy Barnes

Cast: Ken Berry, Bert Convy, Ann Guilbert, Joyce Jameson, Jackie Joseph, Patti Regan, Bob Rodgers, Len Weinrib

Songs: Do a Revue (company)
Where Are Your Children? (company)
Foolin' Ourselves (Convy, Berry)
Las Vegas (Jameson, Convy, Berry, Rodgers)
What Ever Happened? No. 1 (Regan)
Too Long at the Fair (Jameson, Joseph)
Listen to the Beat! (Weinrib, company)

City of the Angels (Jameson, Guilbert, Joseph)
Blocks (Rodgers, Joseph)
What Ever Happened? No. 2 (Regan)
The Fights (Jameson, Rodgers)
Tyler My Boy (Convy)
What Ever Happened? No. 3 (Regan)
One of Those Days - Finale (Joseph, Convy, Berry, company)

BILLY BISHOP GOES TO WAR (May 29, 1980, Morosco Theatre)

Tapestry Records GD 7372 (Canadian) stereo

Music, lyrics, piano accompaniment: John Gray

Cast: Eric Peterson (John Gray, background vocals)

Songs: Off to Fight the Hun
Canada at War
The Good Ship Caledonia (spoken)
Buried Alive in the Mud (spoken)
December Nights
The RE-7 (spoken)
Nobody Shoots No-One in Canada
Lady St. Helier (spoken)
My First Solo Flight (spoken)

In the Sky (1)
As Calm As the Ocean
Friends Ain't S'posed to Die
General Sir Hugh M. Trenchard (spoken)
The Empire Soiree
In the Sky (2)

Note: Recorded live, March, 1979, Torento, Canada.

BILLY NONAME (March 2, 1970, Off Broadway, Truck and Warehouse Theatre)

Roulette Records SROC-11 stereo

Music, lyrics: Johnny Brandon; musical direction: Sammy Benskin

Cast: Donny Burks, Thommie Bush, Doris DeMendez, Eugene Edwards, Marilyn Johnson, Roger Lawson, Urylee Leonardos, Joni Palmer, Andrea Saunders, Andy Torres, Glory Van Scott, Alan Weeks, Hattie Winston

Songs: King Joe (Burks, company)
Billy Noname (Burks)
Boychild (Burks)
A Different Drummer (Burks, company)
Look Through the Window (Winston)
It's Our Time Now! (Burks, Weeks, Lawson, Torres, Bush)
Hello World (Winston, Burks)
At the End of the Day (Leonardos)
I Want to Live (Burks)

Manchild (Burks, Winston, Weeks)
Color Me White (Lawson, Saunders, Torres, DeMendez, Bush, Palmer, Burks, Weeks)
We're Gonna Turn On Freedom (Weeks, company)
Mother Earth (Van Scott)
Movin' (Burks, company)
The Dream (Johnson, company)
Black Boy (Burks)
Burn Baby Burn (Weeks, Edwards, Leonardos, Burks, company)

BLOOMER GIRL (October 5, 1944, Shubert Theatre)

Decca DL 8015 mono reissued: MCA 1536E

Music: Harold Arlen; lyrics: E.Y. Harburg; musical direction: Leon Leonardi

Cast: Harold Arlen, David Brooks, Hubert Dilworth, Toni Hart, Celeste Holm, Richard Huey, Joan McCracken, Mabel Taliaferro, Dooley Wilson

Songs: When the Boys Come Home (girls, chorus)
Evelina (Brooks, Holm)
Welcome Hinges (Taliaferro, Brooks, chorus)
The Farmer's Daughter (men)
It Was Good Enough for Grandma (Holm, girls)
The Eagle and Me (Wilson, chorus)
Right As the Rain (Holm, Brooks)
T'morra' T'morra' (McCracken)

The Rakish Young Man with the Whiskahs (Holm, chorus)
Sunday in Cicero Falls (Holm, chorus)
I Got a Song (Huey, Dilworth, Wilson, chorus)
Satin Gown and Silver Shoe (Holm)
Liza Crossing the Ice (Hart, chorus)
Never Was Born (McCracken, chorus)
Man for Sale (Arlen)
Finale (Holm, Brooks, chorus)

Note: Harold Arlen did not appear in the stage production.

THE BODY BEAUTIFUL (January 23, 1958, Broadway Theatre)

Blue Pear Records BP 1008 mono

Music: Jerry Bock; lyrics: Sheldon Harnick; musical direction: Milton Greene

Cast: Tony Atkins, Dorothy Aull, Mace Barrett, Edward Becker, Armand Boney, Mindy Carson, Richard Chitos, Bob Daley, Richard De Bella, Jack DeLon, Kathie Forman, Steve Forrest, Edmond Gaynes, Betty Graham, Buzz Halliday, Tommy Halloran, William Hickey, Louis Kosman, Mary Louise, Mara Lynn, Barbara McNair, Mitchell Nutick, Broc Peters, Albert Popwell, Tom Raskin, Bill Richards, Jeff Roberts, Harry Lee Rogers, Jane Romano, Lonnie Sattin, Helen Silver, Knute Sullivan, Jack Warden, Alan Weeks, Bob Wiensko

Songs: Overture (orchestra)
Where Are They? (Warden, men)
The Body Beautiful (Carson, Daley, Kosman, Nutick, Richards, Rogers)
Pffft! (Forrest, Hickey)
Fair Warning (McNair, Sattin, Aull, Graham, Halliday, Louise, Barrett, DeLon, Raskin, Sullivan)
Leave Well Enough Alone (Carson)
Blonde Blues (Warden)

Uh-Huh, Oh Yeah! (Atkins, Boney, Chitos, De Bella, Gaynes, Halloran, Roberts, Weeks)
All of These and More (Carson, Forrest, ensemble)

Nobility (Becker, Daley, DeLon, Peters, Popwell, Raskin, Sullivan, Wiensko)
The Body Beautiful (Carson)
Entr'acte (orchestra)
Summer Is (Forman, chorus)
The Honeymoon is Over (Lynn, Romano, Silver)
Just My Luck (Carson, kids)
All of These and More (reprise) (McNair, Sattin)
Art of Conversation (Hickey, chorus)
Gloria (Warden, Lynn)
A Relatively Simple Affair (Carson, McNair)
Finale (company)

Note: A live recording.

THE BOY FRIEND (September 30, 1954, Royale Theatre)

RCA LOC 1018 mono

Music, lyrics: Sandy Wilson; musical direction: Anton Coppola

Cast: Ruth Altman, Julie Andrews, Eric Berry, Paulette Girard, John Hewer, Geoffrey Hibbert, Dilys Lay, Bob Scheerer, Ann Wakefield

Songs: Overture (orchestra)
Perfect Young Ladies (Girard, girls)
The Boy Friend (Andrews, ensemble)
Fancy Forgetting (Altman, Berry)
Won't You Charleston with Me? (Wakefield, Scheerer)
I Could Be Happy with You (Andrews, Hewer)
Sur La Plage (ensemble)

A Room in Bloomsbury (Andrews, Hewer)
The You Don't Want to Play with Me Blues (Altman, Berry, girls)
Safety in Numbers (Wakefield, boys)
The Riviera (Wakefield, Scheerer, ensemble)
It's Never too Late to Fall in Love (Hibbert, Lay)
Carnival Tango (orchestra)
Poor Little Pierrette (Altman, Andrews)
Finale (company)

THE BOY FRIEND (Revival, April 14, 1970, Ambassador Theatre)

Decca DL 79177 stereo reissued: MCA 1537

Musical direction: Jerry Goldberg

Cast: Barbara Andres, Jeanne Beauvais, Judy Carne, Sandy Duncan, Harvey Evans, Simon McQueen, Leon Shaw, David Vaughn, Ronald Young

Songs: Overture (orchestra)
Perfect Young Ladies (Andres, girls)

The Boy Friend (Carne, company)
Won't You Charleston with Me? (Duncan, Evans)
Fancy Forgetting (Beauvais, Shaw)
I Could Be Happy with You (Carne, Young)
Sur La Plage (Duncan, Evans, company)
A Room in Bloomsbury (Carne, Young)
It's Nicer in Nice (Andres, company)

You Don't Want to Play with Me Blues (Beauvais, Shaw, girls)
Safety in Numbers (Duncan, boys)
Finale, Act II - I Could Be Happy with You (Carne, company)
The Riviera (Duncan, Evans, company)
It's Never too Late to Fall in Love (Vaughn, McQueen)
Carnival Tango (orchestra)
Poor Little Pierrette (Beauvais, Carne)
Finale (company)

BOY MEETS BOY (September 17, 1975, Off Broadway, Actors Playhouse)

JO Records 13 stereo reissued: AEI 1102

Music, lyrics: Bill Solly; musical direction: David Friedman

Cast: Joe Barrett, Jan Crean, David Gallegly, Rita Gordon, Monica Grignon, Richard King, Paul Ratkevich, Bobby Reed, Dan Rounds, Raymond Wood

Songs: Boy Meets Boy (chorus)
Party in Room 203 (chorus)
Giving It Up for Love (Barrett, Ratkevich)
Me (Wood, Crean, Grignon, King, Reed, Rounds)
The English Rose (Crean, Grignon, King, Reed, Rounds)
Marry an American (chorus)
It's a Boy's Life (Barrett, Gallegly)
Does Anybody Love You? (Gallegly)
You're Beautiful (Gallegly, chorus)
Let's (Barrett, chorus)

Just My Luck (Barrett, Wood, girls chorus)
It's A Dolly (Gordon, chorus)
What Do I Care? (Gallegly)
Clarence's Turn (Wood)
Does Anybody Love You? (Barrett, Gallegly)
Finale (company)

THE BOYS FROM SYRACUSE (Revival, April 15, 1963, Off Broadway, Theatre Four)

Capitol Records STAO 1933 stereo

Music: Richard Rodgers; lyrics: Lorenz Hart; musical direction: Rene Wiegert

Cast: Danny Carroll, Cathryn Damon, Stuart Damon, Clifford David, Ellen Hanley, Fred Kimbrough, Julienne Marie, Karen Morrow, Richard Nieves, Gary Oakes, Matthew

Tobin, Rudy Tronto

Songs: Opening (Tronto, Carroll)
I Had Twins (Tobin, Oakes, Kimbrough, Nieves, ensemble)
Dear Old Syracuse (S. Damon)
What Can You Do with a Man (Morrow, Tronto)
Falling in Love with Love (Hanley)
The Shortest Day of the Year (David)
This Can't Be Love (S. Damon, Marie)

Ladies of the Evening (Oakes, company)
He and She (Morrow, Carroll)
You Have Cast Your Shadow on the Sea (S. Damon, Marie)
Come with Me (David, Oakes, Nieves, men)
Sing for Your Supper (Hanley, Marie, Morrow)
Oh, Diogenes! (C. Damon, company)
Finale (company)

BRAVO GIOVANNI (May 19, 1962, Broadhurst Theatre)

Columbia KOS 2200 stereo

Music: Milton Schafer; lyrics: Ronny Graham; musical direction: Anton Coppola

Cast: Nino Banome, Rico Froehlich, George S. Irving, Maria Karnilova, Michele Lee, Buzz Miller, David Opatoshu, Cesare Siepi, Gene Varrone

Songs: Overture (chorus, orchestra)
Rome (Siepi)
Urite (Irving, ensemble)
Breachy's Law (Siepi, Opatoshu)
I'm All I've Got (Lee)
The Arguement (Siepi, Irving)
Signora Pandolfi (Opatoshu, Karnilova, Miller, Varrone, Banome, Froehlich)
The Kangaroo (Karnilova, chorus)
If I Were the Man (Siepi)

Steady, Steady (Lee)
We Won't Discuss It (Siepi, Opatoshu)
Ah! Camminare (Varrone)
Virtue, Arrivederci (Irving)
Bravo, Giovanni (Siepi, chorus)
One Little World Apart (Lee)
Miranda (Siepi)
Finale (chorus)

BREAKFAST AT TIFFANY'S (Close during previews, final performance: December 14, 1966, Majestic Theatre)

S.P.M. Records (Society for the Preservation of Musicals) CO 4788 mono

Music, lyrics: Bob Merrill; based upon Truman Capote's novella; musical direction: Stanley Lebowsky

Cast: Richard Chamberlain, Sally Kellerman, Larry Kert, Art

Lund, Mary Tyler Moore

Songs: Overture (orchestra)
Holly Golightly (Chamberlain)
Breakfast at Tiffany's (Moore)
When Daddy Came Home (Moore, Chamberlain)
Freddy Chant (Moore)
Lament for Ten Men (male group)
Home for Wayward Girls (Kellerman, Moore)
Who Needs Her (Chamberlain)
You've Never Kissed Her (Lund)

The Girl Who Used to Be (Lund, Moore)
Who Needs Her (reprise)(Chamberlain, Moore)
Holly Golightly (reprise) (Chamberlain)
Stay with Me (Kert)
Grade 'A' Treatment (Moore, Kert)
Same Mistakes (Moore)
Stay with Her (Chamberlain)

Note: A live recording.

BRIGADOON (March 13, 1947, Ziegfeld Theatre)

RCA LSO 1001(e) mono reissued: AYL 1-3901E

Music: Frederick Loewe; lyrics: Alan Jay Lerner; musical direction: Franz Allers

Cast: Delbert Anderson, Marion Bell, Pamela Britton, David Brooks, Hayes Gordon, Earl Redding, Shirley Robbins, Lee Sullivan, Jeff Warren

Songs: Overture (orchestra)
Once in the Highlands (Anderson, chorus)
Brigadoon (chorus)
Down on MacConnachy Square (Warren, Redding, Robbins, Gordon, chorus)
Waitin' for My Dearie (Bell, girls)
I'll Go Home with Bonnie Jean (Sullivan)
The Heather on the Hill (Brooks, Bell)

Come to Me, Bend to Me (Sullivan)
Almost Like Being in Love (Brooks, Bell)
There But for You Go I (Brooks)
My Mother's Wedding Day (Britton)
From This Day On (Brooks, Bell)
Brigadoon (company)

BRING BACK BIRDIE (March 5, 1981, Martin Beck Theatre)

Original Cast Records OC 8132 stereo

Music: Charles Strouse; lyrics: Lee Adams; musical direction: Milton Rosenstock

Cast: Marcel Forestieri, Betsy Friday, Maurice Hines, Maria Karnilova, Robin Morse, Donald O'Connor, Rebecca

Renfroe, Chita Rivera

Songs: Overture (orchestra)
Twenty Happy Years (Rivera, O'Connor)
Movin' Out (Morse, children)
Half of a Couple (Morse, girls)
I Like What I Do (Rivera)
Bring Back Birdie (Hines, children)
Baby, You Can Count on Me (O'Connor)
A Man Worth Fightin' For (Rivera, men)
You Can Never Go Back (Forestieri)
--- Back in Show Biz Again (O'Connor, Friday, Renfroe)
Middle Age Blues (O'Connor)
Inner Peace (Rivera, chorus)
There's a Brand New Beat in Heaven (Hines, chorus)
Well, I'm Not (Rivera)
When Will Grown-ups Grow Up? (Morse, children)
Young (O'Connor)
I Love 'Em All (Karnilova, boys)
Bring Back Birdie - Finale (Forestieri, company)
Rosie (O'Connor, Rivera, chorus)

Note: Final song from Bye Bye Birdie score.

BUBBLING BROWN SUGAR (March 2, 1976, ANTA Theatre)

H and L Records HL-69011-698 stereo reissued: Amherst AMH3310 CD

Music: Eubie Blake, Duke Ellington, Benny Goodman, Arthur Herzog, Earl 'Fatha' Hines, Danny Holgate, Emme Kemp, Lillian Lopez, W.B. Overstreet, Maceo Pickard, Edgar Sampson, Billy Strayhorn, Fats Waller, Chick Webb, Bert Williams; lyrics: Billy Higgins, Earl 'Fatha' Hines, Danny Holgate, Billie Holiday, Emme Kemp, Lillian Lopez, Irving Mills, Mitchell Parish, Maceo Pickard, Andy Razef, Alex Rogers, Noble Sissle, Paul Francis Webster; musical direction: Danny Holgate

Cast: Joseph Attles, Ethel Beatty, Carolyn Byrd, Chip Garnett, Avon Long, Josephine Premice, Barry Preston, Vivian Reed

Songs: Stompin' at the Savoy (orchestra) music: Sampson, Goodman, Webb
Take the 'A' Train (orchestra) music: Strayhorn
Bubbling Brown Sugar (company) music, lyrics: Holgate, Kemp, Lopez
Nobody (Long) music: Williams; lyrics: Rogers
His Eye is on the Sparrow (Byrd, company) arranged: Holgate
Swing Low, Sweet Chariot (Byrd, company) arranged: Holgate
Sophisticated Lady (Garnett) music: Ellington; lyrics: Mills, Parish
Stormy Monday Blues (Byrd) music, lyrics: Hines
In Honeysuckle Time, When Emaline Said She'd be Mine (Long, Attles) music: Blake; lyrics: Sissle

--- Sweet Georgia Brown (Reed) music, lyrics: Pickard
Honeysuckle Rose (Premice, Long) music: Waller;
lyrics: Razaf
I Got It Bad (Beatty) music: Ellington; lyrics: Webster
Harlem Makes Me Feel! (Preston) music, lyrics: Kemp
There'll Be Some Changes Made (Premice) music:
Overstreet; lyrics: Higgins
God Bless the Child (Reed) music: Herzog; lyrics:
Holiday
It Don't Mean a Thing (company) music: Ellington;
lyrics: Mills

BY JUPITER (Revival, January 19, 1967, Off Broadway, Theatre Four)

RCA LSO 1137 stereo

Music: Richard Rodgers; lyrics: Lorenz Hart; based on Julian F. Thompson's The Warrior's Husband; musical direction: Milton Setzer

Cast: Jackie Alloway, Emory Bass, Irene Byatt, Ronnie Cunningham, Bob Dishy, Norma Doggett, Rosemarie Heyer, Robert R. Kaye, Richard Marshall, Sheila Sullivan

Songs: For Jupiter and Greece (men)
Ride Amazon Ride (women)
Jupiter Forbid (Alloway, Byatt, Cunningham, Doggett, chorus)
Life with Father (Dishy, Byatt)
Nobody's Heart (Sullivan)
In the Gateway of the Temple of Minerva (Kaye)
Here's a Hand (Kaye, Sullivan)
Finale of Act I (Alloway, Byatt, Dishy, Cunningham, chorus)
--- Wait Till You See Her (Kaye, men)
The Boy I Left Behind Me (Heyer, women)
Ev'rything I've Got (Alloway, Dishy)
Bottoms Up (Alloway, Sullivan, Marshall, Bass, chorus)
Careless Rhapsody (Sullivan, Kaye)
Now That I've Got My Strength (Dishy)
Ev'rything I've Got (reprise) (Alloway)
Jupiter Forbid (reprise) (company)

BY THE BEAUTIFUL SEA (April 8, 1954, Majestic Theatre)

Capitol S 531 mono

Music: Arthur Schwartz; lyrics: Dorothy Fields; musical direction: Jay Blackton

Cast: Mae Barnes, Shirley Booth, Wilbur Evans,Richard France, Thomas Gleason, Mary Harmon, Larry Howard, Cindy Robbins, Eddie Roll, Gloria Smith, Libi Staiger

Songs: Overture (orchestra)

The Sea Song (Booth, ensemble)
Old Enough to Love (France)
Coney Island Boat (Booth, ensemble)
Alone too Long (Evans)
Happy Habit (Barnes)
Good Time Charlie (Harmon, Robbins, Smith, Howard, Roll, France)

I'd Rather Wake Up by Myself (Booth)
Hooray for George the Third (Gleason, Staiger, ensemble)
Hang Up (Barnes, ensemble)
More Love Than Your Love (Evans)
Lottie Gibson Specialty (Booth)
Throw the Anchor Away (ensemble)
Finale (Evans, Booth, company)

BYE BYE BIRDIE (April 14, 1960, Martin Beck Theatre)

Columbia KOS 2025 stereo reissued: CSP COS 2025

Music: Charles Strouse; lyrics: Lee Adams; musical direction: Elliot Lawrence

Cast: Jessica Albright, Johnny Borden, Dick Gautier, Sharon Lerit, Paul Lynde, Marijane Maricle, Chita Rivera, Dick Van Dyke, Susan Watson

Songs: Overture (orchestra)
An English Teacher (Rivera, Van Dyke)
The Telephone Hour (teenagers)
How Lovely to Be a Woman (Watson)
Put On a Happy Face (Van Dyke)
Normal American Boy (Rivera, Van Dyke, ensemble)
One Boy (Watson, Albright, Lerit, Rivera)
Honestly Sincere (Gautier)

Hymn for a Sunday Evening (Lynde, Maricle, Watson, Borden)
One Last Kiss (Gautier, ensemble)
What Did I Ever See in Him? (Rivera, Watson)
A Lot of Livin' to Do (Gautier, Watson, teenagers)
Kids (Lynde, Maricle)
Baby, Talk to Me (Van Dyke, quartet)
Spanish Rose (Rivera)
Kids (reprise) (Lynde, Maricle, Borden, ensemble)
Rosie (Van Dyke, Rivera)

CABARET (November 20, 1966, Broadhurst Theatre)

Columbia KOS 3040 stereo CD

Music: John Kander; lyrics: Fred Ebb; based on the play by John van Druten and stories by Christopher Isherwood; musical direction: Harold Hastings

Cast: Bert Convy, Mary Ehara, Jack Gilford, Joel Grey, Jill Haworth, Lotte Lenya, Rita O'Connor, Robert Sharp

Songs: Willkommen (Grey, company)
So What? (Lenya)
Don't Tell Mama (Haworth, girls)
Telephone Song (Convy, company)
Perfectly Marvelous (Convy, Haworth)
Two Ladies (Grey, O'Connor, Ehara)
It Couldn't Please Me More (Lenya, Gilford)
Tomorrow Belongs to Me (Sharp, Grey, men)

Entr'acte (band)
Why Should I Wake Up? (Convy)
The Money Song (Grey, girls)
Married (Lenya, Gilford)
Meeskite (Gilford)
If You Could See Her (The Gorilla Song) (Grey)
What Would You Do? (Lenya)
Cabaret (Haworth)
Finale (company)

CABIN IN THE SKY (October 25, 1940, Martin Beck Theatre)

AEI Records 1107 mono

Music: Vernon Duke; lyrics: John Latouche; musical direction: Max Meth

Cast: Ethel Waters

Songs: Overture (orchestra)
Taking a Chance on Love (Waters)
Honey in the Honeycomb (Waters)
Cabin in the Sky (Waters)
Love Turned the Light Out (Waters)

CABIN IN THE SKY (Revival, January 21, 1964, Off Broadway, Greenwich Mews Theatre)

Capitol SW 2073 stereo

Musical direction: Sy Oliver

Cast: Helen Ferguson, Bernard Johnson, Sam Laws, Rosetta Le Noire, Ketty Lester, Tony Middleton, Harold Pierson, Morton Winston

Songs: Wade in the Water (Ferguson, cast)
Cabin in the Sky (Le Noire, Middleton)
Make Way (Ferguson, Laws)
The Man Upstairs (Laws)
Taking a Chance on Love (Le Noire)
Do What You Want to Do (Johnson, Pierson, Winston)
We'll Live All Over Again (Le Noire)
Gospel: Great Day (cast)

Honey in the Honeycomb (Lester)
Love Me Tomorrow (Lester, Middleton)
Not a Care in the World (Le Noire, Middleton)
Not So Bad to be Good (Laws)

Do What You Want to Do (reprise) (Lester, Pierson, Winston)
Love Turned the Light Out (Le Noire)
Living It Up (Lester, Middleton)
Savanna (Le Noire, cast)

LA CAGE AUX FOLLES (August 21, 1983, Palace Theatre)

RCA HBC 1-4824 stereo CD

Music, lyrics: Jerry Herman; musical direction: Donald Pippin

Cast: Gene Barry, Jay Garner, George Hearn, Merle Louise, Elizabeth Parrish, William Thomas, Jr., John Weiner

Songs: Prelude (orchestra)
We Are What We Are (company)
A Little More Mascara (Hearn, company)
With Anne on My Arm (Weiner)
With You on My Arm (Barry, Hearn)
Song on the Sand (La da da da) (Barry)
La Cage aux Folles (Hearn, company)

I Am What I Am (Hearn)
Song on the Sand (reprise) (Barry, Hearn)
Masculinity (Barry, Hearn, company)
Look Over There (Barry)
Cocktail Counterpoint (Barry, Louise, Weiner, Garner, Thomas)
The Best of Times (Parrish, Hearn, company)
Look Over There (reprise)(Weiner, Barry)
Finale (company)

CALL ME MADAM (October 12, 1950, Imperial Theatre)

RCA LOC 1000 mono reissued: CBM 1-2032

Music, lyrics: Irving Berlin; musical direction: Jay Blackton

Cast: Ralph Chambers, Pat Harrington, Paul Lukas, Russell Nype, Dinah Shore, Galina Talva, Jay Velie

Songs: Overture (orchestra)
Mrs. Sally Adams (chorus)
The Hostess with the Mostes' on the Ball (Shore)
Washington Square Dance (Shore, chorus)
Welcome to Lichtenburg (Lukas, chorus)
Can You Use Any Money Today? (Shore)
Marrying for Love (Shore, Lukas)
The Ocarina (Talva, chorus)

It's a Lovely Day Today (Nype, Talva)
The Best Thing for You (Shore)
Something to Dance About (Shore, chorus)
Once Upon a Time Today (Nype)
They Like Ike (Harrington, Chambers, Velie)
You're Just in Love (Shore, Nype)

Note: Dinah Shore replaced Ethel Merman for this recording,

due to contractual problems. Merman recorded her own studio version, available on MCA 2055E.

CALL ME MISTER (April 18, 1946, National Theatre)

Decca 7005 mono reissued: Columbia CSP X 14877

Music, lyrics: Harold Rome; musical direction: Lehman Engel

Cast: Paula Bane, Bill Callahan, Harry Clark, Chandler Cowles, Betty Garrett, Jules Munshin, Danny Scholl, Lawrence Winters

Songs: Going Home Train (Winters, male chorus)
Along with Me (Scholl, Bane, chorus)
Little Surplus Me (Garrett)
The Red Ball Express (Winters, male quartet)
Military Life (Munshin, Cowles, Clark)
Call Me Mister (Callahan)
Yuletide, Park Avenue (Garrett, vocal septet)
When We Meet Again (Bane, chorus)
The Face on the Dime (Winters)
South America, Take It Away (Garrett, male trio)

CAMBRIDGE CIRCUS (October 6, 1964, Plymouth Theatre)

Parlophone (British) PCS 3046 stereo

Music: Bill Oddie, Hugh MacDonald, David Palmer; Written by the cast; musical direction: Hugh MacDonald

Cast: Tim Brooke-Taylor, Anthony Buffery, John Cleese, David Hatch, Jo Kendall, Bill Oddie, Chris Stuart-Clark

Songs: Green Line Bus (Brook-Taylor, Hatch, Oddie)
Patients for the Use Of (Kendall, Stuart-Clark, Brooke-Taylor, Oddie) spoken
Boring Sexy Song (Buffery, Kendall, Brooke-Taylor)
Great Moments in British Theatre (Cleese, Buffery, Hatch, Kendall, Brooke-Taylor, Stuart-Clark) spoken
Pride and Joy (Kendall)
B.B.C.B.C. (Hatch, Cleese) spoken
Sing Sing (Oddie, Cleese, Kendall, Buffery, Brooke-Taylor)

Boring Straight Song (Oddie)
Sway a Jest (Brooke-Taylor, Stuart-Clark)
Those Were the Days (Oddie) spoken
O.H.M.S. (Oddie, Cleese, Buffery, Brook-Taylor, Hatch)
Judge Not (Cleese, Oddie, Brooke-Taylor, Buffery, Hatch, Stuart-Clark) spoken

Note: London cast recording; Anthony Buffery and Chris Stuart-Clark replaced for Broadway production by Graham Chapman and Jonathan Lynn.

CAMELOT (December 3, 1960, Majestic Theatre)

Columbia KOS 2031 stereo reissued: Columbia JS 32602 CD

Music: Frederick Loewe; lyrics: Alan Jay Lerner; based on *The Once and Future King* by T.H. White; musical direction: Franz Allers

Cast: Julie Andrews, Mary Sue Berry, Richard Burton, John Cullum, Robert Goulet, James Gannon, Roddy McDowall, Bruce Yarnell

Songs: Overture (orchestra)
I Wonder What the King Is Doing Tonight (Burton)
The Simple Joys of Maidenhood (Andrews)
Camelot (Burton)
Follow Me (Berry)
The Lusty Month of May (Andrews, chorus)
C'est Moi (Goulet)
Then You May Take Me to the Fair (Andrews, Cullum, Gannon, Yarnell)
How to Handle a Woman (Burton)

If Ever I Would Leave You (Goulet)
Parade (orchestra)
Before I Gaze at You Again (Andrews)
The Seven Deadly Virtues (McDowall)
What Do the Simple Folk Do (Andrews, Burton)
Fie on Goodness! (men)
I Loved You Once in Silence (Andrews)
Guenevere (chorus)
Camelot (reprise) (Burton)

CAN-CAN (May 7, 1953, Shubert Theatre)

Capitol S 452 mono

Music, lyrics: Cole Porter; musical direction: Milton Rosenstock

Cast: Hans Conried, Peter Cookson, Lilo, Erik Rhodes, Gwen Verdon

Songs: Introduction - Maidens Typical of France (girls)
Never Give Anything Away (Lilo, girls)
Quadrille (orchestra)
C'est Magnifique (Lilo, Cookson)
Come Along with Me (Rhodes, Conried)
Live and Let Love (Lilo)
I Am in Love (Cookson)

If You Loved Me Truly (Verdon, Conried, cast)
Montmart' (cast)
Allez-vous-en, Go Away (Lilo)
Never, Never Be an Artist (Conried, cast)
It's All Right with Me (Cookson)
Every Man Is a Stupid Man (Lilo)
I Love Paris (Lilo)
Can-Can (Lilo, cast)

Note: "The Garden of Eden Ballet", recorded in 1959 in stereo was issued on Painted Smiles PS 1364, Ballet on Broadway; musical direction: Lehman Engel

CANDIDE (December 1, 1956, Martin Beck Theatre)

Columbia OS 2350 stereo

Music: Leonard Bernstein; lyrics: Richard Wilbur; additional lyrics: John Latouche, Dorothy Parker; based on Voltaire's satire; musical direction: Samuel Krachmalnick

Cast: Max Adrian, George Blackwell, William Chapman, Barbara Cook, Robert Mesrobian, William Olvis, Irra Petina, Thomas Pyle, Norman Roland, Robert Rounseville, Robert Rue

Songs: Overture (orchestra)
The Best of All Possible Worlds (Adrian, Cook, Rounseville, chorus)
Oh, Happy We (Rounseville, Cook)
It Must Be So (Rounseville)
Mazurka (orchestra)
Glitter and Be Gay (Cook)
You Were Dead, You Know (Rounseville, Cook)
My Love (Olvis, Cook, Petina)
I Am Easily Assimilated (Petina, Cook, Blackwell, Pyle, chorus)

Quartet Finale (Rounseville, Cook, Olvis, Petina)
Quiet (Cook, Olvis, Petina, Rue)
Eldorado (Rounseville, chorus)
Bon Voyage (Olvis, chorus)
What's the Use? (Petina, Roland, Chapman, Mesrobian, chorus)
Gavotte (Petina, Rounseville, Adrian, Cook)
Finale: Make Our Garden Grow (Rounseville, Cook, chorus)

CANDIDE (Revival, December 18, 1973, Off Broadway, Chelsea Theatre Center; transferred, Broadway, March 5, 1974, Broadway Theatre)

Columbia S2X 32923 (two records) stereo

Additional lyrics: Stephen Sondheim; musical direction: John Mauceri

Cast: Mark Baker, Gail Boggs, Maureen Breenan, Jim Corti, Sam Freed, June Gable, Lynne Gannaway, Chip Garnett, Robert Henderson, David Horwitz, Becky McSpadden, Carolann Page, Deborah St. Darr, Renee Semes, Lewis J. Stadlen

Songs: Overture (orchestra)
Life Is Happiness Indeed (Baker, Breenan, Freed, St. Darr)
Parade (orchestra)

The Best of All Possible Worlds (Stadlen, Baker, Breenan, Freed, St. Darr)
Oh Happy We (Baker, Breenan)
It Must Be So (Baker)
O Miserere (Page, Gannaway, Boggs, Garnett)
Oh Happy We (reprise) (Baker, Breenan)
Glitter and Be Gay (Breenan)
Auto Da Fe (What a Day) (company)
This World (Baker)
You Were Dead, You Know (Baker, Breenan)
The Rich Jew and the Grand Inquisitor - spoken
I Am Easily Assimilated (Gable, Corti, Henderson, Horwitz)
I Am Easily Assimilated (reprise) (Gable, Baker, Breenan)
My Love (Stadlen, Freed)
Barcarolle (Upon a Ship at Sea) (Gable)
Alleluia (company)
Sheep's Song (McSpadden, Semes, Corti, St. Darr)
Bon Voyage (Stadlen, company)
The Best of All Possible Worlds (reprise) (Gable, Baker, St. Darr, Semes, McSpadden)
Constantinople: You Were Dead, You Know (reprise) (Baker, Breenan)
Barcarolle (reprise) (Gable)
Finale: Make Our Garden Grow (company)

CANDIDE (Revival, October 13, 1982, A New York City Opera Production, New York State Theatre)

New World Records NW 340/341 (two records) stereo CD

Additional lyrics: Stephen Sondheim; musical direction: John Mauceri

Cast: Ivy Austin, Ralph Bassett, James Billings, Robert Brubaker, Rhoda Butler, Joyce Castle, Maris Clement, Maria Donaldi, David Eisler, Jack Harrold, John Lankston, William Ledbetter, Erie Mills, Scott Reeve, Don Yule

Songs: Overture (orchestra)
Fanfare (Lankston) spoken
Life Is Happiness Indeed (Eisler, Mills, Reeve, Clement) lyrics: Sondheim
The Best of All Possible Worlds (Lankston, Eisler, Mills, Reeve, Clement, chorus)
Happy Instrumental (orchestra)
Oh, Happy We (Eisler, Mills)
Candide Begins His Travels (orchestra)
It Must Be So (Candide's Meditation) (Eisler)
Westphalian Fanfare (orchestra)
Chorale (chorus)
Battle Music (orchestra)
It Must Be So (reprise) (orchestra)
Entrance of the Jew (orchestra)
Glitter and Be Gay (Mills)

Earthquake Music (orchestra)
Dear Boy (Lankston, male chorus)
Auto-da-Fe (What a Day) (Brubaker, Austin, Butler, Yule, Ledbetter, Donaldi, Wills, Castle, Billings, Harrold, chorus)
Candide's Lament (Eisler)
You Were Dead, You Know (Eisler, Mills)
Travel (to the Stables) (orchestra)
I Am Easily Assimilated (Castle, Yule, Ledbetter, Bassett, chorus)
Quartet Finale (Eisler, Mills, Castle, Lankston, chorus)

Entr'acte (orchestra)
Ballad of the New World (Eisler, chorus)
My Love (Lankston, Reeve)
Barcarolle (chorus)
Alleluia (Eisler, Reeve, Lankston, chorus)
Eldorade (orchestra)
Sheep Song (Austin, Butler, Brubaker, Clement, Eisler, chorus) lyrics: Sondheim

---

Governor's Waltz (orchestra)
Bon Voyage (Lankston, chorus)
Quiet (Castle, Clement, Eisler)
Constantinople (orchestra)
What's the Use (Harrold, Billings, Lankston, chorus)
Finale: Make Our Garden Grow (Eisler, Mills, Castle, Clement, Reeve, Lankston, company)

CANTERBURY TALES (February 3, 1969, Eugene O'Neill Theatre)

Capitol SW 229 stereo

Music: Richard Hill, John Hawkins; lyrics: Nevill Coghill; based on a translation of Chaucer by Mr. Coghill; musical direction: Oscar Kosarin

Cast: Hermione Baddeley, Roy Cooper, Sandy Duncan, Ed Evanko, Ann Gardner, Martyn Green, Bruce Hyde, Evelyn Page, George Rose, Suzan Sidney, Edwin Steffe

Songs: Overture (orchestra)
Chaucer's Prologue (Green)
Song of Welcome (Steffe, company)
Goodnight Hymn (company)
Canterbury Day (company)
Pilgrim Riding Music (orchestra)
I Have a Noble Cock (Evanko)
Darling, Let Me Teach You How to Kiss (Hyde)
There's the Moon (Evanko, Duncan)
It Depends On What You're At (Baddeley, Page, company)
Love Will Conquer All (Gardner, Sidney, company)
Beer Is Best (company)
Mug Dance (orchestra)

Come On and Marry Me, Honey (Baddeley, company)
Where Are the Girls of Yesterday (steffe, company)
Hymen, Hymen (company)
If She Never Loved Before (Rose)

I'll Give My Love a Ring (Evanko, Duncan)
Pear Tree Quintet (Rose, Cooper, Evanko, Duncan, Gardner)
I Am All A-Blaze (Evanko)
What Do Women Want (Hyde)
April Song (company)
Love Will Conquer All (Gardner)
Chaucer's Epilogue (Green, company)

CARMELINA (April 8, 1979, St. James Theatre)

Original Cast Records OS 8019 stereo

Music: Burton Lane; lyrics: Alan Jay Lerner; musical direction: Don Jennings

Cast: Georgia Brown, Jossie De Guzman, Grace Keagy, Bernie Knee, Gordon Ramsey, Howard Ross, Paul Sorvino

Songs: Overture (orchestra)
Prayer (Brown, Sorvino)
It's Time for a Love Song (Sorvino)
Why Him? (Brown)
I Must Have Her (Sorvino)
Someone in April (Brown, Keagy)
Signora Campbell (Keagy, Brown, chorus)

Love Before Breakfast (Brown, Sorvino)
Yankee Doodles Are Coming to Town (chorus)
One More Walk Around the Garden (Ramsey, Ross, Knee)
All That He Wants Me to Be (De Guzman)
Carmelina (Sorvino)
The Image of Me (Knee, Ramsey, Ross)
I'm a Woman (Brown)
Finale (Brown, Sorvino)

Note: Paul Sorvino and Bernie Knee replace Cesare Siepi and John Michael Smith of the original cast.

CARMEN JONES (December 2, 1943, Broadway Theatre)

Decca DL 9021 mono reissued: MCA 1531E

Music: Georges Bizet; lyrics: Oscar Hammerstein II; based on Bizet's opera Carmen; musical direction: Joseph Littau

Cast: Glenn Bryant, Carlotta Franzell, June Hawkins, Dick Montgomery, Jessica Russell, Luther Saxon, Muriel Smith, Randall Steplight

Songs: Prelude (orchestra)
Lift 'em Up and Put 'em Down (chorus)
Dat's Love (Smith, chorus)
Der's a Cafe on de Corner (Smith, Saxon)
Beat Out Dat Rhythm on a Drum (Hawkins, chorus)
Stan' Up and Fight (Bryant, chorus)

Whizzin' Away Along de Track (Smith, Hawkins, Russell,

Montgomery, Steplight)
Diz Flower (Saxon)
My Joe (Franzell)
Dat's Our Man (chorus)
Finale (Smith, Saxon, chorus)

CARNIVAL (April 13, 1961, Imperial Theatre)

MGM Records E 39460C stereo

Music, lyrics: Bob Merrill; musical direction: Saul Schechtman

Cast: Anna Maria Alberghetti, Kaye Ballard, Henry Lascoe, James Mitchell, Pierre Olaf, Jerry Orbach

Songs: Opening - Direct from Vienna (Ballard, Lascoe, chorus)
Mira (Can You Imagine That?) (Alberghetti)
Sword, Rose and Cape (Mitchell, men)
A Very Nice Man (Alberghetti)
I've Got to Find a Reason (Orbach)
Yes, My Heart (Alberghetti, chorus)
Humming (Ballard, Lascoe)
Theme from Carnival (Alberghetti)

Grand Imperial Cirque de Paris (Olaf, chorus)
Her Face (Orbach)
Yum, Ticky, Ticky, Tum, Tum (Alberghetti, puppets)
The Rich (Alberghetti, puppets)
Beautiful Candy (Alberghetti, puppets, chorus)
Everybody Likes You (Orbach)
I Hate Him (Alberghetti)
Her Face (reprise) (Orbach)
It Was Always You (Mitchell, Ballard)
It Was Always You (reprise) (Ballard)
She's My Love (Orbach)
Theme from Carnival (puppet, orchestra)

Note: Carnival Theme title: Love Makes the World Go Round

CAROUSEL (April 19, 1945, Majestic Theatre)

Decca DLP 8003 mono reissued: MCA 37093E

Music: Richard Rodgers; lyrics: Oscar Hammerstein II; based on Ferenc Molnar's Liliom; musical direction: Joseph Littau

Cast: Connie Baxter, Jan Clayton, Jean Darling, Christine Johnson, Eric Mattson, John Raitt, Murvyn Vye

Songs: The Carousel Waltz (orchestra)
You're a Queer One, Julie Jordan (Clayton, Darling)
Mister Snow (Darling, girls chorus)
If I Loved You (Clayton, Raitt)
Soliloquy (Raitt)

June Is Bustin' Out All Over (Johnson, Darling, chorus)
When the Children Are Asleep (Mattson, Darling)
Blow High, Blow Low (Vye, male chorus)

This Was a Real Nice Clambake (Mattson, Darling, chorus)
There's Nothin' So Bad for a Woman (Vye, Baxter, girls chorus)
What's the Use of Wond'rin' (Clayton)
The Highest Judge of All (Raitt, Johnson, Clayton)
You'll Never Walk Alone (Johnson, chorus)

CAROUSEL (Revival, August 10, 1965, New York State Theatre)

RCA LSO 1114 stereo

Musical direction: Franz Allers

Cast: Eileen Christy, Katherine Hilgenberg, Jerry Orbach, John Raitt, Reid Shelton, Susan Watson

Songs: The Carousel Waltz (orchestra)
You're a Queer One, Julie Jordan (Christy, Watson)
If I Loved You (Raitt, Christy)
June Is Bustin' Out All Over (Watson, Hilgenberg, chorus)

Mister Snow (Watson, Shelton, chorus)
Blow High, Blow Low (Raitt, Orbach, chorus)
When the Children Are Asleep (Watson, Shelton)
Soliloquy (Raitt)
A Real Nice Clambake (Christy, Watson, Shelton, Hilgenberg, chorus)
What's the Use of Wond'rin' (Christy)
You'll Never Walk Alone (Hilgenberg)
The Highest Judge of All (Raitt)
Finale Ultimo (company)

CATS (October 7, 1982, Winter Garden Theatre)

Geffen Records 2GHS 2031 (two records) stereo CD

Music: Andrew Lloyd Webber; lyrics: T.S. Eliot, additional material, Trevor Nunn; musical direction: Rene Wiegert

Cast: Betty Buckley, Rene Ceballos, Wendy Edmead, Steven Gelfer, Harry Groener, Stephen Hanan, Janet L. Hubert, Reed Jones, Donna King, Anna McNeely, Terrence V. Mann, Hector Jaime Mercado, Cynthia Onrubia, Ken Page, Timothy Scott, Bonnie Simmons

Songs: Prologue (orchestra)
Jellicle Songs for Jellicle Cats (company)
The Naming of Cats (company)
The Invitation to the Jellicle Ball (Onrubia, Scott, company)
The Old Gumbie Cat (McNeely, Ceballos, King, Simmons)
The Rum Tum Tugger (Mann, company)
Grizabella, the Glamour Cat (Buckley, Edmead, King, company)

Bustopher Jones (Hanan, McNeely, Simmons, King, company)

Mungojerrie and Rumpleteazer (Scott)
Old Deuteronomy (Groener, Mann, Page, company)
The Jellicle Ball (company)
Grizabella (Buckley)

The Moment of Happiness (Page, Hubert)
Gus: the Theatre Cat (Simmons, Hanan)
Growltiger's Last Stand (Hanan, Simmons, Groener, Jones, Mann, Mercado, Scott, Gelfer, company)
Skimbleshanks the Railroad Cat (Jones, company)

Macavity (Edmead, King)
Mr. Mistoffolees (Scott, Mann, company)
Memory (Onrubia, Buckley)
The Journey to the Heaviside Layer (company)
The Ad-dressing of Cats (Page, company)

CELEBRATION (January 22, 1969, Ambassador Theatre)

Capitol SW 198 stereo

Music: Harvey Schmidt; lyrics: Tom Jones; musical direction: Rod Derefinko

Cast: Keith Charles, Michael Glenn-Smith, Ted Thurston, Susan Watson

Songs: Celebration (Charles, chorus)
Orphan in the Storm (Glenn-Smith, chorus)
Survive (Charles, chorus)
Somebody (Watson, chorus)
Bored (Thurston)
My Garden (Glenn-Smith, chorus)
Where Did It Go? (Thurston, chorus)

Love Song (Watson, Charles, Thurston, Glenn-Smith, chorus)
I'm Glad to See You've Got What You Want (Watson, Glenn-Smith)
It's You Who Make Me Young (Thurston, chorus)
Not My Problem (Charles, chorus)
Fifty Million Years Ago (Glenn-Smith, Charles)
Under the Tree (Watson, chorus)
Winter and Summer (chorus)
Celebration - Finale (chorus)

CHARLOTTE SWEET (August 12, 1982, Off Broadway, Cheryl Crawford Theatre)

John Hammond Records W2X-38680 (two records) stereo

Music: Gerald Jay Markoe; lyrics: Michael Colby; musical direction: Jan Rosenberg

Cast: Mara Beckerman, Lynn Eldredge, Jeffrey Keller, Timothy Landfield, Merle Louise, Michael McCormick, Polly Pen, Christopher Seppe

Songs: At the Music Hall (McCormick, cast)

Charlotte Sweet (Landfield, Beckerman, cast)
A Daughter of Valentine's Day (Beckerman, cast)
Forever (Seppe, Beckerman)
Liverpool Sunset (cast)
Layers of Underwear (Landfield, Eldredge, Keller, Beckerman)
Quartet Agnonistes (Eldredge, Keller, Beckerman, Landfield)
Forever (reprise) (Keller, Eldredge)

We Strut Out Our Band (Keller)
The Circus of Voices (Keller, Eldredge, Pen, Louise, McCormick, Beckerman)
Keep It Low (Eldredge, McCormick, Pen)
Bubbles in Me Bonnet (Louise)
Vegetable Reggie (McCormick)
My Baby and Me (Pen)
A-Weaving (Beckerman, Louise, Pen)

What a Girl (cast)
Your High Note! (Beckerman, Keller, Eldredge)
Katina/The Darkness (Keller)
Act One Closing (orchestra)
On It Goes (cast)
You See in Me a Bobby (Landfield, Keller, Eldredge)
A Christmas Buche (Beckerman, Louise, Pen, McCormick)
The Letter (Me Charlotte Dear) (Seppe)
Dover (Pen)
Volley of Indecision (Pen, McCormick)
Good Things Come (Louise)

You're Right! (Beckerman)
It Could Only Happen in the Theatre (Pen, Landfield, Louise, McCormick)
Lonely Canary (Beckerman)
Queenly Comments (Seppe, Keller, Eldredge, Landfield, Beckerman)
Suprise! Suprise! (cast)
The Reckoning (cast)
Farewell to Auld Lang Syne - Finale (cast)

CHICAGO (June 1, 1975, Forty-Sixth Street Theatre)

Arista 9005 stereo reissued: ALB 68346

Music: John Kander; lyrics: Fred Ebb; based on the play by Maurine Dallas Watkins; musical direction: Stanley Lebowsky

Cast: Mary McCarty, Barney Martin, M. O'Haughey, Jerry Orbach, Chita Rivera, Gwen Verdon

Songs: Overture (orchestra)
All That Jazz (Rivera, company)
Funny Honey (Verdon, Martin)
Cell Block Tango (Rivera, girls)
When You're Good to Mama (McCarty)
All I Care About (Orbach, girls)
A Little Bit of Good (O'Haughey)
We Both Reached for the Gun (Orbach, O'Haughey, Verdon, company)

Roxie (Verdon, boys)
I Can't Do It Alone (Rivera)
My Own Best Friend (Verdon, Rivera)
Me and My Baby (Verdon, boys)
Mr. Cellophane (Martin)
When Velma Takes the Stand (Rivera, boys)
Razzle Dazzle (Orbach, company)
Class (Rivera, McCarty)
Nowadays (Verdon, Rivera)
All That Jazz (reprise) (Rivera, company)

Note: Liza Minnelli, who replaced Gwen Verdon for some weeks, recorded:

Columbia 3-10178 (45rpm) My Own Best Friend
All That Jazz

A CHORUS LINE (May 21, 1975, Off Broadway, Public Theatre; transferred, Broadway, October 19, 1975, Shubert Theatre)

Columbia JS 33581 stereo CD

Cast: Renee Baughman, Carole Bishop, Pamela Blair, Wayne Cilento, Kay Cole, Nancy Lane, Priscilla Lopez, Donna McKechnie, Don Percassi

Songs: I Hope I Get It (company)
I Can Do That (Cilento)
At the Ballet (Bishop, Lane, Cole)
Sing! (Baughman, Percassi)
Hello Twelve, Hello Thirteen, Hello Love (company)
Nothing (Lopez)

The Music and the Mirror (McKechnie)
Dance: Ten; Looks: Three (Blair)
One (company)
What I Did for Love (Lopez, company)
One (reprise) (company)

CHRISTINE (April 28, 1960, Forty-Sixth Street Theatre)

Columbia OS 2026 stereo

Music: Sammy Fain; lyrics: Paul Francis Webster; based on the novel *My Indian Family* by Hilda Wernher; musical direction: Jay Blackton

Cast: Nancy Andrews, Bhaskar, Leslye Hunter, Phil Leeds, Morley Meredith, Maureen O'Hara, Janet Pavek, Barbara Webb

Songs: Overture (orchestra)
Welcome Song (Andrews, Leeds, Bhaskar, company)
My Indian Family (O'Hara, company)
A Doctor's Soliloquy (Meredith)
UNICEF Song (children)
My Little Lost Girl (O'Hara, Meredith)

I'm Just a Little Sparrow (Hunter, company)
How to Pick a Man and a Wife (Andrews, Leeds)
The Lovely Girls of Akbarabad (Webb, company)
Room in My Heart (O'Hara)

The Divali Festival (company)
I Never Meant to Fall in Love (Meredith, O'Hara)
Freedom Can Be a Most Uncomfortable Thing (Andrews, company)
Ireland Was Never Like This (O'Hara)
He Loves Her (Pavek)
Christine (Meredith)
I Love Him (O'Hara)
Freedom Can Be a Most Uncomfortable Thing (reprise) (Andrews, Leeds)
The Woman I Was Before (O'Hara)
A Doctor's Soliloquy (reprise) (O'Hara, Meredith)
I Never Meant to Fall in Love - Finale (O'Hara, Meredith)

CHRISTY (October 14, 1975, Off Broadway, Bert Wheeler Theatre)

Original Cast Records OC 7913 stereo

Music: Lawrence J. Blank; lyrics: Bernie Spiro; based on John M. Synge's The Playboy of the Western World; musical direction: Robert Billig

Cast: John Canary, Jimi Elmer, Bette Forsyth, Marie Ginnetti, Lynn Kearney, Martha T. Kearns, Bebe Sacks Landis, Gene Lefkowitz, Brian Pizer, Alexander Sokoloff, Bee Swanson

Songs: Christy (Elmer)
To Please the Woman in Me (Forsyth, Kearns, Kearney, Ginnetti, Landis)
Grain of the Salt of the Earth (Sokoloff, Lefkowitz, Pizer, Forsyth, Elmer)
Until the Likes of You (Elmer, Forsyth)
Picture Me (Elmer)
The Morning After (Forsyth)

Rumors (Kearns, Kearney, Ginnetti, Landis, Swanson)
One Fell Swoop (Elmer, Kearns, Kearney, Ginnetti, Landis, Swanson)
All's Fair (Swanson, Canary)
The Heart's a Wonder (Forsyth, Elmer)
Down the Hatch (Sokoloff, Lefkowitz, Pizer, Swanson)
Gallant Little Swearers (Sokoloff, Elmer, Forsyth, ensemble)
Until the Likes of You (Forsyth)

Note: Gene Lefkowitz replaces Bill Hedge of the original cast.

CINDY (March 19, 1964, Off Broadway, Gate Theatre)

ABC-Paramount Records ABCS-OC-2 stereo

Music, lyrics: Johnny Brandon; musical direction: Sammy Benskin

Cast: Dena Dietrich, Johnny Harmon, Tommy Karaty, Sylvia Mann, Joe Masiell, Jacqueline Mayro, Frank Nastasi, Thelma Oliver, Lizbeth Pritchett, Mike Sawyer, Mark Stone, Amelia Varney

Songs: Once Upon a Time (Oliver, Karaty, Stone)
Let's Pretend (Mayro, Harmon)
Is There Something to What He Said? (Mayro)
Papa, Let's Do It Again (Mann, Nastasi)
A Genuine Feminine Girl (Mayro)
Cindy (Harmon)
Think Mink (Varney, Dietrich)
Tonight's the Night (Oliver, Karaty, Stone)

Who Am I? (Masiell, Mayro)
If You've Got It, You've Got It (Dietrich, Varney, Mann, Nastasi)
The Life That I Have Planned for Him (Pritchett)
If It's Love (Masiell, Mayro)
Got the World in the Palm of My Hand (Masiell)
Call Me Lucky (Harmon)
Laugh It Up (Mayro)
What a Wedding (Sawyer, Pritchett, Nastasi, Mann, Masiell, Dietrich, Varney)

CLUES TO A LIFE (February 3, 1982, Off Broadway, Vineyard Theatre)

Original Cast Records OC 8237 stereo

Music: Marty Palitz, Alec Wilder; lyrics: Roger Bracket, William Engvick, Fran Landesman, Loonis McGlohon, Alec Wilder; musical direction: E. Martin Perry

Cast: Christine Andreas, D'Jamin Bartlett, Keith David, Craig Lucas

Songs: Overture (orchestra)
The Echoes of My Life (Andreas) music: Wilder; lyrics: Bracket
Photographs (Bartlett) music: Wilder; lyrics: Landesman
That's My Girl (David, Lucas) music: Wilder; lyrics: Engvick
Unbelieveable (Lucas) music: Wilder; lyrics: Engvick
Give Me Time (Andreas) music, lyrics: Wilder
It's So Peaceful in the Country (David) music, lyrics: Wilder
Where Is the One? (Andreas, Bartlett) music, lyrics: Wilder
Don't Deny (Lucas) music: Wilder; lyrics: Engvick
Moon and Sand (Bartlett) music: Wilder; lyrics: Engvick
Where Is the One? (reprise) (company)
I'd Do It Again (David) music, lyrics: Wilder
I'll Be Around (company) music, lyrics: Wilder
While We're Young (Andreas) music: Wilder, Palitz; lyrics: Engvick
---

Night Talk (David) music, lyrics: Wilder
A Long Night (Bartlett) music: Wilder; lyrics: McGlohon
Blackberry Winter (David) music, Wilder; lyrics: McGlohon
I'll Be Around (reprise) (Bartlett)
Trouble Is a Man (Andreas) music: Wilder; lyrics: McGlohon
You Wrong Me (Andreas, Lucas, Bartlett) music, lyrics: Wilder
The Worm Has Turned (Andreas, Lucas, Bartlett) music: Wilder; lyrics: McGlohon
Ellen (David) music: Wilder; lyrics: Engvick
Did You Ever Cross Over to Snedens? (Lucas) music, lyrics: Wilder
Mimosa and Me (Andreas) music: Wilder; lyrics: Engvick
I See It Now (David, Andreas) music: Wilder; lyrics: Engvick
While We're Young (reprise) (company)

COCO (December 18, 1969, Mark Hellinger Theatre)

Paramount Records PMS 1002 stereo

Music: Andre Previn; lyrics: Alan Jay Lerner; musical direction: Robert Emmett Dolan

Cast: Will B. Abel, Rene Auberjonois, Chad Block, Jon Cypher, Jack Dabdoub, Gale Dixon, Robert Fitch, Katharine Hepburn, David Holliday, George Rose, Dan Siretta

Songs: Overture (orchestra)
But That's the Way You Are (Dabdoub)
The World Belongs to the Young (Hepburn, chorus)
Let's Go Home (Holliday)
Mademoiselle Cliche de Paris on the Corner of the Rue Cambon (Hepburn)
The Money Rings Out Like Freedom (Hepburn, chorus)
A Brand New Dress (Dixon)
A Woman Is How She Loves (Holliday)

Gabrielle (Cypher)
Coco (Hepburn)
Fiasco (Auberjonois)
When Your Lover Says Goodbye (Ross)
Ohrbach's, Bloomingdale's, Best and Saks (Hepburn, Abel, Block, Fitch, Siretta)
Always Mademoiselle (Hepburn)

COMPANY (April 26, 1970, Alvin Theatre)

Columbia OS 3550 stereo CD

Music, lyrics: Stephen Sondheim; musical direction: Harold Hastings

Cast: Barbara Barrie, Charles Braswell, Susan Browning, George Coe, John Cunningham, Steve Elmore, Beth

Howland, Dean Jones, Charles Kimbrough, Merle Louise, Donna McKechnie, Pamela Myers, Teri Ralston, Elaine Stritch

Songs: Company (Jones, cast)
The Little Things You Do Together (Stritch, cast)
Sorry-Grateful (Kimbrough, Coe, Braswell, Jones)
You Could Drive a Person Crazy (McKechnie, Browning, Myers)
Have I Got a Girl for You (Braswell, Cunningham, Elmore, Coe, Kimbrough, cast)
Someone Is Waiting (Jones, chorus)
Another Hundred People (Myers, chorus)
Getting Married Today (Howland, Ralston, Elmore, cast)

Side by Side by Side (Jones, cast)
What Would We Do Without You (Jones, cast)
Poor Baby (Barrie, Ralston, Louise, Howland, Stritch, Kimbrough, Coe)
Tick Tock (orchestra)
Barcelona (Jones, Browning)
The Ladies Who Lunch (Stritch)
Being Alive (Jones, cast)
Finale (cast)

Note: Larry Kert replaced Dean Jones for most of the run of this show on Broadway, and recorded:

CBS 70108 (British) Company (Kert, cast)
Sorry-Grateful (Kert, Coe, Kimbrough, Braswell)
Someone Is Waiting (Kert, chorus)
Side by Side by Side (Kert, cast)
What Would We Do Without You (Kert, cast)
Barcelona (Kert, Browning)
Being Alive (Kert, cast)

A CONNECTICUT YANKEE (Revival, November 17, 1943, Martin Beck Theatre)

AEI Records 1138 mono

Music: Richard Rodgers; lyrics: Lorenz Hart; a musical adaption of A Connecticut Yankee in King Arthur's Court by Mark Twain; musical direction: George Hirst

Cast: Robert Chisholm, Dick Foran, Vivienne Segal, Chester Stratton, Vera-Ellen, Julie Warren

Songs: Overture (orchestra)
My Heart Stood Still (Foran, Warren)
Thou Swell (Foran, Warren)
On a Desert Island with Thee (Stratton, Vera-Ellen)
To Keep My Love Alive (Segal)
Can't You Do a Friend a Favor? (Segal, Foran)
I Feel at Home with You (Stratton, Vera-Ellen)
You Always Love the Same Girl (Foran, Chisholm)
Finale (Segal, Foran, chorus)

COTTON PATCH GOSPEL (October 21, 1981, Off Broadway, Lambs Theatre)

Chapin Productions Records CP 101 stereo

Music, lyrics: Harry Chapin; based upon The Cotton Patch Version of Matthew and John by Clarence Jordan; musical direction: Tom Chapin

Cast: Scott Ainslie, Pete Corum, Tom Key, Jim Lauderdale, Michael Mark

Songs: Somethin's Brewing in Gainesville (cast)
I Did It (Key, cast)
Mama Is Here (Mark, cast)
It Isn't Easy (Lauterdale, cast)
Sho Nuff (Key, cast)
Turn It Around (Key, cast)
When I Look Up (cast)
Busy Signals (cast)
Spitball (cast)
Goin' to Atlanta (Key, cast)

Are We Ready (Corum, cast)
You Are Still My Boy (Lauderdale, Mark, cast)
We Gotta Get Organized (Key, cast)
We're Gonna Love It While It Lasts (cast)
Jubilation (Ainslie, cast)
Jud (cast)
The Last Supper (cast)
Thank God for Governor Pilate (Corum, cast)
One More Tomorrow (Ainslie, cast)
Well I Wonder (Key, cast)

THE CRADLE WILL ROCK (June 16, 1937, Venice Theatre; transferred, January 3, 1938, Windsor Theatre)

American Legacy Records T 1001 mono

Music, lyrics: Marc Blitzstein; at piano: Marc Blitzstein

Cast: John Adair, Howard Bird, Blanche Collins, Peggy Coudray, Howard da Silva, George Fairchild, Dulce Fox, Edward Fuller, Maynard Holmes, Ralph MacBane, Frank Marvel, Charles Niemeyer, Marion Rudley, Jules Schmidt, Olive Stanton, Bert Weston

Songs: I'm Checkin' Home Now (Stanton)
Mission Scene (Coudray, Niemeyer)
Croon, Spoon (Holmes, Fox)
The Freedom of the Press (MacBane, Weston)
Honolulu (Holmes, Fox, Weston, MacBane)
Drugstore Scene (Adair, Bird)
Gus and Sadie Love Song (Fairchild, Rudley)

The Rich (Fuller, Schmidt)
Ask Us Again (Fuller, Schmidt, Coudray)
Art for Art's Sake (Fuller, Schmidt)
Nickel Under the Foot (Stanton)
Leaflets (da Silva)

The Cradle Will Rock (da Silva)
Doctor and Ella (Collins, Marvel)
Joe Worker (Collins)
Finale (ensemble)

THE CRADLE WILL ROCK (Revival, November 8, 1964, Off Broadway, Theatre Four)

MGM SE 4289-2 OC (two records) stereo reissued: 2-CRI SD 266

Musical direction: Gershon Kingsley

Cast: Nancy Andrews, Joseph Bova, Hal Buckley, Gordon B. Clarke, Karen Cleary, Clifford David, Dean Dittmann, Rita Gardner, Micki Grant, Nichols Grimes, Peter Meersman, Jerry Orbach, Lauri Peters, Ted Scott, Wayne Tucker, Chris Warfield

Songs: Moll's Song (Peters)
Moll and Gent (Peters, Scott)
Moll and Dick (Peters, Tucker)
Moll and Druggist (Peters, Meersman)
Oh, What a Filthy Night Court! (ensemble)
--- Mrs. Mister and Reverend Salvation (Andrews, Warfield)
Croon-Spoon (Bova, Gardner)
The Freedom of the Press (Dittmann, Clarke)
Let's Do Something (Bova, Gardner)
Honolulu (Dittmann, Bova, Clarke, Gardner)
Drugstore Scene (Meersman, Grimes, Tucker)
--- Gus and Sadie Love Song (Scott, Cleary)
The Rich (Buckley, David)
Ask Us Again (Andrews, Buckley, David)
Art for Art's Sake (Buckley, David)
Nickel Under the Foot (Peters)
Leaflets (Orbach)
--- The Cradle Will Rock (Orbach)
Joe Worker (Grant)
Finale: The Cradle Will Rock (Orbach, Clarke, Peters, Meersman, company)

THE CRADLE WILL ROCK (Revival, May 9, 1983, Off Broadway, American Place Theatre)

Polydor 827 937-1 Y-1 stereo

Musical direction: Michael Barrett

Cast: Dennis Bacigalupi, Brooks Baldwin, Casey Biggs*, Daniel Corcoran*, Leslie Geraci, Patti LuPone*, Anderson Matthews, Randle Mell*, Mary Lou Rosato*, David Schramm*, Norman Snow, Henry Stram, Michele-Denise Woods*

Songs: Moll's Song (LuPone)
I'll Show You Guys (LuPone, Stram)
Solicitin' (LuPone, Bacigalupi)

Hard Times (Rosato)
The Sermon (Schramm, chorus)
Croon Spoon (LuPone, Stram)
The Freedom of the Press (Schramm, Matthews)
Let's Do Something (LuPone, Stram)
Honolulu (Matthews, Schramm, LuPone, Stram)
Summer Weather (Bacigalupi, Corcoran)
Love Duet (Gus and Sadie) (Biggs, Geraci)

Don't Let Me Keep You (Baldwin, Mell)
Ask Us Again (Rosato, Baldwin, Mell)
Art for Art's Sake (Rosato, Baldwin, Mell)
The Nickel Under Your Foot (LuPone)
The Cradle Will Rock (Mell)
Joe Worker (Woods)
Final Scene (Mell, Schramm, LuPone, Bacigalupi, company)

Note: London cast recording. Some cast members (*) appeared in New York.

CRANKS (November 26, 1956, Bijou Theatre)

HMV CLP 1082 (British) mono

Music: John Addison; lyrics: John Cranko; musical direction: Anthony Bowles

Cast: Hugh Bryant, Anthony Newley, Annie Ross, Gilbert Vernon

Songs: Who's Who (and) Adrift (Vernon, Ross, Bryant, Newley)
Where Has Tom Gone? (Bryant, Newley, Ross)
Cold Comfort (Newley)
Passacaglia (orchestra)
Who Is It Always There (Ross, Newley)
Chiromancy (Bryant)
New Blue (Ross)
Valse Anglaise (Ross, Bryant, Newley)

Don't Let Him Know You (Bryant, Newley, Ross)
Sea Song (Bryant)
Telephone Tango (Newley, Ross, Vernon)
I'm the Boy You Should Say "Yes" To (Newley, Ross)
Metamorphosis (Bryant, Ross, Newley, Vernon)
Would You Let Me Know? (Ross, Newley)
Dirge (Bryant)
Arthur, Son of Martha (Vernon, Ross, Newley, Bryant)
Goodnight (Vernon, Ross, Newley, Bryant)

Note: London cast recording. Features same cast and conductor as in New York.

CRY FOR US ALL (April 8, 1970, Broadhurst Theatre)

Project 3 Records TS 1000SD stereo

Music: Mitch Leigh; lyrics: William Alfred, Phyllis Robinson; based on Hogan's Goat by William Alfred; musical direction:

Herbert Grossman

Cast: Steve Arlen, Joan Diener, Helen Gallagher, Darel Glaser, William Griffis, Scott Jacoby, Todd Jones, Tommy Rall, Robert Weede

Songs: Overture (orchestra)
The End of My Race (Arlen)
How Are Ya, Since? (Diener, company)
The Mayor's Chair (Weede)
Verandah Waltz (Diener)
The Wages of Sin (Jacoby, Glaser, Jones)
Who to Love if Not a Stranger (Diener)
Search Your Heart (Arlen)
Cry for Us All (Rall, company)

Swing Your Bag (Gallagher)
That Slavery Is Love (Diener)
The Cruelty Man (Jacoby, Glaser, Jones)
Aggie, Oh Aggie (Weede)
The Leg of the Duck (Rall)
This Cornucopian Land (Arlen, company)
Finale (Griffis, company)

THE CRYSTAL HEART (February 15, 1960, Off Broadway, East 74th Street Theatre)

Blue Pear Records BP 1001 mono

Music: Baldwin Bergersen; lyrics: William Archibald; musical direction: Baldwin Bergersen

Cast: John Baylis, Mildred Dunnock, Bob Fitch, Margot Harley, Barbara Janezic, Katherine Litz, Byron Mitchell, Joc Ross, Jeanne Shea, John Stewart, Virginia Vestoff, Vincent Warren

Songs: Overture (pianos)
A Year and a Day (Baylis)
A Monkey When He Loves (Baylis, Fitch, Warren, Mitchell)
Handsome Husbands (Dunnock, Shea, Litz, Janezic, Harley)
Yes, Aunt (Vestoff)
Agnes and Me (Fitch)
A Girl with a Ribbon (Baylis)
I Must Paint (Vestoff)
I Wanted to See the World (Stewart, Litz)
How Strange the Silence (Shea)

Desperate (Ross, Stewart)
Lovely Island (Litz, Janezic, Harley, Stewart, Vestoff)
Bluebird (Dunnock)
Madam I Beg You (Dunnock, Ross)
My Heart Won't Learn (Shea)
When I Dance with My Love (Vestoff, Stewart)
Lovely Bridesmaids (Litz, Janezic, Harley)
It Took Them (Litz, Janezic, Harley, Fitch, Warren, Mithcell)
D-O-G (Stewart)
Finale (Dunnock, Baylis, company)

CYRANO (May 13, 1973, Palace Theatre)

A and M Records SP 3702 (two records) stereo

Music: Michael J. Lewis; lyrics: Anthony Burgess; based on Cyrano de Bergerac by Edmond Rostand; musical direction: Thomas Pierson

Cast: Leigh Berry, James Blendick, J. Kenneth Campbell, Anita Dangler, Patrick Hines, Mark Lamos, Christopher Plummer, Arnold Soboloff, Louis Turenne

Songs: Overture (orchestra)
Opening Sequence (Lamos, Soboloff, Blendick, Hines, Plummer, company)
Nose Song (Turenne, Campbell, Plummer)
Tell Her (Turenne, Plummer, Berry, Blendick, Dangler)

From Now till Forever (Blendick, Plummer, Soboloff, company)
Bergerac (Plummer, Soboloff, Berry)
No Thank You (Turenne, Blendick, Plummer)
Roxanna (Lamos, Berry, Plummer, company)
It's She and It's Me (Lamos)

You Have Made Me Love (Berry)
Thither, Thother, Thide of The...(Plummer)
Pocapdedious (men)

Paris Cuisine (Plummer, Blendick, men)
Love Is Not Love (Lamos, Berry)
Autumn Carol (Berry, women)
I Never Loved You (Plummer)
Epilog (Plummer)

Note: Recording contains dialog.

DAMES AT SEA (December 20, 1968, Off Broadway, Bouwerie Lane Theatre)

Columbia OS 3330 stereo reissued: CSP AOS 3330

Music: Jim Wise; lyrics: George Haimsohn, Robin Miller; musical direction: Richard J. Leonard

Cast: David Christmas, Steve Elmore, Tamara Long, Joseph R. Sicari, Sally Stark, Bernadette Peters

Songs: Overture (orchestra)
Wall Street (Long)
It's You (Christmas, Peters)
Broadway Baby (Christmas)
That Mister Man of Mine (Long, company)
Choo-Choo Honeymoon (Stark, Sicari)
The Sailor of My Dreams (Peters)
Good Times Are Here to Stay (Stark, company)

Dames at Sea (company)
The Beguine (Long, Elmore)
Raining in My Heart (Peters, company)
Singapore Sue (Sicari, company)

There's Something About You (Christmas, Peters)
The Echo Waltz (Long Stark, Peters, company)
Star Tar (Peters, company)
Let's Have a Simple Wedding (company)

DAMN YANKEES (May 5, 1955, Forty-Sixth Street Theatre)

RCA LOC 1021 mono reissued: AYL 1-3948E

Music, lyrics: Richard Adler, Jerry Ross; based on The Year the Yankees Lost the Pennant by Douglass Wallop; musical direction: Hal Hastings

Cast: Rae Allen, Shannon Bolin, Russ Brown, Ronn Cummins, Cherry Davis, Stephen Douglass, Nathaniel Frey, Jimmie Komack, Albert Linville, Eddie Phillips, Jackie Scholle, Robert Shafer, Jean Stapleton, Gwen Verdon, Ray Walston

Songs: Overture (orchestra)
Six Months Out of Every Year (Bolin, Shafer, company)
Goodbye, Old Girl (Shafer, Douglass)
You've Got to Have Heart (Brown, Komack, Frey, Linville)
Shoeless Joe from Hannibal, Mo. (Allen, men)
A Little Brains - A Little Talent (Verdon)
A Man Doesn't Know (Douglass, Bolin)

Whatever Lola Wants (Verdon)
You've Got to Have Heart (reprise) (Stapleton, Cummins, Scholle, Davis)
Who's Got the Pain (Verdon, Phillips)
The Game (Komack, Frey, men)
Near to You (Douglass, Bolin)
Those Were the Good Old Days (Walston)
Two Lost Souls (Verdon, Douglass)
A Man Doesn't Know (reprise) (Bolin, Shafer)
Finale (company)

DARLING OF THE DAY (January 27, 1968, George Abbott Theatre)

RCA LSO 1149 stereo

Music: Jule Styne; lyrics: E. Y. Harburg; based on Arnold Bennett's Buried Alive; musical direction: Buster Davis

Cast: Brenda Forbes, Teddy Green, Beth Howland, Mitchell Jason, Marc Jordan, Reid Klein, Joy Nichols, Vincent Price, Patricia Routledge, Charles Welch, Peter Woodthorpe

Songs: Overture (orchestra)
He's a Genius (Woodthorpe, Price, Welch)
To Get Out of This World Alive (Price)
It's Enough to Make a Lady Fall in Love (Routledge, Green, Jordan, company)
A Gentleman's Gentleman (Routledge, Green, Price, Jordan, Jason, company)
Let's See What Happens (Routledge)

--- I've Got a Rainbow Working for Me (Price, company)
That Something Extra Special (Routledge)
Money, Money, Money (Green, Jordan, Klein)
Panache (Woodthorpe, Forbes)
What Makes a Marriage Merry (Routledge, Price, Green, Jordan, Nichols, Howland)
Not on Your Nellie (Routledge, Green, Jordan, company)
Sunset Tree (Price, Routledge)
Butler in the Abbey (Price, company)
Finale (company)

A DAY IN HOLLYWOOD A NIGHT IN THE UKRAINE (May 1, 1980, John Golden Theatre)

DRG Records SBL 12580 stereo

Music: Frank Lazarus; lyrics: Dick Vosburgh; additional music, lyrics: Jerry Herman; musical direction: Wally Harper

Cast: Kate Draper, David Garrison, Peggy Hewett, Stephen James, Frank Lazarus, Priscilla Lopez

Songs: Just Go to the Movies (company) music, lyrics: Herman
Famous Feet (James, Lopez, Garrison)
I Love a Film Cliche (Lazarus, company) music: Trevor Lyttleton
Nelson (Hewett) music, lyrics: Herman
It All Comes Out of the Piano (Lazarus)
Richard Whiting Medley:
Ain't We Got Fun (company)
Too Marvelous for Words (Draper)
Japanese Sandman (James, Lopez, Garrison)
On the Good Ship Lollipop (Hewett)
Double Trouble (Hewett)
Louise (James, Lopez, Garrison, Draper)
Sleepy Time Gal (James)
Beyond the Blue Horizon (company)
--- The Best in the World (Lopez) music, lyrics: Herman
Doin' the Production Code (company)
A Night in the Ukraine (company)
Entr'acte - A Night in the Ukraine (reprise) (company)
Samovar the Lawyer (Garrison)
Just Like That (Draper, James)
Again (Draper, James)
Natasha (Garrison, Hewett)
A Night in the Ukraine (reprise) (company)

Note: Some selections on side two include dialog.

DEAR WORLD (February 6, 1969, Mark Hellinger Theatre)

Columbia BOS 3260 stereo

Music, lyrics: Jerry Herman; based on The Madwoman of Chaillot by Jean Giraudoux; musical direction: Donald Pippin

Cast: Jane Connell, Pamela Hall, Angela Lansbury, Carmen Mathews, Milo O'Shea, Kurt Peterson

Songs: Overture (orchestra)
The Spring of Next Year (company)
Each Tomorrow Morning (Lansbury, company)
I Don't Want to Know (Lansbury)
I've Never Said I Love You (Hall)
Garbage (O'Shea, Lansbury, Connell, Mathews, company)
Dear World (Lansbury, company)

I Don't Want to Know (orchestra)
Kiss Her Now (Lansbury)
The Tea Party:
Memory (Mathews)
Pearls (Lansbury, Connell)
Dickie (Connell)
Voices (Mathews)
Thoughts (Lansbury)
And I Was Beautiful (Lansbury)
Each Tomorrow Morning (reprise) (Peterson)
One Person (Lansbury, company)
Finale (company)

THE DECLINE AND FALL OF THE ENTIRE WORLD AS SEEN THROUGH THE EYES OF COLE PORTER (March 30, 1965, Off Broadway, Square East Theatre)

Columbia OS 2810 stereo

Music, lyrics: Cole Porter; musical direction: Skip Redwine

Cast: Carmen Alvarez, Kaye Ballard, William Hickey, Harold Lang, Elmarie Wendel

Songs: I Introduced (Lang, Ballard, Alvarez, Wendell)
I'm a Gigolo (Hickey)
The Leader of the Big-Time Band (Ballard, Alvarez, Wendel)
I Loved Him (Ballard)
I Happen to Like New York (Lang)
What Shall I Do? (Alvarez, Lang, Hickey)
Tomorrow (Ballard, Lang, Alvarez, Hickey, Wendel)

Farming (Ballard, Lang, Alvarez, Hickey, Wendel)
Give Him the OO-LA-LA (Wendel)
Make It Another Old Fashioned Please (Alvarez)
Down in the Depths (Ballard)
Most Gentlemen Don't Like Love (Ballard, Alvarez, Wendel)
Finale (cast):
My Mother Would Love You
Easy to Love
I've Got You Under My Skin
My Heart Belongs to Daddy
Friendship
Well, Did You Evah?
It's All Right with Me
Get Out of Town

It's De-lovely
Ev'ry Time We Say Goodbye
Another Op'nin', Another Show
Always True to You in My Fashion
C'est Magnifique
The Physician
Just One of Those Things
What Is This Thing Called Love
Love for Sale
You're the Top
Begin the Beguine
The Laziest Gal in Town

DEMI-DOZEN (October 11, 1958, Off Broadway, Upstairs at the Downstairs)

Offbeat Records O-4015 mono

Music: Michael Brown, Cy Coleman, Michael Hughes, Bud McCreery, Portia Nelson, Harvey Schmidt, Jay Thompson; lyrics: Michael Brown, Tom Jones, Carolyn Leigh, Bud McCreery, Portia Nelson, Harvey Schmidt, Jay Thompson, Joan Wile; at pianos: Gordon Connell, Stan Keen

Cast: Jean Arnold, Ceil Cabot, Jane Connell, Jack Fletcher, George Hall, Gerry Matthews

Songs: Grand Opening (cast) music: Schmidt; lyrics: Jones
Yes Sirree (Cabot) music: Hughes; lyrics: Wile
Mister Off-Broadway (Fletcher) music: Schmidt; lyrics: Jones
You Fascinate Me So (Arnold) music: Coleman; lyrics: Leigh
Conference Call (Arnold, Matthews, Hall, Fletcher) spoken
The Holy Man and the New Yorker (Matthews) music: Schmidt; lyrics: Jones
The Race of the Lexington Avenue Express (Connell) music: Schmidt; lyrics: Jones
Sunday in New York (Cabot, Matthews) music, lyrics: Nelson
The Intellectuals' Rag (cast) music, lyrics: Thompson

A Seasonal Sonatine (all) music: Schmidt; lyrics: Jones
Summer (Connell, Fletcher)
Autumn (Arnold)
Winter (Cabot)
Spring (Connell, Hall, Matthews)
One and All (Hall) music, lyrics: Schmidt
Portofino (Cabot, Connell, Arnold, Matthews, Hall) music, lyrics: Brown
Guess Who Was There (Fletcher, Arnold) music, lyrics: McCreery
3rd Avenue El (Cabot, Connell, Matthews, Fletcher) music, lyrics: Brown
Statehood Hula (Cabot) music: Schmidt; lyrics: Jones
Grand Finale - Monk's Merrie Minstrel Show! (cast) music, lyrics: McCreery

DESTRY RIDES AGAIN (April 23, 1959, Imperial Theatre)

Decca DL 79075 stereo

Music, lyrics: Harold Rome; based on the story by Max Brand; musical direction: Lehman Engel

Cast: Don Crabtree, Dolores Gray, Andy Griffith, Rosetta LeNoire, Jack Prince, Elizabeth Watts

Songs: Overture (orchestra)
Bottleneck (Crabtree, men)
Ladies (Gray, girls)
Hoop-de-Dingle (Prince, chorus)
Tomorrow Morning (Griffith)
Ballad of the Gun (Griffith, Prince)
I Know Your Kind (Gray)
I Hate Him (Gray)
Rose Lovejoy of Paradise Alley (men)
Anyone Would Love You (Griffith, Gray)

Once Knew a Fella (Griffith, men)
Every Once in a While (men)
Fair Warning (Gray)
Are You Ready, Gyp Watson? (Gray, chorus)
Not Guilty (men)
Only Time Will Tell (Griffith, chorus)
Respectability (Watts, girls)
That Ring on the Finger (Gray, LeNoire, girls)
Once Knew a Fella (reprise) (Griffith, Gray)
I Say Hello (Gray)
Ballad of the Gun - Finale (chorus)

Note: An additional orchestral selection, 'The Whip Dance,' is included on the 'Music from Shubert Alley' album, Sinclair OSS 2250 (recorded November 13, 1959).

DIME A DOZEN (October 18, 1962, Off Broadway, Plaza 9)

Cadence Records CLP 26063 (two records) stereo

Music: Michael Brown, Leslie Davison, Jay Foote, Jack Holmes, Bud McCreery, Sam Pottle, June Reizner, Claibe Richardson, William Roy, Rod Warren; lyrics: Michael Brown, William Brown, Leslie Davison, Jack Holmes, Bud McCreery, June Reizner, Allison Roulston, Maxwell Edward Siegel, Rod Warren, Tom Whedon, Bruce Williamson, Seymour Zogott; at pianos: Robert Colston, William Roy

Cast: Susan Browning, Jack Fletcher, Gerry Matthews, Rex Robbins, Fredricka Weber, Mary Louise Wilson

Songs: Introduction (Julius Monk) spoken
Dime a Dozen (cast) music: Roy; lyrics: W. Brown
Ode to an Eminent Daily (Wilson, Weber, Fletcher, Robbins) music: Roy; lyrics: Williamson
Philatelic (Wilson, Robbins) spoken
Something Good Like You (Weber) music: Pottle; lyrics: Whedon

Barry's Boys (Fletcher, Robbins, Matthews) music, lyrics: Reizner
Cholesterol Love Song (Browning) music, lyrics: Reizner
From the Top (Robbins, Fletcher) spoken

Collecting of the Plaid (cast) music, lyrics: Davison
Requiem for Everyone (Matthews, Robbins) music, lyrics: McCreery
P.T. Boat (Wilson, Robbins, Matthews, Fletcher) spoken
Ten Percent Banlon (Weber, Fletcher) music, lyrics: Davison
Battle Hymn of the Rialto (Robbins) music: Foote; lyrics: Roulston
Slow Down Moses (cast) music, lyrics: M. Brown

Marching for Peace (cast) music, lyrics: Davison
Bless This School (Weber, Matthews) music: Roy; lyrics: Siegel
The Minnows and the Sharks (Weber) music: Foote; lyrics: Roulston
H.M.S. Brownstone (Browning, Matthews) spoken
Johnny Come Lately (Browning) music: Richardson; lyrics: Zogott
Barry's Boys (reprise) (Fletcher, Robbins, Matthews)

Thor (Robbins, Fletcher) music, lyrics: Holmes
Alumnae Report (Wilson) music: Foote; lyrics: Roulston
Lincoln Center (Matthews) music, lyrics: Warren
Don't Be Absurd (Robbins, Weber, Fletcher, Wilson) spoken
The Plaza Waltz-Waltz (cast) music, lyrics: M. Brown

DO BLACK PATENT LEATHER SHOES REALLY REFLECT UP? (May 27, 1982, Alvin Theatre)

CBS Special Products DP 18852 stereo

Music, lyrics: James Quinn, Alaric Jans; based upon a novel by John R. Powers; musical direction: Larry Hochman

Cast: Eileen Blackman, Mary Buehrle, Louis DiCrescenzo, Carol Estey, Susann Fletcher, Peter Heuchling*, Patti Hoffman, Max Showalter, Don Stitt*, Russ Thacker*

Songs: Overture (orchestra)
Prologue (Thacker)
Get Ready, Eddie (company)
The Greatest Gift (Hoffman, chorus)
Little Fat Girls (Blackman, Thacker)
It's the Nuns (chorus)
Cookie Cutters (Estey, Blackman)
Queen of the May (chorus)
Patron Saints (Thacker, Showalter)
Private Parts (Showalter, boys)
How Far is Too Far (chorus)

Entr'acte (orchestra)
Patent Leather Shoes Ballet (chorus)
Doo-Waa, Doo-Wee (DiCrescenzo, chorus)
I Must Be in Love (Thacker)
Friends, the Best of (Blackman, Thacker)

The Greatest Gift (reprise) (Hoffman, Showalter, Blackman, Thacker)
Mad Bomber (Stitt, Heuchling, DiCrescenzo, Fletcher, chorus)
Late Bloomer (Thacker, Buehrle)
Friends, the Best of (reprise) (Blackman, Thacker)
Thank God (Thacker, company)

Note: This album was recorded in 1985 with some cast members (*) from the New York production.

DO I HEAR A WALTZ? (March 18, 1965, Forty-Sixth Street Theatre)

Columbia KOS 2770 stereo

Music: Richard Rodgers; lyrics: Stephen Sondheim; based on The Time of the Cuckoo by Arthur Laurents; musical direction: Frederick Dvonch

Cast: Elizabeth Allen, Carol Bruce, Stuart Damon, Fleury D'Antonakis, Sergio Franchi, Jack Manning, Julienne Marie, Madeline Sherwood

Songs: Someone Woke Up (Allen, chorus)
This Week Americans (Bruce)
What Do We Do? We Fly! (Allen, Sherwood, Manning, Damon, Marie)
Someone Like You (Franchi)
Bargaining (Franchi, Allen)
Thinking (Allen, Franchi)
No Understand (Bruce, Damon, D'Antonakis)
Take the Moment (Franchi)

Here We Are Again (Allen, chorus)
Moon in My Window (Marie, Bruce, Allen)
We're Gonna Be All Right (Damon, Marie)
Do I Hear a Waltz? (Allen)
Stay (Franchi)
Perfectly Lovely Couple (cast)
Thank You So Much (Allen, Franchi)

DO RE MI (December 26, 1960, St. James Theatre)

RCA LSOD 2002 stereo

Music: Jule Styne; lyrics: Betty Comden, Adolph Green; musical direction: Lehman Engel

Cast: David Burns, Nancy Dussault, George Givot, George Mathews, John Reardon, Phil Silvers, Nancy Walker

Songs: Overture (orchestra)
Waiting, Waiting (Walker)
All You Need is a Quarter (chorus)
Take a Job (Silvers, Walker)
It's Legitimate (Silvers, Givot, Mathews, Burns, chorus)

I Know About Love (Reardon)
Cry Like the Wind (Dussault)
Ambition (Silvers, Dussault)

Fireworks (Reardon, Dussault)
What's New at the Zoo (Dussault, chorus)
Asking for You (Reardon)
The Late, Late Show (Silvers)
Adventure (Silvers, Walker)
Make Someone Happy (Reardon)
All of My Life (Silvers)
Finale (company)

DOCTOR SELAVY'S MAGIC THEATRE (November 23, 1972, Off Broadway, Mercer-O'Casey Theatre)

United Artists Records UA LA 196 G stereo

Music: Stanley Silverman; lyrics: Tom Hendry; musical direction: Stanley Silverman

Cast: Denise Delapenha, Mary Delson, Jessica Harper, George McGrath, Steve Menken, Jackie Paris, Barry Primus, Robert Schlee, Amy Taubin

Songs: Jingle (girls)
First Day's Treatment (McGrath) spoken
The More You Get (Primus)
Money in the Bank (Harper, Primus)
Swinging at the Stock Exchange (McGrath, cast)
Life on the Inside (Taubin)
Second Day's Treatment (McGrath) spoken
I Live by My Wits (Primus)
Three Menu Songs (Delson, Schlee, cast)
Bankrupt Blues (Menken)
Future for Sale (Delapenha)
Strawberry-Strawberry (Harper, Menken)
Let's Hear It for Daddy Moola (Delapenha, cast)
Life on the Inside (reprise) (Taubin, Schlee)

Third Day's Treatment (McGrath) spoken
Every New Beginning (Menken, girls)
Poor Boy (Primus, Delapenha, Schlee)
Dearest Man (Delson, Taubin)
Fourth Day's Treatment (McGrath) spoken
Where You Been Hiding Till Now (Delapenha, men)
He Lives by His Wits (Menken, McGrath, Schlee)
Fireman's Song (Primus)
Requiem (Harper, Delapenha, cast)
Fifth Day's Treatment (McGrath) spoken
Life on the Inside (reprise) (Taubin, Delapenha, Harper)

Note: Barry Primus replaced Ron Farber for this recording.

A DOLL'S LIFE (September 23, 1982, Mark Hellinger Theatre)

Original Cast Records OC 8241 stereo reissued: CBS Special Products P 18846

Music: Larry Grossman; lyrics: Betty Comden, Adolph Green; musical direction: Paul Gemignani

Cast: Peter Gallagher, George Hearn, Betsy Joslyn, Barbara Lang, Norman A. Large, Edmund Lyndeck, David Vosburgh

Songs: Overture (orchestra)
Prologue (Joslyn, company)
A Woman Alone (Joslyn, Gallagher, Large, company)
Letter to the Children (Joslyn)
New Year's Eve (Lyndeck, Hearn, Vosburgh, Large)
New Year's Eve (reprise) (Gallagher, Joslyn)
Stay with Me, Nora (Gallagher, Joslyn)
She Thinks That's the Answer (Lang, company)
The Arrival (Lang, company)
Loki and Baldur (Gallagher, chorus)
You Interest Me (Hearn)
The Departure (Lang, company)
Letter from Klemnacht (Lang)

Learn to be Lonely (Joslyn)
Rats and Mice and Fish (women)
Jailer, Jailer (Joslyn, women)
Rare Wines (Lyndeck, Joslyn)
No More Mornings (Joslyn, company)
There She Is (Hearn, Lyndeck, Gallagher)
Power (Joslyn)
Letter to the Children (reprise) (Joslyn)
At Last (Hearn)
The Grand Cafe (company)
Finale (Can You Hear Me Now?) (Joslyn, company)

DONNYBROOK! (May 18, 1961, Forty-Sixth Street Theatre)

Kapp Records KD-8500-S stereo

Music, lyrics: Johnny Burke; based on The Quiet Man by Maurice Walsh; musical direction: Clay Warnick

Cast: Darrell J. Askey, Sibyl Bowan, Grace Carney, Alfred DeSio, Eddie Ericksen, Joan Fagan, Eddie Foy, James Gannon, Susan Johnson, Art Lund, Bruce MacKay, Clarence Nordstrom, Charles C. Welch

Songs: Overture (orchestra)
Sez I (Fagan, Askey, DeSio, Gannon, MacKay, Nordstrom)
The Day the Snow is Meltin' (Ericksen)
Sad Was the Day (Johnson, ensemble)
Donneybrook (ensemble)
Ellen Roe (Lund)
The Lovable Irish (Lund, Welch)
I Wouldn't Bet One Penny (Foy, Johnson)

He Makes Me Feel I'm Lovely (Fagan)
I Have My Own Way (Lund)
A Toast to the Bride (Nordstrom)
Wisha Wurra (Foy, DeSio, Gannon, MacKay, Nordstrom)
A Quiet Life (Lund)
Mr. Flynn (Johnson, Bowan, Carney)

Dee-Lightful Is the Word (Foy, Johnson)
For My Own (Fagan)
Finale (company)

DON'T BOTHER ME, I CAN'T COPE (April 19, 1972, Off Broadway, Playhouse Theatre)

Polydor Records PD 6013 stereo

Music, lyrics: Micki Grant; musical direction: Danny Holgate

Cast: Alberta Bradford, Alex Bradford, Charles Campbell, Hope Clarke, Micki Grant, Bobby Hill, Arnold Wilkerson

Songs: I Gotta Keep Movin' (Alex Bradford, company)
Harlem Streets (Hill, company)
Lookin' Over from Your Side (Hill, company)
Don't Bother Me, I Can't Cope (company)
Fighting for Pharoah (Alex Bradford, Hill, Alberta Bradford, Campbell)
Good Vibrations (Alex Bradford, company)
You Think I Got Rhythm? (company)
They Keep Coming (company)
My Name is Man (Wilkerson, company)

Love Power (Hill, Clarke, company)
Questions (Grant)
It Takes a Whole Lot of Human Feeling (Grant)
You Think I Got Rhythm? (reprise) (Wilkerson, Grant, company)
Time Brings About a Change (Wilkerson, Grant, company)
So Little Time (Grant)
Thank Heaven for You (Hill, Grant)
All I Need (Alberta Bradford, company)
I Gotta Keep Movin' (reprise) (Grant, Alex Bradford, company)

DON'T PLAY US CHEAP (May 16, 1972, Ethel Barrymore Theatre)

Stax Records STS 2-3006 (two records) stereo

Music, lyrics: Melvin Van Peebles; musical direction: Harold Wheeler

Cast: Thomas Anderson, Joshie Jo Armstead, Nate Barnett, Frank Carey, Robert Dunn, Rhetta Hughes, Joe Keyes, Jr., Mabel King, Avon Long, Geo. ("Ooppee") McCurn, Esther Rolle, Jay Vanleer

Songs: You Cut Up the Clothes in the Closet of My Dreams (Armstead, company)
Break That Party and Opening (Long, Keyes, company)
The Eight Day Week (Anderson, company)
Saturday Night (company)
The Browsers Thing (orchestra)
The Book of Life (Dunn, company)

Quittin Time (McCurn, company)

Ain't Love Grand (orchestra)
I'm a Bad Character (Keyes, company)
Know Your Business (orchestra)
Feast on Me (King, company)

Ain't Love Grand (reprise) (Hughes, company)
Break That Party (orchestra)
Someday It Seems That It Just Don't Even Pay to Get Out of Bed (Barnett, Carey)
Quartet (orchestra)
The Phony Game (Long, company)

It Makes Nô Difference (Rolle, company)
Bad Character Bossa Nova (orchestra)
Quartet (reprise) (Hughes, Rolle, Long, Keyes, Barnett, Carey, Vanleer)
The Washingtons Thing (orchestra)
(If You See a Devil) Smash Him (company)

Note: This album is labeled 'original cast and soundtrack.'

DOONESBURY (November 21, 1983, Biltmore Theatre)

MCA Records 6129 stereo

Music: Elizabeth Swados; lyrics: Garry Trudeau; based on Doonesbury by Garry Trudeau; musical direction: Jeff Waxman

Cast: Barbara Andres, Gary Beach, Reathel Bean, Ralph Bruneau, Kate Burton, Laura Dean, Mark Linn-Baker, Albert Macklin, Keith Szarabajka, Lauren Tom

Songs: Prologue - Graduation (Bean, Bruneau, Szarabajka, Dean, Linn-Baker, Macklin)
Just One Night (Bruneau)
I Came to Tan (Macklin, ensemble)
Guilty (Beach, ensemble)
I Can Have It All (Dean, ensemble)
Get Together (Burton, ensemble)
Baby Boom Boogie Boy (Linn-Baker, Bean, ensemble)
Another Memorable Meal (Bruneau, Szarabajka, Dean, Linn-Baker, Macklin, Burton, Andres)

Just a House (ensemble)
Complicated Man (Tom, Dean)
Real Estate (Beach, Macklin)
Mother (Burton, Andres)
It's the Right Time to be Rich (Szarabajka, Bean)
Muffy and the Topsiders (Dean, Bruneau, Linn-Baker, Macklin)
Just One Night (Bruneau, Burton)
Graduation (ensemble)

DOWNRIVER (December 22, 1975, Off Broadway, St. Clement's Church Theatre)

Take Home Tunes Records THT 7811 stereo

Music, lyrics: John Braden; based on The Adventures of

Huckleberry Finn by Mark Twain; musical direction: Jeff Waxman

Cast: Donald Arrington, Michael Corbett, Richard Dunne, Alvin Fields, Marcia McLain, Robert Price

Songs: Bound Away (Dunne)
Till Our Good Luck Comes Along (Dunne, Fields)
The Musicale (Arrington)
Come Home, Runaway (Fields)
He's on His Way, Hallelujah! (chorus)

River Rats (Arrington, Price, Dunne)
Just Like Love (Dunne, McLain)
What a Grand Day for an Auction Sell (Arrington, chorus)
Downriver (Dunne)
Tom and Huck's Argument (Corbett, Dunne)
Shine Down. Lord (Fields, chorus)
Finale (Dunne)

Note: Marcia McLain is the only original cast member to sing on this recording.

DRAT! THE CAT! (October 10, 1965, Martin Beck Theatre)

Blue Pear Records BP 1005 mono

Music: Milton Schafer; lyrics: Ira Levin; musical direction: Herbert Grossman

Cast: Jane Connell, Charles Durning, Sandy Ellen, Jack Fletcher, David Gold, Elliott Gould, Lu Leonard, Gene Varrone, Lesley Ann Warren

Songs: Drat! The Cat! (company)
My Son, Uphold the Law (Gold, men)
Holmes and Watson (Warren, Gould)
She Touched Me (Gould)
Wild and Reckless (Warren)
She's Roses (Gould, Leonard)
Ballet: Ignoble Theft of the Idol's Eyes (company)
Dancing with Alice (Gould, Warren, Connell, Fletcher, company)

Drat! The Cat! (reprise) (Connell, Fletcher, company)
Purefoy's Lament (Gould)
A Fox Upon the Traitor's Brow (Durning, Varrone, Ellen, men)
Deep in Your Heart (Gould)
Money, Money (Connell, Fletcher) spoken
Let's Go (Warren, Gould)
It's Your Fault (Connell, Fletcher)
Ballet: The Upside-Down Thief (company)
Today Is a Day for a Band to Play (Durning, Varrone, Ellen, company)
I Like Him (Warren)
Justice Triumphant (company)

Note: A live recording.

DREAMGIRLS (December 20, 1981, Imperial Theatre)

Geffin Records GHSP 2007 stereo CD

Music: Henry Krieger; lyrics: Tom Eyen; musical direction: Yolanda Segovia

Cast: Obba Babatunde, Deborah Burrell, Clevant Derricks, Loretta Devine, Tony Franklin, Ben Harney, Jennifer Holliday, Sheryl Lee Ralph

Songs: Move (You're Steppin' on My Heart) (Holliday, Devine, Ralph)
Fake Your Way to the Top (Derricks, Holliday, Devine, Ralph)
Cadillac Car (company)
Steppin' to the Bad Side (Harney, Derricks, Babatunde, Franklin, Devine, Holliday, Ralph, company)
Family (Holliday, Babatunde, Derricks, Devine, Harney, Ralph)
Dreamgirls (Ralph, Devine, Holliday)
Press Conference (Ralph, Harney, company)
And I Tell You I'm Not Going (Holliday)

Ain't No Party (Devine)
When I First Saw You (Harney, Ralph)
I Am Changing (Holliday)
I Meant You No Harm (Derricks)
The Rap (Derricks)
Firing of Jimmy (Derricks, Harney, Devine, company)
I Miss You Old Friend (Babatunde, Holliday)
One Night Only (Holliday, Ralph, Devine, Burrell, company)
Hard to Say Goodbye, My Love (Ralph, Devine, Burrell)

DRESSED TO THE NINES (September 29, 1960, Off Broadway, Upstairs at the Downstairs)

MGM Records SE 3914 OC stereo

Music: Michael Barr, Michael Brown, Jack Holmes, Ray Jessel, William Roy, Jack Urbant, G. Wood; lyrics: Michael Brown, Jack Holmes, Ray Jessel, Dion McGregor, Michael McWhinney, William Roy, Jack Urbant, G. Wood; at pianos: Carl Norman, William Roy

Cast: Ceil Calbot, Gordon Connell, Bill Hinnant, Gerry Matthews, Pat Ruhl, Mary Louise Wilson

Songs: Overture (pianos)
Gala Opening:
The Theatre's in the Dining Room (cast) music: Roy; lyrics: McWhinney
Dressed to the Nines (cast) music, lyrics: Roy
Tiny Town (Cabot, Matthews) music, lyrics: Holmes
And That Was He and She (Wilson, Connell) spoken
Sociable Amoeba (Hinnant) music, lyrics: Urbant

Con Edison (Cabot, Hinnant, Matthews) spoken in rhythm
Come In and Browse (Connell) music, lyrics: Wood
The Hate Song (Cabot, Hinnant) music: Barr; lyrics: Wood
A Word from Our Sponsor (Cabot, Ruhl, Wilson, Connell, Hinnant, Matthews) spoken

---

Bring Back the Roxy to Me (Connell, Hinnant, Matthews) Music, lyrics: Brown
Nanny (Cabot) music, lyrics: Jessel
Smoke (Wilson, Matthews) spoken
Names (Wilson) music, lyrics: Holmes
Billy's Blues (Ruhl) music, lyrics: Roy
Ft. Lauterdale (Matthews) music: Roy; lyrics: McWhinney
Unexpurgated Version (Matthews, Ruhl, Connell) spoken
Finale: Dressed to the Nines (cast)

Note: A live recording.

DUDE, THE HIGHWAY LIFE (October 9, 1972, Broadway Theatre)

Kilmarnock Records KIL 72007 stereo

Music: Galt MacDermot; lyrics: Gerome Ragni; musical direction: Thomas Pierson

Cast: Salome Bey, Alan Braunstein, Nell Carter, Jim Farrell, Leta Galloway, David Lasley, Nat Morris

Songs: The Highway Life: Going (orchestra)
So Long, Dude (Carter)
The Days of This Life (Morris, Farrell)
I Am Who I Am (Galloway)
I'm Small (Braunstein)
Pears and Apples (Bey)

Wa Wa Wa (Carter)
Suzie Moon (Carter)
Humdrum Life (Galloway, Lasley, Carter, Farrell, Morris, Bey Braunstein)
Weeping (Farrell)
Air Male (Morris, Carter, Bey, Galloway)
Un-Do (Bey)
Dude, All Dude (Carter, Galloway, Farrell)
The Highway Life: Coming (orchestra)

EARL OF RUSTON (May 5, 1971, Billy Rose Theatre)

Capitol ST 465 stereo

Music, lyrics: Peter Link, C.C. and Ragan Courtney; musical direction: none credited

Cast: 'The Salvation Company'

Songs: Just Your Old Friend
R.U.S.T.O.N.
The Guitar Song

Silver's Theme
--- It's Easy to be Lonely
The Revival
Earl is Crazy
Earl Was Ahead
Just Your Old Friend (reprise)

Note: Vocals are uncredited. 'The Salvation Company' is made up of Yolanda Bavan, C.C. Courtney, Ragan Courtney, Boni Enten, Marta Heflin, Peter Link, Joe Morton, Anne Rachel.

ERNEST IN LOVE (May 4, 1960, Off Broadway, Gramercy Arts Theatre)

Columbia OS 2027 stereo

Music: Lee Pockriss; lyrics: Anne Croswell; based on Oscar Wilde's The Importance of Being Earnest; musical direction: Liza Redfield

Cast: Louis Edmonds, Christina Gillespie, George Hall, Margot Harley, John Irving, Lucy Landau, Leila Martin, Gerrianne Raphael, Sara Seegar, Alan Shayne

Songs: Overture (orchestra)
Come Raise Your Cup (Shayne, Hall, ensemble)
How Do You Find the Words? (Irving)
The Hat (Martin, Harley)
Mr. Bunbury (Edmonds, Irving)
Perfection (Irving, Martin)
--- A Handbag Is Not a Proper Mother (Seegar, Irving)
A Wicked Man (Raphael)
Metaphorically Speaking (Landau, Hall)
You Can't Make Love (Shayne, Gillespie)
Lost (Edmonds, Raphael)
My Very First Impression (Martin, Raphael)
The Muffin Song (Edmonds, Irving)
My Eternal Devotion (Martin, Raphael, Edmonds, Irving)
The Muffin Song (reprise) (Irving, Edmonds, Raphael, Martin)
Ernest in Love (Irving, Martin, Raphael, Edmonds, Shayne, Gillespie, Landau, Hall)

EUBIE! (September 20, 1978, Ambassador Theatre)

Warner Brothers Records HS 3267 stereo

Music: Eubie Blake; lyrics: Jim Europe, Micki Grant, F.E. Miller, Andy Razaf, Noble Sissle; musical direction: Vicki Carter

Cast: Ethel Beatty, Terry Burrell, Lynnie Godfrey, Gregory Hines, Maurice Hines, Mel Johnson, Jr., Lonnie McNeil, Janet Powell, Marion Ramsey, Alaina Reed, Jeffery V. Thompson

Songs: Charleston Rag/Shuffle Along (company) lyrics: Sissle
In Honeysuckle Time (McNeil, company) lyrics: Sissle
I'm Just Wild about Harry (Godfrey, Powell, girls) lyrics: Sissle
Daddy (Godfrey) lyrics: Sissle
I'm a Great Big Baby (Thompson) lyrics: Razaf
My Handyman Ain't Handy No More (Reed) lyrics: Razaf
Low Down Blues (G. Hines) lyrics: Sissle
Gee, I Wish I Had Someone to Rock Me in the Cradle of Love (Beatty) lyrics: Sissle
Low Down Blues/Cradle of Love Duet (G. Hines, Beatty)

Dixie Moon (Johnson, company) lyrics: Sissle
Weary (Burrell, company) lyrics: Razaf
Roll Jordan (Reed, Powell, company) lyrics: Razaf, Grant
Memories of You (Beatty) lyrics: Razaf
If You've Never Been Vamped by a Brownskin, You've Never Been Vamped at All (Ramsey, company) lyrics: Sissle
You Got to Git the Gittin While the Gittin's Good (M. Hines) lyrics: Miller
I'm Craving for that Kind of Love (Godfrey) lyrics: Sissle
Goodnight Angeline (Beatty, Johnson, McNeil, Powell) lyrics: Sissle, Europe
Finale (company)

EVITA (September 25, 1979, Broadway Theatre)

MCA Records MCA2-11007 (two records) stereo CD

Music: Andrew Lloyd Webber; lyrics: Tim Rice; musical direction: Rene Wiegert

Cast: Bob Gunton, Patti LuPone, Jane Ohringer, Mandy Patinkin, Mark Syers

Songs: A Cinema in Buenos Aires, 26 July 1952 (film soundtrack and announcer) spoken
Requiem for Evita (company)
Oh What a Circus (Patinkin)
Don't Cry for Me Argentina (LuPone, girls)
On This Night of a Thousand Stars (Patinkin, Syers)
Eva and Magaldi (LuPone, Syers, Patinkin, chorus)
Buenos Aires (LuPone, Patinkin)
Goodnight and Thank You (Patinkin, LuPone, Syers, men)

The Art of the Possible (LuPone, men)
Charity Concert/I'd Be Suprisingly Good for You (Syers, Patinkin, LuPone, Gunton)
Another Suitcase in Another Hall (Lupone, Ohringer, Patinkin)
Peron's Latest Flame (Patinkin, LuPone, men)
A New Argentina (Gunton, LuPone,company)

On the Balcony of the Casa Rosada (Patinkin, Gunton, company)
Don't Cry for Me Argentina (reprise) (LuPone, company)
High Flying, Adored (Patinkin, LuPone)
Rainbow High (LuPone, chorus)

Rainbow Tour (Gunton, Patinkin, LuPone, men)
The Actress Hasn't Learned (LuPone, Patinkin, company)
And the Money Keeps Rolling In (and Out) (Patinkin, company)
--- Santa Evita (Patinkin, men, children)
Waltz for Eva and Che (Patinkin, LuPone)
She Is a Diamond (Patinkin, Gunton, men)
Dice are Rolling (Gunton, LuPone)
Eva's Final Broadcast (Patinkin, LuPone)
Montage (Patinkin, Syers, LuPone, Gunton, company)
Lament (LuPone, Patinkin, company)

FADE OUT FADE IN (May 26, 1964, Mark Hellinger Theatre)

ABC Records ABCS OC-3 stereo

Music: Jule Styne; lyrics: Betty Comden, Adolph Green; musical direction: Colin Romoff

Cast: Carol Burnett, Jack Cassidy, Tiger Haynes, Lou Jacobi, Mitchell Jason, Tina Louise, Dick Patterson

Songs: Overture (orchestra)
Oh Those Thirties (Cassidy)
It's Good to be Back Home (Burnett)
Fear (Patterson, Jason, Cassidy, men)
Call Me Savage (Burnett, Patterson)
The Usher from the Mezzanine (Burnett)
I'm with You (Burnett, Cassidy)
My Fortune is My Face (Cassidy)
--- Lila Tremaine (Burnett)
Go Home Train (Burnett)
Close Harmony (Cassidy, Jacobi, Louise, men)
You Mustn't Be Discouraged (Burnett, Haynes)
The Dangerous Age (Jacobi)
L.Z. in Quest of His Youth (orchestra)
My Heart Is Like a Violin (Cassidy)
The Fiddler and the Fighter (Cassidy, ensemble)
Fade Out - Fade In (Burnett, Patterson)
Finale (company)

THE FAGGOT (June 18, 1973, Off Broadway, Truck and Warehouse Theatre)

Blue Pear Records BP 1008 mono

Music, lyrics: Al Carmines; at piano: Al Carmines

Cast: Peggy Atkinson, Essie Borden, Lou Bullock, Al Carmines, Marilyn Child, Tony Clark, Frank Coppola, Lee Guilliatt, Bruce Hopkins, Julie Kurnitz, Philip Owens, David Pursley, Bill Reynolds, Ira Siff, David Summers

Songs: Women with Women - Men with Men (company)
The Hustler: A Five Minute Opera (Pursley, Reynolds)
I'll Take My Fantasy (Clark, Summers, company)

Hari Krishna (Siff, Owens, Hopkins, Reynolds)
Desperation (Hopkins, Borden, company)
A Gay Bar Cantata (Child, Bullock, Clark, Coppola, Owens, Pursley, Summers)

Nookie Time (Guilliant, company)
Your Way of Loving (Carmines, Siff)
Ordinary Things (Guilliant, Atkinson)
Art Song (Kurnitz, Borden, Child)
What Is a Queen (Owens, company)
Everyone Is Different (company)
Finale (company)

A FAMILY AFFAIR (January 27, 1962, Billy Rose Theatre)

United Artists UAS 5099 stereo

Music, lyrics: James Goldman, John Kander, William Goldman; musical direction: Stanley Lebowsky

Cast: Shelley Berman, Morris Carnovsky, Gino Conforti, Jack De Lon, Rita Gardner, Eileen Heckart, Larry Kert, Linda Lavin, Alice Nunn, Bill McDonald, Bibi Osterwald, Beryl Towbin

Songs: Overture (chorus)
Anything for You (Kert, Gardner)
Beautiful (Berman)
My Son the Lawyer (Heckart, chorus)
Every Girl Wants to Get Married (Gardner, Towbin)
Right Girls (Berman, De Lon, chorus)
Kalua Bay (Heckart, Carnovsky)
There's a Room in My House (Kert, Gardner)
Football Game (Towbin, chorus)

Harmony (Osterwald, Conforti, Lavin, De Lon)
Now Morris (Carnovsky, Heckart)
Wonderful Party (Kert, McDonald, Lavin)
Revenge (Berman, Nunn, chorus)
Summer Is Over (Heckart)
What I Say Goes (Kert)
I'm Worse Than Anybody (Berman, Heckart, Carnovsky)

FANNY (November 4, 1954, Majestic Theatre)

RCA LOC 1015 mono

Music, lyrics: Harold Rome; based on the trilogy of Marcel Pagnol; musical direction: Lehman Engel

Cast: Nejla Ates, Mohammed El Bakkar, Florence Henderson, Ezio Pinza, Edna Preston, Gerald Price, Lloyd Reese, Walter Slezak, William Tabbert

Songs: Overture (orchestra)
Never Too Late for Love (Slezak, girls)
Cold Cream Jar Song (Slezak)
Octopus Song (Price)

Restless Heart (Tabbert, chorus)
Why Be Afraid to Dance (Pinza, chorus)
Shika Shika (Ates, El Bakkar, chorus)
Welcome Home (Pinza)
I Like You (Pinza, Tabbert)

I Have to Tell You (Henderson)
Fanny (Tabbert)
Montage (chorus)
Be Kind to Your Parents (Henderson, Reese)
Panisse and Son (Slezak)
Wedding Dance (chorus)
Finale Act I (chorus)
Birthday Song (Henderson, Preston, chorus)
To My Wife (Slezak)
The Thought of You (Henderson, Tabbert)
Love Is a Very Light Thing (Pinza)
Other Hands, Other Hearts (Pinza, Henderson, Tabbert)

THE FANTASTICKS (May 3, 1960, Off Broadway, Sullivan Street Playhouse)

MGM E 3872 OC reissued: Polydor 821943 1 Y-1 CD

Music: Harvey Schmidt; lyrics: Tom Jones; musical direction: Julian Stein

Cast: Rita Gardner, William Larsen, Kenneth Nelson, Jerry Orbach, Hugh Thomas

Songs: Overture (orchestra)
Try to Remember (Orbach)
Much More (Gardner)
Metaphor (Nelson, Gardner)
Never Say No (Larsen, Thomas)
It Depends on What You Pay (Orbach, Larsen, Thomas)
You Wonder How These Things Begin (Orbach)
Soon It's Gonna Rain (Nelson, Gardner)

Rape Ballet (company)
Happy Ending (Thomas, Larsen, Gardner, Nelson)
This Plum Is Too Ripe (Gardner, Nelson, Larsen, Thomas)
I Can See It (Nelson, Orbach)
Plant a Radish (Larsen, Orbach)
Round and Round (Orbach, Gardner, company)
There Is a Curious Paradox (Orbach)
They Were You (Nelson, Gardner)
Try to Remember (Orbach, company)

FESTIVAL (May 16, 1979, Off Broadway, City Center Downstairs)

Original Cast Records OC 7916 stereo

Music: Stephen Downs; lyrics: Stephen Downs, Randal Martin; based on the chantefable Aucassin and Nicolette; musical direction: David Spear

Cast: Bill Hutton, Tina Johnson, Maureen McNamara, Michael

Magnusen, Lindy Nisbet, Roxann Parker, Michael Rupert, Leon Stewart, Robin Taylor, John Windsor

Songs: Overture (orchestra)
Our Song (Rupert, company)
The Ballad of Oh (Rupert)
For the Love (Rupert, company)
Beata Biax (Beautiful, Beautiful) (Hutton, company)
Just Like You (Magnusen, Hutton)
Special Day (McNamara, Hutton)
The Time Is Come (Rupert, McNamara, Hutton)
Roger the Ox (Stewart)
When the Lady Passes (Hutton, Taylor, Johnson, Windsor, company)

Gifts to You (McNamara, Hutton, company)
The Escape (Quintet) (company)
The Pirates' Song (Rupert, company)
I Can't Remember (Windsor, Stewart, Rupert, Magnusen, McNamara)
One Step Further (Johnson, Taylor, Parker, Nisbet, McNamara, company)
Through Love's Eyes (Magnusen, Hutton)
Let Him Love You (McNamara, Parker)
The Ceremony (Rupert, McNamara, Hutton, company)
I Speak of Love (Rupert)
Finale: Our Song (reprise) (company)

FIDDLER ON THE ROOF (September 22, 1964, Imperial Theatre)

RCA LSO 1093 stereo CD

Music: Jerry Bock; lyrics: Sheldon Harnick; based on Sholem Aleichem's stories; musical direction: Milton Greene

Cast: Beatrice Arthur, Sue Babel, Bert Convy, Tanya Everett, Leonard Frey, Michael Granger, Maria Karnilova, Paul Lipson, Joanna Merlin, Julia Migenes, Zero Mostel, Austin Pendleton, Carol Sawyer

Songs: Tradition (Mostel, chorus)
Matchmaker, Matchmaker (Merlin, Migenes, Everett)
If I Were a Rich Man (Mostel)
Sabbath Prayer (Mostel, Karnilova, chorus)
To Life (Mostel, Granger, men)
Miracle of Miracles (Pendleton)

Tevye's Dream (Mostel, Karnilova, Babel, Sawyer, chorus)
Sunrise, Sunset (Mostel, Karnilova, chorus)
Now I Have Everything (Convy, Migenes)
Do You Love Me? (Mostel, Karnilova)
Far From the Home I Love (Migenes, Mostel)
Anatevka (Mostel, Karnilova, Arthur, Granger, Frey, Lipson)

Note: The CD version contains two additional selections:

Wedding Dance (chorus)
The Rumor (Arthur, chorus)

FINIAN'S RAINBOW (January 10, 1947, Forty-Sixth Street Theatre)

Columbia OL 4062 mono reissued: OS 2080

Music: Burton Lane; lyrics: E.Y. Harburg; musical direction: Ray Charles

Cast: Lorenzo Fuller, Alan Gilbert, Jerry Laws, Ella Logan, Delores Martin, Donald Richards, Lewis Sharp, Maude Simmons, David Wayne

Songs: Overture (orchestra)
This Time of the Year (Gilbert, chorus)
How Are Things in Glocca Morra? (Logan)
If This Isn't Love (Logan, Richards, chorus)
Look to the Rainbow (Logan, Richards, chorus)
Old Devil Moon (Logan, Richards)

Something Sort of Grandish (Logan, Wayne)
Necessity (Martin, Simmons, chorus)
When the Idle Poor Become the Idle Rich (Logan, chorus)
The Begat (Fuller, Laws, Sharp)
When I'm Not Near the Girl I Love (Wayne)
That Great Come and Get It Day (Logan, Richards, chorus)

FINIAN'S RAINBOW (Revival, April 27, 1960, Off Broadway, City Center; transferred: May 23, 1960, Forty-Sixth Street Theatre)

RCA LSO 1057 stereo

Musical direction: Max Meth

Cast: Carol Brice, Sorrell Brooke, Jeannie Carson, Bill Glover, Colonel Tiger Haynes, Bobby Howes, Jerry Laws, Biff McGuire, Howard Morris

Songs: Overture (orchestra)
This Time of Year (chorus)
How Are Things in Glocca Morra? (Carson)
Look to the Rainbow - Dance (orchestra)
Look to the Rainbow (Carson, McGuire, chorus)
Something Sort of Grandish (Morris, Carson)
When the Idle Poor Become the Idle Rich (Carson, chorus)

If This Isn't Love (McGuire, Carson, Howes, chorus)
Old Devil Moon (McGuire, Carson)
Necessity (Brice, chorus)
Something Sort of Grandish (Morris)
The Begat (Brooke, Laws, Haynes, Glover)
When I'm Not Near the Girl I Love (Morris)
That Great Come-and-Get-It-Day (McGuire, Carson, Brice, chorus)

FIORELLO! (November 23, 1959, Broadhurst Theatre)

Capitol WAO 1321 stereo

Music: Jerry Bock; lyrics: Sheldon Harnick; musical direction: Hal Hastings

Cast: Tom Bosley, Howard da Silva, Nathaniel Frey, Ellen Hanley, Bob Holiday, Eileen Rodgers, Pat Stanley, Patricia Wilson

Songs: Overture (orchestra)
On the Side of the Angels (Holiday, Frey, Wilson)
Politics and Porker (da Silva, men)
Unfair (Bosley, girls)
Marie's Law (Wilson, Frey)
The Name's La Guardia (Bosley, company)
The Bum Won (da Silva, men)
I Love a Cop (Stanley)

'Til Tomorrow (Hanley, company)
Home Again (company)
When Did I Fall in Love (Hanley)
Gentleman Jimmy (Rodgers, girls)
Little Tin Box (da Silva, men)
The Very Next Man (Wilson)
Finale (Bosley, Wilson, company)

FIRST IMPRESSIONS (March 19, 1959, Alvin Theatre)

Columbia OS 2014 stereo

Music, lyrics: Robert Goldman, Glenn Paxton, George Weiss; based on Jane Austin's _Pride and Prejudice_ and the play by Helen Jerome; musical direction: Frederick Dvonch

Cast: Polly Bergen, Lois Bewley, Hermione Gingold, Farley Granger, Ellen Hanley, Christopher Hewett, Donald Madden, Phyllis Newman, Lauri Peters, Lynn Ross

Songs: Overture (orchestra)
Five Daughters (Gingold)
I'm Me (Bergen, Newman, Bewley, Ross, Peters)
Have You Heard the News? (Gingold, ensemble)
Polka; The Assembly Dance (orchestra)
A Perfect Evening (Granger, Bergen)
As Long as There's a Mother (Gingold, Newman, Bewley, Ross, Peters)
Love Will Find Out the Way (Bergen)
A Gentleman Never Falls Wildly in Love (Granger)
Fragrant Flower (Hewett, Bergen)

I Feel Sorry for the Girl (Newman, Madden, ensemble)
I Suddenly Find It Agreeable (Bergen, Granger)
This Really Isn't Me (Bergen)
Wasn't It a Simply Lovely Wedding? (Bergen, Gingold, Hewett, Hanley, ensemble)
A House in Town (Gingold)
The Heart Has Won the Game (Granger)
Dance (orchestra)
Let's Fetch the Carriage (Bergen, Gingold)
Finale (company)

FIVE AFTER EIGHT (December 6, 1979, Off Broadway, Cubiculo Theatre)

Original Cast Records OC 8027 stereo

Music, lyrics: Michael Bitterman; musical direction: Ron Williams

Cast: Sally Funk, James Paul Handakas, Dena Olstad, Arthur Alan Sorenson, Barbara Walker

Songs: Closing Song (company)
Spirit Song (company)
What I'm Looking For (Funk, Walker)
A Quartet with a Smile (company)
I Know You're Here Jeannine (Olstad)
You Better Watch Out for Me (Funk, Olstad, Walker)
It's Not Working Out (Olstad)
If We Spend Our Lives in a Fishbowl (Sorenson, Walker)
Nothing Can Stand In My Way (Olstad)

We're Not Who We Think We Are (company)
Unanswered Questions (company)
If There's Anything Left of Us (Sorenson, Funk)
That's What Love Does to Me (Olstad)
25 Years (Walker)
Still Here with Me (Sorenson)
Besancon (Funk)
The Perfect Imbalance (Handakas, Sorenson, Walker)
What Is Funny (Sorenson)
New York Finale (company)

FLAHOOLEY (May 14, 1951, Broadhurst Theatre)

Capitol S 284 mono reissued: T-11649

Music: Sammy Fain; lyrics: E.Y. Harburg; special material for Yma Sumac: Moises Vivanco; musical direction: Maurice Levine

Cast: Barbara Cook, Irwin Corey, Jerome Courtland, Fay DeWitt, Marilyn Ross, Yma Sumac

Songs: Prologue (orchestra)
You, Too, Can Be a Puppet (chorus)
Here's to Your Illusions (Cook, Courtland)
Telephone Switchboard Scene (operators)
B.G. Bigelow, Inc. (chorus)
Najala's Lament (Sumac)
Who Says There Ain't No Santa Claus? (Courtland, Cook, chorus)
Flahooley (DeWitt, Ross, chorus)
The World Is Your Balloon (Cook, Courtland, puppets)
Najala's Song of Joy (Sumac)

He's Only Wonderful (Cook, Courtland)
Inner Office Scene (chorus)
Jump, Little Chillun'! (chorus)
Consternation (chorus)
No More Flahooleys! (chorus)

Spirit of Capsulanti (Ross, chorus)
Come Back, Little Genie (Cook)
Birds (Sumac)
The Springtime Cometh (Corey)
Finale (company)

FLORA THE RED MENACE (May 11, 1965, Alvin Theatre)

RCA LSO 1111 stereo

Music: John Kander; lyrics: Fred Ebb; based on the novel *Love Is Just Around the Corner* by Lester Atwell; musical direction: Hal Hastings

Cast: Danny Carroll, James Cresson, Cathryn Damon, Bob Dishy, Jamie Donnelly, Dortha Duckworth, Stephanie Hill, Robert Kaye, Joe E. Marks, Liza Minnelli, Marie Santell, Mary Louise Wilson

Songs: Overture (orchestra)
Unafraid (Minnelli, ensemble)
All I Need (Is One Good Break) (Minnelli, ensemble)
Not Every Day of the Week (Minnelli, Dishy)
Sign Here (Dishy, Minnelli)
The Flame (Wilson, Dishy, ensemble)
Palomino Pal (Duckworth, Cresson)

A Quiet Thing (Minnelli)
Hello Waves (Dishy, Minnelli)
Dear Love (Minnelli)
Express Yourself (Damon, Dishy)
Knock Knock (Wilson, Cresson)
Sing Happy (Minnelli)
You Are You (Marks, Minnelli, Kaye, Hill, Donnelly, Santell, Carroll)

FLOWER DRUM SONG (December 1, 1958, St. James Theatre)

Columbia OS 2009 stereo

Music: Richard Rodgers; lyrics: Oscar Hammerstein II; based on the novel by C.Y. Lee; musical direction: Salvatore Dell'Isola

Cast: Pat Adiarte, Larry Blyden, Cely Carrillo, Anita Ellis, Juanita Hall, Luis Robert Hernandez, Arabella Hong, Ed Kenney, Baayork Lee, Keye Luke, Susan Lynn, Rose Quong, Linda Ribuca, Yvonne Ribuca, Jack Soo, Pat Suzuki, Miyoshi Umeki, Conrad Yama

Songs: Overture (orchestra)
You Are Beautiful (Kenney, Hall)
A Hundred Million Miracles (Umeki, Yama, Luke, Hall, Quong)
I Enjoy Being a Girl (Suzuki)
I Am Going to Like It Here (Umeki)
Like a God (Kenney)

Chop Suey (Hall, Adiarte, ensemble)
Don't Marry Me (Blyden, Umeki)

Entr'acte (orchestra)
Grant Avenue (Suzuki, ensemble)
Love, Look Away (Hong)
Fan Tan Fanny (Ellis)
Gliding Through My Memoriee (Soo)
Grant Avenue (reprise) (Suzuki, ensemble)
The Other Generation (Hall, Luke)
Sunday (Suzuki, Blyden)
The Other Generation (reprise) (Adiarte, Lynn, Lee, L. Ribuca, Y. Ribuca, Hernandez, Carrillo)
Wedding Parade and Finale (ensemble)

FLY BLACKBIRD (February 5, 1962, Off Broadway, Mayfair Theatre)

Mercury OCS 6206 stereo

Music: C. Bernard Jackson; lyrics: C. Bernard Jackson, James Hatch; musical direction: Gershon Kingsley

Cast: John Anania, Helen Blout, Jack Crowder, Robert Guillaume, Avon Long, Mary Louise, Thelma Oliver, Leonard Parker, William Sugihara, Glory Van Scott

Songs: Overture (orchestra)
Everything Comes to Those Who Wait (Long, men)
Now (students)
I'm Sick of the Whole Damn Problem (Anania, Long)
The Right Way (Long)
Couldn't We (Louise, Guillaume)
The Housing Cha Cha (students)
Natchitoches, Louisiana (Blout, Parker)
The Gong Song (Oliver, Van Scott, Sugihara)

Fly Blackbird (Oliver, students)
Rivers to the South (Guillaume, Crowder, students)
Lilac Tree (Louise, Guillaume, students)
Mr. Boy (Anania, Crowder, troupe)
Old White Tom (Guillaume, troupe)
Who's the Fool (Long)
Wake Up (Guillaume, Louise, company)

FOLIES BERGERE (June 2, 1964, Broadway Theatre)

Audio Fidelity AFSD 6135 stereo

Music: Henri Betti (others); musical direction: Jo Basile

Cast: Patachou, Georges Ulmer

Songs: Folle de Broadway - Bonjour Paris (orchestra)
Darling, Be Careful (La Trapeziste) (Ulmer)
Quartier Latin (orchestra)
Mon Manege a Moi (Patachou)
Can Can (orchestra)

Opening, Act II (orchestra)
Pigalle (Patachou)
Hands Dance (orchestra)
What Now My Love? (En Maintenant?) (Patachou)
La Musique (orchestra)
Finale, Act II (orchestra)

FOLLIES (April 4, 1971, Winter Garden Theatre)

Capitol SO 761 stereo

Music, lyrics: Stephen Sondheim; musical direction: Harold Hastings

Cast: Michael Bartlett, Dorothy Collins, Yvonne De Carlo, Fifi d'Orsay, Harvey Evans, Justine Johnston, Mary McCarty, John McMartin, Victoria Mallory, Arnold Moss, Gene Nelson, Rita O'Connor, Kurt Peterson, Suzanne Rogers, Marti Rolph, Virginia Sandifur, Ethel Shutta, Alexis Smith

Songs: Prologue (orchestra - Arnold Moss) spoken
Beautiful Girls (Bartlett, company)
Don't Look at Me (Collins, McMartin)
Waiting for the Girls Upstairs (Nelson, McMartin, Smith, Collins, Evans, Peterson, Sandifur, Rolph)
Ah, Paris! (d'Orsay)
Broadway Baby (Shutta)
The Road You Didn't Take (McMartin)
In Buddy's Eyes (Collins)
Who's That Woman? (McCarty, company)
I'm Still Here (De Carlo)

Too Many Mornings (McMartin, Collins)
The Right Girl (Nelson)
Could I Leave You? (Smith)
You're Gonna Love Tomorrow (Peterson, Sandifur)
Love Will See Us Through (Evans, Rolph)
The God-Why-Don't-You-Love-Me-Blues (Nelson, Rogers, O'Connor)
Losing My Mind (Collins)
The Story of Lucy and Jessie (Smith)
Live, Laugh, Love (McMartin, company)
Finale (company)

Note: An additional original cast selection, recorded live, March 11, 1973, is included on Warner Brothers Records (2WS 2705) Sondheim - A Musical Tribute:

One More Kiss (Johnston, Mallory)

A concert version, recorded live September 6 and 7, 1985, was issued on RCA HBC 2 7128 and CD.

FORBIDDEN BROADWAY (January 15, 1982, Off Broadway, Palsson's Supper Club)

DRG Records SBL 12585 stereo

A musical revue which parodies popular Broadway show selections and stars. Concept, parody lyrics: Gerard Alessandrini; musical direction: Fred Barton

Cast: Gerard Alessandrini, Fred Barton, Bill Carmichael, Nora Mae Lyng, Chloe Webb

Songs: Forbidden Broadway (company) music, lyrics: Alessandrini
Non Piu Andrai (Mozart)
Amadeus (Carmichael)
Don't Cry for Me, Argentina (Webber, Rice)
Don't Cry for Me (Lyng)
Tomorrow (Strouse, Charnin)
Annie's Favorite Showtune (Webb)
Pirates of Penzance Sequence (Gilbert, Sullivan)
(Alessandrini, Carmichael, Lyng)
Be Italian (Yeston)
Be a Catholic (Webb, Carmichael, Alessandrini)
Triplets (Schwartz, Dietz)
(Carmichael, Alessandrini, Lyng)

Beautiful Girls (Sondheim)
Bankable Stars (Carmichael)
That's Entertainment (Schwartz, Dietz)
I'm Entertainment (Lyng)
Angela Lansbury Sequence
Mame: If He Walked into My Life (Herman)
If the Show Had Run Past Labor Day (Webb)
Audition Sequence
Soliloquy from Carousel (Rodgers, Hammerstein)
(Alessandrini)
They're Playing Our Song (Hamlish, Sager)
I'm Sick of Playing Their Songs (Barton)
Merman and Martin Sequence
It's Delovely (Porter)
It's De-Merman (Lyng)
My Heart Belongs to Daddy (Porter)
I'm Larry Hagman's Mother (Webb)
Mutual Admiration Society (Dubey, Karr)
Mutual Aggravation Society (Lyng, Webb)
Carol Channing Sequence
Call on Dolly (Herman)
Call on Carol (Alessandrini, Carmichael)
Diamonds Are a Girl's Best Friend (Styne, Robin)
Dolly Is a Girl's Best Friend (Webb)
Hello, Dolly! (Herman)
Oh, No, Carol! (Alessandrini, Carmichael, Webb)
Tradition (Bock, Harnick)
Ambition (Alessandrini, company)
Climb Ev'ry Mountain (Rodgers, Hammerstein) company
Forbidden Broadway (reprise) company

42nd STREET (August 25, 1980, Winter Garden Theatre)

RCA CBL 1 3891 stereo CD

Music: Harry Warren; lyrics: Al Dubin; based on a novel by Bradford Ropes; musical direction: John Lesko

Cast: Joseph Bova, Danny Carroll, James Congdon, Carole Cook, Tammy Grimes, Jeri Kansas, Ginny King, Jerry Orbach, Karen Prunczik, Lee Roy Reams, Wanda Richert

Songs: Overture (orchestra)
Audition (Carroll, ensemble)
Shadow Waltz (Grimes, girls)
Young and Healthy (Reams, Richert)
Go Into Your Dance (Cook, Richert, Prunczik, Carroll, King, Kansas)
You're Getting to Be a Habit with Me (Grimes, Reams, Richert, ensemble)
Getting Out of Town (Congdon, Bova, Cook, Prunczik, Grimes, ensemble)
Dames (Reams, ensemble)
We're in the Money (Prunczik, Richert, King, Kansas, Reams, ensemble)

Sunny Side to Every Situation (Prunczik, ensemble)
Lullaby of Broadway (Orbach, company)
About a Quarter to Nine (Grimes, Richert)
Shuffle Off to Buffalo (Prunczik, Bova, Cook, girls)
42nd Street (Richert, Reams, ensemble)
Finale: 42nd Street (Orbach)
Bows (company)

FOUR BELOW STRIKES BACK (January 28, 1960, Off Broadway, Downstairs at the Upstairs)

Offbeat Records 0-4017 mono

Music: Michael Brown, Ronny Graham, Bud McCreery, Walter Marks, Edward C. Redding, William Roy, Bruce Williamson, C. Wood; lyrics: Louis Botto, Michael Brown, Ronny Graham, Tom Jones, Bud McCreery, Walter Marks, Edward C. Redding, William Roy, Bruce Williamson, G. Wood; Robert Colston, Paul Trueblood at pianos.

Cast: Nancy Dussault, George Furth, Jenny Lou Law, Cy Young

Songs: Introduction (Julius Monk) spoken
Overture (pianos)
Opening (cast) music, lyrics: McCreery
Leave Your Mind Alone (Dussault, Young) music, lyrics: Graham
Mr. X (Law, Furth) spoken
It's a Wonderful Day to be Seventeen (Dussault) msuic: Graham; lyrics: Jones
The Castro Tango! (Law Furth) music, lyrics: Williamson
Charlie Chan (Dussault) music, lyrics: Roy
The Sitwells (Law, Young, Furth) music, lyrics: McCreery
Merry-Go, Merry-Go-Round (Law) music, lyrics: Wood
Jefferson Davis Tyler's General Store (Dussault, cast) music, lyrics: Redding
---
Four Seasons (cast) music: Roy; lyrics: Botto
Speak No Love (Young) music, lyrics: Redding
The Constant Nymphet (Law, Dussault) spoken
Man Tan (Law) music, lyrics: Graham

Lola Montez (Young, Dussault) music, lyrics: Brown
Family Fallout Shelter (Furth) music, lyrics: Williamson
Literary Time (Young, Law) spoken
Love, Here I Am (Dussault) music, lyrics: Marks
Payola (cast) music: Roy; lyrics: Williamson

Note: A live recording.

FOXY (February 16, 1964, Ziegfeld Theatre)

S.P.M. Records (Society for the Preservation of Musicals)
CO 4636 mono

Music: Robert Emmett Dolan; lyrics: Johnny Mercer; suggested by Ben Jonson's Volpone; musical direction: Donald Pippin

Cast: Larry Blyden, Cathryn Damon, John Davidson, Edward Greenhalgh, Robert H. Harris, Gerald Hiken, Bert Lahr, Julienne Marie

Songs: Overture (orchestra)
Prologue (Blyden)
Many Ways to Skin a Cat (Lahr, Blyden)
Rollin' in Gold (Damon, ensemble)
Money Isn't Everything (Lahr, Blyden, Harris, Hiken, Greenhalgh, ensemble)
Larceny and Love (Damon, Blyden)
Ebenezer McAfee III (ensemble)
Talk to Me, Baby (Marie, Davidson)

This Is My Night to Howl (Hiken, Davidson, ensemble)
Bon Vivant (Lahr, ensemble)
It's Easy When You Know How (Blyden)
Run, Run, Run Cinderella (Marie)
I'm Way Ahead of the Game (Damon, Blyden)
A Case of Rape (Marie, Davidson, ensemble)
In Loving Memory (Lahr, Blyden, Harris, Hiken, Greenhalgh, ensemble)
Finale (Lahr, Blyden, ensemble)

Note: A live recording.

FUNNY GIRL (March 26, 1964, Winter Garden Theatre)

Capitol SVAS 2059 stereo

Music: Jule Styne; lyrics: Bob Merrill; musical direction: Milton Rosenstock

Cast: Sydney Chaplin, John Lankston, Kay Medford, Danny Meehan, Jean Stapleton, Barbra Streisand

Songs: Overture (orchestra)
If a Girl Isn't Pretty (Stapelton, Medford, Meehan, ensemble)
I'm the Greatest Star (Streisand)

Coronet Man (Streisand)
Who Taught Her Everything (Medford, Meehan)
His Love Makes Me Beautiful (Lankston, Streisand, ensemble)
I Want to Be Seen with You Tonight (Chaplin, Streisand)
Henry Street (ensemble)
People (Streisand)

You Are Woman (Chaplin, Streisand)
Don't Rain on My Parade (Streisand)
Sadie, Sadie (Streisand, ensemble)
Find Yourself a Man (Meehan, Streisand, ensemble)
Rat-Tat-Tat-Tat (Meehan, Streisand, ensemble)
Who Are You Now? (Streisand)
The Music That Makes Me Dance (Streisand)
Don't Rain on My Parade (Streisand)

A FUNNY THING HAPPENED ON THE WAY TO THE FORUM (May 8, 1962, Alvin Theatre)

Capitol SWAO 1717 stereo

Music, lyrics: Stephen Sondheim; musical direction: Harold Hastings

Cast: David Burns, John Carradine, Brian Davies, Jack Gilford, Ronald Holgate, Ruth Kobart, Preshy Marker, Zero Mostel

Songs: Overture (orchestra)
Comedy Tonight (Mostel, company)
Love, I Hear (Davies)
Free (Mostel, Davies)
Lovely (Davies, Marker)
Pretty Little Picture (Mostel, Davies, Marker)

Everybody Ought to Have a Maid (Burns, Mostel, Gilford, Carradine)
I'm Calm (Gilford)
Impossible (Burns, Davies)
Bring Me My Bride (Holgate, Mostel, company)
That Dirty Old Man (Kobart)
That'll Show Him (Marker)
Lovely (Mostel, Gilford)
Funeral Sequence (Mostel, Holgate, company)
Finale (company)

THE GAY LIFE (November 18, 1961, Shubert Theatre)

Capitol SWAO 1560 stereo

Music, lyrics: Arthur Schwartz, Howard Dietz; musical direction: Herbert Greene

Cast: Elizabeth Allen, Jeanne Bal, Walter Chiari, Barbara Cook, Lu Leonard, Jules Munshin, Loring Smith

Songs: Overture (orchestra)
What a Charming Couple (ensemble)

Why Go Anywhere at All (Bal)
Bring Your Darling Daughter (Munshin, ensemble)
Now I'm Ready for a Frau (Chiari, Munshin)
Magic Moment (Cook)
Who Can? You Can (Chiari, Cook)
Oh, Mein Liebchen (ensemble)
The Label on the Bottle (Cook)

This Kind of a Girl (Chiari, Cook)
The Bloom Is Off the Rose (Munshin, men)
I'm Glad I'm Single (Munshin, men)
Something You Never Had Before (Cook)
You Will Never Be Lonely (Leonard, Smith, ensemble)
You're Not the Type (Chiari, Cook)
Come A-Wandering with Me (Allen)
I Never Had a Chance (Chiari, Munshin)
I Wouldn't Marry You (Cook)
For the First Time (Chiari)
Finale (ensemble)

GENTLEMEN PREFER BLONDES (December 8, 1949, Ziegfeld Theatre)

Columbia OL 4290 mono reissued: CSP AOS 2310

Music: Jule Styne; lyrics: Leo Robin; based on the book by Anita Loos; musical direction: Milton Rosenstock

Cast: Yvonne Adair, Cholly Atkins, Eric Brotherson, Carol Channing, Honi Coles, Rex Evans, George S. Irving, Jack McCauley, Alice Pearce

Songs: Overture (orchestra)
It's High Time (Adair, chorus)
Bye Bye Baby (Channing, McCauley, chorus)
A Little Girl from Little Rock (Channing)
Just a Kiss Apart (Adair, Brotherson)
I Love What I'm Doing (Adair)
Scherzo (orchestra)
It's Delightful Down in Chile (Channing, Evans, chorus)

You Say You Care (Adair, Brotherson)
I'm A'Tingle, I'm A'Glow (Irving)
Sunshine (Adair, Brotherson, chorus)
Diamonds Are a Girl's Best Friend (Channing)
Mamie is Mimi (Coles, Atkins, chorus)
Homesick Blues (Channing, Adair, Pearce, McCauley, Brotherson, Irving)
Gentlemen Prefer Blondes (Channing, McCauley)
Keeping Cool with Coolidge (Adair, company)

Note: For 1974 revival, see Lorelei.

GEORGE M! (April 10, 1968, Palace Theatre)

Columbia KOS 3200 stereo

Music, lyrics: George M. Cohan; musical direction: Jay Blackton

Cast: Loni Ackerman, Jonelle Allen, Jacqueline Alloway, Susan

Batson, Danny Carroll, Jerry Dodge, Jamie Donnelly, Harvey Evans, Joel Grey, Betty Ann Grove, Angela Martin, Jill O'Hara, Bernadette Peters

Songs: Overture (orchestra)
Musical Moon (Dodge, Grove)
Oh, You Wonderful Boy (Peters)
All Aboard for Broadway (Grey, Dodge, Peters, Grove)
Musical Comedy Man (Grey, Dodge, Grove, Peters, chorus)
Twentieth Century Love (Grey, Dodge, Grove, Peters, Donnelly)
My Town (Grey)
Billie (O'Hara)
Push Me Along in My Pushcart (company)
Ring to the Name of Rosie (Peters, bell ringers)
Popularity (orchestra)

Give My Regards to Broadway (Grey, company)
Forty-Five Minutes from Broadway (Grey, Ackerman)
So Long, Mary (Grey, Evans, Ackerman, Carroll, Martin)
Down by the Erie (Allen, Batson, company)
Mary (Alloway)
All Our Friends (Evans, Grey, company)
Yankee Doodle Dandy (Grey, company)
Nellie Kelly, I Love You (Grey, Peters, company)
Harrigan (Grey, company)
Over There (Grey)
You're a Grand Old Flag (Grey, company)
Finale: Yankee Doodle Dandy (reprise) (Grey, company)
Epilogue:
Dancing Our Worries Away (Grey, company)
The Great Easter Sunday Parade (company)
Hannah's a Hummer (men)
Barnum and Bailey Rag (company)
The American Ragtime (company)
All In the Wearing (women)
I Want to Hear a Yankee Doodle Tune (Grey, company)
Give My Regards to Broadway (reprise) (Grey, company)

GERTRUDE STEIN'S FIRST READER (December 15, 1969, Off Broadway, Astor Place Theatre)

Polydor 24-7002 stereo

Music: Ann Sternberg; words: Gertrude Stein; piano: Ann Sternberg

Cast: Michael Anthony, Joy Garrett, Frank Giordano, Ann Sternberg, Sandra Thornton

Songs: Genius (Thornton)
A Dog (Sternberg, company)
Wild Pen (Writing Lesson) (Garrett, Thornton)
Johnny and Jimmy (Giordano, Anthony)
The Blackberry Vine (Anthony, Thornton, Giordano, Garrett)
Big Bird (Sternberg, company)
Jenny (Thornton)
The Three Sisters Who Are Not Sisters (company)

Wildflowers (Sternberg, company)
Sunshine (entire company)
Soldier (Anthony)
Baby Benjamin (Giordano)
How They Do, Do (Garrett)
In a Garden (Anthony, Garrett, Giordano)
Be Very Careful (entire company)

GIGI (November 13, 1973, Uris Theatre)

RCA ABL 1-0404 stereo

Music: Frederick Loewe; lyrics: Alan Jay Lerner; based on the novel by Colette; musical direction: Ross Reimueller

Cast: Howard Chitjian, Alfred Drake, George Gaynes, Maria Karnilova, Daniel Massey, Agnes Moorehead, Karin Wolfe

Songs: Overture (orchestra)
Thank Heaven for Little Girls (Drake)
It's a Bore (Drake, Massey)
The Earth and Other Minor Things (Wolfe)
Paris Is Paris Again (Drake)
She Is Not Thinking of Me (Massey)
I Remember It Well (Drake, Karnilova)
The Night They Invented Champage (Karnilova, Massey, Wolfe)

Gigi (Massey)
The Contract (Moorehead, Karnilova, Gaynes, Chitjian)
In This Wide, Wide World (Wolfe)
I'm Glad I'm Not Young Anymore (Drake)
Finale (orchestra)
Thank Heaven for Little Girls (reprise) (Drake)

THE GIRL IN PINK TIGHTS (March 5, 1954, Mark Hellinger Theatre)

Columbia ML 4890 mono reissued: CSP AOL 4890

Music: Sigmund Romberg; lyrics: Leo Robin; musical direction: Sylvan Levin

Cast: David Atkinson, Lydia Fredericks, Charles Goldner, Jeanmaire, Kalem Kermoyan, Brenda Lewis, John Stamford

Songs: Overture (orchestra)
That Naughty Show from Gay Paree (ensemble)
Lost in Loveliness (Atkinson)
I Promised Their Mothers (Goldner, girls)
Up in the Elevated Railway (Jeanmaire, Atkinson, ensemble)
In Paris and in Love (Jeanmaire, Atkinson)

You've Got to Be a Little Crazy (Lewis, Fredericks, Kermoyan, Stamford)
Free to Love (Jeanmaire)
Out of the Way! (ensemble)
Roll Out the Hose, Boys (men)

Overture to Act II (ensemble)
My Heart Won't Say Goodbye (Atkinson)
We're All in the Same Boat (ensemble)
Love Is the Funniest Thing (Lewis, Goldner)
The Cardinal's Guard Are We (Lewis, ensemble)
Going to the Devil (Jeanmaire) Finale (ensemble)

Note: "Pas de Deux", recorded 1959 by Lehman Engel in stereo, issued on Painted Smiles PS 1364: Ballet on Broadway.

THE GIRL WHO CAME TO SUPPER (December 8, 1983, Broadway Theatre)

Columbia KOS 2420 stereo

Music, lyrics: Noel Coward; based on a play by Terence Rattigan; musical direction: Jay Blackton

Cast: Roderick Cook, Jose Ferrer, Florence Henderson, Carey Nairnes, Tessie O'Shea, Sean Scully

Songs: Carpathian National Anthem: Yasni Kozkolai (ensemble)
My Family Tree (Ferrer, Cook)
I've Been Invited to a Party (Henderson)
Sir or Ma'am (Cook, Henderson)
Soliloquies (Ferrer, Henderson)
Lonely (Ferrer)
Here and Now (Henderson)
London Is a Little Bit of All Right (O'Shea, ensemble)
What Ho, Mrs. Brisket (O'Shea, ensemble)
Don't Take Our Charlie for the Army (O'Shea, ensemble)
Saturday Night at the Rose and Crown (O'Shea, ensemble)

Coronation Chorale (Henderson, Ferrer, company)
How Do You Do, Middle Age? (Ferrer)
When Foreign Princes Come to Visit Us (Nairnes, men)
Curt, Clear and Concise (Ferrer, Cook)
This Time It's True Love (Henderson, Ferrer)
"The Coconut Girl" selections: (Henderson, Scully)
Welcome to the Pootzie Van Doyle
The Coconut Girl
Paddy MacNeil and His Automobile
Swing Song
Six Lillies of the Valley
The Walla Walla Boola
I'll Remember Her (Ferrer)

GODSPELL (May 17, 1971, Off Broadway, Cherry Lane Theatre)

Bell Records 1102 stereo reissued: Arista ALB 68304

Music, new lyrics: Stephen Schwartz; based upon the Gospel According to St. Matthew; musical direction: Stephen Schwartz

Cast: Lamar Alford, Jesse Cutler, Peggy Gordon, David Haskell, Joanna Jonas, Richard LaBonte, Robin Lamont, Gilmer McCormick, Sonia Manzano, Jeffrey Mylett, Stephen Nathan, Steve Reinhardt, Herb Simon

Songs: Prepare Ye the Way of the Lord (Haskell, company)
Save the People (Nathan, company)
Day by Day (Lamont, company)
Learn Your Lessons Well (McCormick)
Bless the Lord (Jonas, company)
All for the Best (Nathan, Haskell)
All Good Gifts (Alford, company)
Light of the World (Simon, Gordon, Mylett, Lamont, company)

Turn Back, O Man (Manzano, company)
Alas for You (Nathan)
By My Side (Gordon, McCormick, company)
We Beseech Thee (Mylett, company)
On the Willows (Reinhardt, LaBonte, Cutler)
Finale (Nathan, company)
Day by Day (reprise) (company)

THE GOLDEN APPLE (March 11, 1954, Off Broadway, Phoenix Theatre)

RCA LOC 1014 mono reissued: Elektra EKL 5000

Music: Jerome Morass; lyrics: John Latouche; musical direction: Hugh Ross

Cast: Kaye Ballard, Stephen Douglass, Priscilla Gillette, Martha Larrimore, Dean Michener, Portia Nelson, Bibi Osterwald, Geraldine Viti, Jack Whiting

Songs: Overture (orchestra)
My Love Is on the Way (Gillette)
The Heroes Come Home (chorus)
It Was a Glad Adventure (Douglass, men)
Come Along Boys (chorus)
It's the Going Home Together (Gillette, Douglass)
Mother Hare's Prophecy (Larrimore, Douglass, Gillette)
Helen Is Always Willing (company)
The Judgement of Paris (Osterwald, Viti, Nelson, Larrimore)
Lazy Afternoon (Ballard)

The Departure for Rhododendron (company)
My Picture in the Papers (Ballard, men)
Hector's Song (Whiting)
Wind Flowers (Gillette)
Store-Bought Suit (Douglass)
Calypso (Viti, Whiting, Douglass)
Scylla and Charybdis (Whiting, Michener)
Goona-Goona (Osterwald, chorus)
Doomed, Doomed, Doomed (Nelson, chorus)
Circe (Larrimore, Whiting, Douglass, chorus)
Ulysses' Soliloquy (Douglass, chorus)
Finale:
The Sewing Bee (Osterwald, Viti, Nelson)
The Tirade (Gillette, Douglass)
Going Home Together (Douglass, Gillette, company)

Note: Narration by Jack Whiting.

GOLDEN BOY (October 20, 1964, Majestic Theatre)

Capitol SVAS 2124 stereo

Music: Charles Strouse; lyrics: Lee Adams; based on the play by Clifford Odets; musical direction: Elliot Lawrence

Cast: Johnny Brown, Billy Daniels, Sammy Davis, Louis Gossett, Terrin Miles, Kenneth Tobey, Paula Wayne

Songs: Workout (men)
Night Song (Davis)
Everything's Great (Tobey, Wayne)
Gimme Some (Miles, Davis)
Stick Around (Davis)
Don't Forget 127th Street (Brown, Davis, company)
Lorna's Here (Wayne)
This Is the Life (Daniels, Davis, company)

Golden Boy (Wayne)
While the City Sleeps (Daniels)
Colorful (Davis)
I Want to Be with You (Davis, Wayne)
Can't You See It (Davis)
No More (Davis, company)
Finale (Gossett, Davis)

THE GOLDEN LAND - see page 259

GOLDEN RAINBOW (February 4, 1968, Shubert Theatre)

Calendar Records KOS 1001 stereo

Music, lyrics: Walter Marks; based on a play by Arnold Schulman; musical direction: Elliot Lawrence

Cast: Eydie Gorme, Scott Jacoby, Steve Lawrence, Joseph Sirola

Songs: Overture (orchestra)
24 Hours a Day (company)
We Got Us (Lawrence, Jacoby)
He Needs Me Now (Gorme)
Kid (Lawrence)
For Once in Your Life (Gorme, Lawrence, company)
Taking Care of You (Gorme, Jacoby)
I've Gotta Be Me (Lawrence)

Entr'acte (orchestra)
Taste (Sirola, company)
Desert Moon (Gorme, Lawrence)
All in Fun (Gorme, Lawrence)
It's You Again (Gorme)
He Needs Me Now (reprise) (Gorme)
Golden Rainbow (Lawrence)
How Could I Be So Wrong (Gorme)
Finale: We Got Us (Gorme, Lawrence, Jacoby)

GOLDILOCKS (October 11, 1958, Lunt-Fontanne Theatre)

Columbia OS 2007 stereo

Music: Leroy Anderson; lyrics: Joan Ford, Jean and Walter Kerr; musical direction: Lehman Engel

Cast: Don Ameche, Richard Armbruster, Nathaniel Frey, Margaret Hamilton, Russell Nype, Pat Stanley, Elaine Stritch, Gene Varrone

Songs: Overture (orchestra)
Lazy Moon (company)
Give the Little Lady a Great Big Hand (Stritch, company)
Save a Kiss (Nype, Stritch)
No One'll Ever Love You (Stritch, Ameche)
Who's Been Sitting in My Chair? (Stritch)
There Never Was a Woman (Ameche)
The Pussy Foot (Stanley, company)

Lady in Waiting (Stanley, Nype, company)
Where Is the Beast in You? (Stritch)
Shall I Take My Heart and Go (Nype)
I Can't Be in Love (Ameche)
Bad Companions (Frey, Hamilton, Armbruster, Varrone)
I Never Know When (Stritch)
Two Years in the Making (Frey, Hamilton, chorus)
Heart of Stone (company)

GOODTIME CHARLEY (March 3, 1975, Palace Theatre)

RCA ARL 1-1011 stereo

Music: Larry Grossman; lyrics: Hal Hackady; musical direction: Arthur B. Rubinstein

Cast: Ed Becker, Susan Browning, Rhoda Butler, Peggy Cooper, Jay Garner, Joel Grey, Grace Keagy, Nancy Killmer, Hal Norman, Ann Reinking, Charles Rule, Richard B. Shull, Brad Tyrrell, Louis Zorich

Songs: Overture (orchestra)
History (Tyrrell, Norman, Keagy, Butler, Rule, Cooper, Killmer, Becker, ensemble)
Goodtime Charley (Grey)
Voices and Visions (Reinking)
Bits and Pieces (Grey, Reinking)
To Make the Boy a Man (Reinking)
Why Can't We All Be Nice (Grey)

Born Lover (Grey)
I Am Going to Love (the Man You're Going to Be) (Reinking)
Castles of the Loire (Reinking, ensemble)
You Still Have a Long Way to Go (Reinking, Grey)
Merci, Bon Dieu (Browning, Shull)
Confessional (Zorich, Garner)
One Little Year (Reinking)
I Leave the World (Grey)
Finale (Grey, Reinking, ensemble)

THE GRAND TOUR (January 11, 1979, Palace Theatre)

Columbia JS 35761 stereo

Music, lyrics: Jerry Herman; based upon the original play Jacobowsky and the Colonel by Franz Werfel and the American play based on the same by S. N. Behrman; musical direction: Wally Harper

Cast: Chevi Colton, Joel Grey, Ron Holgate, Travis Hudson, Florence Lacey, Gene Varrone, Stephen Vinovich

Songs: Overture (orchestra)
I'll Be Here Tomorrow (Grey)
For Poland (Holgate, Grey, chorus)
I Belong Here (Lacey)
Marianne (Holgate)
We're Almost There (Lacey, Vinovich, Grey, Holgate, Hudson, Varrone, chorus)
More and More/Less and Less (Lacey, Holgate)

One Extraordinary Thing (Grey, Lacey, Holgate, Vinovich, Colton)
Mrs. S. L. Jacobowsky (Grey)
Mazeltov (Grey, Varrone, chorus)
I Think, I Think (Holgate)
Marianne (reprise) (Grey)
You I Like (Grey, Holgate)
I Belong Here (reprise) (Lacey)
I'll Be Here Tomorrow (reprise) (Grey)
You I Like (reprise) (chorus)

THE GRASS HARP (November 2, 1971, Martin Beck Theatre)

Painted Smiles PS 1354 stereo

Music: Claibe Richardson; lyrics: Kenward Elmslie; based on the novel by Truman Capote; musical direction: Theodore Saidenberg

Cast: Carol Brice, Barbara Cook, Ruth Ford, Karen Morrow, Max Showalter, Russ Thacker

Songs: Overture (orchestra)
Dropsy Cure Weather (Cook, Brice, Thacker)
Floozies (Thacker)
Think Big Rich (Showalter)
If There's Love Enough (Brice)
Yellow Drum (Cook, Thacker, Brice)
Marry with Me (Brice)
Chain of Love (I've Always Been in Love) (Cook)

This One Day (Thacker)
The Babylove Miracle Show:
Call Me Babylove (Morrow)
Walk into Heaven (Morrow)
Hang a Little Moolah on the Washline (Morrow, company)
Talkin' in Tongues (Morrow)

Whooshin' Through My Flesh (Morrow, Cook, Brice, Thacker, company)
Walk into Heaven (reprise) (Morrow)
The Indian Blues (Brice, company)
What Do I Do Now (Ford)
Reach Out (Cook, Morrow, Brice, Thacker, company)
Finale: Yellow Drum (Cook, company)

GREASE (February 14, 1972, Off Broadway, Eden Theatre; transferred June 7, 1972, Broadhurst Theatre)

MGM 1SE-34 OC stereo reissued: Polydor 827-548-1 Y-1

Music, lyrics: Jim Jacobs, Warren Casey; musical direction: Louis St. Louis

Cast: Adrienne Barbeau, Walter Bobbie, Barry Bostwick, James Canning, Carole Demas, Katie Hanley, Tom Harris, Ilene Kristen, Dorothy Leon, Timothy Meyers, Kathi Moss, Alan Paul, Marya Small, Garn Stephens

Songs: Alma Mater (Leon, Kristen, Harris)
Alma Mater (Parody) (students)
Summer Nights (Demas, Bostwick, students)
Those Magic Changes (Canning, students)
Freddy, My Love (Hanley, Stephens, Small, Barbeau)
Greased Lightin' (Meyers, boys)
Mooning (Bobbie, Stephens)
Look at Me, I'm Sandra Dee (Barbeau)
We Go Together (students)

It's Raining on Prom Night (Demas, Moss)
Born to Hand-Jive (Paul, company)
Beauty School Dropout (Paul, Small, chorus)
Alone at a Drive-In Movie (Bostwick, boys)
Rock 'N' Roll Party Queen (Canning, Bobbie)
There Are Worse Things I Could Do (Barbeau)
Look at Me, I'm Sandra Dee (reprise) (Demas)
All Choked Up (Demas, Bostwick, company)
We Go Together (reprise) (company)

GREENWICH VILLAGE, U.S.A. (September 28, 1960, Off Broadway, One Sheridan Square)

20th Fox TCF-105-2S (two records) stereo reissued: AEI 1129

Music: Jeanne Bargy; lyrics: Jeanne Bargy, Frank Gehrecke, Herb Corey; musical direction: Bill Costa

Cast: Jack Betts, Saralou Cooper, Pat Finley, Judy Guyll, Dawn Hampton, James Harwood, Jane A. Johnston, Burke McHugh, James Pompeii, Ken Urmston

Songs: Greenwich Village, U.S.A. (cast)*
It's A Nice Place to Visit (McHugh)
Ladies of the House (Finley, Hampton, Johnston)*
How Can Anyone So Sweet (Pompeii)

Sunday Brunch (cast)*
Love Me (Cooper)*

How About Us Last Nite (Betts, Johnston)*
Brownstone (Hampton)*
BLT (Finley, Harwood)
That's How You Get Your Kicks (McHugh, Cooper, Finley, Guyll, Hampton)*
Miss Hi-Fie (Johnston)*
Living Pictures (cast)
N.Y.U. (Finley, Guyll, Hampton, Harwood, Johnston, McHugh, Pompeii, Urmston)*

Off Broadway Broads (Finley, Guyll, Johnston)
Shopkeepers Trio (McHugh, Pompeii, Urmston)*
Baby You Bore Me (Betts, Guyll)
Birth of a Beatnik (orchestra)*
Espresso House (Johnston, Harwood)* spoken
Week-End Shopping (Cooper, Finley, Pompeii, Urmston)*
Tea Party (Cooper)
What Do They Know About Love Uptown (Finley, Urmston, Guyll, Pompeii)

It Pays to Advertise (Johnston)*
We Got Love (Hampton)*
When the Village Goes to Sleep (Harwood)*
Finale: Save the Village (cast)*

Note: Introductions by Burke McHugh. Fox Records originally issued a one record 'highlights' version (SFX-4005) with starred (*) numbers.

GREENWILLOW (March 8, 1960, Alvin Theatre)

RCA LSO 2001 stereo reissued: CSP P 13974

Music, lyrics: Frank Loesser; based on the novel by B.J. Chute; musical direction: Abba Bogin

Cast: Lynn Brinker, Lee Cass, William Chapman, Brenda Harris, Cecil Kellaway, Pert Kelton, Ellen McCown, Bruce MacKay, John Megna, Anthony Perkins, Jan Tucker

Songs: Overture (orchestra)
A Day Borrowed from Heaven (Perkins, ensemble)
The Music of Home (MacKay, Perkins, chorus)
Dorrie's Wish (McCown)
Gideon Briggs, I Love You (Perkins, McCown)
Summertime Love (Perkins, chorus)
Greenwillow Walk (orchestra)
Walking Away Whistling (McCown)
The Sermon (Kellaway, Chapman)
Greenwillow Christmas (Carol) (chorus)

Could've Been a Ring (Kelton, Cass)
Never Will I Marry (Perkins)
Faraway Boy (McCown)
Clang Dang the Bell (Perkins, Kelton, Brinker, Tucker, Harris, Megna)
What a Blessing (Kellaway)
He Died Good (chorus)

Summertime Love (reprise) (Perkins)
Finale (company)

GRIND (April 16, 1985, Mark Hellinger Theatre)

Polydor 827 072-1 Y-1 stereo CD

Music: Larry Grossman; lyrics: Ellen Fitzhugh; musical direction: Paul Gemignani

Cast: Leilani Jones, Stubby Kaye, Sharon Murray, Timothy Nolan, Ben Vereen, Carol Woods

Songs: Overture (orchestra)
This Must Be the Place (company)
A Sweet Thing Like Me (Jones, girls)
I Get Myself Out (Kaye)
My Daddy Always Taught Me to Share (Vereen)
All Things to One Man (Jones)
The Line (Vereen, girls)
Katie, My Love (Nolan)
The Grind (Kaye, company)

Why, Mama, Why (Jones, Vereen)
This Crazy Place (Vereen, company)
Who Is He? (Jones)
Never Put It in Writing (Kaye)
I Talk, You Talk (Nolan)
Timing (Murray)
These Eyes of Mine (Woods, company)
New Man (Vereen)
Down (Nolan)
Finale (company)

GUYS AND DOLLS (November 24, 1950, Forty-Sixth Street Theatre)

Decca DLP 8036 mono reissued: MCA 37094E

Music, lyrics: Frank Loesser; based on a story and characters by Damon Runyon; musical direction: Irving Actman

Cast: Robert Alda, Isabel Bigley, Vivian Blaine, Douglas Deane, Stubby Kaye, Sam Levene, Pat Rooney, Sr., Johnny Silver

Songs: Runyonland Music (orchestra)
Fugue for Tinhorns (Kaye, Silver, Deane)
Follow the Fold (Bigley, chorus)
The Oldest Established (Levene, Kaye, Silver, chorus)
I'll Know (Alda, Bigley)
A Bushel and a Peck (Blaine, girls)
Adelaide's Lament (Blaine)
Guys and Dolls (Kaye, Silver)
If I Were a Bell (Bigley)
My Time of Day (Alda)

I've Never Been in Love Before (Alda, Bigley)
Take Back Your Mink (Blaine, girls)

More I Cannot Wish You (Rooney)
Luck Be a Lady (Alda, men)
Sue Me (Blaine, Levene)
Sit Down, You're Rockin' the Boat (Kaye, chorus)
Marry the Man Today (Blaine, Bigley)
Guys and Dolls (reprise) (chorus)

GUYS AND DOLLS (Revival, July 21, 1976, Broadway Theatre)

Motown M6-876S1 stereo

Musical direction: Howard Roberts

Cast: Bardell Conner, Irene Datcher, Norma Donaldson, Robert Guillaume, Ernestine Jackson, Sterling McQueen, Marion Moore, Ken Page, Christophe Pierre, James Randolph, Emett 'Babe' Wallace

Songs: Overture - Runyonland (company)
Fugue for Tinhorns (Page, Pierre, McQueen)
Follow the Fold (Jackson, Wallace, Datcher, Moore, Conner)
The Oldest Established (Page, Pierre, Guillaume, men)
I'll Know (Randolph, Jackson)
Bushel and a Peck (Donaldson, girls)
Adelaide's Lament (Donaldson)
Guys and Dolls (Page, Pierre)
If I Were a Bell (Jackson, Randolph)

Entr'acte (orchestra)
My Time of Day (Randolph)
I've Never Been in Love Before (Randolph, Jackson)
Take Back Your Mink (Donaldson, girls)
More I Cannot Wish You (Wallace)
Luck Be a Lady Tonight (Randolph, men)
Adelaide's Lament (reprise) (Donaldson) (and) Sue Me (Guillaume)
Sit Down, You're Rockin' the Boat (Page, chorus)
Adelaide's Lament (reprise) (Donaldson) (and) I've Never Been in Love Before (reprise) (Jackson)
Marry the Man Today (Jackson, Donaldson)
Guys and Dolls (reprise) (company)

GYPSY (May 21, 1959, Broadway Theatre)

Columbia OS 2017 stereo reissued: S 32607 CD

Music: Jule Styne; lyrics: Stephen Sondheim; suggested by the memoirs of Gypsy Rose Lee; musical direction: Milton Rosenstock

Cast: Lane Bradbury, Sandra Church, Faith Dane, Chotzi Foley, Maria Karnilova, Jack Klugman, Jacqueline Mayro, Ethel Merman, Karen Moore, Paul Wallace

Songs: Overture (orchestra)
Let Me Entertain You (Mayro, Moore, Merman)

Some People (Merman)
Small World (Merman, Klugman)
Baby June and Her Newsboys (Mayro, Moore, boys)
Mr. Goldstone, I Love You (Merman)
Little Lamb (Church)
You'll Never Get Away from Me (Merman, Klugman)
--- Dainty June and Her Farmboys (Bradbury, Church, boys)
If Mama Was Married (Church, Bradbury)
All I Need Is the Girl (Wallace)
Everything's Coming Up Roses (Merman)
Together Wherever We Go (Merman, Klugman, Church)
You Gotta Have a Gimmick (Dane, Foley, Karnilova)
Let Me Entertain You (Church)
Rose's Turn (Merman)

Note: *Gypsy* was revived September 23, 1974, at the Winter Garden Theatre, starring Angela Lansbury. The only cast recording, however, was the London one, issued on RCA LBL 1-5004.

HAIR (October 17, 1967, Off Broadway, Public Theatre)

RCA LSO 1143 stereo

Music: Galt MacDermot; lyrics: Gerome Ragni, James Rado; musical direction: John Morris

Cast: Jonelle Allen, Susan Batson, Linda Compton, Walker Daniels, Steve Dean, Sally Eaton, Suzannah Evans, Paul Jabara, Marijane Maricle, Jill O'Hara, Shelley Plimpton, Gerome Ragni, Alma Robinson, Arnold Wilkerson

Songs: Ain't Got No (Daniels, Ragni, Dean, Wilkerson, company)
I Got Life (Daniels, Maricle)
Air (Eaton, Plimpton, Allen)
Going Down (Ragni, company)
Hair (Daniels, Ragni, company)
Dead End (O'Hara, company)
Frank Mills (Plimpton)
Hare Krishna (company)
--- Where Do I Go? (Daniels, company)
Electric Blues (Evans, Compton, Jabara)
Easy to Be Hard (Evans, Compton, Jabara, company)
Manchester (Daniels)
White Boys (Allen, Batson, Robinson)
Black Boys (Compton, Plimpton, Evans)
Walking in Space (company)
Aquarius (company)
Good Morning Starshine (O'Hara, company)
Exanaplanetooch (Daniels)
The Climax (O'Hara)

HAIR (Revival, April 29, 1968, Biltmore Theatre)

RCA LSO 1150 stereo

Musical direction: Galt MacDermot

Cast: Donnie Burks, Steve Curry, Mary Davis, Ronald Dyson, Sally Eaton, Walter Harris, Diane Keaton, Lynn Kellogg, Jonathan Kramer, Emmaretta Marks, Melba Moore, Natalie Mosco, Suzannah Norstrand, Shelley Plimpton, James Rado, Gerome Ragni, Lamont Washington

Songs: Aquarius (Dyson, company)
Donna (Ragni, company)
Hashish (company)
Sodomy (Curry, company)
Colored Spade (Washington, company)
Manchester England (Rado, company)
I'm Black (Washington, Curry, Ragni, Rado)
Ain't Got No (Curry, Washington, Moore, company)
Air (Eaton, Plimpton, Moore, company)
Initials (company)
I Got Life (Rado, company)
Hair (Rado, Ragni, company)
My Conviction (Kramer)
Don't Put It Down (Ragni, Curry)
Frank Mills (Plimpton)
Be-In (company)

Where Do I Go? (Rado, company)
Black Boys (Keaton, Norstrand, Mosco)
White Boys (Moore, Davis, Marks)
Easy to Be Hard (Kellogg)
Walking in Space (company)
Abie Baby (Washington, Dyson, Burks, Davis)
Three-Five-Zero-Zero (company)
What a Piece of Work Is Man (Dyson, Harris)
Good Morning Starshine (Kellogg, Moore, Rado, Ragni)
The Flesh Failures (Let the Sun Shine In) (Rado, Kellogg, Moore, company)

HALF A SIXPENCE (April 25, 1965, Broadhurst Theatre)

RCA LSO 1110 stereo

Music, lyrics: David Heneker; based on H.G. Wells' Kipps; musical direction: Stanley Lebowsky

Cast: Norman Allen, Grover Dale, James Grout, Polly James, Will Mackenzie, Tommy Steele

Songs: Overture (orchestra)
All in the Cause of Economy (Steele, Mackenzie, Allen, Dale)
Half a Sixpence (Steele, James)
Money to Burn (Steele, men)
A Proper Gentleman (Steele, Mackenzie, Allen, Dale, girls)
She's Too Far Above Me (Steele)

If the Rain's Got to Fall (Steele, Dale, Mackenzie, Allen, girls)
Long Ago (Steele, James)

Flash, Bang, Wallop! (Steele, James, Grout, Dale, Mackenzie, Allen, girls)
I Know What I Am (James)
The Party's on the House (Steele, Dale, Mackenzie, Allen, girls)
Finale (company)

HALF-PAST WEDNESDAY (April 6, 1962, Off Broadway, Orpheum Theatre)

Columbia CS 8717 stereo reissued: Harmony HS 14560

Music: Robert Colby; lyrics: Robert Colby, Nita Jonas; a new musical version of Rumpelstiltskin; musical direction: Julian Stein

Cast: Dom De Luise, Robert Fitch, Sean Garrison, Audre Johnston, David Winters

Songs: Prologue - I've Got a Goose (cast)
What's the Fun of Being King (Dom De Luise)
You're the Sweet Beginning (Garrison, Johnston)
Who? Where? What? (Winters)
The Spinning Song (Winters, Johnston)
If You Did It Once (cast)
How Lovely, How Lovely (Johnston, Garrison)
The Spinning Song (reprise) (Winters)

Grandfather (De Luise, Fitch)
To Whit - To Whoo (Winters)
What's the Name of 'What's His Name?' (cast)
Companionship (Winters)
We Know a Secret Secret (cast)
Finale (cast)

Note: Recording includes dialog.

HALLELUJAH, BABY! (April 26, 1967, Martin Beck Theatre)

Columbia KOS 3090 stereo

Music: Jule Styne; lyrics: Betty Comden, Adolph Green; musical direction: Buster Davis

Cast: Clifford Allen, Allen Case, Hope Clarke, Marilyn Cooper, Lillian Hayman, Winston DeWitt Hemsley, Robert Hooks, Sandra Lein, Saundra McPherson, Garrett Morris, Kenneth Scott, Barbara Sharma, Leslie Uggams, Alan Weeks

Songs: Overture (orchestra)
My Own Morning (Uggams)
The Slice (Hooks, Uggams, Allen, Morris, Scott, Weeks)
Feet Do Yo' Stuff (Uggams, Hemsley, Weeks, Clarke, Lein, McPherson)
Watch My Dust (Hooks)
Smile, Smile (Uggams, Hooks, Hayman)
Witches' Brew (Uggams, Sharma, Cooper)
Being Good (Uggams)

--- I Wanted to Change Him (uggams)
Another Day (Case, Hooks, Sharma, Uggams)
Talking to Yourself (Uggams, Hooks, Case)
Hallelujah, Baby! (Uggams, Hemsley, Weeks)
Not Mine (Case)
I Don't Know Where She Got It (Hayman, Case, Hooks)
Now's the Time (Uggams, company)

THE HAPPIEST GIRL IN THE WORLD (April 3, 1961, Martin Beck Theatre)

Columbia KOS 2050 stereo

Music: Jacques Offenbach; lyrics: E.Y. Harburg; lightly based on Lysistrata; musical direction: Robert DeCormier

Cast: Lu Leonard, Cyril Ritchard, Janice Rule, Dran Seitz, Nancy Windsor, Bruce Yarnell

Songs: Overture (orchestra)
The Glory That Is Greece (Ritchard, Yarnell, ensemble)
The Happiest Girl in the World (Seitz, Yarnell)
The Greek Marine (Rithcard, ensemble)
Shall We Say Farewell? (Seitz)
Never Be-Devil the Devil (Ritchard)
Whatever That May Be (Rule, ensemble)
Eureka (Rule, ensemble)
The Oath (Seitz, ensemble)
Viva la Virtue (Ritchard, Rule)
--- Finale, Act I (ensemble)
Adrift on a Star (Seitz, Yarnell)
That'll Be the Day (ensemble)
How Soon, Oh Moon? (Windsor, Seitz, ensemble)
Love-Sick Serenade (Ritchard, Leonard)
Five Minutes of Spring (Yarnell)
Never Trust a Virgin (Ritchard, ensemble)
Entrance of the Courtesans (ensemble)
Vive la Virtue (reprise) (Ritchard, Rule)
Finale (ensemble)

HAPPY HUNTING (December 6, 1956, Majestic Theatre)

RCA LOC 1026 mono

Music: Harold Karr; lyrics: Matt Dubey; musical direction: Jay Blackton

Cast: Leon Belasco, Mary Finney, Virginia Gibson, Fernando Lamas, Ethel Merman, Gordon Polk

Songs: Opening (chorus)
Don't Tell Me (Polk, Gibson)
It's Good to Be Here (Merman, chorus)
Mutual Admiration Society (Merman, Gibson)
It's Like a Beautiful Woman (Lamas)
The Wedding-of-the-Year Blues (Finney, chorus)

Mr. Livingstone (Merman)
If'n (Polk, Gibson, chorus)
This Is What I Call Love (Merman)

Entr'acte (chorus)
A New-Fangled Tango (Merman, Gibson, Belasco, chorus)
She's Just Another Girl (Polk)
The Game of Love (Merman)
Happy Hunting (Merman, chorus)
I'm a Funny Dame (Merman)
This Much I Know (Lamas)
Everyone Who's "Who's Who" (chorus)
Grande Finale (chorus)

THE HAPPY TIME (January 18, 1968, Broadway Theatre)

RCA LSO 1144 stereo

Music: John Kander; lyrics: Fred Ebb; suggested by characters in the stories of Robert L. Fontaine; musical direction: Oscar Kosarin

Cast: Robert Goulet, Julie Gregg, Mike Rupert, David Wayne

Songs: The Happy Time (Goulet, family)
He's Back (family)
Catch My Garter (girls)
Tomorrow Morning (Goulet, Wayne, Rupert, girls)
Please Stay (Rupert, Goulet)
I Don't Remember You (Goulet)
St. Pierre (Goulet, glee club)
Without Me (Rupert, schoolboys)

Among My Yesterdays (Goulet)
The Life of the Party (Wayne, girls, schoolboys)
Seeing Things (Goulet, Gregg)
A Certain Girl (Wayne, Goulet, Rupert)
Finale (Goulet, company)

HARD JOB BEING GOD (May 15, 1972, Off Broadway, Edison Theatre)

GWP Records ST 2036 stereo

Music, lyrics: Tom Martel; musical direction: John O'Reilly

Cast: Dorothy Lerner, Tom Martel, John O'Reilly, Tom Troxell, Joe Valentine, Susie Walcher

Songs: Hard Job Being God (Martel, chorus)
Moses' Song (Valentine)
The Ten Plagues (Troxell, Valentine)
Passover (O'Reilly, Valentine, Troxell)
Ruth (Walcher, chorus)

You're on Your Own (Martel)
A Psalm of Peace (Lerner, chorus)
I'm Countin' on You (Troxell, Martel)
Shalom! L'chaim! (chorus)
Amos Gonna Give You Hell (Walcher, chorus)

What Do I Have to Do? (Martel, chorus)
A Psalm of Peace (reprise) (Lerner)
A Hard Job Being God (reprise) (Martel, chorus)

Note: Tom Martel is the only cast member on this recording (c1971) to appear in the New York production.

HAZEL FLAGG (February 11, 1953, Mark Hellinger Theatre)

RCA LOC 1010 mono reissued: RCA CBM 1-2207

Music: Jule Styne; lyrics: Bob Hilliard; based on a story by James Street and the film Nothing Sacred; musical direction: Pembroke Davenport

Cast: Dean Campbell, Helen Gallagher, John Howard, Benay Venuta, Jack Whiting

Songs: Overture (orchestra)
A Little More Heart (Venuta, chorus)
The World Is Beautiful Today (Gallagher)
The Rutland Bouce (orchestra)
I'm Glad I'm Leaving (Gallagher, chorus)
Hello, Hazel (Venuta, chorus)
Every Street's a Boulevard in Old New York (Whiting)

How Do You Speak to an Angel? (Howard)
Autograph Chant (chorus)
I Feel Like I'm Gonna Live Forever (Gallagher)
You're Gonna Dance with Me, Willie (Gallagher, chorus)
Who Is the Bravest? (male chorus)
Salome (Campbell, chorus)
Everybody Loves to Take a Bow (Venuta, Whiting, male chorus)
Laura De Maupassant (Gallagher)
Finale (company)

HELLO, DOLLY! (January 16, 1964, St. James Theatre)

RCA LSO 1087 stereo

Music, lyrics: Jerry Herman; based on The Matchmaker by Thornton Wilder; musical direction: Shepard Coleman

Cast: Eileen Brennan, David Burns, Carol Channing, Jerry Dodge, Igors Gavon, Sondra Lee, Charles Nelson Reilly

Songs: Overture (orchestra)
I Put My Hand In (Channing, company)
It Takes a Woman (Burns, company)
Put On Your Sunday Clothes (Reilly, Dodge, Channing, Gavon)
Ribbons Down My Back (Brennan)
Motherhood (Channing, Brennan, Lee)
Dancing (Channing, Reilly, Dodge, Lee, Brennan, company)

Before the Parade Passes By (Channing, company)

Elegance (Brennan, Reilly, Lee, Dodge)
Hello, Dolly! (Channing, company)
It Only Takes a Moment (Reilly, Brennan, company)
So Long Dearie (Channing)
Finale (Burns, Channing, company)

HELLO, DOLLY! (All black cast, November 12, 1967, St. James Theatre)

RCA LSO 1147 stereo

Musical direction: Saul Schechtman

Cast: Pearl Bailey, Cab Calloway, Chris Calloway, Jack Crowder, Winston DeWitt Hemsley, Roger Lawson, Emily Yancy

Songs: Overture (orchestra)
I Put My Hand In (Bailey, company)
It Takes a Woman (Cab Calloway, company)
Put On Your Sunday Clothes (Crowder, Hemsley, Bailey, Lawson)
Ribbons Down My Back (Yancy)
Motherhood (Bailey, Yancy, Chris Calloway)
Dancing (Bailey, Crowder, Hemsley, Yancy)

Before the Parade Passes By (Bailey, company)
Elegance (Yancy, Crowder, Chris Calloway, Hemsley)
Hello, Dolly! (Bailey, company)
It Only Takes a Moment (Crowder, Yancy, company)
So Long Dearie (Bailey)
Finale (Cab Calloway, Bailey, company)

HELLO, DOLLY! (New songs added, March 28, 1970, St. James Theatre)

Bar-Mike Records (45rpm) No number stereo Goldie Hawkins, Wayne Sanders: double pianos; Bill Halfacre: bass

Cast: Ethel Merman

Songs: World, Take Me Back (Merman)
Love, Look in My Window (Merman)

HENRY, SWEET HENRY (October 23, 1967, Palace Theatre)

ABC Records OC-4 stereo

Music, lyrics: Bob Merrill; based upon the novel The World of Henry Orient by Nora Johnson; musical direction: Shepard Coleman

Cast: Don Ameche, Carol Bruce, Louise Lasser, Laried Montgomery, Alice Playten, Neva Small, Robin Wilson

Songs: Overture (orchestra)

Academic Fugue (girls)
In Some Little World (Wilson)
Pillar to Post (Ameche, Lasser)
Here I Am (Wilson)
I Wonder How It Is (Small, chorus)
Nobody Steps on Kafritz (Playten)
Henry, Sweet Henry (Wilson, Small)
Woman in Love (Wilson, Small)
--- People Watchers (Montgomery, chorus)
Weary Near to Dyin' (Wilson, chorus)
Poor Little Person (Pleyten, chorus)
I'm Blue Too (Wilson, Small)
To Be Artistic (Ameche, Bruce)
Do You Ever Go to Boston (Wilson)
Here I Am (Wilson)
Finale (company)

HER FIRST ROMAN (October 20, 1968, Lunt-Fontanne Theatre)

S.P.M. Records (Society for the Preservation of Musicals)
CO 7751 mono

Music, lyrics: Ervin Drake; based on Bernard Shaw's Caesar and Cleopatra; musical direction: Peter Howard

Cast: Cal Bellini, Richard Kiley, Bruce MacKay, Claudia McNeil, Brooks Morton, Leslie Uggams

Songs: Prologue (orchestra)
Hail Sphinx (Kiley)
Save Me from Caesar (Uggams, Kiley)
Many Young Men from Now (Uggams)
March (soldiers)
He Pleasures Me (Uggams, McNeill)
Rome (Kiley)
--- Her First Roman (MacKay, Morton, soldiers)
Magic Carpet (Uggams)
The Dangerous Age (MacKay, Morton)
The Things We Think We Are (Kiley, Uggams, Morton, Bellini)
I Cannot Make Him Jealous (Uggams)
Evil Companions (MacKay, Kiley, Uggams, Morton, Bellini, soldiers)
In Vino Veritas (Kiley, MacKay, Morton, Bellini)
Just for Today (Uggams)
Finale: Her First Roman (soldiers)

Note: A live recording.

HERE'S LOVE (October 3, 1963, Shubert Theatre)

Columbia KOS 2400 stereo

Music, lyrics: Meredith Willson; based on the film Miracle on 34th Street; musical direction: Elliot Lawrence

Cast: Kathy Cody, Fred Gwynne, Cliff Hall, Valerie Lee, Laurence Naismith, Janis Paige, Paul Reed, Arthur Rubin, Craig Stevens

Songs: Overture (orchestra)
The Big Clown Balloons (chorus)
Parade (includes 'O Come All Ye Faithful') (chorus)
Arm in Arm (Paige, Lee)
You Don't Know (Paige)
The Bugle (Naismith, Cody)
Here's Love (Naismith, ensemble)

My Wish (Stevens, Paige)
Pine Cones and Holly Berries (Naismith, Paige, Gwynne) (includes 'It's Beginning to Look a Lot Like Christmas')
Look Little Girl (Stevens, Paige)
Expect Things to Happen (Naismith, Lee)
Love Can Take Me Again (waltz) (orchestra)
She Hadda Go Back (Stevens, men)
That Man Over There (Reed, chorus)
My State (Reed, Rubin, Gwynne, Paige, Hall)
Finale (company)

HIGH BUTTON SHOES (October 9, 1947, Century Theatre)

RCA Camden 457 mono reissued: RCA LSO 1107(e)

Music: Jule Styne; lyrics: Sammy Cahn; based on Stephen Longstreet's short stories; musical direction: Milt Rosenstock

Cast: Mark Dawson, Nanette Fabray, Lois Lee, Jack McCauley, Phil Silvers, Johnny Stewart

Songs: Can't You Just See Yourself in Love with Me? (Dawson, Lee)
There's Nothing Like a Model 'T' (Silvers, Fabray, McCauley, Lee, Stewart, chorus)
You're My Girl (Dawson, Lee)
Get Away for a Day in the Country (McCauley, Stewart, chorus)

Papa, Won't You Dance with Me? (Fabray, McCauley, chorus)
On a Sunday by the Sea (Silvers, chorus)
I Still Get Jealous (Fabray, McCauley)
Nobody Ever Died for Dear Old Rutgers (Dawson, Silvers, men)

Note: 'The Bathing Bēauty Ballet', recorded in 1959 in stereo was issued on Painted Smiles PS 1364, Ballet on Broadway; musical direction: Lehman Engel.

HIGH SPIRITS (April 7, 1964, Alvin Theatre)

ABC Records OC 1 stereo

Music, lyrics: Hugh Martin, Timothy Gray; based upon Blithe Spirit by Noel Coward; musical direction: Fred Werner

Cast: (the voice of Timothy Gray), Tammy Grimes, Beatrice Lillie, Louise Troy, Edward Woodward

Songs: Overture (orchestra)
Was She Prettier Than I? (Troy)
The Bicycle Song (Lillie, ensemble)
You'd Better Love Me (Grimes)
Where Is the Man I Married? (Woodward, Troy)
Go into Your Trance (Lillie, ensemble)
Forever and a Day (Grimes, Woodward, Gray)
Something Tells Me (Grimes)

I Know Your Heart (Woodward, Grimes)
Faster than Sound (Grimes, ensemble)
If I Gave You (Woodward, Troy)
Talking to You (Lillie)
Home Sweet Heaven (Grimes)
Something Is Coming to Tea (Lillie, ensemble)
What in the World Did You Want? (Grimes, Troy, Woodward)
Something Tells Me (reprise) (company)

HOUSE OF FLOWERS (December 30, 1954, Alvin Theatre)

Columbia OL 4969 mono reissued: OS 2320

Music: Harold Arlen; lyrics: Harold Arlen, Truman Capote; based on a short story by Truman Capote; musical direction: Jerry Arlen

Cast: Pearl Bailey, Miriam Burton, Diahann Carroll, Juanita Hall, Dolores Harper, Ada Moore, Enid Mosier, Rawn Spearman

Songs: Overture (orchestra)
Waitin' (Harper, Moore, Mosier)
One Man Ain't Quite Enough (Bailey)
A Sleepin' Bee (Carroll, Harper, Moore, Mosier)
Bamboo Cage (Harper, Moore, Mosier, chorus)
House of Flowers (Carroll, Spearman)
Two Ladies in de Shade of de Banana Tree (Moore, Mosier, chorus)

What Is a Friend For? (Bailey)
Slide "Boy" Slide (Hall, chorus)
I'm Gonna Leave Off Wearing My Shoes (Carroll, chorus)
Has I Let You Down (Bailey, Harper, Moore, Mosier)
I Never Has Seen Snow (Carroll)
Turtle Song (Carroll, Spearman, chorus)
Don't Like Goodbyes (Bailey)
Mardi Gras (Burton, chorus)

HOUSE OF FLOWERS (Revival, January 28, 1968, Off Broadway, Theatre De Lys)

United Artists Records UAS 5180 stereo

Musical direction: Joseph Raposo

Cast: Yolande Bavan, Hope Clarke, Tom Helmore, Robert Jackson, Charles Moore, Novella Nelson, Thelma Oliver, Carla Pinza, Josephine Premice

Songs: Preface: Smellin' of Vanilla (company)
A Sleepin' Bee (Bavan, Oliver, Clarke)
Somethin' Cold to Drink (Premice)
House of Flowers (Jackson, Bavan)
Two Ladies in de Shade of de Banana Tree (Oliver, Clarke)
Don't Like Goodbyes (Bavan)
Jump de Broom (Moore, company)

Smellin' of Vanilla (reprise) (Oliver, Clarke, Nelson, company)
Waitin' (Oliver, Clarke)
Woman Never Understan' (Jackson)
I Never Has Seen Snow (Bavan)
Madame Tango's Particular Tango (Nelson, Pinza, Clarke, Oliver)
What Is a Friend For? (Helmore, Premice)
A Sleepin' Bee (reprise) (Jackson)
I Never Has Seen Snow (reprise) (Bavan)
Finale: Two Ladies in de Shade of de Banana Tree (Premice, Clarke, Oliver, company)

THE HOUSEWIVES' CANTATA (February 17, 1980, Off Broadway, Theatre Four)

Original Cast Records OC 8133 stereo

Music: Mira J. Spektor; lyrics: June Siegel; musical direction: Bob Goldstone

Cast: Lawrence Chelsi, Maida Meyers, Mira J. Spektor, Sharon Talbot

Songs: What Is a Woman? (Spektor, Chelsi)
Dirty Dish Rag (Meyers, Talbot, Spektor)
Early Morning Rain (Meyers, Chelsi) lyrics: C. Spektor
M.C.P. Song (cast)
Song of the Bourgeoise Hippie (Talbot)
Sex (cast)
Guinevere Among the Grapefruit Peels (Meyers, Talbot, Spektor)
Suburban Rose (Spektor)
Little Women (Chelsi)

Open Road (Meyers)
Our Apartment (cast)
Someday Blues (Spektor, Chelsi)
Adultery Waltz (Talbot, Chelsi)
Lullaby (Meyers)
Mr. Fixer (Spektor)
Divorce Lament (Talbot, Chelsi)
Legs (Talbot)
White House Resident (Chelsi)
New Song (cast)

Note: Sharon Talbot is the only New York cast member.

HOW NOW, DOW JONES (December 7, 1967, Lunt-Fontanne Theatre)

RCA LSO 1142 stereo

Music: Elmer Bernstein; lyrics: Carolyn Leigh; musical direction: Peter Howard

Cast: Charlotte Jones, Marlyn Mason, Anthony Roberts, Hiram Sherman, Sammy Smith, Fran Stevens, Brenda Vaccaro, Mara Worth

Songs: A-B-C (Vaccaro, company)
They Don't Make 'em Like That Anymore (Mason, Vaccaro)
Live a Little (Roberts, Mason)
The Pleasure's About to Be Mine (Roberts, Mason)
A Little Investigation (Sherman, company)
Walk Away (Mason)
Gawk, Tousle and Shucks (Roberts, company)
Shakespeare Lied (Mason, Vaccaro, Smith)

Step to the Rear (Roberts, Jones, company)
Big Trouble (Mason)
Rich Is Better (Smith, Stevens, Worth, company)
Just for the Moment (Mason)
He's Here (Vaccaro)
Touch and Go (Roberts, Mason)
Finale (company)

HOW TO STEAL AN ELECTION (October 13, 1968, Off Broadway, Pocket Theatre)

RCA LSO 1153 stereo

Music, lyrics: Oscar Brand; musical direction: Bhen Lanzaroni

Cast: D.R. Allen, Barbara Anson, Beverly Ballard, Ed Crowley, Clifton Davis, Carole Demas, Del Hinkley, Thom Koutsoukos, Bill McCutcheon

Songs: The Plumed Knight (Crowley)
Clay and Frelinghuysen (Anson, Ballard, Crowley)
Silent Cal (Anson, Ballard, Crowley, Hinkley, Koutsoukos, McCutcheon)
Nobody's Listening (Davis)
Comes the Right Man (Demas)
How to Steal an Election (Allen, Crowley, Hinkley)
Van Buren (Koutsoukos)
With Tippecanoe and Tyler Too (McCutcheon, ensemble)
Grover (Hinkley)
Lincoln and Soda (Ballard)
With Lincoln and Liberty (Crowley, Hinkley)
He's the Right Man (Allen, ensemble)

Down Among the Grass Roots (Allen, ensemble)
Grant (Crowley, Hinkley, Koutsoukos, McCutcheon)
Lucky Lindy (Anson, Ballard)
Charisma (Allen)
Get Out the Vote (ensemble)
Mr. Might've Been (Demas, Davis)

We're Gonna Win (Demas, Davis, ensemble)
More of the Same (Demas, Davis)

HOW TO SUCCEED IN BUSINESS WITHOUT REALLY TRYING (October 14, 1961, Forty-Sixth Street Theatre)

RCA LSO 1066 stereo

Music, lyrics: Frank Loesser; based on the book by Shepherd Mead; musical direction: Elliot Lawrence

Cast: Ruth Kobart, Mara Landi, Virginia Martin, Robert Morse, Paul Reed, Charles Nelson Reilly, Bonnie Scott, Sammy Smith, Claudette Sutherland, Rudy Vallee

Songs: Overture (orchestra)
How to (Morse)
Happy to Keep His Dinner Warm (Scott)
Coffee Break (Reilly, Sutherland, company)
The Company Way (Morse, Smith, Reilly, company)
A Secretary Is Not a Toy (Reed, company)
Been a Long Day (Morse, Scott, Sutherland)
Grand Old Ivy (Morse, Vallee)

Paris Original (Scott, Sutherland, Landi, company)
Rosemary (Morse, Scott, Reilly)
Cinderella, Darling (Sutherland, company)
Love From a Heart of Gold (Vallee, Martin)
I Believe in You (Morse, company)
Brotherhood of Man (Morse, Smith, Kobart, company)
Finale (Scott, company)

I CAN GET IT FOR YOU WHOLESALE (March 22, 1962, Shubert Theatre)

Columbia KOS 2180 stereo

Music, lyrics: Harold Rome; based on the novel by Jerome Weidman; musical direction: Lehman Engel

Cast: Francine Bond, Kelly Brown, Marilyn Cooper, Wilma Curley, Elliott Gould, James Hickman, Jack Kruschen, Harold Lang, Ken Le Roy, Bambi Linn, Luba Lisa, Barbara Monte, Sheree North, William Reilly, Lillian Roth, Barbra Streisand, Pat Turner, Edward Verso

Songs: Overture (orchestra)
I'm Not a Well Man (Kruschen, Streisand)
The Way Things Are (Gould)
When Gemini Meets Capricorn (Cooper, Gould)
Momma, Momma, Momma (Gould, Roth)
The Sound of Money (North, Gould, Monte, Reilly, Verso)
Too Soon (Roth)
The Family Way (Roth, Gould, Cooper, Lang, Linn, LeRoy)
Who Knows? (Cooper)

Ballad of the Garment Trade (Streisand, Cooper, Linn, Gould, Lang, LeRoy, chorus)

Have I Told You Lately? (LeRoy, Linn)
A Gift Today (Gould, Roth, LeRoy, Cooper, chorus)
Miss Marmelstein (Streisand)
A Funny Thing Happened (Cooper, Gould)
What's In It for Me? (Lang)
Eat a Little Something (Roth)
What Are They Doing to Us Now? (Streisand, Brown, Hickman, Turner, Lisa, Curley, Bond)

I CAN'T KEEP RUNNING IN PLACE (May 14, 1981, Off Broadway, Westside Arts Theatre)

Painted Smiles PS 1346 stereo

Music, lyrics: Barbara Schottenfeld; musical direction: Robert Hirschhorn

Cast: Evalyn Baron, Joy Franz, Helen Gallagher, Bev Larson, Phyllis Newman, Marcia Rodd

Songs: I'm Glad I'm Here (company)
Don't Say Yes If You Want to Say No (Rodd, company)
I Can't Keep Running in Place (Franz)
I'm on My Own (Rodd)
More of Me to Love (Newman, Baron)
I Live Alone (Gallagher)

I Can Count on You (Baron, company)
Penis Envy (Rodd, company)
Get the Answer Now (Larsen, company)
What If We (Rodd)
Almosts, Maybes and Perhapses (Gallagher)
Where Will I Be Next Wednesday Night? (company)

Note: The part sung by Phyllis Newman was performed on stage by Jennie Ventriss.

I DO! I DO! (December 5, 1966, Forty-Sixth Street Theatre)

RCA LSO 1128 stereo

Music: Harvey Schmidt; lyrics: Tom Jones; based on The Fourposter by Jan de Hartog; musical direction: John Lesko

Cast: Mary Martin, Robert Preston

Songs: All the Dearly Beloved (Martin, Preston)
Together Forever (Martin, Preston)
I Do! I Do! (Martin, Preston)
Goodnight (Martin, Preston)
I Love My Wife (Preston)
Something Has Happened (Martin)
My Cup Runneth Over (Martin, Preston)
Love Isn't Everything (Martin, Preston)
Nobody's Perfect (Martin, Preston)

A Well Known Fact (Preston)
Flaming Agnes (Martin)

The Honeymoon Is Over (Martin, Preston)
Where Are the Snows (Martin, Preston)
When the Kids Get Married (Martin, Preston)
The Father of the Bride (Preston)
What Is a Woman? (Martin)
Someone Needs Me (Martin)
Roll Up the Ribbons (Martin, Preston)
This House (Martin, Preston)

I HAD A BALL (December 15, 1964, Martin Beck Theatre)

Mercury OCS 6210 stereo

Music, lyrics: Jack Lawrence, Stan Freeman; musical direction: Pembroke Davenport

Cast: Buddy Hackett, Richard Kiley, Rosetta Le Noire, Luba Lisa, Karen Morrow, Steve Roland

Songs: Overture (orchestra)
Garside the Great (Hackett) spoken
Coney Island U.S.A. (company)
The Other Half of Me (Kiley)
Addie's at It Again (Lisa, chorus)
I Got Everything I Want (Morrow)
Dr. Freud (Hackett)
Think Beautiful (Le Noire, Morrow, chorus)
Faith (Kiley, chorus)

Can It Be Possible? (Kiley, Morrow, Roland, Lisa)
Neighborhood (Le Noire, chorus)
The Affluent Society (Kiley, Roland)
I Had a Ball (Morrow, chorus)
Almost (Morrow)
Fickle Finger of Faith (Kiley)
You Deserve Me (Hackett, Roland, Lisa)
You Deserve Me (reprise) (Hackett)
Fickle Finger of Faith (reprise) (Hackett, company)

I LOVE MY WIFE (April 17, 1977, Ethel Barrymore Theatre)

Atlantic Records SD 19107 stereo

Music: Cy Coleman; lyrics: Michael Stewart; from a play by Luis Rego; musical direction: John Miller

Cast: Lenny Baker, Ken Bichel, Joanna Gleason, Ilene Graff, Michael Mark, John Miller, James Naughton, Joe Saulter

Songs: We're Still Friends (company)
Monica (Baker, Gleason, Miller, Mark, Saulter, Bichel)
By Threes (Naughton, Baker, Miller)
Love Revolution (Graff)
A Mover's Life (Baker, Miller, Mark, Saulter, Bichel)
Someone Wonderful I Missed (Gleason, Graff)
Sexually Free (Baker, Graff, Naughton)

Hey There, Good Times (Miller, Mark, Saulter, Bichel)
By the Way If You Are Free Tonight (Miller, Mark, Saulter, Bichel)
Lovers on Christmas Eve (Gleason, Naughton, Bichel)
Scream (Miller, Mark, Saulter, Bichel)
Ev'rybody Today Is Turning On (Baker, Naughton)
Married Couple Seeks Married Couple (Baker, Graff, Naughton, Gleason)
I Love My Wife (Baker, Naughton)
In Conclusion (Baker, Naughton)
Bows - Hey There, Good Times (reprise) (company)

I REMEMBER MAMA (May 31, 1979, Majestic Theatre)

Polydor 827 336 1 Y-1 stereo CD

Music: Richard Rodgers; lyrics: Martin Charnin, Raymond Jessel; based upon the play by John Van Druten; musical direction: Bruce Pomahac

Cast: Joanna Borman, Charlotte Edwards, George Hearn, Sally Ann Howes, George S. Irving, Ann Morrison, Sian Phillips, Rachael Ann Roberts, Patricia Routledge, Elizabeth Seal, Gay Soper, Tim Woodman

Songs: I Remember Mama (Morrison)
A Little Bit More (Howes, Hearn, children)
A Writer Writes at Night (Morrison, Howes)
Ev'ry Day (Comes Something Beautiful) (Howes, Hearn, company)
You Could Not Please Me More (Howes, Hearn)
A Most Disagreeable Man (Routledge, Seal, Soper)
Uncle Chris (Routledge, Seal,Soper)
Lullaby (Howes)
Easy Come, Easy Go (Irving, men, children)
It Is Not the End of the World (Hearn, Howes, children)

Entr'acte (orchestra)
Mama Always Makes It Better (Morrison, Edwards, Woodman, Roberts, Borman)
When? (Howes)
Fair Trade (Phillips, Howes, Morrison, chorus)
I Write, You Read (Fair Trade - reprise) (Howes, Phillips)
It's Going to Be Good to Be Gone (Irving, Seal, Soper. Routledge)
Time (Howes)
You Could Not Please Me More (reprise) (Hearn, Howes)
Finale (Morrison)

Note: This studio recording was made in 1985. George Hearn and George S. Irving are the only cast members to appear in the New York production.

ILLYA DARLING (April 11, 1967, Mark Hellinger Theatre)

United Artists UAS 9901 stereo

Music: Manos Hadjidakis; lyrics: Joe Darion; based on the film Never on Sunday; musical direction: Karen Gustafson

Cast: Orson Bean, Despo, Nikos Kourkoulos, Melina Mercouri, Titos Vandis

Songs: Bouzouki Nights (chorus)
Piraeus, My Love (Mercouri, men)
Golden Land (Bean, ensemble)
Illya Darling (Vandis, ensemble)
Medea Tango (Mercouri, men)
I'll Never Lay Down Anymore (Despo)
Never on Sunday (Mercouri, ensemble)

Entracte (orchestra)
Love, Love, Love (Mercouri)
I Think She Needs Me (Bean)
Dear Mr. Schubert (Mercouri)
Heaven Help the Sailors on a Night Like This (ensemble)
After Love (Kourkoulos)
Yorgo's Dance (orchestra)
Ya Chara (Vandis, Despo, Kourkoulos, Mercouri, company)

I'M GETTING MY ACT TOGETHER AND TAKING IT ON THE ROAD (June 14, 1978, Off Broadway, Public Theatre)

Columbia CSP X 14885 stereo

Music: Nancy Ford; lyrics: Gretchen Cryer; accompanied by the Liberated Man's Band, no director credited

Cast: Betty Aberlin, Gretchen Cryer, Margot Rose, Don Scardino

Songs: Natural High (Cryer, company)
Miss America (Cryer, company)
Put in a Package and Sold (Cryer, Rose, Aberlin)
Smile (Cryer, Rose, Aberlin, company)
Dear Tom (Cryer)

Old Friend (Cryer)
Strong Woman Number (Rose, Cryer)
Feel the Love (Aberlin, Rose, Scardino)
Lonely Lady (Cryer)
In a Simple Way I Love You (Scardino)
Happy Birthday (Cryer, company)
Natural High (reprise) (Cryer, company)

IN CIRCLES (November 5, 1967, Off Broadway, Cherry Lane Theatre)

Avant Garde Records AV 108 stereo

Music: Al Carmines; Words: Gertrude Stein; piano: Al Carmines

Cast: Theo Barnes, Al Carmines, Jacque Lynn Colton, Lee Crespi, Lee Guilliatt, James Hilbrandt, Julie Kurnitz, George McGrath, Arlene Rothlein, Elaine Summers, David

Tice, David Vaughn, Arthur Williams, Nancy Zala

Songs: Papa Dozes, Mama Blows Her Noses (company)
A Morning Celebration (company)
Round and Around (Colton, company)
Cut Wood (Summers, company)
Crimson (company)
In Circles (company)
Writing to a Girl (company)
Mrs. De Moncey Has Adopted a Child (company)
The Balcony (company)
An Inner Circle (company)
Messages Are Received (Carmines, company)
I Saw What I Saw (Vaughn, company)
Do Not Despair (company)
From Tangier to the Moon (company)

Water (company)
Flags (Rothlein, company)
Realize (How Do You Like Morocco?) (company)
How Do You Recognize Hats (company)
The Singing Bird (company)
A Religious Circle (Carmines, company)
I Remembered That I Need Not Give Her Flowers (company)
Circular Dancing (company)
Can You See the Moon? (company)
A Circlette of Kisses (company)
I Can Hear Alice (company)
Circles (company)

Note: No titles or vocals are listed. Some spoken words.

IN TROUSERS (February 21, 1979, Off Broadway, Playwrights Horizon)

Original Cast Records OC 7915 stereo

Music, lyrics: William Finn; musical direction: Michael Starobin

Cast: Alison Fraser, Joanna Green, Mary Testa, Chip Zien

Songs: Marvin's Giddy Seizures (cast)
How the Body Falls Apart (Fraser, Green, Testa)
Your Lips and Me (Fraser)
My High School Sweetheart (cast)
Set Those Sails (Fraser, Green, Testa)
My Chance to Survive the Night (Zien)
I Am Wearing a Hat (cast)
How Marvin Eats His Breakfast (cast)
A Breakfast over Sugar (Zien, Fraser)
Whizzer Going Down (cast)

High School Ladies at 5 O'Clock (Fraser, Green, Testa)
The Rape of Miss Goldberg by Marvin (Zien, Testa)
The Nausea before the Game (cast)
Love Me for What I Am (Fraser)
How America Got It's Name (Zien)
Your Lips and Me (reprise) (Fraser)

Marvin Takes a Victory Shower (cast)
Another Sleepless Night (cast)
In Trousers - The Dream (cast)

INNER CITY - A STREET CANTATA (December 19, 1971, Ethel Barrymore Theatre)

RCA LSO 1171 stereo

Music: Helen Miller; lyrics: Eve Merriam; based on The Inner City Mother Goose by Eve Merriam; musical direction: Clay Fullum

Cast: Joy Garrett, Carl Hall, Delores Hall, Fluffer Hirsch, Linda Hopkins, Paulette Ellen Jones, Larry Marshall, Allan Nicholls, Florence Tarlow

Songs: Fee Fi Fo Fum (Hopkins)
Now I Lay Me (D. Hall, C. Hall, Nicholls)
Hushaby (Jones)
My Mother Said (Jones)
Nub of the Nation (cast)
Urban Mary (cast)
City Life (Tarlow)
One Misty Moisty Morning (Marshall)
If Wishes Were Horses (D. Hall)
Deep in the Night (Hopkins)
Jeremiah Obadiah (Marshall)
Riddle Song (cast)
Shadow of the Sun (cast)
Boys and Girls Come Out to Play (cast)
Lucy Locket (Hirsch)
Wisdom (Marshall)
--- The Hooker (You Make It Your Way) (Garrett)
Law and Order (D. Hall)
The Dealer (You Push It Your Way) (Nicholls)
Kindness (Nicholls)
As I Went Over (Nicholls)
Apartment House (cast)
There Was a Little Man (cast)
Who Killed Nobody? (cast)
It's My Belief (Hopkins)
Street Sermon (C. Hall)
The Great If (C. Hall)
On This Rock (cast)
The Great If (reprise) (cast)

INSIDE U.S.A. (April 30, 1948, New Century Theatre)

RCA K 14 (78 rpm) mono reissued: Box Office Records 19733

Music: Arthur Schwartz; lyrics: Howard Dietz; suggested by John Gunter's book of the same title; musical direction: Russ Cass

Cast: Jack Haley, Beatrice Lillie

Songs: Inside U.S.A. (chorus)
Come, O Come (Lillie, chorus)
Rhode Island Is Famous for You (Haley, chorus)
Atlanta (Lillie)
First Prize at the Fair (Haley, chorus)
At the Mardi Gras (Lillie, chorus)

Note: Other songs recorded at the same time by non-cast members are included on this album.

INTERNATIONAL SOIREE (March 12, 1958, Bijou Theatre)

Audio Fidelity AFSD 5881 stereo

Music, lyrics: various; musical direction: Jo Basile

Cast: Patachou

Songs: Overture: Potpourri-Patachou (orchestra)
A Paris (Patachou)
Piano du Pauvre (Patachou)
I'm in Love with a Wonderful Guy (Patachou)
Mon Homme (Patachou)
Rue Lepic (Patachou)

Bravo Margot (Patachou)
Complainte de la Butte (Patachou)
Only for Americans (Patachou)
Fascination (Patachou)
Potpourri (Patachou, chorus)
Girl Chase (orchestra)

IRENE (Revival, March 13, 1973, Minskoff Theatre)

Columbia KS 32266 stereo

Music: Harry Tierney; lyrics: Joseph McCarthy; additional music, lyrics: Charles Gaynor, Otis Clements; musical direction: Jack Lee

Cast: Carmen Alvarez, George S. Irving, Patsy Kelly, Jeanne Lehman, Monte Markham, Ted Pugh, Debbie Reynolds, Meg Scanlon, Janie Sell, Ruth Warrick, Penny Worth

Songs: Overture (Lehman, Worth, Scanlon)
The World Must Be Bigger Than an Avenue (Reynolds)
What Do You Want to Make Those Eyes at Me For? (chorus)
The Family Tree (Warrick, women)
Alice Blue Gown (Reynolds)
They Go Wild, Simply Wild Over Me (Irving)
An Irish Girl (Reynolds, chorus)
Mother, Angel, Darling (Reynolds, Kelly)
The Riviera Rage (orchestra)

I'm Always Chasing Rainbows (Reynolds)
The Last Part of Ev'ry Party (chorus)
We're Getting Away with It (Alvarez, Sell, Irving, Pugh)
Irene (Markham, men)

The Great Lover Tango (Markham, Alvaraz, Sell)
You Made Me Love You (Reynolds, Markham)
You Made Me Love You (reprise) (Kelly, Irving)
Finale (Reynolds, Markham, company)

IRMA LA DOUCE (September 29, 1960, Plymouth Theatre)

Columbia OS 2029 stereo

Music: Marguerite Monnot; English lyrics: Julian More, David Heneker, Monty Norman; musical direction: Stanley Lebowsky

Cast: Stuart Damon, George Del Monte, Fred Gwynne, George S. Irving, Aric Lavie, Zack Matalon, Keith Michell, Clive Revill, Elizabeth Seal, Osborne Smith, Rudy Tronto

Songs: Overture (orchestra)
Valse Milieu (Revill, Seal)
Sons of France (Irving, Gwynne, Matalon, Lavie, Smith, Damon)
The Bridge of Caulaincourt (Seal, Michell)
Our Language of Love (Seal, Michell)
She's Got the Lot (Irving, company)
Dis-donc, dis-donc (Seal, company)
Le Grisbi Is le Root of le Evil in Man (Michell, Revill, Matalon, Lavie, Smith, Damon)
The Wreck of a Mec (Michell)

That's a Crime (Revill, company)
From a Prison Cell (Michell, Matalon, Lavie, Smith, Damon)
Irma-la-Douce (Seal, company)
There Is Only One Paris for That (Michell, company)
Artic Ballet (orchestra)
The Freedom of the Seas (company)
But (Michell, Irving, Tronto, Del Monte, Gwynne)
Christmas Child (company)

IS THERE LIFE AFTER HIGH SCHOOL? (May 7, 1982, Ethel Barrymore Theatre)

Original Cast Records OC 8240 stereo

Music, lyrics: Craig Carnilia; suggested by the book by Ralph Keyes; musical direction: Bruce Coughlin

Cast: Raymond Baker, Cynthia Carle, Alma Cuervo, Sandy Faison, Harry Groener, Philip Hoffman, David Patrick Kelly, Maureen Silliman, James Widdoes

Songs: The Kid Inside (company)
Things I Learned in High School (Groener)
Second Thoughts (Baker, Silliman, Widdoes, Kelly, Faison)
Nothing Really Happened (Cuervo, women)
Beer (Baker, Kelly, Groener)
Diary of a Homecoming Queen (Silliman)

For Them (Hoffman, company)
Thousands of Trumpets (Widdoes, company)
Reunion (company)
High School All Over Again (Kelly, company)
Fran and Janie (Faison, Silliman)
I'm Glad You Didn't Know Me (Carle, Hoffman)
The Kid Inside (reprise) (company)

IT'S A BIRD...IT'S A PLANE...IT'S SUPERMAN (March 29, 1966, Alvin Theatre)

Columbia KOS 2970 stereo

Music: Charles Strouse; lyrics: Lee Adams; based upon the comic strip; musical direction: Harold Hastings

Cast: Jack Cassidy, Don Chastain, The Flying Lings, Bob Holiday, Linda Lavin, Patricia Marand, Michael O'Sullivan

Songs: Overture (orchestra) spoken: Holiday, Marand
Doing Good (Holiday)
We Need Him (Cassidy, Marand, Holiday, company)
It's Superman (Marand)
We Don't Matter at All (Chastain, Marand)
Revenge (O'Sullivan)
The Woman for the Man (Cassidy)
You've Got Possibilities (Lavin)
What I've Always Wanted (Marand)
--- Entr'acte (orchestra)
It's Supernice (company)
So Long, Big Guy (Cassidy)
The Strongest Man in the World (Holiday)
Ooh, Do You Love You! (Lavin)
You've Got What I Need (Cassidy, O'Sullivan)
It's Superman (reprise) (company)
I'm Not Finished Yet (Marand)
Pow! Bam! Zonk! (Holiday, the Flying Lings)
Finale (company)

JACQUES BREL IS ALIVE AND WELL AND LIVING IN PARIS (January 22, 1968, Off Broadway, Village Gate)

Columbia D2S 779 (two records) stereo

Music: Jacques Brel; English lyrics, additional material: Eric Blau, Mort Shuman; musical direction: Wolfgang Knittel

Cast: Shawn Elliott, Mort Shuman, Elly Stone, Alice Whitfield

Songs: Marathon (company)
Alone (Elliott)
Madeleine (company)
I Loved (Stone)
Mathilde (Shuman)
Bachelor's Dance (Elliott)

Timid Frieda (Whitfield, company)
My Death (Stone, company)
Jackie (Shuman)
Desperate Ones (company)
Sons of ... (Stone)

Amsterdam (Shuman, company)
The Bulls (Elliott, company)
Old Folks (Stone, company)
Marieke (Stone, company)
Brussels (Whitfield, company)

Fanette (Elliott)
Funeral Tango (Shuman)
You're Not Alone (Stone)
Next (Shuman, company)
Carousel (Stone, company)
If We Only Have Love (company)

JAMAICA (October 31, 1957, Imperial Theatre)

RCA LSO 1103 stereo reissued: Time/Life P 16377

Music: Harold Arlen; lyrics: E.Y. Harburg; musical direction: Lehman Engel

Cast: Joe Adams, Ossie Davis, Hugo Dilworth, Adelaide Hall, Lena Horne, Ricardo Montalban, Josephine Premice, Augustine Rios

Songs: Overture (orchestra)
Savannah (Montalban, men)
Push de Button (Horne, chorus)
Savannah's Wedding Day (Adams, Dilworth, Hall, Rios, chorus)
Pretty to Walk With (Horne, chorus)
Incompatibility (Montalban, Rios, Adams, Dilworth, chorus)
Little Biscuit (Davis, Premice)
Cocoanut Sweet (Horne)
For Every Fish (There's a Little Bigger Fish) (Hall, chorus)

Pity de Sunset (Horne, Montalban)
Hooray for de Yankee Dollar (Premice, chorus)
What Good Does It Do? (Montalban, Davis, Rios)
Monkey in the Mango Tree (Montalban, men)
Take It Slow, Joe (Horne)
Ain't It de Truth? (Horne)
Leave de Atom Alone (Premice, women)
I Don't Think I'll End It All Today (Horne, Montalban, chorus)
Napoleon (Horne)
Savannah (reprise) (Horne, Montalban, chorus)

Note: "Beach Ballet", recorded in 1959 in stereo was issued on Painted Smiles PS 1364, Ballet on Broadway; musical direction: Lehman Engel.

JENNIE (October 17, 1963, Majestic Theatre)

RCA LSO 1083 stereo

Music: Arthur Schwartz; lyrics: Howard Dietz; suggested by Laurette by Marguerite Courtney; musical direction: John Lesko

Cast: Robin Bailey, Jack De Lon, Mary Martin, Ethel Shutta, George Wallace

Songs: Overture (orchestra)
Waitin' for the Evening Train (Martin, Wallace)
When You're Far Away from New York Town (De Lon, company)
I Still Look at You That Way (Martin)
For Better or Worse (Shutta)
Born Again (Martin, De Lon, company)
Over Here (Bailey, Martin)
Before I Kiss the World Goodbye (Martin)

Sauce Diable (orchestra)
Where You Are (Bailey, Martin)
See Seattle (Wallace)
High Is Better Than Low (Wallace, Martin, company)
The Night May Be Dark (Martin, Shutta)
I Believe in Takin' a Chance (Wallace, De Lon)
Lonely Nights (Martin)
Before I Kiss the World Goodbye (reprise) (Martin, company)

JERICO-JIM CROW (January 12, 1964, Off Broadway, The Sanctuary)

Folkways Records FL 9671 mono

Words, music: Langston Hughes, Paul Campbell, traditional sources; musical direction: Hugh Porter

Cast: Joseph Attles, William Cain, Dorothy Drake, Micki Grant, Rosalie King, Metrogene Myles, Gilbert Price

Songs: A Meeting Here Tonight (ensemble)
I'm On My Way (Attles, ensemble)
I Been 'buked and I Been Scorned (King)
Such a Little King (Grant, King)
Is Massa Gwine to Sell Us Tomorrow? (Price, chorus)
How Much Do You Want Me to Bear? (Drake)
Where Will I Lie Down? (Grant, Price)
Follow the Drinking Gourd (Myles, chorus)
John Brown's Body (chorus)
Battle Hymn of the Republic (chorus)
Slavery Chain Done Broke At Last (Grant, ensemble)
Oh, Freedom (Grant, chorus)
Go Down, Moses (Drake)
Ezekiel Saw the Wheel (Attles, chorus)
Stay in the Field (Attles, chorus)
Freedom Land (Price)
God's Gonna Cut You Down (Price, Drake, ensemble)
Better Leave Segregation Alone (Cain)

My Mind on Freedom (Grant, Price, chorus)
We Shall Overcome (Grant, Price)
Freedom Land (reprise) (Grant, Price)
The Battle of Old Jim Crow (Grant, Price, ensemble)
Come and Go with Me (Drake, chorus)

JEROME KERN GOES TO HOLLYWOOD (January 23, 1986, Ritz Theatre)

Safari Records Jerome 1 stereo

Music: Jerome Kern; lyrics: Bernard Dougall, Dorothy Fields, Ira Gershwin, Oscar Hammerstein II, Otto Harbach, Jimmy McHugh, Johnny Mercer, M.E. Rourke, P.G. Wodehouse; musical direction: Clive Chaplin

Cast: Elaine Delmar, David Kernan, Liz Robertson, Elisabeth Welch

Songs: The Song is You (cast) lyrics: Hammerstein
I've Told Every Little Star (cast) lyrics: Hammerstein
I'll Be Hard to Handle (Robertson) lyrics: Dougall
Smoke Gets in Your Eyes (Welch) lyrics: Harbach
Yesterdays (Robertson, Kernan) lyrics: Harbach
I Won't Dance (cast) lyrics: Hammerstein, Harbach
I'm Old Fashioned (Delmar) lyrics: Mercer
Dearly Beloved (Robertson) lyrics: Mercer
Pick Yourself Up (Delmar, Robertson) lyrics: Fields
She Didn't Say Yes (Welch) lyrics: Harbach
The Folks Who Live on the Hill (Kernan) lyrics: Hammerstein
Long Ago and Far Away (cast) lyrics: Gershwin

Lovely to Look At (Welch, Robertson) lyrics: Fields, McHugh
Just Let Me Look at You (Welch, Roberston) lyrics: Fields
Remind Me (Delmar) lyrics: Fields
The Last Time I Saw Paris (Kernan) lyrics: Hammerstein
Ol' Man River (Kernan, Robertson, Welch) lyrics: Hammerstein
Why Was I Born? (Welch) lyrics: Hammerstein
Bill/Can't Help Lovin' Dat Man of Mine (Robertson, Delmar) lyrics: Wodehouse, Hammerstein/ Hammerstein
All the Things You Are (cast) lyrics: Hammerstein
They Didn't Believe Me (cast) lyrics: Rouke

Note: London cast recording. Scott Holmes replaced David Kernan for the New York production.

JERRY'S GIRLS (December 18, 1985, St. James Theatre)

Polydor 820 207-1 Y-2 (two records) stereo CD

Music, lyrics: Jerry Herman; musical direction: Janet Glazener

Cast: Ellyn Arons, Carol Channing, Deborah Graham, Jerry Herman, Suzanne Ishee, Andrea Mc Ardle, Diana Myron, Laura Soltis, Leslie Uggams, Helena-Joyce Wright

Songs: Overture (orchestra)
Jerry's Girls (It's Today/Mame)(Arons, Wright, Graham, Myron, Soltis, Ishee)
It Takes a Woman (Ishee, ensemble)
Put On Your Sunday Clothes (Channing, ensemble)
It Only Takes a Moment (Uggams)
Wherever He Ain't (McArdle)
We Need a Little Christmas (Arons, Graham, Ishee, Myron, Soltis, Channing)
I Won't Send Roses (Uggams)
Tap Your Troubles Away (Channing, Uggams, ensemble)

Two-a-Day (McArdle)
Bosom Buddies (Uggams, Channing)
The Man in the Moon (ensemble)
So Long Dearie (McArdle)
Take It All Off (Arons, Soltis, Ishee, Channing)
Two-a-Day (reprise) (Channing, McArdle, ensemble)
Shalom (Uggams)
Milk and Honey (Uggams, ensemble)
Showtune (Ishee, Arons, McArdle, ensemble)
If He Walked into My Life (Uggams)
Hello, Dolly! (Wright, Arons, Myron, McArdle, Ishee, Soltis, Graham, Channing, Uggams)

Entr'acte (orchestra)
Just Go to the Movies (Myron, Soltis, Arons, Ishee, Wright, Graham)
Movies Were Movies (Uggams)
Look What Happened to Mabel (McArdle)
Nelson (Channing, Ishee)
Just Go to the Movies (reprise) (Uggams, ensemble)
Time Heals Everything (McArdle)
It's Today (Channing, ensemble)
Mame (Arons, Graham, Ishee, Myron, Soltis)
Kiss Her Now (Uggams, Wright)

That's How Young I Feel (orchestra)
Gooch's Song (McArdle)
Before the Parade Passes By (Channing)
I Don't Want to Know (Uggams)
Jerry's New Girl (Ishee, Myron, Wright, Arons, Graham, Soltis)
La Cage aux Folles (Channing, ensemble)
Song on the Sand (McArdle, Arons, Myron)
I Am What I Am (Uggams)
The Best of Times (Channing, Uggams, McArdle, ensemble)
Jerry's Turn: (Herman, girls)
You're My Best Girls
Hundreds of Girls
Mame
Hello, Dolly!
Jerry's Girls (reprise) (company)

Note: This album recorded in 1984 prior to New York engagement. Leslie Uggams and Ellyn Arons are the only cast members to appear in New York.

JESUS CHRIST SUPERSTAR (October 12, 1971, Mark Hellinger Theatre)

Decca DL7-1503 stereo

Music: Andrew Lloyd Webber; lyrics: Tim Rice; musical direction: Marc Pressel

Cast: Paul Ainsley, Steven Bell, Bob Bingham, Alan Braunstein, Barry Dennen, Yvonne Elliman, Jeff Fenholt, Michael Jason, Phil Jethro, Michael Meadows, Ben Vereen

Songs: Heaven on Their Minds (Vereen)
Everything's Alright (Elliman, Fenholt, Vereen, chorus)
This Jesus Must Die (Bingham, Jethro, Braunstein, Meadows, Bell)
Hosanna (Bingham, Fenholt, chorus)
Pilate's Dream (Dennen)
I Don't Know How to Love Him (Elliman)
Gethsemane (Fenholt)

King Herod's Song (Ainsley, chorus)
Could We Start Again Please (Elliman, Jason, chorus)
Judas' Death (Vereen, Bingham, Jethro, chorus)
Trial Before Pilate (Dennen, Bingham, Fenholt, chorus)
Superstar (Vereen, chorus)
John Nineteen : Forty-One (orchestra)

JIMMY (October 23, 1969, Winter Garden Theatre)

RCA LSO 1162 stereo

Music, lyrics: Bill, Patti Jacob; based on the novel, Beau James by Gene Fowler; musical direction: Milton Rosenstock

Cast: Edward Becker, Dorothy Claire, Jack Collins, Carol Conte, Clifford Fearl, Paul Forrest, Anita Gillette, William Griffis, Frank Gorshin, Henry Lawrence, Stanley Simmonds, Evan Thompson, Julie Wilson

Songs: Overture (orchestra)
Will You Think of Me Tomorrow? (Gorshin)
The Little Woman (Griffis, Collins, Gorshin)
The Darlin' of New York (Collins, Griffis, Thompson, Wilson, Gorshin, company)
Oh, Gee! (Gillette)
The Walker Walk (Claire, Gorshin, company)
That Old Familiar Ring (Gillette, Gorshin)
The Walker Walk (reprise) (Collins, company)
I Only Wanna Laugh (Wilson)

Riverside Drive (Gorshin, company)
What's Out There for Me? (Gorshin)
The Squabble Song (Gorshin, Gillette)
One in a Million (Gorshin, Gillette)
It's a Nice Place to Visit (Forrest, Simmonds, Becker, Lawrence, Fearl, Conte, company)
The Charmin' Son-of-a-Bitch (Wilson)
Jimmy (Gillette)
Life Is a One Way Street (Gorshin)
Our Jimmy (Collins, Gorshin, Wilson, Thompson, Griffis, Claire, company)

JOAN (June 19, 1972, Off Broadway, Circle in the Square)

Judson Records JU 1001 (two records) stereo

Music, lyrics: Al Carmines; piano: Al Carmines

Cast: Emily Adams, Jeffrey Apter, Essie Borden, Al Carmines, Joe Cecil, Lee Guilliatt, Teresa King, Julie Kurnitz, Phyllis MacBryde, Tracy Moore, Sandy Padilla, Ira Siff, David Vaughn, Margaret Wright

Songs: Praise the Lord (chorus)
Come On Joan (Moore, chorus)
It's So Nice (Guilliatt, Siff, Moore)
Go Back (MacBryde, Padilla)
They Call Me the Virgin Mary (Borden, Guilliatt)
The Woman I Love (Moore)

Did I Complain? (Adams)
Five Billion Years Ago (Guilliatt)
Joan, I'm a Rag Doll (Siff)
Country of the Mind (Siff)
I Live a Little (Borden, chorus)
What I Wonder (Guilliatt, chorus)

Religious Establishment (Vaughn, Cecil, Apter)
In My Silent Universe (Siff)
Joan, I Am Here (chorus)
Take Courage, Daughter (Kurnitz, chorus)
River of Roses (Carmines, chorus)
I'm Madame Margaret, the Therapist (Wright, chorus)

Look at Me, Joan (chorus)
Hi There, Joan (Cecil)
Despair (King)
Faith Is Such a Simple Thing (Guilliatt, chorus)
I've Changed (Adams)
Praise the Lord (Guilliatt, chorus)

Note: This recording includes spoken dialog.

JOSEPH AND THE AMAZING TECHNICOLOR DREAMCOAT (November 18, 1981, Off Broadway, Entermedia Theatre; transferred, January 27, 1982, Royale Theatre)

Chrysalis CHR 1387 stereo

Music: Andrew Lloyd Webber; lyrics: Tim Rice; musical direction: David Friedman

Cast: David Ardao, Laurie Beechman, Kenneth Bryan, Tom Carder, Bill Hutton, Robert Hyman, Randon Lo, Steve McNaughton, Charlie Serrano, Gordon Stanley, Harry Tarallo

Songs: Prologue - You Are What You Feel (Beechman)
Jacob and Sons (Beechman, chorus)
Joseph's Coat (The Coat of Many Colors) (Stanley, Hutton, Beechman, men)
Joseph's Dreams (Beechman, Hutton, men)

Poor, Poor Joseph (Beechman, Hutton, chorus)
One More Angel in Heaven (McNaughton, men)
Potiphar (Ardao, Lo, Hutton, women)
Close Every Door (Hutton)
--- Go, Go, Go Joseph (Beechman, Tarallo, Bryan, Hutton)
Pharaoh Story (Beechman, women)
Poor Poor Pharaoh (Beechman, Bryan, Hutton, chorus)
Song of the King (Carder)
Pharaoh's Dream Explained (Hutton)
Stone the Crows (Beechman, Carder, Hutton, girls)
Those Canaan Days (Hyman, men)
The Brothers Come to Egypt (Beechamn, Hutton, men)
Grovel, Grovel (Hutton, Beechamn, men)
Who's the Thief? (Hutton, Beechaman, chorus)
Benjamin Calypso (Serrano, men)
Joseph All the Time (Beechman, Hutton, men)
Jacob in Egypt (Beechman)
Any Dream Will Do (Hutton)

JOY (January 27, 1970, Off Broadway, New Theatre)

RCA LSO 1166 stereo

Music, lyrics: Oscar Brown, Jr.; musical direction: uncredited

Cast: Oscar Brown, Jr., Jean Pace, Norman Shobey, Sivuca

Songs: Time (Brown)
What Is a Friend (Brown, Sivuca, Shobey)
Funny Feelin' (Pace)
Under the Sun (Pace)
Wimmen's Ways (Brown)
Brown Baby (Pace)
--- Mother Africa's Day (Brown, Sivuca)
A New Generation (Brown, Pace)
Sky and Sea (Sivuca)
If I Only Had (Pace)
Nothing But a Fool (Brown, Sivuca)
Much As I Love You (Brown, Sivuca, Shobey)
Afro Blue (Pace)
Funky World (Brown)

JUNO (March 9, 1959, Winter Garden Theatre)

Columbia OS 2013 stereo

Music, lyrics: Marc Blitzstein; based on Sean O'Casey's Juno and the Paycock; musical direction: Robert Emmett Dolan

Cast: Monte Amundsen, Nancy Andrews, Shirley Booth, Melvyn Douglas, Loren Driscoll, Rico Froehlich, Beulah Garrick, Robert Hoyem, Jack MacGowran, Julian Patrick, Arthur Rubin, Robert Rue, Jean Stapleton, Sada Thompson

Songs: Overture (orchestra)
We're Alive (ensemble)

I Wish It So (Amundsen)
Song of the Ma (Booth)
We Can Be Proud (Rubin, Froehlich, Rue, Patrick)
Daarlin' Man (Douglas, MacGowran, ensemble)
One Kind Word (Driscoll)
Old Sayin's (Booth, Douglas)
What Is the Stars (Douglas, MacGowran)
You Poor Thing (Stapleton, Andrews, Thompson, Garrick)
On a Day Like This (Booth, Douglas, MacGowran, Amundsen, ensemble)
My True Heart (Amundsen)
Bird Upon the Tree (Booth, Amundsen)
Music in the House (Douglas, ensemble)
It's Not Irish (Rubin, Douglas, Froehlich, Rue)
The Liffey Waltz (ensemble)
Hymn (Hoyem, ensemble)
Johnny (orchestra)
You Poor Thing (reprise)(Stapleton, Andrews, Thompson, Garrick)
For Love (Amundsen)
Where? (Booth)
Finale: We're Alive (ensemble)

JUST FOR OPENERS (November 3, 1965, Off Broadway, Upstairs at the Downstairs)

Upstairs at the Downstairs UD 37W56 stereo

Music: Rod Warren, others; lyrics: Michael McWhinney, others; musical direction: Michael Cohen

Cast: Betty Aberlin, Richard Blair, Stockton Brigel, R.G. Brown, Fannie Flagg, Madeline Kahn

Songs: Just for Openers (company)
The Telephone Hang-Up (Aberlin, Kahn)
New York without Bob (Brown)
The Adaptations (company)
The Second-Best Man (Aberlin, Brown, Brigel)
Mr. Know-It-All (Blair)
You're a Big Boy Now (company)
Anyone Who's Anyone (Aberlin, Kahn, Blair, Brigel)
Christmas Shopping (Flagg, Brigel)
America the Beautiful (Kahn)
Space Age (Kahn)
Where Did We Go Wrong? (Flagg, Brown)
The Waitress (Flagg, Blair)
The "Dolly" Sisters (Aberlin, Kahn, Flagg)
Finale: Just for Openers (company)

KA-BOOM! (November 20, 1980, Off Broadway, Carter Theater)

CYM Records 8130 stereo

Music: Joe Ercole; lyrics: Bruce Kluger; musical direction: John Lehman

Cast: Ben Agresti, Judith Bro, John Hall, Ken Ward, Valerie Williams, Andrea Wright

Songs: Overture (orchestra)
Now We Pray (company)
Oh, Lord (company)
A Little Bit O' Glitter (Hall)
Maybe for Instance (Bro)
With a World to Conquer (Williams)
Smile (Wright)
Let Me Belive in Me (Ward)
A Few Get Through (Bro)
Ballad of Adam and Evie (Hall, Williams)
Gimme a 'G' (Wright)
Finale (company)

Believe Us - Receive Us (company)
The Soft Spot (Hall, Bro)
You Are You (ensemble)
The Light Around the Corner (ensemble)
Those ABC's (Wright, company)
Judgment Day (Hall, company)
Bump and Grind for God (Williams, company)
Let Me Believe in Me (reprise) (Ward, company)
Let the Show Go On! (Agresti, company)

Note: Valerie Williams and Ben Agresti were not in the New York cast.

KARL MARX PLAY (April 2, 1973, Off Broadway, American Place Theatre)

Kilmarnock KIL 72010 stereo

Music: Galt MacDermot; lyrics: Rochelle Owens; musical direction: Galt MacDermot

Cast: Ralph Carter, Harold Gould, Norman Matlock, Linda Mulrean, Phyllis Newman, Louie Piday, Jamie Sanchez, Linda Swenson

Songs: Overture (orchestra)
My Knees Are Weak (Matlock)
Tavern Scene:
There Was a Hen (Sanchez, girls)
O Mistress Mine (Matlock)
White Sheeting (Matlock)
Hello, Hello (Gould)
Jenny von Westphalen (Newman)
So I Give You (ensemble)
Dying Child (Gould)
Jenny Is Like an Angel (Newman, girls)
Interlude (orchestra)

Pretty Women (Matlock)
Tempting Salome (Newman)
It's Me They Talk About (Gould)
He Eats (Matlock, girls)
Red Leather Wrist Watch (Carter)

Holy Mystery (Carter, Newman, girls)
Baby Johann (Gould)
Comes the Revolution (ensemble)
Ya Ta Ta (Gould, ensemble)
We Doubt You Papa (Carter, Matlock, Sanchez, ensemble)
The Hand of Fate (Matlock)
Finale: World Creation (Newman, chorus)

Note: Phyllis Newman, Harold Gould and Jamie Sanchez did not appear in the New York production.

KEAN (November 2, 1961, Broadway Theatre)

Columbia KOS 2120 stereo

Music, lyrics: Robert Wright, George Forrest; from a comedy by Jean-Paul Satre; musical direction: Pembroke Davenport

Cast: Alfred DeSio, Alfred Drake, Oliver Gray, Christopher Hewett, Robert Penn, Arthur Rubin, Truman Smith, Lee Venora, Joan Weldon

Songs: Overture: Penny Plain, Twopence Colored (DeSio)
Man and Shadow (Drake)
Mayfair Ensemble (ensemble)
Sweet Danger (Weldon, Drake)
Queue at Drury Lane (ensemble)
Penny Plain, Twopence Colored (reprise) (DeSio, ensemble)
King of London (ensemble)
To Look Upon My Love (Drake, Smith)
Let's Improvise (Drake, Verona)
Elena (Drake, Rubin, ensemble)

The Fog and the Grog (Hewett, Penn, Rubin, Drake, ensemble)
Civilized People (Drake, Verona, Weldon, Smith)
Service for Service (Drake, Weldon)
Willow, Willow, Willow (Verona)
Chime In! (DeSio, Hewett, Penn, Rubin, ensemble)
Swept Away (Weldon, Drake)
Apology (Drake, Gray)

THE KING AND I (March 29, 1951, St. James Theatre)

Decca DL 9008 mono reissued: MCA 2028E

Music: Richard Rodgers; lyrics: Oscar Hammerstein II; based on Margaret Landon's Anna and the King of Siam; Musical direction: Frederick Dvonch

Cast: Yul Brynner, Larry Douglas, Gertrude Lawrence, Doretta Morrow, Dorothy Sarnoff

Songs: Overture (orchestra)
I Whistle a Happy Tune (Lawrence)
My Lord and Master (Morrow)
Hello Young Lovers (Lawrence)

March of the Siamese Children (orchestra)
A Puzzlement (Brynner)
--- Getting to Know You (Lawrence, chorus)
We Kiss in a Shadow (Morrow, Douglas)
Shall I Tell You What I Think of You? (Lawrence)
Something Wonderful (Sarnoff)
I Have Dreamed (Morrow, Douglas)
Shall We Dance? (Lawrence, Brynner)

THE KING AND I (Revival, July 6, 1964, New York State Theatre)

RCA LSO 1092 stereo

Musical direction: Franz Allers

Cast: James Harvey, Darren McGavin, Patricia Neway, Frank Porretta, Rise Stevens, Lee Venora

Songs: Overture (orchestra)
I Whistle a Happy Tune (Stevens, Harvey)
My Lord and Master (Venora)
Hello, Young Lovers! (Stevens)
March of the Siamese Children (orchestra)
A Puzzlement (McGavin)
Getting to Know You (Stevens, chorus)
--- We Kiss in a Shadow (Venora, Porretta)
Shall I Tell You What I Think of You? (Stevens)
Something Wonderful (Neway)
I Have Dreamed (Venora, Porretta)
The Small House of Uncle Thomas (Venora, chorus)
Shall We Dance? (Stevens, McGavin)
Something Wonderful (reprise) (chorus)

THE KING AND I (Revival, May 2, 1977, Uris Theatre)

RCA ABL 1-2610 stereo CD

Musical direction: Milton Rosenstock

Cast: Alan Amick, June Angela, Yul Brynner, Hye-Young Choi, Gene Profanato, Constance Towers, Martin Vidnovic

Songs: Overture (orchestra)
Arrival at Bangkok (men)
I Whistle a Happy Tune (Amick, Towers)
My Lord and Master (Angela)
Hello, Young Lovers (Towers)
March of the Siamese Children (orchestra)
Children Sing, Priests Chant (men, children)
A Puzzlement (Brynner)
The Royal Bangkok Academy (children)
Getting to Know You (Towers, women, children)
So Big a World (Brynner)
We Kiss in a Shadow (Vidnovic, Angela)
--- A Puzzlement (reprise) (Profanato, Amick)
Shall I Tell You What I Think of You? (Towers)

Something Wonderful (Choi)
Finale to Act I (company)
Western People Funny (Choi, women)
Dance of Anna and Sir Edward (orchestra)
I Have Dreamed (Vidnovic, Angela)
Song of the King (Brynner, Towers)
Shall We Dance? (Towers, Brynner)
Finale (Towers, Brynner, Profanato)

KING OF HEARTS (October 22, 1978, Minskoff Theatre)

Original Cast Records OC 8028 stereo

Music: Peter Link; lyrics: Jacob Brackman; based on the motion picture screenplay; musical direction: Peter Link

Cast: Pamela Blair, Marilyn D'Honau, Bob Gunton, Rex David Hays, A. Lacoonis, Michael McCarty, Millicent Martin, Don Scardino, Gordon Weiss

Songs: Prologue (Hays, Scardino, company)
Here Comes Mine (Scardino)
St. Anne's (Martin, D'Honau, Lacoonis, company)
Transformation Suite (company)
Gate Theme (company)
Deja Vu (Martin, Weiss, company)
Promenade (company)
Deja Vu (reprise) (Martin)
Down at Madeline's (Martin, McCarty, Gunton, company)
Nothing Only Love (Blair, Scardino)
King of Hearts (Blair, Gunton, Martin, company)
Mrs. Draba (Scardino)

Close Upon the Hour (Scardino)
Coronation (McCarty, Scardino, company)
With My Friends (Scardino, company)
Raoul's Grande Cirque (Gunton, company)
Going Home Tomorrow (soldiers)
Somewhere is Here (Martin)
Quartet (Martin, Gunton, Blair, Scardino)
A Day in Our Life (Martin, Gunton, company)
Finale (Scardino)

KISMET (December 3, 1953, Ziegfeld Theatre)

Columbia OL 4850 mono reissued: OS 2060

Music: from Alexander Borodin; lyrics: Robert Wright, George Forrest; based on the play by Edward Knoblock; musical direction: Louis Adrian

Cast: Lucy Andonian, Henry Calvin, Joan Diener, Alfred Drake, Hal Hackett, Richard Kiley, Richard Oneto, Doretta Morrow

Songs: Overture (orchestra)
Sands of Time (Oneto, chorus)

Rhymes Have I (Drake, Morrow)
Fate (Drake)
Bazaar of the Caravans (chorus)
Not Since Ninevah (Diener, Calvin, chorus)
Baubles, Bangles and Beads (Morrow, Oneto, chorus)
Stranger in Paradise (Morrow, Kiley)
He's in Love (Hackett, chorus)

Gesticulate (Drake, Diener, Calvin, chorus)
Night of My Nights (Kiley, chorus)
Was I Wazir? (Calvin, chorus)
Rahadlakum (Drake, Diener, Andonian, chorus)
And This Is My Beloved (Drake, Morrow, Kiley, Calvin)
The Olive Tree (Drake)
Zubbediya, Samaris' Dance (Andonian, chorus)
Finale: Sands of Time (reprise) (Drake, Morrow, Kiley, chorus)

KISMET (Revival, June 22, 1965, New York State Theatre)

RCA LSO 1112 stereo

Musical direction: Franz Allers

Cast: Anita Alpert, Richard Banke, Henry Calvin, Alfred Drake, Anne Jeffreys, Albert Toigo, Rudy Vejar, Lee Venora

Songs: Overture (orchestra)
Sands of Time (Vejar, chorus)
Rhymes Have I (Drake, Venora)
Fate (Drake)
Not Since Ninevah (Jeffreys, Calvin, chorus)
Baubles, Bangles and Beads (Venora, chorus)
Stranger in Paradise (Venora, Banke)
He's in Love (Toigo, chorus)

Gesticulate (Drake, Jeffreys, Calvin, chorus)
Bored (Drake, Jeffreys)
Night of My Nights (Banke, chorus)
Was I Wazir? (Calvin, chorus)
Rahadlakum (Drake, Jeffreys, Alpert, chorus)
And This Is My Beloved (Drake, Venora, Banke, Calvin)
The Olive Tree (Drake)
Zubbediya (Alpert)
Finale (Drake, Venora, Banke, chorus)

KISS ME, KATE (December 30, 1948, Century Theatre)

Columbia ML 4140 mono reissued: OL 4140

Music, lyrics: Cole Porter; musical direction: Pembroke Davenport

Cast: Harry Clark, Edwin Clay, Fred Davis, Jack Diamond, Alfred Drake, Lorenzo Fuller, Annabelle Hill, Lisa Kirk, Harold Lang, Patricia Morison, Eddie Sledge, Charles Wood

Songs: Overture (orchestra)
Another Op'nin', Another Show (Hill, chorus)
Why Can't You Behave (Kirk, Lang)
Wunderbar (Drake, Morison)
So in Love (Morison)
We Open in Venice (Drake, Morison, Kirk, Lang)
Tom, Dick or Harry (Kirk, Lang, Clay, Wood)
I've Come to Wive It Wealthily in Padua (Drake, chorus)
I Hate Men (morison)

Were Thine That Special Face (Drake)
Too Darn Hot (Fuller, Sledge, Davis)
Where Is the Life That Late I Led? (Drake)
Always True to You in My Fashion (Kirk)
Bianca (Lang)
So in Love (reprise) (Drake)
Brush Up Your Shakespeare (Clark, Diamond)
I Am Ashamed That Women Are So Simple (Morison) lyrics: William Shakespeare
Finale: Kiss Me, Kate (Drake, Morison)

Note: Drake, Morison, Kirk, Lang and Fuller re-recorded this score in stereo for Capitol Records (STAO-1267) in 1959.

KITTIWAKE ISLAND (October 12, 1960, Off Broadway, Martinique Theatre)

Blue Pear Records BP 1003 mono

Music: Alec Wilder; lyrics: Arnold Sundgaard; musical direction: Joseph Stecko

Cast: David Canary, Reid Klein, Joe Lautner, Don Liberto, Kathleen Murray, G. Wood, Caroline Worth

Songs: Were This to Prove a Feather in My Cap (Lautner)
It Doesn't Look Deserted to Me (female chorus)
Can This Be a Toeprint? (Lautner)
Good Morning Dr. Puffin (Murray)
I'd Gladly Walk to Alaska (Murray)
The Smew Song (Lautner, Murray)
Under a Tree (Liberto, Klein, Canary, male chorus)
Never Try Too Hard (Murray)
Good Morning Dr. Sparrow (Wood)

I Delight in the Sight of My Lydia (Wood)
Robinson Crusoe (Liberto, Worth)
Nothing Is Working Out Right (Lautner, Murray, Wood)
If Love's Like a Lark (Murray, Lautner)
When One Deems a Lady Sweet (Wood)
When a Robin Leaves Chicago (Lautner)
So Raise the Banner High (chorus)
It's So Easy to Say (chorus)

THE KOSHER WIDOW (October 31, 1959, Off Broadway, Anderson Theatre)

Golden Crest Records 4018 mono

Music: Sholom Secunda; lyrics: Molly Picon, Sheldon Secunda; musical direction: Sholom Secunda

Cast: Bruce Adler, Julius Adler, Henrietta Jacobson, Irving Jacobson, Molly Picon, Esta Saltzman, Mae Schoenfeld, Muni Serebroff, Ann Winters

Songs: Overture (orchestra)
Gantz Long Island Redt (All Long Island Gossips) (J. Adler, Slatzman, Winters)
An Akteritzeh (An Actress) (Picon)
Oib S'iz Bashert (What's Destined to Be) (Picon, Serebroff)
Di Belles fun Belle Harbor (The Belles of Belle Harbor) (Schoenfeld, H. Jacobson)
Am Yisroel Chai (Israel Shall Live) (Picon, ensemble)

Le Chayim (To Health) (I. Jacobson, Serebroff)
Mazel-Tov (Good Luck) (I. Jacobson, Schoenfeld, Saltzman, J. Adler, B. Adler, H. Jacobson)
M'Nemt Eich Oif Der Hutska (They've Gotcha on the Hutska) (Picon)
Ich Darf Dich (I Need You) (Picon, B. Adler)

KWAMINA (October 23, 1961, Fifty-Fourth Street Theatre)

Capitol SW 1645 stereo

Music, lyrics: Richard Adler; musical direction: Colin Romoff

Cast: Isa Arnal, Joseph Attles, Ethel Ayler, Terry Carter, Scott Gibson, Robert Guillaume, Victor Harison, Lillian Hayman, Lee Hooper, Sally Ann Howes, Mary Louise, Rosalie Maxwell, Brock Peters, Helen Phillips, Mike Quashie, Charles Queenan, Mal Scott, George Tipton, Gordon Watkins

Songs: The Cocoa Bean Song (Guillaume, Gibson, Watkins, company)
Welcome Home (Gibson, Scott, Hooper, Quashie, company)
The Sun is Beginning to Crow (company)
Did You Hear That? (Howes, Carter)
You're As English As (Howes)
Seven Sheep, Four Red Shirts, and a Bottle of Gin (Attles, Gibson, Queenan, Tipton, company)
Nothing More to Look Forward To (Guillaume, Ayler)

What's Wrong with Me? (Howes)
Something Big (company)
Ordinary People (Howes, Carter)
A Man Can Have No Choice (Peters)
What Happened to Me Tonight? (Howes)
One Wife (Hayman, Maxwell, Arnal, Harison, Hooper, Louise, Phillips)
Another Time, Another Place (Howes)

LADY IN THE DARK (January 21, 1941, Alvin Theatre)

RCA LPV 503 mono

Music: Kurt Weill; lyrics: Ira Gershwin; musical direction: Leonard Joy

Cast: Gertrude Lawrence

Songs: Oh Fabulous One (male chorus)
Huxley (Lawrence, men)
Girl of the Moment (male chorus)
One Life to Live (Lawrence)
This Is New (Lawrence)
The Princess of Pure Delight (Lawrence)
The Saga of Jenny (Lawrence, men)
My Ship (Lawrence)

THE LAST SWEET DAYS OF ISAAC (January 26, 1970, Off Broadway, Eastside Playhouse)

RCA LSO 1169 stereo

Music: Nancy Ford; lyrics: Gretchen Cryer; musical direction: Clay Fullum

Cast: Charles Collins, C. David Colson, Louise Heath, John Long, Austin Pendleton, Fredricka Weber

Songs: The Elevator
Overture (the Zeitgeist)
The Last Sweet Days of Isaac (Pendleton, the Zeitgeist)
A Transparent Crystal Moment (Pendleton, Weber, the Zeitgeist)
My Most Important Moments Go By (Weber, Pendleton)
Love, You Came to Me (Pendleton, Weber, the Zeitgeist)
Finale (Pendleton, Weber, Zeitgeist)

I Want to Walk to San Francisco
I Want to Walk to San Francisco (company)
I Can't Live in Solitary (Long, the Zeitgeist)
Herein Lie the Seeds of Revolution (Collins, the Zeitgeist)
Touching Your Hand Is Like Touching Your Mind (Pendleton, the Zeitgeist)
Somebody Died Today (Colson, the Zeitgeist)
Yes, I Know That I'm Alive (Heath, the Zeitgeist)
Finale (company)

Note: 'The Zeitgeist' indicates a backup group of singers.

LEADER OF THE PACK (April 8, 1985, Ambassador Theatre)

Elektra 960409-1-Q (two records) stereo

Music, lyrics: Ellie Greenwich, friends; based on a play by Melanie Mintz; musical direction: Jimmy Vivino

Cast: Patrick Cassidy, Pattie Darcy, Annie Golden, Ellie

Greenwich, Jasmine Guy, Lon Hoyt, Darlene Love, Keith McDaniel, Dinah Manoff, Gina Taylor, Barbara Yeager

Songs: Overture (orchestra)
Be My Baby (Golden, girls)
Wait 'Til My Bobby Gets Home (Love, company)
A...My Name Is Ellie (Manoff)
Jivette Boogie Beat (Manoff, Yeager, Guy)
Why Do Lovers Break Each Others' Hearts (Love, company)
--- Today I Met the Boy I'm Going to Marry (Love, company)
I Wanna Love Him So Bad (Manoff, girls)
Do Wah Diddy (Cassidy, men)
And Then He Kissed Me (Manoff, girls)
Hanky Panky (Cassidy, men)
Not Too Young to Get Married (Love, girls)
Chapel of Love (company)
--- Baby I Love You (Golden, girls)
Leader of the Pack (Golden, company)
Look of Love (Darcy)
Christmas - Baby Please Come Home (Love, girls)
I Can Hear Music (Golden, Darcy, McDaniel, Hoyt)
--- Rock of Rages (Manoff)
Keep It Confidential (Taylor, company)
Da Doo Ron Ron (Greenwich, men)
What a Guy (Greenwich, company)
Maybe I Know (Greenwich, girls)
River Deep, Mountain High (Love, company)
We're Gonna Make It (After All) (Greenwich, Love, Golden, company)

LEAVE IT TO JANE (Revival, May 25, 1959, Off Broadway, Sheridan Square Playhouse)

Strand SLS 1002 stereo reissued: Stet DS 15002

Music: Jerome Kern; lyrics: Guy Bolton, P.G. Wodehouse; musical direction: Joseph Stecko

Cast: Jeanne Allen, Dorothy Greener, Angelo Mango, Art Matthews, Kathleen Murray, George Segal, Jan Speers, Ray Tudor

Songs: Overture (orchestra)
Good Old Atwater (chorus)
Wait Till Tomorrow (Murray, men)
Just You Watch My Step (Mango, Allen, girls)
Leave It to Jane (Murray, Mango, Allen, chorus)
The Siren's Song (Murray, girls)
--- There It Is Again (Matthews, Speers, Murray, girls)
Cleopatterer (Greener)
The Crickets are Calling (Murray, Matthews, chorus)
Finale: Act One (company)
Opening: Act Two (Allen, chorus)
Sir Galahad (Mango, Greener, Tudor)
The Sun Shines Brighter (Mango, Allen, girls)
I'm Going to Find a Girl (Segal, Mango, Tudor)
Poor Prune (Greener)

The Sun Shines Brighter (reprise) (Mango, Allen)
Finale (Murray, Matthews, company)

LET IT RIDE! (October 12, 1961, Eugene O'Neill Theatre)

RCA LSO 1064 stereo

Music, lyrics: Jay Livingston, Ray Evans; based on a play by John Cecil Holm and George Abbot; musical direction: Jay Blackton

Cast: Larry Alpert, Harold Gary, George Gobel, Stanley Grover, Sam Levene, Albert Linville, Barbara Nichols, Stanley Simmonds, Paula Stewart, Ted Thurston, Maggie Worth

Songs: Overture (orchestra)
Run, Run, Run (company)
The Nicest Thing (Stewart)
Hey Jimmy Joe John Jim Jack (Gobel)
Broads Ain't People (Gobel, Gary, Alpert, Linville)
Let It Ride (Levene, company)
I'll Learn Ya (Gobel, company)
Love, Let Me Know (Stewart, Grover)
Happy Birthday, Erwin (girls)

Everything Beautiful (Gobel, girls)
Who's Doing What to Erwin? (Stewart, Thurston, Grover, Worth)
I Wouldn't Have Had To (Nichols)
There's Something About a Horse (company)
He Needs You (Gobel, Alpert, Linville, Levene)
Just an Honest Mistake (Thurston, Simmonds, company)
His Own Little Island (Gobel)
If Flutterby Wins (Gobel, Levene, Alpert, Linville, Gary, company)
Finale (company)

LET MY PEOPLE COME (January 8, 1974, Off Broadway, Village Gate)

Libra Records LR 1069 stereo

Music, lyrics: Earl Wilson, Jr.; musical direction: Billy Cunningham

Cast: Tobie Columbus, Lorraine Davidson, Marty Duffy, Joe Jones, Larry Paulette, Peachena, Shezwae Powell, Christine Rubens

Songs: Opening Number (company)
Give It to Me (Davidson)
I'm Gay (Duffy, Jones)
Come in My Mouth (Columbus)
Dirty Words (company)
Linda, Georgina, Marilyn and Me (Rubens)
I Believe My Body (company)

Take Me Home with You (Paulette)
Choir Practice (company)
And She Loved Me (Powell, Peachena)
The Cunnilingus Champion of Co. C (Paulette, Rubens, Jones)
Doesn't Anybody Love Anymore (Powell)
Let My People Come (company)

LI'L ABNER (November 15, 1956, St. James Theatre)

Columbia OL 5150 mono reissued: CSP AOL 5150

Music: Gene de Paul; lyrics: Johnny Mercer; based on characters created by Al Capp; musical dirction: Lehman Engel

Cast: Edith Adams, Carmen Alvarez, Marc Breaux, Pat Creighton, Lillian D'Honau, Bonnie Evans, Hope Holiday, Stubby Kaye, Ralph Linn, Robert McClure, Jack Matthew, Peter Palmer, George Reeder, Howard St. John, Stanley Simmonds, Deedee Wood

Songs: Overture (orchestra)
A Typical Day (ensemble)
If I Had My Druthers (Palmer, Adams, Breaux, Linn, Matthew, McClure, Reeder)
Jubilation T. Cornpone (Kaye, ensemble)
Rag Offen the Bush (ensemble)
Namely You (Adams, Palmer)
Unnecessary Town (Adams, Palmer, ensemble)

The Country's in the Very Best of Hands (Palmer, Kaye, chorus)
Oh, Happy Day (Simmonds, Reeder, Linn, Breaux)
I'm Past My Prime (Adams, Kaye)
Love in a Home (Palmer, Adams)
Progress Is the Root of All Evil (St. John)
Put 'Em Back (Alvarez, Creighton, D'Honau, Evans, Holiday, Wood)
The Matrimonial Stomp (Kaye, ensemble)

Note: "Sadie Hawkins Ballet", recorded in 1959 in stereo was issued on Painted Smiles PS 1364, Ballet on Broadway; musical direction: Lehman Engel

LITTLE MARY SUNSHINE (November 18, 1959, Off Broadway, Orpheum Theatre)

Capitol SWAO 1240 stereo

Music, lyrics: Rick Besoyan; musical direction: Glenn Osser

Cast: John Aniston, Eileen Brennan, William Graham, John McMartin, Elizabeth Parrish, Mario Siletti, Elmarie Wendel

Songs: Overture (orchestra)
The Forest Rangers (Aniston, Graham, rangers)

Little Mary Sunshine (Brennan, rangers)
Look for a Sky of Blue (Brennan, rangers)
You're the Fairest Flower (Graham)
In Izzenschnooken on the Lovely Essenzook Zee (Parrish)
Playing Croquet (girls)
Swinging (girls)
How Do You Do? (rangers)
\---
Tell a Handsome Stranger (girls, rangers)
Once in a Blue Moon (McMartin, Wendel)
Every Little Nothing (Parrish, Brennan)
Colorado Love Call (Graham, Brennan)
Such a Merry Party (Wendel, rangers, girls)
Naughty, Naughty Nancy (Brennan, girls)
Mata Hari (Wendel, girls)
Do You Ever Dream of Vienna? (Parrish, Siletti)
Coo Coo (Brennan)
Finale (company)

LITTLE ME (November 17, 1962, Lunt-Fontanne Theatre)

RCA LSO 1078 stereo

Music: Cy Coleman; lyrics: Carolyn Leigh; based on a novel by Patrick Dennis; musical direction: Charles Sanford

Cast: Nancy Andrews, Sid Caesar, Mickey Deems, Joey Faye, Mort Marshall, Virginia Martin, Swen Swenson, Peter Turgeon

Songs: Overture (orchestra)
The Truth (Andrews, Turgeon, chorus)
The Other Side of the Tracks (Martin)
I Love You (Caesar, Martin, chorus)
The Other Side of the Tracks (reprise) (Martin)
Deep Down Inside (Caesar, Martin, Deems, chorus)
Be a Performer! (Faye, Marshall, Martin)
Dimples (Martin, chorus)
Boom-Boom (Caesar, chorus)
\---
I've Got Your Number (Swenson)
Real Live Girl (Caesar)
Real Live Girl (reprise) (men)
Poor Little Hollywood Star (Martin)
Little Me (Andrews, Martin)
Goodbye - The Prince's Farewell (Caesar, Deems, chorus)
Here's to Us (Andrews, chorus)

A LITTLE NIGHT MUSIC (February 25, 1973, Shubert Theatre)

Columbia KS 32265 stereo CD

Music, lyrics: Stephen Sondheim; suggested by a film by Ingmar Bergman; musical direction: Harold Hastings

Cast: Len Cariou, Patricia Elliott, Beth Fowler, Hermione Gingold, Laurence Guittard, D. Jamin-Bartlett, Glynis Johns, Judy Kahan, Mark Lambert, Barbara Lang, Victoria

Mallory, Teri Ralston, Benjamin Rayson, Gene Varrone

Songs: Overture and Night Waltz (Rayson, Ralston, Lang, Varrone, Fowler)
Now (Cariou)
Later (Lambert)
Soon (Mallory, Lambert, Cariou)
The Glamorous Life (Kahan, Johns, Gingold, Ralston, Fowler, Lang, Rayson, Varrone)
Remember? (Rayson, Ralston, Fowler, Varrone, Lang)
You Must Meet My Wife (Cariou, Johns)
Liaisons (Gingold)

In Praise of Women (Guittard)
Every Day a Little Death (Elliott, Mallory)
A Weekend in the Country (company)
The Sun Won't Set (Lang, Fowler, Ralston, Rayson, Varrone)
It Would Have Been Wonderful (Cariou, Guittard)
Perpetual Anticipation (Ralston, Fowler, Lang)
Send in the Clowns (Johns)
The Miller's Son (Jamin-Bartlett)
Finale: Send in the Clowns; Night Waltz (Johns, Cariou)

LITTLE SHOP OF HORRORS (July 28, 1982, Off Broadway, Orpheum Theatre)

Geffen Records GHSP 2020 stereo

Music: Alan Menken; lyrics: Howard Ashman; based upon the film by Roger Corman; musical direction: Robert Billig

Cast: Hy Anzell, Sheila Kay Davis, Ellen Greene, Leilani Jones, Franc Luz, Ron Taylor, Leigh Warren, Lee Wilkof

Songs: Prologue: Little Shop of Horrors (Warren, Davis, Jones)
Skid Row: Downtown (company)
Da-Doo (Warren, Davis, Jones)
Grow for Me (Wilkof)
Ya Never Know (Anzell, Wilkof, Warren, Davis, Jones)
Mushnick and Son (Anzell, Wilkof)
Dentist! (Luz, Warren, Davis, Jones)
Somewhere That's Green (Greene)

Feed Me: Git It (Wilkof, Taylor)
Now: It's Just the Gas (Wilkof, Luz)
Closed for Renovation (Wilkof, Greene, Anzell)
Suddenly Seymour (Wilkof, Greene, Warren, Davis, Jones)
Suppertime (Taylor)
The Meek Shall Inherit (company)
Sominex/Suppertime II (Greene, Taylor, Wilkof)
Finale: Don't Feed the Plants (company)

THE LITTLEST REVUE (May 22, 1956, Off Broadway, Phoenix Theatre)

Epic LN 3275 mono reissued: Painted Smiles PS 1361

Music: Michael Brown, Vernon Duke, Sheldon Harnick, Bud McCreery, John Strauss, Charles Strouse; lyrics: Lee Adams, Michael Brown, Sammy Cahn, Kenward Elmslie, Sheldon Harnick, John Latouche, Bud McCreery, Ogden Nash, Charles Strouse; musical direction: Will Irwin

Cast: Beverly Bozeman, Joel Grey, Tammy Grimes, George Marcy, Tommy Morton, Charlotte Rae

Songs: Overture (orchestra)
Opening Number (company) music: Strauss; lyrics: Latouche, Elmslie
The Shape of Things (Rae) music, lyrics: Harnick
Madly in Love (Grimes) music: Duke; lyrics: Nash
I Lost the Rhythm (Grey) music, Lyrics: Strouse
Game of Dance (Marcy, Bozeman, Morton) music: Sol Berkowitz; dialogue: Don Meyer
Third Avenue El (Morton, chorus) music, Lyrics: Brown
I Want to Fly Now and Pay Later (Morton) music: Duke; lyrics: Nash
Summer Is A-Commin' In (Rae) music: Duke; lyrics: Latouche
You're Far from Wonderful (Grey) music: Duke; lyrics: Nash
Good Little Girls (Bozeman, Morton, Marcy) music: Duke; lyrics: Cahn
Spring Doth Let Her Colours Fly (Rae, Morton, Marcy) music: Strouse; lyrics: Adams
I'm Glad I'm Not a Man (Grimes) music: Duke; lyrics: Nash
Love Is Still in Town (Marcy) music: Duke; lyrics: Nash
The Power of Negative Thinking (company) music, lyrics: McCreery

Note: The Painted Smiles reissue contains two additional songs:
Backer's Audition (company)
Born too Late (Morton)

LOOK MA, I'M DANCIN'! (January 29, 1948, Adelphi Theatre)

Decca DL 5231 mono reissued: Columbia Special Products X14879

Music, lyrics: Hugh Martin; musical direction: Pembroke Davenport

Cast: Sandra Deel, Harold Lang, Hugh Martin, Bill Shirley, Nancy Walker

Songs: Gotta Dance (Lang, chorus)
I'm the First Girl in the Second Row (Walker)
I'm Not So Bright (Lang)
I'm Tired of Texas (Walker, chorus)
Tiny Room (Shirley)
The Little Boy Blues (Martin, Deel)
If You'll Be Mine (Walker, Shirley)
Shauny O'Shay (Deel, chorus)

Note: This album was recorded while the show was in rehearsal, and Harold Lang and Nancy Walker are the only cast members of the New York production. "Mlle. Scandale Ballet", recorded in 1959 in stereo, was issued on Painted Smiles PS 1364, Ballet on Broadway; musical direction: Lehman Engel

LORELEI (January 27, 1974, Palace Theatre)

MGM Records M3G-55 stereo

Music: Jule Styne; lyrics: Leo Robin; new lyrics: Betty Comden, Adolph Green; based on Gentlemen Prefer Blondes by Anita Loos; musical direction: Milton Rosenstock

Cast: Carol Channing, Bob Fitch, Jack Fletcher, Tamara Long, John Mineo, Peter Palmer, Lee Roy Reams

Songs: Overture (orchestra)
Looking Back (Channing)
Bye Bye Baby (Channing, Palmer, chorus)
A Little Girl from Little Rock (Channing)
I Love What I'm Doing (Long)
It's Delightful Down in Chile (Channing, Fletcher, chorus)
I Won't Let You Get Away (Reams)

Keeping Cool with Coolidge (Reams, chorus)
Men (Channing)
Mamie is Mimi (Channing, Mineo, Fitch, chorus)
Diamonds Are a Girl's Best Friend (Channing)
Lorelei (Channing, chorus)
Homesick Blues (Channing, Palmer, chorus)
'Looking Back' ...on...'Diamonds' (Channing)
Lorelei Finale (Channing, chorus)

Note: This is a revised version of Gentlemen Prefer Blondes (1949). A pre-Broadway recording was issued on Verve MV-5097-OC which differs from the above.

LOST IN THE STARS (October 30, 1949, Music Box Theatre)

Decca DL 8028 mono reissued: MCA 2071E

Music: Kurt Weill; lyrics: Maxwell Anderson; based on Alan Paton's novel Cry, the Beloved Country; musical direction: Maurice Levine

Cast: Herbert Coleman, Todd Duncan, Sheila Guyse, Inez Matthews, Frank Roane

Songs: The Hills of Ixopo (Roane, chorus)
Thousands of Miles (Duncan)
Train to Johannesburg (Roane, chorus)
Thousands of Miles (reprise) (Duncan)
The Search (spoken)
The Little Gray House (Duncan, chorus)
Who'll Buy? (Guyse)

Trouble Man (Matthews)
Murder in Parkwold (chorus)
Fear (chorus)

Lost in the Stars (Duncan, chorus)
O Tixo, Tixo, Help Me (Duncan)
Stay Well (Matthews)
Cry, the Beloved Country (Roane, chorus)
Big Mole (Coleman, chorus)
Chapel Scene (Duncan) spoken
A Bird of Passage (chorus)
Thousands of Miles (reprise) (Duncan, chorus)

Note: This recording includes spoken dialog.

LOVERS (January 27, 1975, Off Broadway, Players Theatre)

Golden Gloves PG-723 mono

Music: Steve Sterner; lyrics: Peter del Valle; musical direction: Steve Sterner

Cast: Reathel Bean, Mike Cascone, John Ingle, Martin Rivera, Robert Serva, Gary Sneed

Songs: Lovers (cast)
Look at Him (Cascone, Rivera)
Make It (Serva, Ingle)
I Don't Want to Watch TV (cast)
Twenty Years (cast)
Somebody, Somebody Hold Me (Serva)
Belt and Leather (Serva, Ingle)

Hymn (Celebrate) (cast)
Somehow I'm Taller (Cascone, cast)
Role-Playing (Cascone, Rivera)
The Trucks (Ingle, cast)
Help Him Along (Sneed, cast)
You Came to Me As a Young Man (Bean)
Finale (cast)

LOVESONG (October 5, 1976, Off Broadway, Village Gate)

Orignal Cast Records OC 8022 stereo

Music: Michael Valenti; lyrics: various writers and poets; musical direction: Michael Valenti

Cast: Melanie Chartoff, Sigrid Heath, Robert Manzari, Jess Richards

Songs: What Is Love? (cast) lyrics: Sir Walter Raleigh
When I Was One-and-Twenty (Manzari, Richards, cast) lyrics: A.E. Houseman
Bid Me Love (cast) lyrics: Robert Herrick
A Birthday (Heath) lyrics: Christina Rossetti
Sophia (Richards) lyrics: Edwin Dulchin
To My Dear and Loving Husband (Heath, Richards) lyrics: Anne Bradstreet

I Remember (Richards) lyrics: Thomas Hood
April Child (Chartoff, cast) lyrics: Kenneth Pressman
Song (cast) lyrics: Thomas Lodge
What Is a Woman Like? (Manzari) lyrics: anonymous
Let the Toast Pass (cast) lyrics: Richard Brinsley Sheridan
Echo (cast) lyrics: anonymous
A Rondelay (Heath, Richards, Manzari) lyrics: Peter Anthony Motteaux
Just Suppose (Manzari, Chartoff) lyrics: Edwin Dulchin
Open All Night (Chartoff) lyrics: James Agee
Young I Was (Manzari) lyrics: anonymous
Jenny Kiss'd Me (Richards) lyrics: Leigh Hunt
The Fair Dissenter Lass (Heath) lyrics: John Lewin
Blood Red Roses (Manzari, cast) lyrics: John Lewin
So, We'll Go No More A-Roving (cast) lyrics: George Gordon, Lord Byron
An Epitaph (cast) lyrics: Richard Crashaw

Note: Robert Manzari replaces Ty McConnell of the original cast.

LUTE SONG (February 6, 1946, Plymouth Theatre)

Decca DL 8030 mono

Music: Raymond Scott; lyrics: Bernard Hanighen; based on _Pi-Pa-Ki_ by Kao-Tong-Kia; musical direction: Raymond Scott

Cast: Mary Martin

Songs: Mountain High, Valley Low (Martin)
Vision Song (Martin)
Bitter Harvest (Martin)
See the Monkey (Martin)
Where You Are (Martin)
Imperial March (orchestra)
Dirge (orchestra)

MACK AND MABEL (October 6, 1974, Majestic Theatre)

ABC Records H 830 stereo

Music, lyrics: Jerry Herman; musical direction: Donald Pippin

Cast: Lisa Kirk, Bernadette Peters, Robert Preston, Stanley Simmonds

Songs: Overture (orchestra)
Movies Were Movies (Preston)
Look What Happened to Mabel (Peters, company)
Big Time (Kirk)
I Won't Send Roses (Preston)
I Won't Send Roses (reprise) (Peters)
I Wanna Make the World Laugh (Preston, company)
Wherever He Ain't (Peters)

Hundreds of Girls (Preston, girls)
When Mabel Comes in the Room (Simmonds, company)
My Heart Leaps Up (Preston)
Time Heals Everything (Peters)
Tap Your Troubles Away (Kirk, girls)
I Promise You a Happy Ending (Preston)

THE MAD SHOW (January 9, 1966, Off Broadway, New Theatre)

Columbia OS 2930 stereo

Music: Mary Rodgers; lyrics: Marshall Barer, Larry Siegel, Stephen Sondheim, Steven Vinaver; based on Mad Magazine; musical direction: Sam Pottle

Cast: MacIntyre Dixon, Linda Lavin, Dick Libertini, Paul Sand, Jo Anne Worley

Songs: Overture (orchestra)
Opening Number (company) lyrics: Barer
Academy Awards for Parents (company) spoken
Eccch! (company) lyrics: Barer
The Boy from ... (Lavin) lyrics: Sondheim (as Esteban Ria Nido)
Well It Ain't (Libertini) lyrics: Siegel
Misery Is (Lavin, Dixon, Sand) lyrics: Barer
Handle with Care (Dixon, Libertini, Worley) spoken
Hate Song (company) lyrics: Vinaver

Entr'acte (orchestra)
You Never Can Tell (Lavin, Dixon, Worley) lyrics: Vinaver
The Real Thing (Sand) lyrics: Barer
Looking for Someone (Lavin) lyrics: Barer
Kiddie T.V. (company) spoken
The Gift of Maggie (and others) (Worley) lyrics: Barer
Football in Depth (Sand, Dixon, Libertini) spoken
Finale (company) spoken

Note: "The Real Thing" half speed (normal) recorded by Don Meehan.

MAGGIE FLYNN (October 23, 1968, ANTA Theatre)

RCA LSOD 2009 stereo

Music, lyrics: Hugh Peretti, Luigi Creatore, George David Weiss; musical direction: John Lesko

Cast: Sybil Bowan, Jack Cassidy, Austin Colyer, Jennifer Darling, William James, Shirley Jones, Robert Kaye, Stanley Simmonds

Songs: Overture (orchestra)
Nice Cold Mornin' (Jones, children)
I Wouldn't Have You Any Other Way (Jones, boys)

Learn How to Laugh (Cassidy, chorus)
Maggie Flynn (Cassidy)
The Thank You Song (Jones, Darling, children)
Look Around Your Little World (Kaye, Cassidy)
Maggie Flynn (reprise) (Cassidy, Jones, children, boys)
I Won't Let It Happen Again (Jones)
--- How About a Ball? (Cassidy, Jones, Bowan, ladies)
Pitter Patter (Cassidy)
They're Never Gonna Make Me Fight (Colyer, Simmonds, James, men)
Why Can't I Walk Away (Cassidy)
The Game of War (children)
Mr. Clown (Cassidy, Jones, children, chorus)
Pitter Patter (reprise) (Jones)
Finale (Jones, Cassidy)

THE MAGIC SHOW (May 28, 1974, Cort Theatre)

Bell Records 9003 stereo

Music, lyrics: Stephen Schwartz; musical direction: Stephen Reinhardt

Cast: Cheryl Barnes, Doug Henning, Robert LuPone, Annie McGreevey, Anita Morris, Loyd Sannes, Dale Soules, Ronald Stafford, David Ogden Stiers

Songs: Up to His Old Tricks (company)
Solid Silver Platform Shoes (Barnes, McGreevey)
Lion Tamer (Soules)
Style (Stiers, company)
Two's Company (Barnes, McGreevey)
--- Charmin's Lament (Morris)
The Goldfarb Variations (Barnes, Stiers, McGreevey, LuPone, Morris)
West End Avenue (Soules)
Sweet, Sweet, Sweet (Morris, LuPone, Sannes, Stafford, Henning)
Before Your Very Eyes (Barnes, McGreevey)
Finale (company)

MAKE A WISH (April 18, 1951, Winter Garden Theatre)

RCA LOC 1002 mono reissued: CMB 1-2033

Music, lyrics: Hugh Martin; based on The Good Fairy by Ferenc Molnar; musical direction: Milton Rosenstock

Cast: Dean Campbell, Stephen Douglass, Nanette Fabray, Helen Gallagher, Harold Lang

Songs: Overture (orchestra)
The Tour Must Go On (Campbell, chorus)
I Wanna Be Good 'n' Bad (Fabray, girls)
What I Was Warned About (Fabray)
Suits Me Fine (Lang, Gallagher)

Hello, Hello, Hello (chorus)
Tonight You Are in Paree (chorus)
Who Gives a Sou? (Douglass, Fabray, Lang, Gallagher, chorus)
Make a Wish (Fabray, Douglass)
I'll Never Make a Frenchman Out of You (Gallagher, Lang)

Paris, France (Douglass, chorus)
When Does This Feeling Go Away? (Douglass)
Over and Over (Fabray, chorus)
The Sale - Ballet (orchestra)
That Face! (Lang, Gallagher, chorus)
Take Me Back to Texas with You (Fabray, Gallagher, Lang)
Make a Wish - Finale (Fabray, company)

MAME (May 24, 1966, Winter Garden Theatre)

Columbia KOS 3000 stereo CD

Music, lyrics: Jerry Herman; based on the novel Auntie Mame by Patrick Dennis and the play by Lawrence and Lee; musical direction: Donald Pippin

Cast: Beatrice Arthur, Charles Braswell, Jane Connell, Jerry Lanning, Angela Lansbury, Frankie Michaels, Sab Shimono

Songs: Overture (orchestra)
St. Bridget (Connell, Michaels)
It's Today (Lansbury, company)
Open a New Window (Lansbury, company)
The Man in the Moon (Lansbury, Arthur, girls)
My Best Girl (Michaels, Lansbury)
We Need a Little Christmas (Lansbury, Michaels, Connell, Shimono)

Mame (Braswell, company)
The Letter (Michaels, Lanning)
Bosum Buddies (Lansbury, Arthur)
Gooch's Song (Connell)
That's How Young I Feel (Lansbury, company)
If He Walked into My Life (Lansbury)
Finale (Lansbury, company)

MAN OF LA MANCHA (November 22, 1965, Off Broadway, ANTA Washington Square Theatre)

Kapp KRS 4505 stereo reissued: MCA 2018 CD

Music: Mitch Leigh; lyrics: Joe Darion; musical direction: Neil Warner

Cast: Gino Conforti, Joan Diener, Irving Jacobson, Richard Kiley, Eleanor Knapp, Ray Middleton, Robert Rounseville, Harry Theyard, Mimi Turque

Songs: Overture (orchestra)
Man of La Mancha (Kiley, Jacobson)
It's All the Same (Diener, ensemble)

Dulcinea (Kiley, ensemble)
I'm Only Thinking of Him (Turque, Rounseville, Knapp)
I Really Like Him (Jacobson, Diener)
What Do You Want of Me? (Diener)
The Barber's Song (Conforti)
Golden Helmet (Kiley, Conforti, Jacobson, ensemble)

To Each His Dulcinea (Rounseville)
The Impossible Dream (Kiley)
Little Bird, Little Bird (Theyard, ensemble)
The Dubbing (Middleton, Kiley, Diener, Jacobson)
The Abduction (Theyard)
Aldonza (Diener, Kiley)
A Little Gossip (Jacobson)
Dulcinea (reprise) (Diener)
The Impossible Dream (reprise) (Diener, Kiley)
Man of La Mancha (reprise) (Kiley, Jacobson)
The Psalm (Rounseville)
Finale (company)

MAN WITH A LOAD OF MISCHIEF (November 6, 1966, Off Broadway, Jan Hus Playhouse)

Kapp Records KRS 5508 stereo

Music: John Clifton; lyrics: John Clifton, Ben Tarver; adapted from the play by Ashley Dukes; musical direction: Sande Campbell

Cast: Alice Cannon, Lesslie Nicol, Tom Noel, Reid Shelton, Raymond Thorne, Virginia Vestoff

Songs: Overture (orchestra)
Wayside Inn (Noel)
The Rescue (Noel, Nicol)
Goodbye, My Sweet (Vestoff)
Romance! (Cannon, Thorne, Noel, Nicol)
Lover Lost (Vestoff)
Once You're Had a Little Taste (Cannon)
Any Other Way (Nicol, Noel)
Hulla-Baloo-Balay (Shelton)

You'd Be Amazed (Vestoff, Shelton, Thorne)
A Friend Like You (Vestoff, Thorne)
Come to the Masquerade (Shelton)
Man with a Load of Mischief (Vestoff)
Come to the Masquerade (reprise) (Shelton)
What Style! (Noel)
A Wonder (Vestoff)
Make Way for My Lady (Shelton)
Forget! (Cannon, Thorne)
Little Rag Doll (Cannon)
Man with a Load of Mischief (reprise) (Vestoff)
Make Way for My Lady (reprise) (Vestoff, Shelton, Noel, Nicol)

MARCH OF THE FALSETTOS (April 1, 1981, Off Broadway, Playwrights Horizons)

DRG Records SBL 12581 stereo CD

Music, lyrics: William Finn; musical direction: Michael Starobin

Cast: Stephen Bogardus, Alison Fraser, James Kushner, Michael Rupert, Chip Zien

Songs: Four Jews in a Room Bitching (men)
A Tight-Knit Family (Rupert)
Love is Blind (Fraser, Zien, cast)
The Thrill of First Love (Rupert, Bogardus)
Marvin at the Psychiatrist (Rupert, Zien, Kushner)
My Father's a Homo (Kushner)
Everyone Tells Jason to See a Psychiatrist (Rupert, Fraser, Kushner, Bogardus)
This Had Better Come to a Stop (cast)
Please Come to My House (Fraser, Zien, Kushner)
Jason's Therapy - Part One (Kushner, Zien, cast)

Jason's Therapy - Part Two (Kushner, Zien, cast)
A Marriage Proposal (Zien)
A Tight-Knit Family (reprise) (Rupert, Zien)
Trina's Song (Fraser)
March of the Falsettos (men)
The Chess Game (Rupert, Bogardus)
Making a Home (Fraser, Zien, Bogardus)
The Games I Play (Bogardus)
Marvin Hits Trina (cast)
I Never Wanted to Love You (cast)
Father to Son (Rupert, Kushner)

MARRY ME A LITTLE (March 12, 1981, Off Broadway, Actors Playhouse)

RCA ABL 1-4159 stereo

Music, lyrics: Stephen Sondheim; musical direction: E. Martin Perry

Cast: Suzanne Henry, Craig Lucas

Songs: Saturday Night (Henry, Lucas)
Two Fairy Tales (Henry, Lucas)
All Things Bright and Beautiful (Henry, Lucas)
Bang! (Henry, Lucas)
All Things Bright and Beautiful - Part 2 (Henry, Lucas)
The Girls of Summer (Henry)
Uptown, Downtown (Lucas)
So Many People (Henry, Lucas)

Your Eyes are Blue (Henry, Lucas)
A Moment with You (Henry, Lucas)
Marry Me a Little (Henry)
Happily Ever After (Lucas)
Pour le Sport (Henry, Lucas)
Silly People (Lucas)
There Won't Be Trumpets (Henry)
It Wasn't Meant to Happen (Henry, Lucas)

Who Could Be Blue? (Lucas)
Little White House (Henry)

MASK AND GOWN (September 10, 1957, John Golden Theatre)

AEI Records 1178 mono

Special music, lyrics: June Carroll, Dorothea Freitag, Ronny Graham, Arthur Siegel; musical direction: Dorothea Freitag

Cast: T.C. Jones

Songs: The Circus Is Over (ensemble)
T.C. on T.V. - Your Money or Your Life (Jones) spoken
Catch! (Jones, cast)
Ten Cents a Dance (Jones)
T.C. on Hollywood (Jones) spoken
T.C. on Certain Singers (Jones)

On Certain Singers - continuation (Jones)
T.C.-on-Avon (Jones, cast)
The Circus is Over (reprise) (ensemble)
You Better Go Now (Jones, cast)
I'll Be Seeing You (Jones)
T.C. Jones - Himself (Jones) spoken

Note: A live recording.

MASS (June 26, 1972, Metropolitan Opera House)

Columbia M2 31008 (two records) stereo

Music: Leonard Bernstein; Text from the Liturgy of the Roman Mass; additional texts, Stephen Schwartz, Leonard Bernstein; musical director: Leonard Bernstein

Cast: David Cryer, Ed Dixon, Eugene Edwards, Tom Ellis, Joy Franz, Carl Hall, Lee Hooper, Larry Marshall, Gina Penn, Mary Bracken Phillips, Marion Ramsey, Louis St. Louis, Alan Titus, Ronald Young

Songs: A Simple Song (Titus)
I Don't Know (Young, Hall)
Easy (Edwards, Franz, Dixon, Ramsey, St. Louis)

Gloria Tibi (Titus)
Thank You (Hooper)
The Word of the Lord (Titus)
God Said (Marshall, ensemble)

Non Credo (Cryer)
Hurry (Penn)
World Without End (Phillips)
I Believe in God (Ellis)
Our Father (Titus)
I Go On (Titus)

Things Get Broken (Titus)
Secret Songs (ensemble)

Note: This recording was made prior to the New York production with some minor cast changes.

MAYOR - THE MUSICAL (May 13, 1985, Off Broadway, Village Gate)

New York Music Records NYM 21 stereo CD

Music, lyrics: Charles Strouse; based on Mayor by Edward I. Koch; musical direction: Michael Kosarin

Cast: Douglas Bernstein, Marion J. Caffey, Keith Curran, Nancy Giles, Ken Jennings, Ilene Kristen, Kathryn McAteer, Lenny Wolpe

Songs: Overture (orchestra)
Mayor (Wolpe)
You Can Be a New Yorker Too! (Curran, Bernstein, company)
You're Not the Mayor (McAteer, Caffey, Jennings)
March of the Yuppies (Giles, Curran, Bernstein, company)
Hootspa (Wolpe, Curran, Jennings)
What You See Is What You Get (Giles, Wolpe)
Ballad (Kristen, Curran)

I Want to Be the Mayor (Bernstein)
The Last 'I Love New York' Song (company)
Good Times (Kristen, Giles, Curran, Jennings, Bernstein, Wolpe)
I'll Never Leave You (Caffey, McAteer, Kristen, Curran)
How'm I Doin'? (Wolpe, Jennings, company)
Finale (Wolpe, company)
My City (company)
Bows (company)

ME AND JULIET (May 28, 1953, Majestic Theatre)

RCA LOC 1012 mono

Music: Richard Rodgers; yrics: Oscar Hammerstein II; musical direction: Salvatore Dell'Isola

Cast: Isabel Bigley, Mark Dawson, Bob Fortier, Bill Hayes, Jackie Kelk, Joan McCracken, Arthur Maxwell

Songs: Overture (orchestra)
A Very Special Day (Bigley)
That's the Way It Happens (Bigley, Hayes)
Marriage Type Love (Maxwell, chorus)
Keep It Gay (Dawson, chorus)
No Other Love (Bigley, Hayes)
The Big Black Giant (Hayes)

It's Me (McCracken, Bigley)
Intermission Talk (Kelk, chorus)
It Feels Good (Dawson)
We Deserve Each Other (McCracken, Fortier)
I'm Your Girl (Bigley, Hayes)
Finale (company)

ME AND MY GIRL (August 10, 1986, Marquis Theatre)

MCA Records 6196 stereo CD

Music: Noel Gay; lyrics: L. Arthur Rose, Douglas Furber; musical direction: Stanley Lebowsky

Cast: Jane Connell, George S. Irving, Timothy Jerome, Robert Lindsay, Maryann Plunkett, Jane Summerhays, Thomas Toner, Nick Ullett

Songs: Overture (orchestra)
A Weekend at Hareford (ensemble)
Thinking of No One but Me (Summerhays, Ullett)
The Family Solicitor (Jerome, family)
Me and My Girl (Lindsay, Plunkett)
An English Gentleman (Toner, staff)
You Would If You Could (Summerhays, Lindsay)
Hold My Hand (Lindsay, Plunkett, chorus)
Once You Lose Your Heart (Plunkett)

The Lambeth Walk (Lindsay, Plunkett, company)
The Sun Has Got His Hat On (Ullett, Summerhays, ensemble)
Take It on the Chin (Plunkett)
Song of Hareford (Connell, Lindsay, ensemble)
Love Makes the World Go Round (Lindsay, Irving, ensemble)
Once You Lose Your Heart (reprise) (Plunkett)
Leaning on a Lamp Post (Lindsay)
Finale (company)

THE ME NOBODY KNOWS (May 18, 1970, Off Broadway, Orpheum Theatre)

Atlantic Records SD 1566 stereo

Music: Gary William Friedman; lyrics: Will Holt; based on the book edited by Stephen M. Joseph; musical direction: Edward Strauss

Cast: Beverly Ann Bremers, Northern J. Calloway, Irene Cara, Gerri Dean, Jose Fernandez, Douglas Grant, Melanie Henderson, Devin Lindsay, Carl Thoma, Hattie Winston

Songs: Introduction (Henderson)
Dream Babies (Dean)
Light Sings (Lindsay, company)
This World (company)
How I Feel (Bremers, Fernandez)
The White Horse (Calloway)
If I Had a Million Dollars (company)

Sounds (Winston, Bremers)
The Tree (Fernandez)
Something Beautiful (Henderson)
Sounds (reprise) (Winston, Bremers)

Black (Grant, Thoma, Cara, Calloway, Dean, Winston, Henderson, Lindsay)
War Babies (Calloway)
Let Me Come In (company)

THE MEGILLA OF ITZIK MANGER (October 9, 1968, John Golden Theatre)

Columbia OS 3270 stereo

Music: Dov Seltzer; English commentaries: Joe Darion; musical direction: Dov Seltzer

Cast: Mike Burstein, Pesach Burstein, Lillian Lux

Songs: Overture and Prologue (company)
Der Nigun Fun der Megilla/Theme of the Megilla (company)
Dem Melech's Sudeh/The King's Party (company)
Vashti's Kloglid/Vashti's Last Mile (Lux)
Der Alter Nussenboim/The Walnut Tree (company)
Di Elegiye Fun Fastrigosso/Fastrigosso's Lament (M. Burstein)
In Droissen Iz a Regen/Song of the Rain (company)
Flits Fegelech/Fly, Little Bird (M. Burstein, company)

Gevald/The Gevald Aria (company)
Kum Arain In Shenk/The Tailor's Drinking Song (company)
S'a Mechaye/The King's Song (P. Burstein)
Das Lid Fun der Goldener Paveh/The Golden Peacock (company)
Dos Shneider Lid/Tailor's Song (company)
Mir Velen Nisht Fasten/Revolutionary Song (company)
Fastrigosso's Mame/A Mother's Tears (Lux)
Der Fetter Mord'che Heist/Uncle Mordechai Is So Smart (M. Burstein, Lux)
Chiribim (company)
Lechaim/A Toast to the Players (company)

MERRILY WE ROLL ALONG (November 16, 1981, Alvin Theatre)

RCA CBL 1-4197 stereo CD

Music, lyrics: Stephen Sondheim; from the play by George S. Kaufman, Moss Hart; musical direction: Paul Gemignani

Cast: Jason Alexander, Marianna Allen, Donna Marie Elio, Sally Klein, David Loud, Ann Morrison, Lonny Price, Jim Walton

Songs: Overture (orchestra)
The Hills of Tomorrow (company)
Merrily We Roll Along - 1980 (company)
Rich and Happy (Walton, guests)
Merrily We Roll Along - 1979 - 1975 (company)
Old Friends (Morrison, Price)
Like It Was (Morrison)

Merrily We Roll Along - 1974 - 1973 (trio)
Franklin Shepard, Inc. (Price)
Old Friends (Morrison, Walton, Price)
Not a Day Goes By (Walton)

Now You Know (Morrison, company)
Merrily We Roll Along - 1964 - 1962 (Elio, company)
Good Thing Going (Price, Walton, company)
Merrily We Roll Along - 1961 - 1960 (company)
Bobby and Jackie and Jack (Price, Klein, Walton, Loud)
Not a Day Goes By (reprise) (Walton, Morrison)
Opening Doors (Walton, Price, Morrison, Alexander, Allen, Klein)
Our Time (Walton, Price, Morrison, company)
The Hills of Tomorrow (reprise) (company)

Note: The following additional selection is included on A Collector's Sondheim, RCA CRL 4-5359:

It's a Hit! (Alexander, Walton, Morrison, Price)

THE MERRY WIDOW (Revival, October 7, 1944, City Center)

Decca DLP 8004 mono

Music: Franz Lehar; lyrics: Adrian Ross; musical direction: Isaac Van Grove

Cast: Kitty Carlisle, Wilbur Evans, Felix Knight, Lisette Verea

Songs: The Merry Widow Overture (orchestra)
In Marsovia (Carlisle, male chorus)
Maxim's (Evans)
Finale of Act I (Carlisle, Evans, chorus)
Down in Dear Marsovia (chorus)

Vilia (Carlisle, male chorus)
Women (Evans, Knight, male chorus)
Love in My Heart (Knight)
Finale of Act II (Carlisle, Evans, chorus)
The Girls at Maxim's (Verea, chorus)
I Love You So (The Merry Widow Waltz) (Carlisle, Evans)
Finale (Carlisle, Evans, chorus)

Note: Studio recording, with Lisette Verea being the only member of the stage cast.

THE MERRY WIDOW (Revival, August 17, 1964, New York State Theatre)

RCA LSO 1094 stereo

New lyrics: Foreman Brown; musical direction: Franz Allers

Cast: Sig Arno, Mischa Auer, Luce Ennis, Robert Goss, Marion Haraldson, Joseph Leon, Patrice Munsel, Frank Porretta, Wood Romoff, Rudy Vejar, Joan Weldon, Bob Wright

Songs: Overture (orchestra)
When in France (Goss, Vejar, Weldon, Haraldson, Ennis, Auer, chorus)
Respectable Wife (Weldon, Porretta)
Who Know the Way to My Heart? (Munsel, Goss, Vejar, chorus)
Maxim's (Wright, chorus)
Riding on a Carousel (Munsel, Wright)
Finale Act I (Munsel, Wright, chorus)

Vilia (Munsel, chorus)
Women (Auer, Arno, Leon, Romoff, Goss, Vejar)
Romance (Porretta, Weldon)
Finale Act II (Munsel, Wright, Porretta, Weldon, chorus)
Girl at Maxim's (Munsel, chorus)
I Love You So (The Merry Widow Waltz) (Munsel, Wright, chorus)

THE MERRY WIDOW (Revival, April 2, 1978, A New York City Opera Production, New York State Theatre)

Angel S 37500 stereo

Lyrics: Sheldon Harnick; musical direction: Julius Rudel

Cast: James Billings, Harlan Foss, Glenys Fowles, Thomas Jamerson, Alan Kays, Henry Price, Beverly Sills, David Rae Smith, Alan Titus

Songs: Anna's Entrance (Sills, Jamerson, Kays, men)
Oh Fatherland (Maxim's) (Titus)
Do Listen, Please (Fowles, Price)
Act I Finale (Sills, Titus, Jamerson, Kays, Fowles, chorus)
Dances (chorus)

Vilia (Sills, chorus)
Heia! See the Horseman Come (Sills, Titus)
Ev'ry Woman (Titus, Smith, Kays, Jamerson, Foss, Billings)
Just As a Rosebud Blossoms (Fowles, Price)
Act II Finale (Titus, Smith, Sills, Fowles, Price, Billings, chorus)
Grisette Song (Fowles, female chorus)
Tres Parisien (Billings, chorus)
Strings Are Sighing (Waltz) (Titus, Sills)
Act III Finale (company)

MEXICAN HAYRIDE (January 28, 1944, Winter Garden Theatre)

Decca DL 5232 mono reissued: Columbia CSP X-14878

Music, lyrics: Cole Porter; musical direction: Harry Sosnik

Cast: Wilbur Evans, June Havoc, Corinna Mura

Songs: Sing to Me, Guitar (Mura, chorus)

Carlotta (Mura, male chorus)
I Love You (Evans)
Girls (Evans, girls chorus)
There Must Be Some One for Me (Havoc)
Abracadabra (Havoc, male chorus)
Count Your Blessings (Havoc, male chorus)
What a Crazy Way to Spend Sunday (chorus)

MILK AND HONEY (October 10, 1961, Martin Beck Theatre)

RCA LSO 1065 stereo

Music, lyrics: Jerry Herman; musical direction: Max Goberman

Cast: Juki Arkin, Mimi Benzell, Molly Picon, Tommy Rall, Robert Weede

Songs: Overture (orchestra)
Shalom (Weede, Bensell)
Independence Day Hora (company)
Milk and Honey (Rall, Arkin, company)
There's No Reason in the World (Weede)
Chin Up, Ladies (Picon, women)
That Was Yesterday (Benzell, company)

Let's Not Waste a Moment (Weede)
The Wedding (Benzell, Weede, company)
Like a Young Man (Weede)
I Will Follow You (Rall)
Hymn to Hymie (Picon)
As Simple As That (Benzell, Weede)
Finale (company)

MINNIE'S BOYS (March 26, 1970, Imperial Theatre)

Project 3 Records TS 6002 SD stereo

Music: Larry Grossman; lyrics: Hal Hackady; musical direction: John Berkman

Cast: Jacqueline Britt, Jean Bruno, Daniel Fortus, Arny Freeman, Merwin Goldsmith, Alvin Kupperman, Julie Kurnitz, Mort Marshall, Irwin Pearl, Gary Raucher, Richard B. Shull, Lewis J. Stadlen, Shelley Winters

Songs: Overture (orchestra)
Five Growing Boys (Winters, company)
Rich Is (Marshall, Winters, Freeman, Stadlen, Fortus, Pearl, Kupperman, Raucher)
Empty (Freeman)
The Four Nightingales (Stadlen, Fortus, Kupperman)
Underneath It All (Shull, girls)
Mama, a Rainbow (Fortus, Winters)
You Don't Have to Do It for Me (Winters, Fortus, Stadlen, Pearl, Kupperman)

Where Was I When They Passed Out Luck? (Stadlen, Kupperman, Fortus, Pearl)

You Remind Me of You (Stadlen, Kurnitz)
They Give Me Love (Winters)
Minnie's Boys (Britt, Goldsmith, Bruno, Winters, Marshall, company)
Be Happy! (Winters, Fortus, Kupperman, Pearl, Raucher)
The Act - Finale (Winters, Stadlen, Fortus, Pearl, Kupperman, company)

MISS LIBERTY (July 15, 1949, Imperial Theatre)

Columbia ML 4220 mono

Music, lyrics: Irving Berlin; musical direction: Jay Blackton

Cast: Eddie Albert, Ethel Griffies, Mary McCarty, Allyn McLerie, Johnny V. R. Thompson

Songs: Overture (orchestra)
I'd Like My Picture Took (McCarty)
The Most Expensive Statue in the World (ensemble)
Little Fish in a Big Pond (Albert, McLerie)
Let's Take an Old-Fashioned Walk (Albert, McLerie)
Homework (McCarty)
Paris Wakes Up and Smiles (Thompson)

Only for Americans (Griffies)
(Just One Way to Say) I Love You (Albert, McLerie)
You Can Have Him (McCarty, McLerie)
The Policeman's Ball (McCarty)
Falling Out of Love Can Be Fun (McCarty)
Give Me Your Tired, Your Poor (McLerie) words: Emma Lazarus

MR. PRESIDENT (October 20, 1962, St. James Theatre)

Columbia KOS 2270 stereo

Music, lyrics: Irving Berlin; musical direction: Jay Blackton

Cast: David Brooks, Wiza D'Orso, Nanette Fabray, Anita Gillette, Stanley Grover, Jack Haskell, Robert Ryan, Jerry Strickler, Jack Washburn

Songs: Opening (Brooks)
Let's Go Back to the Waltz (Fabray, chorus)
In Our Hide-Away (Fabray, Ryan)
The First Lady (Fabray)
Meat and Potatoes (Haskell, Grover)
I've Got to Be Around (Haskell)
The Secret Service (Gillette)
It Gets Lonely in the White House (Ryan)
Is He the Only Man in the World (Fabray, Gillette)
They Love Me (Fabray, chorus)

Pigtails and Freckles (Haskell, Gillette)
Don't Be Afraid of Romance (Washburn)
Laugh It Up (Fabray, Ryan, Gillette, Strickler)
Empty Pockets Filled with Love (Haskell, Gillette)

Glad to Be Home (Fabray, chorus)
You Need a Hobby (Fabray, Ryan)
The Washington Twist (Gillette)
Song for a Belly Dancer (D'Orso, girls)
I'm Gonna Get Him (Fabray, Gillette)
This Is a Great Country (Ryan, company)

MR. WONDERFUL (March 22, 1956, Broadway Theatre)

Decca DL 9032 mono

Music, lyrics: Jerry Bock, Larry Holofcener, George Weiss; musical direction: Morton Stevens

Cast: Jack Carter, Sammy Davis, Jr., Olga James, Hal Loman, Pat Marshall, Will Mastin Trio, Chita Rivera

Songs: Overture (orchestra)
1617 Broadway (Rivera, Loman, chorus)
Without You I'm Nothing (Carter, Marshall)
Jacques d'Iraque (Mastin Trio, chorus)
Mr. Wonderful (James)
Ethel, Baby (James, Davis)
Charlie Welch (Carter, chorus)
Too Close for Comfort (Davis)

Talk to Him (Marshall, James)
There (Davis)
Miami (Marshall, chorus)
Without You I'm Nothing (reprise) (Carter, Davis)
I'm Available (Rivera)
I've Been too Busy (James, Carter, Marshall, Davis)
Sing You Sinners (Davis) music, lyrics: W. Franke Harling, Sam Coslow
Mr. Wonderful - finale (company)

MRS. PATTERSON (December 1, 1954, National Theatre)

RCA LOC 1017 mono

Music, lyrics: Charles Sebree, Greer Johnson, James Shelton; musical direction: Abba Bogin

Cast: Helen Dowdy, Eartha Kitt

Songs: Overture (orchestra)
Mrs. Patterson (Kitt)
If I Was a Boy (kitt)
I Wish I Was a Bumble Bee (Dowdy)

Be Good, Be Good, Be Good (Kitt)
Tea in Chicago (Kitt)
My Daddy Is a Dandy (Kitt)

Note: This recording is primarily spoken word.

MIXED DOUBLES (October 19, 1966, Off Broadway, Upstairs at the Downstairs)

UD-37E56-VOL 2 (two records, with BELOW THE BELT) stereo

Music: J.S. Bach, Gene Bissell, Michael Cohen, Ed Kresley, Stephen Lawrence, Jerry Powell, June Reizner, Richard Robinson, James Ruck, Franklin Underwood, Bill Weeden; lyrics: Gene Bissell, David Finkel, Tony Geiss, John Meyer, June Reizner, James Rusk, Drey Shepard, Franklin Underwood, Michael McWhinney, Rod Warren; musical direction: Michael Cohen

Cast: Judy Graubart, Madeline Kahn, Larry Moss, Robert Rovin, Janie Sell, Gary Sneed

Songs: Overture (pianos)
Mixed Doubles (company) music: Bach; lyrics: Warren
New York Is a Festival of Fun (Kahn, Sell, Rovin, Sneed) music, lyrics: Bissell
The Newlyweds (Graubart, Moss) spoken
Questions (Kahn, Rovin, Sneed) music: Kresley; lyrics: Shepard
Mixed Marriages (Sell, Moss) music: Weeden; lyrics: Finkel
Man with a Problem (Graubart, Rovin) spoken
Friendly, Liberal Neighborhood (men) music, lyrics: Reizner

Spoleto (company) music: Powell; lyrics: McWhinney
Sartor Sartoris (Moss, Rovin) music, lyrics: Underwood
Fashion Show (Kahn, Sneed, Graubart) spoken
Bon Voyeur (Moss) music, lyrics: Rusk
Ronald Reagan (ladies) music: Kresley; lyrics: Shepard
Holden and Phoebe (Graubart, Rovin) music: Cohen lyrics: McWhinney
More Questions (Graubart, Kahn, Rovin, Sneed)
The Fat Song (Sell) music, lyrics: Rusk

And a Messenger Appeared (Kahn, company) music, lyrics: Bissell
Britannia Rules (Graubart) music: Powell; lyrics: Warren
Still More Questions (company)
Das Chicago-Song (Kahn) music: Cohen; lyrics: Geiss
Bobby the K (Rovin) music: Robinson; lyrics: McWhinney
Civilian Review Board (Sell, Sneed) spoken

And a Few More Questions (company)
Best Wishes (company) music: Lawrence; lyrics: Meyer

Note: A live recording.

THE MOST HAPPY FELLA (May 3, 1956, Imperial Theatre)

Columbia O3L-240 (three records) mono

Music, lyrics: Frank Loesser; based on Sidney Howard's They Knew What They Wanted; musical direction: Herbert Greene

Cast: Lee Cass, Rico Froehlich, Alan Gilbert, John Henson,

Susan Johnson, Keith Kaldenberg, Roy Lazarus, Shorty Long, Art Lund, Mona Paulee, Arthur Rubin, Jo Sullivan, Robert Weede

Songs: Prelude, Act I (orchestra)*
Ooh, My Feet (Johnson)*
I Know How It Is (Johnson, Sullivan)
Seven Million Crumbs (Johnson)
The Letter (Sullivan)
Somebody Somewhere (Sullivan)*
The Most Happy Fella (Weede, chorus)*
Standing on the Corner (Long, Gilbert, Henson, Lazarus)*

The Letter Theme (Weede, Paulee)
Joey, Joey, Joey (Lund)*
Soon You Gonna Leave Me, Joe (Weede)
Rosabella (Weede)*
Abbondanza (Rubin, Froehlich, Henson)*
Plenty Bambini (Weede)
Sposalizio (chorus)*

Special Delivery! (Cass)
Benvenuta (Rubin, Froehlich, Henson, Lund)
Aren't You Glad? (Sullivan)
Don't Cry (Lund, Sullivan)*
Finale, Act I (orchestra)

Prelude, Act II (orchestra)
Fresno Beauties (Cold and Dead) (men, Sullivan, Lund)
Love and Kindness (Kaldenberg)
Happy to Make Your Acquaintance (Sullivan, Weede, Johnson)*
I Don't Like This Dame (Paulee, Johnson)
Big 'D' (Johnson, Long, chorus)*
How Beautiful the Days (Weede, Sullivan, Paulee, Lund)*

Young People (Paulee, Weede, chorus)
Warm All Over (Sullivan)*
Old People (Weede)
I Like Everybody (Long, Johnson)*
I Know How It Is (reprise) (Johnson)
I Love Him (Sullivan)
Like a Woman Loves a Man (Sullivan)
My Heart Is So Full of You (Weede, Sullivan)*
Hoedown (Weede, Sullivan, chorus)
Mama, Mama (Weede)*

Prelude, Act III (orchestra)
Abbondanza (reprise) (Froehlich, Rubin, Henson)
Goodbye, Darlin' (Johnson, Long)
Song of a Summer Night (Kaldenberg, chorus)*
Please Let Me Tell You (Sullivan)
Tony's Thoughts (Weede)
She Gonna Come Home with Me (Weede, Paulee, Johnson)
I Made a Fist (Long, Johnson)*
Finale (Weede, Sullivan, company)*

Note: Complete recording, including dialog. Some selections (*) are included on a one record version, AOS 2330.

THE MUSIC MAN (December 19, 1957, Majestic Theatre)

Capitol SW 990 stereo

Music, lyrics: Meredith Willson; musical direction: Herbert Greene

Cast: Barbara Cook, Martha Flynn, Eddie Hodges, Pert Kelton, Peggy Mondo, Robert Preston, Helen Raymond, Paul Reed, Adnia Rice, Elaine Swann, Iggie Wolfington

Songs: Overture (orchestra)
Rock Island (Reed, men)
Iowa Stubborn (ensemble)
Ya Got Trouble (Preston, ensemble)
Piano Lesson (Cook, Kelton)
Goodnight My Someone (Cook)
Seventy-Six Trombones (Preston, ensemble)
Sincere (male quartet)
The Sadder-But-Wiser Girl for Me (Preston)
Pick-a-Little, Talk-a-Little (Raymond, Swann, Mondo, Rice, Flynn)
Goodnight Ladies (male quartet)

Marian the Librarian (Preston)
My White Knight (Cook)
Wells Fargo Wagon (Hodges, ensemble)
It's You (male quartet)
Shipoopi (Wolfington, ensemble)
Lida Rose (male quartet)
Will I Ever Tell You (Cook)
Gary, Indiana (Hodges)
Till There Was You (Cook, Preston)
Finale (comapany)

MUSICAL CHAIRS (May 14, 1980, Rialto Theatre)

Original Cast Records OC 8024 stereo

Music, lyrics: Tom Savage; musical direction: Barry Gordon

Cast: Enid Blaymore, Helen Blount, Tom Breslin, Edward Earle, Randall Easterbrook, Scott Ellis, Rick Emery, Joy Franz, Patti Karr, Brandon Maggart, Jess Richards, Tom Urich, Leslie-Anne Wolfe

Songs: Tonight's the Night (company)
My Time (Urich)
Who's Who (company)
If I Could Be Beautiful (Wolfe, boys)
What I Could Have Done Tonight (Maggart, Franz)
There You Are (Emery)
Sally (Ellis, company)
Other People (Franz)

Hit the Ladies (Karr, ladies)
Musical Chairs (Emery, Breslin, Earle)
Suddenly, Love (Richards)
Better Than Broadway (Blaymore, Blount)
Every Time the Music Starts (Easterbrook, company)
My Time (reprise) (Urich)
Finale (company)

MY FAIR LADY (March 15, 1956, Mark Hellinger Theatre)

Columbia OL 5090 mono reissued: CSP AOL 5090

Music: Frederick Loewe; lyrics: Alan Jay Lerner; adapted from Bernard Shaw's Pygmalion; musical direction: Franz Allers

Cast: Julie Andrews, Philippa Bevans, Robert Coote, Gordon Dilworth, Michael King, Rex Harrison, Stanley Holloway, Rod McLennan

Songs: Overture (orchestra)
Why Can't the English? (Harrison)
Wouldn't It Be Loverly (Andrews, ensemble)
With a Little Bit of Luck (Holloway, Dilworth, McLennan)
I'm an Ordinary Man (Harrison)
Just You Wait (Andrews)
The Rain in Spain (Harrison, Andrews, Coote)
I Could Have Danced All Night (Andrews, Bevans)

Ascot Gavotte (ensemble)
On the Street Where You Live (King)
You Did It (Harrison, Coote, Bevans)
Show Me (Andrews, King)
Get Me to the Church on Time (Holloway, Dilworth, McLennan)
A Hymn to Him (Harrison)
Without You (Andrews)
I've Grown Accustomed to Her Face (Harrison)

Note: Principal cast members re-recorded this score in stereo in London, February, 1959.

MY FAIR LADY (Revival, March 25, 1976, St. James Theatre)

Columbia PS 34197 stereo

Musical direction: Theodore Saidenberg

Cast: Christine Andreas, Robert Coote, Jerry Lanning, Sylvia O'Brien, Ian Richardson, George Rose

Songs: Overture (orchestra)
Why Can't the English (Richardson)
Wouldn't It Be Loverly (Andreas, ensemble)
With a Little Bit of Luck (Rose, ensemble)
I'm an Ordinary Man (Richardson)
Just You Wait (andreas)
The Rain in Spain (Richardson, Andreas, Coote, ensemble)
I Could Have Danced All Night (Andreas, O'Brien, maids)

Ascot Gavotte (ensemble)
Embassy Waltz (orchestra)
On the Street Where You Live (Lanning)
You Did It (Richardson, Coote, O'Brien, ensemble)
Show Me (Andreas, Lanning)
Get Me to the Church on Time (Rose, ensemble)
A Hymn to Him (Richardson, Coote)
Without You (Andreas)

I've Grown Accustomed to Her Face (Richardson)

MY ONE AND ONLY (May 1, 1983, St. James Theatre)

Atlantic Records 80110-1-E stereo

Music: George Gershwin; lyrics: Ira Gershwin; musical direction: Jack Lee

Cast: Roscoe Lee Browne, Charles 'Honi' Coles, Jill Cook, Denny Dillon, Bruce McGill, Tommy Tune, Twiggy

Songs: Overture (orchestra)
I Can't Be Bothered Now (Tune, company)
Blah, Blah, Blah (Tune)
Boy Wanted (Twiggy, Cook)
Soon (tune)
Sweet 'n Low Down (Coles, Tune, Twiggy)
He Loves and She Loves (Tune, Twiggy)
's Wonderful (Tune, Twiggy)
Strike Up the Band (Tune)

Entr'acte (orchestra)
In the Swim (girls)
Nice Work If You Can Get It (Twiggy)
My One and Only (Coles, Tune)
Little Jazz Bird (Tune, Twiggy)
Funny Face (Dillon, McGill)
Kickin' the Clouds Away (Browne, company)
How Long Has This Been Going On? (Twiggy, Tune)

Note: 'Little Jazz Bird' was not used in the New York production.

THE MYSTERY OF EDWIN DROOD (August 21, 1985, Off Broadway, Delacorte Theatre; transferred, December 2, 1985, Imperial Theatre)

Polydor 827 969-1 Y-1 stereo CD

Music, lyrics: Rupert Holmes; suggested by the unfinished novel by Charles Dickens; musical direction: Michael Starobin

Cast: Betty Buckley, Patti Cohenour, Jerome Dempsey, Stephen Glavin, Joe Grifasi, John Herrera, Judy Kuhn, Cleo Laine, Howard McGillin, George N. Martin, Donna Murphy, George Rose, Jana Schneider

Songs: There You Are (Rose, Laine, Buckley, McGillin, Cohenour, company)
A Man Could Go Quite Mad (McGillin)
Two Kinsmen (Buckley, McGillin)
Moonfall (Cohenour)
Moonfall Quartet (Cohenour, Schneider, Kuhn, Murphy)
The Wages of Sin (Laine)
Ceylon (Schneider, Herrera, Buckley, McGillin, ensemble)

Both Sides of the Coin (McGillin, Rose)
Perfect Strangers (Buckley, Cohenour)
No Good Can Come from Bad (Herrera, Cohenour, Schneider, Martin, McGillin, Buckley)
Never the Luck (Grifasi)

The Name of Love (Cohenour, McGillin)
Moonfall (reprise) (Cohanour, McGillin, ensemble)
Settling Up the Score (Buckley, Laine, ensemble)
Off to the Races (Rose, Dempsey, Glavin, ensemble)
Don't Quit While You're Ahead (Laine, company)
The Garden Path to Hell (Laine)
Out on a Limerick (Grifasi)
Jasper's Confession (McGillin)
Puffer's Confession (Laine)
The Writing on the Wall (Buckley, company)

Note: The CD version contains the following multiple endings:
Out on a Limerick
1. Rosa Bud (Cohenour)
2. Rev. Crisparkle (Martin)
3. Bazzard (Grifasi)
4. Neville Landless (Herrera)
5. Helena Landless (Schneider)

Murderer's Confession
1. Princess Puffer (Laine)
2. Rosa Bud (Cohenour)
3. Bazzard (Grifasi)
4. Rev. Crisparkle (Martin)
5. Neville Landless (Herrera)
6. Helena Landless (Schneider)

THE NERVOUS SET (May 12, 1959, Henry Miller Theatre)

Columbia OS 2018 stereo

Music: Tommy Wolf; lyrics: Fran Landsman; based on the novel by Jay Landesman; musical direction: Tommy Wolf

Cast: Thomas Aldredge, Del Close, Larry Hagman, Richard Hayes, Gerald Hiken, Tani Seitz

Songs: Overture (orchestra)
Man, We're Beat (company)
New York (Hayes, Aldredge, Seitz)
What's to Lose (Seitz, Hayes)
Stars Have Blown My Way (Seitz, Hayes)
Fun Life (Hayes)
How Do You Like Your Love (Close)
Party Song (company)
Night People (Hayes, Seitz)

Overture, Act 2 (orchestra)
Party Song (company)
I've Got a Lot to Learn About Life (Seitz)
The Ballad of the Sad Young Men (Seitz)
A Country Gentleman (Hayes, Seitz)
Max the Millionaire (Hiken, Hayes, Close, Aldredge)
Travel the Road of Love (Hagman, company)
Laugh, I Though I'd Die (Hayes)

Fun Life (reprise) (company)

NEW FACES OF 1952 (May 16, 1952, Royale Theatre)

RCA LOC 1008 mono reissued: RCA CBM 1-2206

Music: Michael Brown, Ronny Graham, Murray Grand, Sheldon Harnick, Francis Lemarque, Arthur Siegel; lyrics: Elisse Boyd, Michael Brown, June Carroll, Peter De Vries, Herbert Farjean, Ronny Graham, Sheldon Harnick, Francis Lemarque; musical direction: Anton Coppola

Cast: Virginia Bosler, June Carroll, Robert Clary, Allen Conroy, Virginia de Luce, Alice Ghostley, Ronny Graham, Patricia Hammerlee, Eartha Kitt, Joseph Lautner, Paul Lynde, Bill Mullikin, Rosemary O'Reilly

Songs: Opening (Graham, company) music: Graham; lyrics: De Vries
Lucky Pierre (Clary, de Luce, O'Reilly, Hammerlee, Mullikin) music, lyrics: Graham
Boston Beguine (Ghostley; introduction by de Luce) music, lyrics: Harnick
Love Is a Simple Thing (O'Reilly, Clary, Kitt, Carroll; introduction by de Luce) music: Siegel; lyrics: Carroll
Nanty Puts Her Hair Up (Ghostley, Lautner, Bosler, Millikin, Conroy; introduction by de Luce) music: Siegel; lyrics: Farjean
Guess Who I Saw Today (Carroll) music: Grand; lyrics: Boyd
Bal Petit Bal (Kitt; introduction by Clary) music, lyrics: Lemarque
---
Three for the Road (introduction by de Luce) music, lyrics: Graham
It's Raining Memories (Clary)
Waltzing in Vienna (O'Reilly, Lautner)
Take Off the Mask (Ghostley, Graham, company)
Penny Candy (Carroll, company) music: Siegel; lyrics: Carroll
Don't Fall Asleep (O'Reilly) music, lyrics: Graham
I'm in Love with Miss Logan (Clary, O'Reilly, Lautner; introduction by de Luce) music, lyrics: Graham
Monotonous (Kitt) music: Siegel; lyrics: Carroll
Time for Tea (Carroll, Ghostley) music: Siegel; lyrics: Carroll
Lizzie Borden (Lautner, Mulliken, Lynde, Hammerlee, company) music, lyrics: Brown
He Takes Me Off His Income Tax (introductions by de Luce) music: Siegel; lyrics: Carroll

Note: "Time for Tea" was not included on LOC 1008. It was on Painted Smiles, PS 1364, Ballet on Broadway.

NEW FACES OF 1956 (June 14, 1956, Ethel Barrymore Theatre)

RCA LOC 1025 mono

Music: Marshall Barer, Dean Fuller, Ronny Graham, Murray Grand, Harold Karr, Paul Nassau, John Rox, Arthur Siegel; lyrics: Elisse Boyd, Marshall Barer, June Carroll, Matt Dubey, Ronny Graham, Murray Grand, Leslie Julian-Jones, Peter Nassau, John Rox, Sid Silvers; musical direction: Jay Blackton

Cast: Jane Connell, Billie Hayes, Johnny Haymer, Tiger Haynes, Ann Henry, T.C. Jones, Virginia Martin, John Reardon, Amru Sani, Bob Shaver, Maggie Smith, Inga Swenson

Songs: Opening (Jones, company) music, lyrics: Graham
Tell Her (Reardon) music: Siegel; lyrics: Carroll
And He Flipped (Henry) music, lyrics: Rox
Boy Most Likely to Succeed (Swenson) music: Siegel; lyrics: Carroll
Talent (Martin) music, lyrics: Nassau
Mustapha (Abdullah Abu Ben Al Rahjid) (Sani) music: Fuller; lyrics: Barer
The Greatest Invention (Hayes, Haymer) music: Karr; lyrics: Dubey
Isn't She Lovely (Jones, company) music: Fuller, Silvers; lyrics: Barer
---
The White Witch of Jamica (Reardon) music: Siegel; lyrics: Carroll
Don't Wait 'Til It's Too Late to See Paris (Bernard, Reardon) music: Siegel; lyrics: Carroll
April in Fairbanks (Connell) music, lyrics: Grand
Hurry (Sani) music: Grand; lyrics: Boyd
One Perfect Moment (Smith) music: Barer, Fuller; lyrics: Julian-Jones
La Ronde (Haymer, Swenson, Shaver, Martin) music: Fuller; lyrics: Barer
Scratch My Back (Haynes, Henry) music: Fuller; lyrics: Barer

NEW FACES OF 1968 (May 2, 1968, Booth Theatre)

Warner Brothers Records BS 2551 stereo

Music: Michael Cohen, Carl Friberg, Clark Gesner, Ronny Graham, Murray Grand, Fred Hellerman, Alonzo Levister, Sam Pottle, Jerry Powell, Sidney Shaw, Arthur Siegel; lyrics: David Axelrod, June Carroll, Tony Geiss, Clark Gesner, Ronny Graham, Murray Grand, Hal Hackady, Michael McWhinney, Fred Minkoff, Paul Nassau, Sidney Shaw; musical direction: Ted Simons

Cast: Michael K. Allen, Suzanne Astor, Gloria Bleezarde, Trudy Carson, Marilyn Child, Elaine Giftos, Madeline Kahn, Robert Klein, Brandon Maggart, George Ormiston, Rod Perry, Nancie Phillips, Leonard Sillman

Songs: Overture (orchestra)
Welcome (Sillman, Bleezarde)
Opening (company) music, lyrics: Graham
By the Sea (Bleezarde, Maggart) music, lyrics: Gesner
Where Is the Waltz? (Allen) music; Levister; lyrics: Nassau

A New Waltz (Child) music: Hellerman; lyrics: Minkoff
The Girl in the Mirror (Perry) music: Hellerman; lyrics: Minkoff
Luncheon Ballad (Astor, Child, Kahn, Phillips) music: Powell; lyrics: McWhinney
Love Songs: (introduction by Sillman)
Something Big (Ormiston, Giftos) music: Pottle; lyrics: Axelrod
Love in a New Tempo (Klein) music, lyrics: Graham
Hungry (Astor) music, lyrics: Grand
Where Is Me? (Child) music: Siegel; lyrics: Carroll
Tango (Sillman, company) music: Pottle; lyrics: Axelrod

Hullabaloo at Thebes (Sillman, Klein, Astor, Carson, Giftos) music, lyrics: Graham
Prisms (Child) music: Friberg; lyrics: Hackady
You're the One I'm For (Bleezarde, Maggart) music, lyrics: Gesner
#X9RL220(Bleezarde) music: Powell; lyrics: McWhinney
Philosophy (Perry) music: Friberg; lyrics: Hackady
Das Chicago Song (Kahn) music: Cohen; lyrics: Geiss
You Are (Bleezarde, Maggart) music, lyrics: Gesner
Evil (Allen) music, lyrics: Shaw
Die Zusammenfugung (Bleezarde, Maggart, Klein, Kahn, Ormiston) music: Pottle; lyrics: Axelrod

NEW GIRL IN TOWN (May 14, 1957, Forty-Sixth Street Theatre)

RCA LSO 1027 stereo reissued: LSO 1106

Music, lyrics: Bob Merrill; based on Anna Christie by Eugene O'Neill; musical direction: Hal Hastings

Cast: Del Anderson, Lulu Bates, Mark Dawson, H.F. Green, Mara Landi, Eddie Phillips, Cameron Prud'homme, Thelma Ritter, Gwen Verdon, George Wallace

Songs: Overture (orchestra)
Roll Yer Socks Up (Green, chorus)
Anna Lilla (Prud'homme)
Sunshine Girl (Anderson, Phillips, Dawson)
On the Farm (Verdon)
Flings (Ritter, Bates, Landi)
It's Good to Be Alive (Verdon)
Look at 'er (Wallace)
It's Good to Be Alive (reprise) (Wallace)

Yer My Friend Ain'tcha? (Ritter, Prud'homme)
Did You Close Your Eyes? (Verdon, Wallace)
At the Check Apron Ball (chorus)
There Ain't No Flies on Me (chorus)
Ven I Valse (Verdon, Prud'homme, chorus)
Sunshine Girl (reprise) (chorus)
If That Was Love (Verdon)
Chess and Checkers (Ritter, chorus)
Look at 'er (reprise) (Wallace)

A NIGHT IN VENICE (Revival, June 26, 1952, Off Broadway, Jones Beach Marine Theatre)

Everest SDBR 3028 stereo

Music: Johann Strauss; lyrics: Ruth and Thomas Martin; musical direction: Thomas Martin

Cast: Nola Fairbanks, Thomas Tibbett Hayward, Laurel Hurley, David Kurlan, Guen Omeron, Jack Russell, Kenneth Schon, Norwood Smith, Enzo Stuarti

Songs: Overture (orchestra)
Now the Day Is Done (Stuarti, Hayward, chorus)
Spaghetti Song (Stuarti, chorus)
A Lovable Fellow (Smith)
Tarantella (chorus)
We Always Get Our Man (Omeron)
Quintet (Russell, Omeron, Smith, Fairbanks, Hurley)
Gondola Song (Hayward)
Birthday Serenade (Kurlan, chorus)
Gondola Duet (Hayward, ensemble)
Bells of St. Marks (ensemble)
Fireworks Gallop (orchestra)

Ni-nana Duet (Hurley, Hayward, ensemble)
Don't Speak of Love to Me (Fairbanks, Russell)
Now That We Are Alone (Fairbanks, Russell)
Ballet (orchestra)
The Pidgeons of San Marco (female ensemble)
I Can't Find My Wife (Schon)
Women Are Here to Stay (Russell, Omeron, Smith, Fairbanks, Hurley)
Finale (company)

NINE (May 9, 1982, Forty-Sixth Street Theatre)

CBS Records JS 38325 stereo CD

Music, lyrics: Maury Yeston; musical direction: Vincent Fanuele

Cast: Karen Akers, Shelly Burch, Stephanie Cotsirilos, Taina Elg, Cameron Johann, Raul Julia, Liliane Montevecchi, Anita Morris, Kathi Moss, Camille Saviola

Songs: Overture delle Donne (women)
Spa Music (women)
Not Since Chaplin (company)
Guido's Song (Julia, company)
The Germans at the Spa (Saviola, ensemble)
My Husband Makes Movies (Akers)
A Call from the Vatican (Morris)
Only with You (Julia)
Folies Bergeres (Montevecchi, Cotsirilos, company)
Nine (Elg, company)

Be Italian (Ti Voglio Bene) (Moss, boys, company)
The Bells of St. Sebastian (Julia, boys, company)

Unusual Way (Burch)
The Grand Canal (Julia)
Simple (Morris)
Be On Your Own (Akers)
I Can't Make This Movie (Julia)
Waltz from _Nine_ (orchestra)
Getting Tall (Johann)
Reprises (Julia, company)

Note: Cassette package containing over 80 minutes of music also available (JST 38325).

NITE CLUB CONFIDENTIAL (August 29, 1983, Off Broadway, Riverwest Theatre; transferred, May 11, 1984, Off Broadway, The Ballroom)

Confidential Records (No number - matrix: 3048) stereo

New music, lyrics: Dennis Deal, Albert Evans; musical direction: Albert Evans

Cast: Stephen Berger, Fay DeWitt, Steve Gideon, Denise Nolan, Tom Spiroff

Songs: Prologue (Berger, Gideon, Nolin, Spiroff)
Comment Allez-Vous? (Berger, Gideon, Nolin, Spiroff) music, lyrics: Murray Grand
Something's Gotta Give (DeWitt, company) music, lyrics: Johnny Mercer
Love Isn't Born, It's Made (DeWitt, Berger) music: Arthur Schwartz; lyrics: Frank Loesser
Goody, Goody (Berger, Gideon, Spiroff) music: Matt Malneck; lyrics: Johnny Mercer
I Thought About You (Berger) music: Johnny Mercer; lyrics: Jimmy Van Heusen
Put the Blame on Mamie (DeWitt, Berger, Gideon, Spiroff)
The Canarsie Diner (Nolin, Berger, Gideon, Spiroff)

Bonjour (DeWitt, Berger, Gideon, Spiroff)
That Old Black Magic (DeWitt, Berger, Gideon, Spiroff) music: Harold Arlen; lyrics: Johnny Mercer
Crazy New Words (Gideon)
The Long Goodbye (DeWitt)
Club Au Revoir (Berger, Gideon, Nolin, Spiroff)
Ev'rybody's Boppin' (Berger, Gideon, Nolin, Spiroff) music, lyrics: Jon Hendricks
Cloudburst (Berger, Gideon, Nolin, Spiroff) music: Jon Hendricks; lyrics: Leroy Kirkland, Jimmy Harris
The Other One (DeWitt) music: Arthur Siegel; lyrics: June Carroll
Dead End Street (company)

Note: Narration by Stephen Berger.

NO FOR AN ANSWER (January 5, 1941, Off Broadway, Mecca Auditorium)

Theme Records TALP 103 mono reissued: AEI 1140

Music, lyrics: Marc Blitzstein; piano: Marc Blitzstein

Cast: Carol Channing, Bert Conway, Curt Conway, Olive Deering, Norma Green, Lloyd Gough, Michael Loring, Charles Polacheck, Coby Raskin, Hester Sundergard, Martin Wolfson

Songs: The Song of the Bat (Polacheck, chorus)
Take the Book (Polacheck, chorus)
Gina (Sundergard)
Secret Singing (Deering, Gough)
Dimples (Raskin, Channing)
Fraught (Channing, Raskin)
Francie (Green, Loring)
No for an Answer (chorus)

Penny Candy (C. Conway)
Mike (B. Conway)
Purest Kind of a Guy (C. Conway)
Nick (Wolfson)
Make the Heart Be Stone (ensemble)
No for an Answer (reprise) (Wolfson, ensemble)

NO, NO, NANETTE (Revival, January 19, 1971, Forty-Sixth Street Theatre)

Columbia S 30563 stereo

Music: Vincent Youmans; lyrics: Irving Caesar, Otto Harbach; musical direction: Buster Davis

Cast: Loni Zoe Ackerman, Helen Gallagher, Jack Gilford, Ruby Keeler, Patsy Kelly, Pat Lysinger, Roger Rathburn, K.C. Townsend, Bobby Van, Susan Watson

Songs: Overture (orchestra)
Too Many Rings Around Rosie (Gallagher, boys)
I've Confessed to the Breeze (Watson, Rathburn)
Call of the Sea (Van)
I Want to Be Happy (Gilford, Watson, Keeler, chorus)
You Can Dance with Any Girl (Gallagher, Van)
No, No, Nanette (Watson, Rathburn, Kelly, chorus)

Tea for Two (Watson, Rathburn, chorus)
I Want to Be Happy (reprise) (Gilford, Townsend, Ackerman, Lysinger)
Telephone Girlie (Van, Ackerman, Townsend, Lysinger)
Finaletto Act II (company)
"Where-Has-My-Hubby-Gone" Blues (Gallagher, boys)
Waiting for You (Watson, Rathburn)
Take a Little One-Step (Keeler, company)
Finale (company)

NO STRINGS (March 15, 1962, Fifty-Fourth Street Theatre)

Capitol SO 1695 stereo

Music, lyrics: Richard Rodgers; musical direction: Peter Matz

Cast: Noelle Adam, Diahann Carroll, Don Chastain, Alvin Epstein, Mitchell Gregg, Ann Hodges, Richard Kiley, Bernice Massi, Polly Rowles

Songs: The Sweetest Sounds (Carroll, Kiley)
How Sad (Kiley)
Loads of Love (Carroll)
The Man Who Has Everything (Gregg)
Be My Host (Kiley, Massi, Chastain, Epstein, Hodges)
La La La (Adam, Epstein)
You Don't Tell Me (Carroll)

Love Makes the World Go Round (Rowles, Massi)
Nobody Told Me (Kiley, Carroll)
Look No Further (Kiley, Carroll)
Maine (Kiley, Carroll)
An Orthodox Fool (Carroll)
Eager Beaver (Massi, Chastain)
No Strings (Kiley, Carroll)
Finale: The Sweetest Sounds (Kiley, Carroll)

NOW IS THE TIME FOR ALL GOOD MEN (September 26, 1967, Off Broadway, Theatre De Lys)

Columbia OS 3130 stereo

Music: Nancy Ford; lyrics: Gretchen Cryer; musical direction: Stephen Lawrence

Cast: David Cryer, Donna Curtis, Judy Frank, Anne Kaye, Sally Niven, Murray Olson, John Bennett Perry, David Sabin, Steve Skiles, Art Wallace

Songs: What's in the Air? (Cryer, women)
Keep 'em Busy (teachers)
Tea in the Rain (Niven, Cryer)
Halloween Hayride (company)
Katydid (company)
See Everything New (Cryer, Niven)
Stuck-Up (Frank, women)
He Could Show Me (Niven)
All Alone (Cryer)

My Holiday (Niven, Cryer, women)
Down Through History (Skiles, Kaye)
Good Enough for Grandpa (company)
A Simple Life (Sabin)
A Star on the Monument (Wallace, Perry, Olson)
Rain Your Love on Me (Cryer, Niven)
There's Goin' to be a Wedding (company)
Finale: Quintet (Skiles, Cryer, Kaye, Wallace, Curtis)

Note: 'Sally Niven' is a pseudonym for lyricist Gretchen Cryer.

NUNSENSE - see page 260

OF THEE I SING (Revival, May 5, 1952, Ziegfeld Theatre)

Capitol S 350 mono

Music: George Gershwin; lyrics: Ira Gershwin; musical direction: Maurice Levine

Cast: Florenz Ames, Jack Carson, Donald Foster, Howard Freeman, Paul Hartman, Lenore Lonergan, Jonathan Lucas, Mort Marshall, Betty Oakes, J. Pat O'Malley, Robert F. Simon, Loring Smith, Jack Whiting

Songs: Prelude (orchestra)
Wintergreen for President (chorus)
Who Is the Lucky Girl to Be? (girls)
The Dimple on My Knee (chorus)
Because, Because, Because (men)
Never Was There a Girl So Fair (Smith, Foster, Freeman, O'Malley, Simon)
Some Girls Can Bake a Pie (Carson, chorus)
Love Is Sweeping the Country (Lucas, chorus)
Of Thee I Sing (Carson, Oakes, chorus)
Finaletto:
The Supreme Court Judges (Whiting, men)
Here's a Kiss for Cinderella (Carson, Oakes)
I Was the Most Beautiful Blossom (Lonergan, chorus)
Some Girls Can Bake a Pie (reprise) (Carson, Oakes, Lonergan, Whiting, chorus)
Of Thee I Sing (reprise) (chorus)

Hello, Good Morning (chorus)
Mine (Oakes, Carson)
Who Cares (Carson, chorus)
Garcon S'il Vous Plait (chorus)
The Illegitimate Daughter (Ames, Carson, chorus)
Because, Because, Because (reprise) (Longergan)
Who Cares (reprise) (Carson, Oakes)
The Senate Roll Call: Impeachment (Hartman, Ames, Smith, Freeman, O'Malley, Foster, Simon, Marshall)
Jilted (Lonergan, chorus)
I'm About to Be a Mother (Oakes, chorus)
Trumpter Blow Your Horn (company)
Finale (company)

OH, BROTHER! (November 10, 1981, ANTA Theatre)

Original Cast Records OC 8342 stereo

Music: Michael Valenti; lyrics: Donald Driver; musical direction: Peter Howard

Cast: David-James Carroll; Harry Groener, Judy Kaye, Larry Marshall, Mary Mastrantonio, Joe Morton, Alyson Reed, Richard B. Shull, Alan Weeks

Songs: Prologue (Shull, men)
We Love an Old Story (Marshall, men)
I To the World (Carroll, Groener, Morton, Weeks)
How Do You Want Me? (Kaye)
Revolution (chorus)

My World's Comin' Unwrapped (Morton)
That's Him (Mastrantonio, chorus)
Everybody Calls Me by My Name (Groener, chorus)

OPEC Maiden (Groener, chorus)
It's a Man's World (Kaye, Reed, Mastrantonio, chorus)
A Man (Carroll)
How Do You Want Me? (reprise) (Kaye)
Tell Sweet Saroyana (Carroll, Weeks, chorus)
What Do I Tell the People This Time? (Kaye)
OPEC Maiden (reprise) (Mastrantonio, women)
A Loud & Funny Song (Kaye, Reed, Mastrantonio)
Oh, Brother! (company)

OH! CALCUTTA! (June 17, 1969, Off Broadway, Eden Theatre)

Aidart Records 9903 stereo

Music, lyrics: Peter Schickele, Stanley Walden, Robert Dennis; musical direction: Norman Berger

Cast: Raina Barrett, Mark Dempsey, Robert Dennis, Katie Drew-Wilkinson, Boni Enten, Alan Rachins, Leon Russom, Margo Sappington, Peter Schickele, Nancy Tribush, Stanley Walden, George Welbes

Songs: Oh! Calcutta! (company)
Dick and Jane (orchestra)
Sincere Replies (Schickele, Walden, Dennis)
Coming Together, Going Together:
Don't Have a Song to Sing (Enten, Drew-Wilkinson, Dempsey, Russom)
I'm an Actor (Welbes, Rachins, Barrett)
Ballerina (Tribush, Sappington)
I Want It (Schickele, Walden, Dennis)
Freeze Music (orchestra)
I Want It (reprise) (Schickele, Walden, Dennis)
Clarence and Mildred (Schickele, Walden, Dennis)

Oh! Calcutta! (reprise) (orchestra)
Much Too Soon (Schickele, Walden, Dennis)
Green Pants (orchestra)
Jack and Jill (Schickele, Walden, Dennis)
Suite for Five Letters (Dempsey, Drew-Wilkinson, Enten, Tribush, Welbes)
Exchanges of Information (Schickele, Walden, Dennis)
I Like the Look (Tribush, Enten, company)

OH CAPTAIN! (February 4, 1958, Alvin Theatre)

Columbia AOS 2002 stereo

Music, lyrics: Jay Livingston, Ray Evans; based on a screenplay by Alec Coppel; musical direction: Jay Blackton

Cast: Susan Johnson, Bruce MacKay, Jacquelyn McKeever, Louis Polacek, Edward Platt, Tony Randall, Eileen Rodgers, George Ritner, Paul Valentine, Nolan Van Way

Songs: Overture (orchestra)
A Very Proper Town (Randall, ensemble)
Life Does a Man a Favor (Randall, McKeever)
Life Does a Man a Favor (reprise) (Rnadall, Platt, Ritner, MacKay, Polacek, Van Way)
Captain Henry St. James (men)
Three Paradises (Randall)
Surprise (McKeever, ensemble)
Life Does a Man a Favor (reprise) (Randall)
Hey, Madame (Randall)
Femininity (Rodgers)
It's Never Quite the Same (Platt, men)
It's Never Quite the Same (reprise) (McKeever, Platt, crew)

We're Not Children (McKeever, Valentine)
Give It All You Got (Johnson, ensemble)
Love Is Hell (Johnson)
Keep It Simple (Rodgers)
The Morning Music of Montmartre (Johnson, ensemble)
You Don't Know Him (McKeever, Rodgers)
I've Been There and I'm Back (Platt, Randall)
Double Standard (McKeever, Rodgers)
You're So Right for Me (Platt, Rodgers)
All the Time (Randall, McKeever)
Finale (company)

Note: The part sung on this album by Eileen Rodgers was played on the stage by Abbe Lane who recorded:

RCA LSP 1688 Femininity
We're Not Children

OH COWARD! (October 4, 1972, Off Broadway, The New Theatre)

Bell 9001 (two records) stereo

Music, lyrics: Noel Coward; musical direction: Rene Wiegert

Cast: Barbara Cason, Roderick Cook, Jamie Ross

Songs: Overture (orchestra)
Introduction: The Boy Actor (Ross, Cason, Cook) spoken
Something to Do with Spring (Cason, Cook, Ross)
Bright Young People (Cason, Cook, Ross)
Poor Little Rich Girl (Cook, Ross)
Ziegeuner (Cason)
Let's Say Goodbye (Ross)
This Is a Changing World (Ross, Cook, Cason)
We Were Dancing (Cook, Ross, Cason)
Dance Little Lady (Cook, Ross, Cason)
A Room with a View (Cook, Cason, Ross)
Sail Away (Cason, Cook, Ross)
London Pastoral (Ross) spoken
The End of the News (Cason, Cook)
The Stately Homes of England (Ross, Cook)
London Pride (Cason)
Aunt Jessie (Cook) spoken

--- Uncle Harry (Cason, Ross)
Music Hall (Cook) spoken
Chase Me Charlie (Cason)
Saturday Night at the Rose and Crown (Cook, Ross, Cason)
Island of Bolamazoo (Ross, Cook, Cason)
What Ho Mrs. Briskett! (Cook, Cason, Ross)
Has Anybody Seen Our Ship? (Cook, Cason, Ross)
Men About Town (Cook, Ross)
If Love Were All (Cason)
Too Early or Too Late (Cook) spoken
Why Do the Wrong People Travel? (Ross, Cason)
The Passenger's Always Right (Cook, Ross, Cason)
--- Mrs. Worthington (Cook, Ross, Cason)
Mad Dogs and Englishmen (Ross, Cason, Cook)
A Marvelous Party (Cook) spoken)
Design for Dancing (Cason, Ross, Cook) spoken
You Were There (Ross)
Three White Feathers (Cason, Cook)
The Star (Ross) spoken
The Critic (Cook) spoken
The Elderly Actress (Cason) spoken
Gertie (Cook) spoken
Loving (Ross) spoken
I Am No Good at Love (Cook) spoken
Sex Talk (Ross) spoken
A Question of Lighting (Cook, Ross) spoken
--- Mad About the Boy (Cason)
Women (Cook) spoken
Nina (Ross)
Mrs. Wentworth-Brewster (Cook)
World Weary (Cook, Cason, Ross)
Let's Do It (Cook, Cason, Ross) music: Cole Porter
Where Are the Songs We Sung? (Ross)
Someday I'll Find You (Cook)
I'll Follow My Secret Heart (Cason)
If Love Were All (Cook, Ross, Cason)
Play Orchestra Play (Cook Ross, Cason)
I'll See You Again (Cook, Ross, Cason)

OH, KAY! (Revival, April 16, 1960, Off Broadway, East 74th Street Theatre)

20th Fox Records SFX 4003 stereo reissued: Stet DS 15017

Music: George Gershwin; lyrics: Ira Gershwin; musical direction: Dorothea Freitag

Cast: David Daniels, Murray Matheson, Eddie Phillips, Marti Stevens, Bernie West

Songs: Overture (orchestra)
The Woman's Touch (girls)
The Twenties Are Here to Stay (Matheson, Phillips, West)
Home (Daniels)
Stiff Upper Lip (West, Matheson)
Maybe (Stevens, Daniels)
The Pophams (Matheson, girls)

--- Do, Do, Do (Daniels, Stevens)
Clap Yo' Hands (Daniels, company)
Somebody to Watch Over Me (Stevens)
Fidgety Feet (Phillips, girls)
You'll Still Be There (Daniels, Stevens)
Little Jazz Bird (Phillips, girls)
Oh, Kay (Phillips, West, Stevens, girls)
Finale (company)

OH WHAT A LOVELY WAR (September 30, 1964, Broadhurst Theatre)

London Records 25906 stereo

Traditional songs of World War I; musical direction: Alfred Ralston

Cast: Avis Bunnage, Fanny Carby*, John Gower, Myvanwy Jenn*, Colin Kemball*, Brian Murphy*, Mary Preston, Victor Spinetti*

Songs: Overture (orchestra) spoken introduction: Spinetti
Row, Row, Row (ensemble)
Your King and Your Country Want You (Jenn, ladies)
Belgium Put the Kibosh on the Kaiser (Preston)
Are We Downhearted (men)
Hold Your Hand Out Naughty Boy (men)
I'll Make a Man of You (Bunnage)
Pack Up Your Troubles (men)
Hitchy Koo (Carby)
Heilige Nacht (Kemball)
Christmas Day in the Cookhouse (Murphy)
Good Byee (Spinetti)
--- Oh It's a Lovely War (ensemble)
Gassed Last Night (men)
There's a Long Long Trail (Gower)
Hush Here Comes a Whizzbang (men)
They Were Only Playing Leapfrog (men)
I Wore a Tunic (Gower)
Joe Soap's Army (men)
When This Lousy War Is Over (Kemball)
Wash Me in the Water (men)
I Want to Go Home (men)
The Bells of Hell (men)
Keep the Home Fires Burning (Jenn)
La Chanson de Craonne (ensemble)
I Don't Want to Be a Soldier (ensemble)
They Didn't Believe Me (ensemble)

Note: London cast recording, with some (*) cast members who appeared in New York. Vocals are uncredited.

OKLAHOMA! (March 31, 1943, St. James Theatre)

Decca DL 9017 mono reissued: MCA 2030

Music: Richard Rodgers; lyrics: Oscar Hammerstein II; based on

Lynn Riggs' Green Grows the Lilacs; musical direction: Jay Blackton

Cast: Joseph Buloff, Betty Garde, Lee Dixon, Howard da Silva, Alfred Drake, Celeste Holm, Ralph Riggs, Joan Roberts

Songs: Overture (orchestra)
Oh, What a Beautiful Mornin' (Drake)
The Surry with the Fringe on Top (Drake)
Kansas City (Dixon, men)
I Cain't Say No (Holm)
Many a New Day (Roberts, girls)

People Will Say We're in Love (Drake, Roberts)
Pore Jud is Daid (Drake, da Silva)
Out of My Dreams (Roberts, girls)
All er Nothin' (Holm, Dixon, Drake, chorus)
Oklahoma (Drake, chorus)
Finale:
Oh, What a Beautiful Mornin' (reprise) (Roberts, Drake, chorus)
People Will Say We're in Love (reprise) (Drake, Roberts, chorus)

Note: The following additional selections are included on Time Life Records STL AM01:

Lonely Room (Drake)
The Farmer and the Cowmen (Garde, Riggs, chorus)
It's a Scandal (Buloff, chorus)

OKLAHOMA! (Revival, December 13, 1979, Palace Theatre)

RCA CBL 1-3572 stereo CD

Musical direction: Jay Blackton

Cast: Bruce Adler, Christine Andreas, Stephen Crain, Christine Ebersole, Harry Groener, Laurence Guittard, Nick Jolley, Philip Rash, Robert Ray, Martin Vidnovic, Mary Wickes

Songs: Overture (orchestra)
Oh, What a Beautiful Mornin' (Guittard)
Laurey's Entrance (Andreas)
The Surry with the Fringe on Top (Guittard, Andreas, Wickes)
Kansas City (Groener, Wickes, men)
I Cain't Say No (Ebersole)
Many a New Day (Andreas, girls)
It's a Scandal! It's a Outrage! (Adler, men)

People Will Say We're in Love (Andreas, Guittard)
Pore Jud is Daid (Guittard, Vidnovic)
Lonely Room (Vidnovic)
Out of My Dreams (Andreas, girls)
The Farmer and the Cowmen (Rash, Wickes, Groener, Guittard, Jolley, Ray, Crain, Ebersole, ensemble)
All er Nothin' (Groener, Ebersole)
People Will Say We're in Love (reprise) (Guittard, Andreas)

Oklahoma (Guittard, company)
Finale: Oh, What a Beautiful Mornin' (reprise) (company)

OLIVER! (January 6, 1963, Imperial Theatre)

RCA LSOD 2004 stereo CD

Music, lyrics: Lionel Bart; freely adapted from Charles Dickens' Oliver Twist; musical direction: Donald Pippin

Cast: Georgia Brown, Willoughby Goddard, Michael Goodman, Hope Jackman, Alice Playten, Bruce Prochnik, Clive Revill, Danny Sewell

Songs: Food, Glorious Food (boys)
Oliver (Goddard, Jackman, Prochnik, boys)
I Shall Scream (Jackman, Goddard)
Boy for Sale (Goddard)
Where is Love? (Prochnik)
Consider Yourself (Goodman, Prochnik, ensemble)
You've Got to Pick a Pocket or Two (Revill, Prochnik, boys)
It's a Fine Life (Brown, Playten)
Be Back Soon (Revill, Goodman, Prochnik, boys)

Oom-Pah-Pah (Brown, company)
My Name (Sewell)
As Long as He Needs Me (Brown)
Who Will Buy? (Prochnik, chorus)
Reviewing the Situation (Revill)
I'd Do Anything (Goodman, Brown, Prochnik, Playten, Revill)
As Long as He Needs Me (reprise) (Brown)
Reviewing the Situation (reprise) (Revill)
Finale (company)

ON A CLEAR DAY YOU CAN SEE FOREVER (October 17, 1965, Mark Hellinger Theatre)

RCA LSOD 2006 stereo

Music: Burton Lane; lyrics: Alan Jay Lerner; musical direction: Theodore Saidenberg

Cast: John Cullum, Willaim Daniels, Clifford David, Barbara Harris, Barbara Monte, William Reilly, Gerald M. Teijelo, Titos Vandis, Byron Webster

Songs: Overture (chorus)
Hurry! It's Lovely Up Here! (Harris, Cullum)
Tosy and Cosh (Harris)
On a Clear Day (Cullum)
On the S.S. Bernard Cohn (Harris, Monte, Reilly, Teijelo)
Don't Tamper with My Sister (David, Webster, chorus)

She Wasn't You (David)
Melinda (Cullum)
When I'm Being Born Again (Vandis)

What Did I Have That I Don't Have? (Harris)
Wait Till We're Sixty-Five (Daniels, Harris)
Come Back to Me (Cullum)
Finale (cast)

ON THE TOWN (December 28, 1944, Adelphi Theatre)

Decca DL 8030 mono

Music: Leonard Bernstein; lyrics: Betty Comden, Adolph Green; musical directors: Lyn Murray, Camarata, Leonard Joy

Cast: Betty Comden, Adolph Green, Mary Martin, Nancy Walker

Songs: I Feel Like I'm Not Out of Bed Yet (chorus)
New York, New York (chorus)
I Get Carried Away (Comden, Green)
Lucky to be Me (Martin)
Lonely Town (Martin)
I Can Cook Too (Walker)
Ya Got Me (Walker)

Note: Mary Martin was not in the stage production. Bernstein, Comden, Green, and Walker recorded a more complete studio version of this score in stereo in 1960.

ON THE TWENTIETH CENTURY (February 19, 1978, St. James Theatre)

Columbia 35330 stereo

Music: Cy Coleman; lyrics: Betty Comden, Adolph Green; based on plays by Ben Hecht, Charles MacArthur and Bruce Millholland; musical direction: Paul Gemignani

Cast: Tom Batten, Imogene Coca, George Coe, John Cullum, Dean Dittman, Madeline Kahn, Kevin Kline, Hal Norman, Charles Rule, Stanley Simmonds

Songs: Overture (orchestra)
Stranded Again (Rule, Norman, chorus)
On the Twentieth Century (Batten, Simmonds, company)
I Rise Again (Cullum, Coe, Dittman)
Veronique (Kahn, chorus)
Together (Cullum, company)
Never (Kahn, Coe, Dittman)
Our Private World (Kahn, Cullum)
Repent (Coca)
Mine (Cullum, Kline)

I've Got It All (Kahn, Cullum)
Five Zeros (Coe, Dittman, Coca, Cullum)
Sextet (Coe, Dittman, Cullum, Coca, Kahn, Kline)
She's a Nut (company)
Babette (Kahn, chorus)
The Legacy (Cullum)
Lily, Oscar (Kahn, Cullum)
Life Is Like a Train (men)

ON YOUR TOES (Revival, October 11, 1954, Forty-Sixth Street Theatre)

Decca DL 9015 mono reissued: Stet DS 15024E

Music: Richard Rodgers; lyrics: Lorenz Hart; musical direction: Salvatore Dell'Isola

Cast: Ben Astar, Kay Coulter, Joshua Shelley, Elaine Stritch, Bobby Van, Eleanor Williams, Jack Williams, David Winters

Songs: Overture (orchestra)
Two a Day for Keith (J. Williams, E. Williams, Winters)
The 3 B's (Van, chorus)
It's Got to be Love (Van, Coulter)
Too Good for the Average Man (Stritch, Astar)
There's a Small Hotel (Van, Coulter)
The Heart is Quicker Than the Eye (Stritch, Van)
Quiet Night (Shelley, chorus)

Glad to be Unhappy (Coulter, Shelley)
On Your Toes (Coulter, Van, Shelley, chorus)
You Took Advantage of Me (Stritch)
Slaughter on Fifth Avenue (orchestra)
On Your Toes Finale (company)

ON YOUR TOES (Revival, March 6, 1983, Virginia Theatre)

Polydor 813 667-1 Y-1 stereo CD

Musical direction: John Mauceri

Cast: Christine Andreas, Eugene J. Anthony, Betty Ann Grove, George S. Irving, Dina Merrill, Philip Arthur Ross, Lara Teeter, Michael Vita

Songs: Overture (orchestra)
Two a Day for Keith (Anthony, Grove, Ross)
Questions and Answers (The Three B's) (Teeter, chorus)
It's Got to be Love (Andreas, Teeter, chorus)
Too Good for the Average Man (Irving, Merrill)
There's a Small Hotel (Andreas, Teeter)
La Princesse Zenobia Ballet (orchestra)

The Heart Is Quicker Than the Eye (Merrill, Teeter)
Glad to be Unhappy (Andreas)
Quiet Night (Vita, chorus)
On Your Toes (Andreas, chorus)
Slaughter on Tenth Avenue (orchestra)

Note: "Quite Night" a reprise sung by George S. Irving, and extended orchestral selections were included on the British version of this recording, on two records: That's Entertainment Records TER 2 1063, in stereo.

ONCE UPON A MATTRESS (May 11, 1959, Off Broadway, Phoenix Theatre; transferred, November 25, 1959, Alvin Theatre)

Kapp Records KDS 7004 stereo reissued : MCA 37097

Music: Mary Rodgers; lyrics: Marshall Barer; musical direction: Hal Hastings

Cast: Joe Bova, Carol Burnett, Allen Case, Jack Gilford, Ann Jones, Matt Mattox, Harry Snow, Robert Weil, Jane White

Songs: Overture (orchestra)
Many Moons Ago (Snow)
An Opening for a Princess (Bova, ensemble)
In a Little While (Case, Jones)
Shy (Burnett, Bova, ensemble)
Sensitivity (White, Weil)
The Swamps of Home (Burnett, Bova, ensemble)
Normandy (Snow, Mattox, Jones)

Song of Love (Burnett, Bova, ensemble)
Spanish Panic (White)
Happily Ever After (Burnett)
Man to Man Talk (Mattox, Bova)
Very Soft Shoes (Mattox, ensemble)
Yesterday I Loved You (Case, Jones)
Finale (Bova, Mattox, Golford, ensemble)

110 IN THE SHADE (October 24, 1963, Broadhurst Theatre)

RCA LSO 1085 stereo

Music: Harvey Schmidt; lyrics: Tom Jones; based on a play by N. Richard Nash; musical direction: Donald Pippin

Cast: George Church, Stephen Douglass, Will Geer, Robert Horton, Steve Roland, Inga Swenson, Scooter Teague, Lesley Warren

Songs: Gonna Be Another Hot Day (Douglass, chorus)
Lizzie's Comin' Home (Geer, Roland, Teague)
Love, Don't Turn Away (Swenson)
Poker Polka (Douglass, Geer, Roland)
Hungry Men (chorus)
Rain Song (Horton, chorus)
You're Not Foolin' Me (Swenson, Horton)
Raunchy (Swenson, Geer)

A Man and a Woman (Swenson, Douglass)
Old Maid (Swenson)
Everything Beautiful Happens at Night (Church, Teague, Warren, chorus)
Melisande (Horton)
Simple Little Things (Swenson)
Little Red Hat (Warren, Teague)
Is It Really Me? (Swenson, Horton)
Wonderful Music (Douglass, Horton, Swenson)
Rain Song Finale (company)

ONE MO' TIME (October 22, 1979, Off Broadway, Village Gate)

Warner Brothers Records HS 3454 stereo

An evening of 1920's black vaudeville. Musical direction: Orange Kellin

Cast: Vernel Bagneris, Topsy Chapman, Thais Clark, Jabbo Smith, Sylvia 'Kuumba' Williams

Songs: Down in Honky Tonk Town (Bagneris, girls)
Kiss Me Sweet (Bagneris, Chapman)
Miss Jenny's Ball (Clark)
Cake Walkin' Babies from Home (Bagneris, girls)
I've Got What It Takes (Chapman)
C.C. Rider (Clark)
The Graveyard (Bagneris)
He's Funny That Way (Chapman)
Kitchen Man (Williams)
Wait Till You See My Baby Do the Charleston (girls)

Love (Smith)
Louise (Bagneris)
New Orleans Hop Scop Blues (Bagneris)
Everybody Loves My Baby (Chapman)
You've Got the Right Key but the Wrong Key Hole (Williams)
After You've Gone (Clark)
My Man Blues (Williams, Chapman)
Papa De Da Da (Bagneris, girls)
Muddy Waters (Clark)
There'll Be a Hot Time in the Old Town Tonight (cast)

Note: A live recording. Vocals uncredited.

ONE NIGHT STAND (Closed during previews, final performance: October 25, 1980, Nederlander Theatre)

Original Cast Records OC 8134 stereo

Music: Jule Styne; lyrics: Herb Gardner; musical direction: Milton Rosenstock

Cast: Paul Binotto, Catherine Cox, Jeff Keller, Charles Kimbrough, William Morrison, Jack Weston

Songs: Overture (orchestra)
Let Me Hear You Love Me (Kimbrough)
Don't Kick My Dreams Around (Cox)
Go Out Big (Weston)
A Little Travellin' Music Please (Kimbrough)
I'm Writing a Love Song for You (Morrison)
Somebody Stole My Kazoo (Kimbrough, Keller, Binotto, chorus)

Entr'acte (orchestra)
Someday Soon (Morrison)
There Was a Time (Kimbrough, Cox)
For You (Weston)

Long Way from Home (Cox)
Too Old to Be So Young (Kimbrough)
Here Comes Never (Weston)
Finale (Kimbrough, chorus)

ONE TOUCH OF VENUS (October 7, 1943, Imperial Theatre)

Decca DL 79122 mono reissued: AEI 1136

Music: Kurt Weill; lyrics: Ogden Nash; musical direction: Maurice Abravanel

Cast: Kenny Baker, Mary Martin

Songs: I'm a Stranger Here Myself (Martin)
Forty Minutes for Lunch (orchestra)
Westwind (Baker)
Foolish Heart (Martin)
The Trouble with Women (Baker, male quartet)

Speak Low (Martin, Baker)
That's Him (Martin)
Wooden Wedding (Baker)
Venus in Ozone Heights (orchestra)
Finaletto: Speak Low (Martin, Baker)

Note: Original cast member Paula Laurence recorded two additional songs in 1981 in stereo on Painted Smiles Records, PS 1375, Kurt Weill Revisited:

One Touch of Venus
Very Very Very

ONWARD VICTORIA (December 14, 1980, Martin Beck Theatre)

Original Cast Records OC 8135 stereo

Music: Keith Herrmann; lyrics: Charlotte Anker, Irene Rosenberg; musical direction: Patrick Holland

Cast: Beth Austin, Jill Eikenberry, Jim Jansen, Laura Waterbury, Lenny Wolpe, Michael Zaslow

Songs: Overture (orchestra)
In New York the Only Sin Is Being Timid (Eikenberry, Austin, ensemble)
Magnetic Healing (Eikenberry, Austin, Wolpe)
A Taste of Forever (Eikenberry)
I Depend on You (Eikenberry, Austin)
Onward Victoria (Eikenberry, Austin, ensemble)
Changes (Eikenberry)
A Woman Like Beth (Zaslow)
Unescorted Women (Wolpe, Eikenberry, Austin, ensemble)

Love and Joy (Eikenberry, Zaslow)
Every Day I Do a Little Something for the Lord (Jansen)
You Cannot Drown the Dream (Eikenberry, Waterbury, ensemble)

Respectable (Austin)
Another Life (Eikenberry)
Read It in the Weekly (Eikenberry, ensemble)
A Valentine for Beecher (ensemble)
Beecher's Defense (Eikenberry)
Finale (Eikenberry, Austin, Zaslow)

OUT OF THIS WORLD (December 21, 1950, New Century Theatre)

Columbia ML 54390 mono

Music, lyrics: Cole Porter; musical direction: Pembroke Davenport

Cast: Barbara Ashley, David Burns, Priscilla Gillette, Charlotte Greenwood, George Jongeyans, William Redfield

Songs: Overture (orchestra)
Prologue (Redfield)
I Jupiter, I Rex (Jongeyans, ensemble)
Use Your Imagination (Gillette)
Entrance of Juno (ensemble)
Hail, Hail, Hail (Greenwood, ensemble)
I Got Beauty (Greenwood, ensemble)
Where, Oh, Where (Ashley)
I Am Loved (Gillette)
They Couldn't Compare to You (Redfield, girls)

What Do You Think about Men? (Greenwood, Gillette, Ashley)
I Sleep Easier Now (Greenwood)
Climb Up the Mountain (Greenwood, company)
No Lover for Me (gillette)
Cherry Pies Ought to Be You (Redfield, Ashley, Greenwood, Burns)
Hark to the Song of the Night (Jongeyans)
Nobody's Chasing Me (Greenwood)
Finale: Use Your Imagination (reprise) (company)

Note: George Jongeyans later used the name George Gaynes.

OVER HERE! (March 6, 1974, Shubert Theatre)

Columbia KS 32961 stereo

Music, lyrics: Richard M. Sherman, Robert B. Sherman; musical direction: Joseph Klein

Cast: Maxene Andrews, Patty Andrews, MacIntyre Dixon, John Driver, William Griffis, Janie Sell, April Shawhan, Phyllis Somerville, John Travolta, Douglass Watson, Jim Weston, Samuel E. Wright

Songs: Overture (The Beat Begins) (orchestra)
Since You're Not Around (Weston, company)
Over Here! (M. Andrews, P. Andrews, company)
Buy a Victory Bond (company)

Charlie's Place (M. Andrews, company)
Hey Yvette (Watson, Griffis, Dixon)
The Grass Grows Green (Watson)
My Dream for Tomorrow (Shawhan, Driver)
The Good Time Girl (P. Andrews, company)

Wait for Me, Marlena (Sell, company)
We Got It! (P. Andrews, M. Andrews, Sell, company)
Wartime Wedding (P. Andrews, M. Andrews, company)
Don't Shoot the Hooey to Me, Louie (Wright)
Where Did the Good Times Go? (P. Andrews)
Dream Drummin' (Travolta, Sommerville, company)
Soft Music (company)
The Big Beat (P. Andrews, M. Andrews, Sell)
No Goodbyes (P. Andrews, M. Andrews, company)

PACIFIC OVERTURES (January 11, 1976, Winter Garden Theatre)

RCA ARL 1-1367 stereo CD

Music, lyrics: Stephen Sondheim; musical direction: Paul Gemignani

Cast: James Dybas, Timm Fujii, Ernest Harada, Alvin Ing, Genji Ito, Patrick Kinser-Lau, Jae Woo Lee, Mako, Isao Sato, Freda Foh Shen, Yuki Shimoda, Sab Shimono, Mark Hsu Syers, Ricardo Tobia, Gedde Watanabe, Leslie Watanabe, Conrad Yama, Fusako Yoshida

Songs: The Advantages of Floating in the Middle of the Sea (Mako, company)
There Is No Other Way (Ing, Tobia)
Four Black Dragons (Lee, Syers, Mako, company)
Chrysanthemum Tea (Ing, Mako, Syers, Fujii, G. Watanabe, Kinser-Lau, Yama, Lee, Harada, Shen)
Poems (Sato, Shimono)
Welcome to Kanagawa (Harada, Fujii, Kinser-Lau, G. Watanabe, L. Watanabe, Mako)

Someone in a Tree (Dybas, Mako, G. Watanabe, Syers)
Please Hello (Ing, Shimoda, Harada, Mako, Kinser-Lau, Syers, Dybas)
A Bowler Hat (Sato)
Pretty Lady (Kinser-Lau, Fujii, Syers)
Next (Mako, company)

Note: Album credits:

Fusako Yoshida (Voice and Shamisen)
Genji Ito (Shakuhachi)

PAINT YOUR WAGON (November 12, 1951, Shubert Theatre)

RCA LOC 1006 mono

Music: Frederick Loewe; lyrics: Alan Jay Lerner; musical direction: Franz Allers

Cast: James Barton, Tony Bavaar, Olga San Juan, Robert Penn, Rufus Smith, Dave Thomas

Songs: I'm on My Way (Smith, Penn, Thomas, chorus)
Rumson (Penn)
What's Goin' On Here? (San Juan)
I Talk to the Trees (Bavaar)
They Call the Wind Maria (Smith, chorus)
I Still See Elisa (Barton)
How Can I Wait? (San Juan)

In Between (Barton)
Whoop-Ti-Ay! (chorus)
Carino Mio (San Juan, Bavaar)
There's a Coach Comin' In (chorus)
Hand Me Down That Can O' Beans (Penn, chorus)
Another Autumn (Bavaar, Smith)
All for Him (San Juan)
Wand'rin Star (Barton, chorus)

THE PAJAMA GAME (May 13, 1954, St. James Theatre)

Columbia OL 4840 mono reissued: S 32606

Music, lyrics: Richard Adler, Jerry Ross; based on the novel $7\frac{1}{2}$ Cents by Richard Bissell; musical direction: Hal Hastings

Cast: Eddie Foy, Jr., Peter Gennaro, Carol Haney, Buzz Miller, Janis Paige, Stanley Prager, John Raitt, Reta Shaw

Songs: Overture (orchestra)
The Pajama Game (Foy)
Racing with the Clock (Foy, ensemble)
A New Town Is a Blue Town (Raitt)
I'm Not At All in Love (Paige, girls)
I'll Never Be Jelous Again (Foy, Shaw)
Hey There (Raitt)
Her Is (Prager, Haney)
Once-a-Year-Day! (Raitt, Paige, ensemble)

Small Talk (Raitt, Paige)
There Once Was a Man (Raitt, Paige)
Steam Heat (Haney, Miller, Gennaro)
Think of the Time I Save (Foy, girls)
Hernando's Hideaway (Haney, ensemble)
Seven-and-a-Half Cents (Paige, Prager, ensemble)
Finale (company)

PAL JOEY (Revival, January 3, 1952, Broadhurst Theatre)

Capitol S 310 mono

Music: Richard Rodgers; lyrics: Lorenz Hart; based on stories by John O'Hara; musical direction: Max Meth

Cast: Dick Beavers, Lewis Bolyard, Jane Froman, Helen Gallagher, Pat Northrop, Elaine Stritch

Songs: Overture (orchestra)
You Mustn't Kick It Around (Beavers, Gallagher)
I Could Write a Book (Beavers, Northrup)
Chicago (Gallagher, chorus)
That Terrific Rainbow (Gallagher, chorus)
What Is a Man (Froman)
Happy Hunting Horn (Beavers)
Bewitched (Froman)

Pal Joey (Beavers)
Flower Garden of My Heart (Bolyard, Gallagher)
Zip (Stritch)
Plant You Now, Dig You Later (Gallagher, chorus)
In Our Little Den (Froman, Beavers)
Do It the Hard Way (Beavers)
Take Him (Northrup, Froman)
Bewitched (reprise) (Froman)
Finale (company)

Note: Vivienne Segal and Harold Lang, the stars of this production, recorded a studio cast version of the score on Columbia CSP 4364. Jane Froman and Dick Beavers did not appear in the stage production.

PANAMA HATTIE (October 30, 1940, Forty-Sixth Street Theatre)

Decca 203 (78 rpm) mono JJA Records 19732 (LP)

Music, lyrics: Cole Porter; musical direction: Harry Sosnik

Cast: Joan Carroll, Ethel Merman

Songs: My Mother Would Love You (Merman)
I've Still Got My Health (Merman)
Let's Be Buddies (Carroll, Merman)
Make It Another Old Fashioned, Please (Merman)

PARADE (January 20, 1960, Off Broadway, Players Theatre)

Kapp Records KD 7005-S stereo

Music, lyrics: Jerry Herman; musical direction: Jerry Herman

Cast: Dody Goodman, Lester James, Fia Karin, Charles Nelson Reilly, Richard Tone

Songs: Overture (orchestra)
Show Tune (company)
Save the Village (Goodman)
Your Hand in Mine (James, Karin)
Confession to a Park Avenue Mother (Reilly)
Two a Day (Tone)

Just Plain Folks (Goodman, Reilly)
The Antique Man (James)
The Next Time I Love (Karin)
Your Good Morning (James, Karin)
Maria in Spats (Goodman)
Another Candle (Karin)

Jolly Theatrical Season (Goodman, Reilly)
Finale (Parade) (company)

PARIS '90 (March 4, 1952, Booth Theatre)

Columbia ML 4619 mono

Music: Kay Swift, Paul Delmet, Yvette Guilbert; lyrics: Kay Swift; musical direction: Nathaniel Shilkret

Cast: Cornelia Otis Skinner

Songs: Overture (orchestra)
The Waltz I Heard in a Dream (chorus)
Tourne mon Moulin (Skinner) music: Delmet
Lend Me a Bob (Skinner)

Calliope (Skinner, chorus)
St. Lazare (Skinner) music: Guilbert
Mme. Arthur (Skinner) music: Guilbert
Calliope (reprise) (Skinner, chorus)

Note: This recording is primarily spoken word.

A PARTY WITH BETTY COMDEN AND ADOLPH GREEN (December 23, 1958, John Golden Theatre)

Capitol SWAO 1197 stereo

Music: Leonard Bernstein, Saul Chaplin, Roger Edens, Andre Previn, Jule Styne; lyrics: Betty Comden, Adolph Green; musical direction: Peter Howard

Cast: Betty Comden, Adolph Green

Songs: I Said Good Morning (Comden, Green) music: Previn
The Reader's Digest (Comden, Green)
Baroness Basooka (Comden, Green)
New York, New York (Comden, Green) music: Bernstein
Lonely Town (Green) music: Bernstein
Some Other Time (Comden, Green) music: Bernstein
I Get Carried Away (Comden, Green) music: Bernstein
The French Lesson (Comden, Green) music: Edens

Movie Ads (Comden, Green) spoken
If You Hadn't But You Did (Comden) music: Styne
Catch Our Act at the Met (Comden, Green) music: Styne
Oh, My Mysterious Lady (Comden, Green) music: Styne
A Quiet Girl (Green) music: Bernstein
Inspiration (Comden, Green) music: Chaplin
Just in Time (Comden, Green) music: Styne
The Party's Over (Comden, Green) music: Styne

Note: A live recording.

A PARTY WITH BETTY COMDEN AND ADOLPH GREEN (Revival, February

10, 1977, Morosco Theatre)

Stet Records S2L 5177 (two records) stereo

Music: Leonard Bernstein, Saul Chaplin, Cy Coleman, Roger Edens, Andre Previn, Jule Styne; lyrics: Betty Comden, Adolph Green; piano: Paul Trueblood

Cast: Betty Comden, Adolph Green

Songs: I Said Good Morning (Comden, Green) music: Previn
The Reader's Digest (Comden, Green)
The Screen Writers (Comden, Green) spoken
The Beautiful Girl (Comden, Green)
The Banshee Sisters (Comden, Green)
The Baroness Bazooka (Comden, Green)

New York, New York (Comden, Green) music: Bernstein
Lonely Town (Comden, Green) music: Bernstein
Lucky to Be Me (Comden, Green) music: Bernstein
Some Other Time (Comden, Green) music: Bernstein
Carried Away (Comden, Green) music: Bernstein
100 Easy Ways to Lose a Man (Comden) music: Bernstein
Ohio (Comden, Green) music: Bernstein
The Wrong Note Rag (Comden, Green) music: Bernstein

Capital Gains (Green) music: Styne
If (Comden) music: Styne
Catch Our Act at the Met (Comden, Green) music: Styne
The French Lesson (Comden, Green) music: Edens
The Lost Word (Comden) music: Coleman

Captain Hook's Waltz (Green) music: Styne
Never Never Land (Comden) music: Styne
Mysterious Lady (Comden, Green) music: Styne
Simplified Language (Comden, Green) music: Coleman
Inspiration (Comden, Green) music: Chaplin
Just in Time (Comden, Green) music: Styne
Make Someone Happy (Comden, Green) music: Styne
The Party's Over (Comden, Green) music: Styne

Note: Recorded live at the Arena Stage, Washington D.C., May 1, 1977.

PEACE (November 1, 1968, Off Broadway, Judson Memorial Church)

Metromedia Records MP 33001 stereo

Music: Al Carmines; lyrics: Tim Reynolds; adapted from Aristophanes; musical direction: Al Carmines

Cast: Rethel Bean, Essie Borden, Ann Dunbar, Julie Kurnitz, George McGrath, David Pursley, Arlene Rothlein, Maria Santell, David Tice, David Vaughn, Margaret Wright

Songs: Through Excessive Concern (Kurnitz)
Oh God (Bean, Kurnitz)
Trio (McGrath, Kurnitz, Bean)
Oh Daddy Dear (Bean, Borden, Dunbar)
The Gods Have Gone Away (Vaughn, Bean)

Plumbing (Pursley, Tice)
Medley:
I Want to See Peace Again (sextet)
Just Let Me Get My Hands on Peace (sextet)
I Just Can't Help It (sextet)
Don't Do It Mr. Hermes (sextet)
Things Starting to Grow Again (Wright, Santell, ensemble)

Muse, Darling (Wright, ensemble)
Up in Heaven (ensemble)
My Name's Abundance (Santell, ensemble)
You've Got Yourself a Bunch of Women (Wright, ensemble)
All the Dark is Changed to Sunshine (ensemble)
Peace Prayer (McGrath) spoken
Peace Anthem (ensemble)
Poor Mortals (Rothlein, ensemble)
Just Sit Around (Kurnitz, McGrath, ensemble)
Summer's Nice (Kurnitz, ensemble)
America the Beautiful (Wright, ensemble) lyrics: Katherine Lee Bates

PETER PAN (April 24, 1950, Imperial Theatre)

Columbia OL 4312 mono

Music: Leonard Bernstein; lyrics: Leonard Bernstein; based on J.M. Barrie's play; musical direction: Ben Steinberg

Cast: Marcia Henderson, Boris Karloff

Songs: Introduction (orchestra) narration: Torin Thatcher
Who Am I? (Henderson)
The Pirate Song (Karloff, pirates)

Build My House (Henderson)
Peter, Peter (Henderson)
The Plank (Karloff, pirates)

Note: This recording is primarily spoken word.

PETER PAN (October 20, 1954, Winter Garden)

RCA LOC 1019 mono

Music: Mark Charlop; additional music: Jule Styne; lyrics: Carolyn Leigh; additional lyrics: Betty Comden, Adolph Green; musical direction: Louis Adrian

Cast: Margalo Gillmore, Robert Harrington, Sondra Lee, Mary Martin, Kathy Nolan, Cyril Ritchard, Joseph Stafford

Songs: Overture (orchestra)
Prologue (orchestra)
Tender Shepherd(Gillmore, Harrington, Nolan, Stafford)
I've Gotta Crow (Martin, Nolan)
Never, Never Land (Martin, Nolan)
I'm Flying (Martin, Nolan, Harrington, Stafford)

Pirate Song (pirates, boys)
Hook's Tango (Ritchard, pirates)
Indians (indians)
Wendy (Martin, Harrington, Stafford, boys)

Tarantella (Ritchard, pirates)
I Won't Grow Up (Martin, Harrington, Stafford, Nolan, boys)
Oh My Mysterious Lady (Martin, Ritchard)
Ugg-a-Wugg (Martin, Lee, boys, indians)
Distant Melody (Martin, Nolan)
Hook's Waltz (Ritchard, pirates)
I've Gotta Crow (reprise) (Martin, Nolan)
Tender Shepherd (reprise) (Gillmore, Harrington, Nolan, Stafford)
I Won't Grow Up (reprise) (Ritchard, Harrington, Nolan, Stafford)
Never, Never Land (reprise) (Nolan, Martin)

PHILEMON (January 3, 1975, Off Broadway, Portfolio Studio)

Gallery Records OC 1 stereo

Music: Harvey Schmidt; lyrics: Tom Jones; musical direction: Ken Collins

Cast: Michael Glenn-Smith, Virginia Gregory, Dick Latessa, Leila Martin, Howard Ross, Kathrin King Segal

Songs: Within This Empty Space (company)
The Streets of Antioch Stink (Latessa, Ross)
Don't Kiki Me (Segal, Latessa)
I'd Do Almost Anything to Get Out of Here and Go Home (Latessa, Ross)
He's Coming (prisoners)
Antioch Prison (prisoners)
Name: Cockian (Latessa, company)

I Love Order (Ross, company)
My Secret Dream (Glenn-Smith, Latessa, prisoners)
I Love His Face (Gregory, Latessa)
Sometimes (Latessa, prisoners)
The Nightmare (Latessa, company)
The Greatest of These (Martin)
How Free I Feel (Latessa)
Oh, How Easy to Be Scornful! (Ross)
Come with Me (Latessa, Ross, company)
The Greatest of These (reprise) (company)
Within This Empty Space (reprise) (company)

PIANO BAR (June 8, 1978, Off Broadway, Westside Theatre)

Original Cast Records OC 7812 stereo

Music: Rob Fremont; lyrics: Doris Willens; musical direction: Joel Silberman

Cast: Kelly Bishop, Karen De Vito, Steve Elmore, Richard Ryder, Joel Silberman

Songs: Introduction (Silberman)
Sweet Sue's Piano Bar (Silberman, company)
Pideon-hole Time (Elmore, Ryder, De Vito)
Congradulations (De Vito)
Believe Me (Ryder, Bishop)
Tango (Bishop, Ryder)
Everywhere I Go (De Vito)
Dinner at the Mirklines (Elmore)
Scenes from Some Marriages (Silberman, company)
Personals (Silberman)
Nobody's Perfect (company)

One, Two Three (Silberman, company)
Greenspons (De Vito, Bishop)
Moms and Dads (Silberman, company)
Meanwhile Back in Yonkers (Bishop)
Alas, Alack (Ryder, Elmore)
New York Cliche (Elmore, De Vito)
Tomorrow Night (Silberman)
Closing (Silberman, company)

PICKWICK (October 4, 1965, Forty-Sixth Street Theatre)

Philips (British) SAL 3431 stereo

Music: Cyril Ornadel; lyrics: Leslie Bricusse; based on Dickens' posthumous papers of the Pickwick Club; musical direction: Marcus Dodds

Cast: Brendan Barry, Hilda Braid, Ian Burford, Michael Darbyshire*, Jessie Evans, Teddy Green, Gerald James, Julian Orchard*, Oscar Quitak*, Anton Rodgers*, Harry Secombe*, Tony Sympson*, Norman Warwick, Dilys Watling, Robin Wentworth

Songs: Business Is Booming (Warwick, Burford, Barry, company)
Debtors Lament (company)
Talk (Green, company)
That's What I'd Like for Christmas (Secombe, company)
The Pickwickians (Secombe, Orchard, James, Quitak)
A Bit of Character (Rodgers, Orchard, Quitak, James)
There's Something About You (Rodgers, Braid, company)
You Never Met a Feller Like Me (Secombe, Green)
Look into Your Heart (Secombe, Evans)

A Hell of an Election (company)
Very (Rodgers)
Learn a Little Something (Green, Watling)
If I Ruled the World (Secombe, company)
The Trouble with Women (Green, Wentworth)
That's the Law (Secombe, James, Quitak, Orchard, Green, Wentworth, Darbyshire, Sympson)
British Justice (Secombe, company)
Good Old Pickwick (company)
Do As You Would Be Done (Secombe, Rodgers, Evans, Green, company)
If I Ruled the World (reprise) (Secombe)

Note: London cast recording, with some cast members (*) who also appeared in New York.

PIECES OF EIGHT (September 24, 1959, Off Broadway, Upstairs at the Downstairs)

Offbeat Records O-4016 mono

Music: Elisse Boyd, Dave Davenport, Alan Friedman, Bart Howard, Bob Kessler, Bud McCreery, John Meyer, Claibe Richardson, William Roy, Rod Warren, Bruce Williamson; lyrics: Elisse Boyd, Martin Charnin, Bart Howard, Bud McCreery, Dennis Marks, John Meyer, Claibe Richardson, William Roy, Rod Warren; pianos: William Roy, Carl Norman

Cast: Ceil Cabot, Del Close, Gordon Connell, Jane Connell, Gerry Matthews, Estelle Parsons

Songs: Introduction (Julius Monk) spoken
Overture (pianos)
Gala Opening (cast) music, lyrics: McCreery
Happiness Is a Bird (Cabot, Matthews) music, lyrics: Richardson
And Then I Wrote (Close) music: Roy; lyrics: Davenport
Radio City Music Hall (J. Connell, Parsons, Cabot) music, lyrics: Warren
Miss Williams (G. Connell) music, lyrics: Boyd
The Uncle Bergie Evans Show (Parsons, J. Connell, Cabot, Close, Matthews) spoken
Oriental (Cabot) music: Kessler; lyrics: Charnin
Ardent Admirer (J. Connell) music, lyrics: Meyer
Steel Guitars and Barking Seals (cast) music, lyrics: McCreery
---
Election Spectacular (cast) music: various; lyrics: McCreery
Seasons' Greetings (Cabot) music, lyrics: Warren
A Name of Our Own (Close, Matthews, G. Connell) music: Friedman; lyrics: Marks
M'Lady Chatterley (J. Connell) music: Roy; lyrics: Williamson
Farewell (Matthews) music, lyrics: Roy
The Night the Hurricane Struck (Cabot, J. Connell, G. Connell, Matthews) music, lyrics: McCreery
Everybody Wants to Be Loved (Parsons) music, lyrics: Howard
A Conversation Piece (Parsons, Close, G. Connell, Matthews) spoken
Final Reprise (cast)

Note: A live recording.

PIPE DREAM (November 30, 1955, Shubert Theatre)

RCA LOC 1023 mono

Music: Richard Rodgers; lyrics: Oscar Hammerstein II; based on the novel Sweet Thursday by John Steinbeck; musical direction: Salvatore Dell'Isola

Cast: Mike Kellin, William Johnson, Helen Traubel, Judy Tyler,

G.D. Wallace

Songs: Overture (orchestra)
All Kinds of People (Johnson, Kellin)
The Tide Pool (Johnson, Kellin, Wallace)
Everybody's Got a Home but Me (Tyler)
A Lopsided Bus (Wallace, Kellin, chorus)
Bums' Opera (Traubel, chorus)
The Man I Used to Be (Johnson)
Sweet Thursday (Traubel)
Suzy Is a Good Thing (Traubel, Tyler)
All at Once (Johnson)

The Happiest House on the Block (Traubel, chorus)
The Party That We're Gonna Have Tomorrow Night (Wallace, chorus)
Will You Marry Me? (Tyler, Johnson)
Thinkin' (Kellin)
All at Once (reprise) (Traubel)
How Long? (Traubel, chorus)
The Next Time It Happens (Tyler, Johnson)
Finale (company)

PIPPIN (October 23, 1972, Imperial Theatre)

Motown M760L stereo CD

Music, lyrics: Stephen Schwartz; musical direction: Stanley Lebowsky

Cast: Eric Berry, Jill Clayburgh, Leland Palmer, John Rubinstein, Irene Ryan, Ben Vereen

Songs: Magic to Do (Vereen, chorus)
Corner of the Sky (Rubinstein)
War Is a Science (Berry, Rubinstein, men)
Glory (Vereen, men)
Simple Joys (Vereen)
No Time at All (Ryan, chorus)
With You (Rubinstein)

Spread a Little Sunshine (Palmer)
Morning Glow (Rubinstein, chorus)
On the Right Track (Vereen, Rubinstein)
Kind of Woman (Clayburgh, girls)
Extraordinary (Rubinstein)
Love Song (Rubinstein, Clayburgh)
I Guess I'll Miss the Man (Clayburgh)
Finale (company)

THE PIRATES OF PENZANCE (Revival, July 15, 1980, Off Broadway, Delacorte Theatre; transferred, January 8, 1981, Uris Theatre)

Elektra Records VE-601 (two records) stereo

Music: Arthur Sullivan; lyrics: W.S. Gilbert; musical direction: William Elliott

Cast: Tony Azito, Stephen Hanan, Kevin Kline, Alexandra Korey,

Estelle Parsons, Linda Ronstadt, George Rose, Marcie Shaw, Rex Smith

Songs: Pour, O Pour the Pirate Sherry (Kline, Hanan, men)
When Frederic Was a Little Lad (Parsons)
Oh, Better Far to Live and Die (Kline, men)
Oh, False One, You Have Deceived Me! (Parsons, Smith)
Climbing Over Rocky Mountain (girls)
--- Stop, Ladies, Pray! (Smith, girls)
Oh, Is There Not One Maiden Breast (Smith, girls)
Poor Wandering One (Ronstadt, girls)
What Ought We to Do? (Shaw, Korey, girls)
How Beautifully Blue the Sky (Ronstadt, Smith, girls)
Stay, We Must Not Lose Our Senses (Smith, girls, men)
Hold, Monsters! (Ronstadt, Hanan, Rose, girls, men)
I Am the Very Model of a Modern Major-General (Rose, ensemble)
--- Oh, Men of Dark and Dismal Fate (ensemble)
Oh, Dry the Glistening Tear (Ronstadt, girls)
Then Frederic (Rose, Smith)
When the Foreman Bares His Steel (Azito, Ronstadt, men, girls)
Now for the Pirates' Lair! (Smith, Kline, Parsons)
When You Had Left Our Pirate Fold (Parsons, Smith, Kline)
My Eyes Are Fully Open (Smith, Parsons, Kline)
Away, Away! My Heart's on Fire (Parsons, Kline, Smith)
All Is Prepared (Ronstadt, Smith)
--- Stay, Frederic, Stay! (Ronstadt, Smith)
Sorry Her Lot (Ronstadt)
No, I Am Brave (Ronstadt, Azito, men)
When a Felon's Not Engaged In His Employment (Azito, men)
A Rollicking Band of Pirates We (Azito, men)
With Cat-Like Tread, Upon Our Prey We Steal (Hanan, men)
Hush, Hush! Not a Word (Smith, Rose, men)
Sighing Softly to the River (Rose, men)
Finale (company)

PLAIN AND FANCY (January 27, 1955, Mark Hellinger Theatre)

Capitol S 603 mono

Music: Albert Hague; lyrics: Arnold B. Horwitt; musical direction: Franz Allers

Cast: Nancy Andrews, Shirl Conway, Barbara Cook, David Daniels, Richard Derr, Elaine Lynn, Gloria Marlowe, Douglas Fletcher Rodgers, Stefan Schnabel

Songs: Overture (orchestra)
You Can't Miss It (Derr, Conway, ensemble)
It Wonders Me (Marlowe)
Plenty of Pennsylvania (Andrews, Rodgers, Lynn, ensemble)
Young and Foolish (Daniels, Marlowe)
Why Not Katie (Rodgers, men)
It's a Helluva Way to Run a Love Addair (Conway)

This Is All Very New to Me (Cook, ensemble)
Plain We Live (Schnabel, men)
How Do You Raise a Barn (company)
Follow Your Heart (Daniels, Marlowe, Cook)
City Mouse, Country Mouse (Andrews, women)
I'll Show Him (Cook)
Take Your Time and Take Your Pick (Cook, Derr, Conway)
Finale (company)

POLONAISE (October 6, 1945, Alvin Theatre)

RCA Camden CAL 210 mono

Music: Frederic Chopin; adaptions and original numbers: Bronislaw Kaper; lyrics: John Latouche; musical direction: Al Goodman

Cast: Mary Martha Briney, Rose Inghram, Earl Wrightson

Songs: Overture - Polonaise (orchestra)
O Heart of My Country (Wrightson)
Mazurka (orchestra)
Just for Tonight (Briney, Wrightson)
Now I Know Your Face by Heart (Wrightson, Briney, chorus)
The Next Time I Care (Inghram)
I Wonder as I Wonder (Briney)
Wait for Tomorrow (Wrightson, chorus)

Note: Studio cast recording. Rose Inghram is the only member of the New York cast.

PORGY AND BESS (Revival, January 22, 1942, Majestic Theatre)

Decca DL 8042 mono

Music: George Gershwin; lyrics: Du Bose Heyward, Ira Gershwin; founded on the play Porgy by Dorothy and Du Bose Hayward; musical direction: Alexander Smallens

Cast: Anne Brown, Edward Matthews, Harriet Jackson, Todd Duncan, Helen Dowdy, Gladys Goode, William Woolfolk, Georgette Harvey, Avon Long

Songs: Overture (orchestra)
Summertime (Brown, female chorus)
A Woman Is a Sometime Thing (Matthews, Jackson, chorus)
My Man's Gone Now (Brown, chorus)
It Take a Long Pull to Get There (Matthews, male chorus)
I Got Plenty of Nuttin' (Duncan, chorus)
Buzzard Song (Duncan, chorus)
Bess, You Is My Woman (Duncan, Brown, chorus)

It Ain't Necessarily So (Duncan, chorus)
What You Want Wid Bess? (Brown, Duncan)
Strawberry Woman's Call (Dowdy, Goode)
Crab Man's Call (Woolfolk, Harvey)

I Loves You, Porgy (Duncan, Brown)
The Requiem (chorus)
There's a Boat Dat's Leavin' Soon for New York (Long, Brown)
Porgy's Lament and Finale (Duncan, chorus)

PORGY AND BESS (Revival, September 25, 1976, Uris Theatre)

RCA ARL 3-2109 (three records) stereo

Musical direction: John DeMain

Cast: Donnie Rae Albert, Carol Brice, Clamma Dale, Betty Lane, Larry Marshall, Myra Merritt, Wilma Shakesnider, Alexander B. Smalls, Andrew Smith, Mervin Wallace

Songs: Overture (orchestra)
Brown Blues (Dick Hyman, piano)
Summertime (Betty Lane)
A Woman Is a Sometime Thing (Smalls, men)
Here Comes de Honey Man (Wallace)
They Pass By Singin' (Albert)
\---
Oh Little Stars (Albert)
Gone, Gone, Gone (ensemble)
Overflow (ensemble)
My Man's Gone Now (Shakesnider)
Leavin' for the Promised Land (Dale, ensemble)
\---
It Takes a Long Pull to Get There (Smalls, men)
I Got Plenty o' Nuttin' (Albert, ensemble)
Struttin' Style (Brice)
Buzzard Song (Albert, ensemble)
Bess, You Is My Woman Now (Albert, Dale)
Oh, I Can't Sit Down (ensemble)
\---
I Ain't Got No Shame (ensemble)
It Ain't Necessarily So (Marshall, ensemble)
What You Want wid Bess (Dale, Smith)
Oh, Doctor Jesus (Shakesnider, Brice, Wallace, Merritt, Albert)
I Loves You, Porgy (Albert, Dale)
\---
Oh, He'venly Father (ensemble)
Oh, de Lawd Shake de Heavens (ensemble)
Oh, Dere's Somebody Knockin' at de Do (ensemble)
A Red Headed Woman (Smith, ensemble)
Clara, Clara (ensemble)
\---
There's a Boat Dat's Leavin' Soon for New York (Marshall, Dale)
Good Mornin', Sistuh! (ensemble)
Oh Bess, Oh Where's My Bess (Albert, Shakesnider, Brice)
Oh Lawd, I'm on My Way (Albert, ensemble)

PREPPIES (August 9, 1983, Off Broadway, Promenade Theatre)

Alchemy Records AL 1001-D stereo

Music, lyrics: Gary Portnoy, Judy Hart Angelo; musical direction: Jeff Lodin

Cast: Dennis Bailey, Beth Fowler, Tom Hafner, Michael Ingram, Kathleen Rowe McAllen, David Sabin, Bob Walton

Songs: People Like Us (company)
Chance of a Lifetime (Sabin, Ingram, Fowler, Hafner)
One Step Away (Fowler)
Summertime (company)
Fairy Tales (Walton, McAllen, Bailey, company)
Parents' Farewell (company)
Bells (company)
Moving On (company)

Summertime (reprise) (boys)
We've Got Each Other (Ingram, Fowler)
Gonna Run (Walton)
No Big Deal (company)
Worlds Apart (Walton, McAllen)
Loot (Bailey, company)
Poeple Like Us (reprise) (company)

PROMENADE (June 4, 1969, Off Broadway, Promenade Theatre)

RCA LSO 1161 stereo

Music: Al Carmines; lyrics: Maria Irene Fornes; musical direction: Al Carmines

Cast: Margo Albert, Shannon Bolin, Michael Davis, Glenn Kezer, Ty McConnell, Alice Playten, Gilbert Price, Sandra Schaeffer, Al Settimio, Florence Tarlow, Carrie Wilson

Songs: Promenade Theme (orchestra)
Unrequited Love (Albert, Wilson, Playten, Settimio, ensemble)
The Cigarette Song (Schaeffer, McConnell, Price)
A Flower (Albert)
Isn't That Clear? (Kezer, ensemble)
Two Little Angels (Bolin, McConnell, Price, Schaeffer)
Four (Albert, Wilson, Playten, Kezer, Davis, Settimio)
Chicken Is He (Tarlow)
The Passing of Time (McConnell, Price)
Crown Me (Schaeffer, McConnell, Price)

Capricious and Fickle (Playten)
The Moment Has Passed (Wilson)
Little Fool (Davis, ensemble)
The Clothes Make the Man (Schaeffer, McConnell, Price)
A Poor Man (McConnell, Price)
Listen, I Feel (Schaeffer)
I Saw a Man (Bolin)
All Is Well in the City (McConnell, Price, ensemble)

PROMISES, PROMISES (December 1, 1968, Shubert Theatre)

United Artists UAS 9902 stereo

Music: Burt Bacharach; lyrics: Hal David; based on the screen play <u>The Apartment</u> by Billy Wilder and I.A.L. Diamond; musical direction: Harold Wheeler

Cast: A. Larry Haines, Neil Jones, Baayork Lee, Donna McKechnie, Marion Mercer, Vince O'Brien, Rita O'Connor, Jill O'Hara, Dick O'Neill, Jerry Orbach, Kay Oslin, Paul Reed, Margo Sappington, Norman Shelly, Julane Stites, Edward Winter

Songs: Overture (orchestra)
Half As Big As Life (Orbach)
Upstairs (Orbach)
You'll Think of Someone (Orbach, O'Hara)
Our Little Secret (Orbach, Winter)
She Likes Basketball (Orbach)
Knowing When to Leave (O'Hara)
Wanting Things (Winter)

Turkey Lurkey Time (McKechnie, Sappington, Lee)
A Fact Can Be a Beautiful Thing (Orbach, Mercer)
Grapes of Roth (orchestra)
Whoever You Are (O'Hara)
Where Can You Take a Girl? (Reed, Shelly, O'Brien, O'Neill)
Christmas Day (Winter, Oslin, O'Connor, Stites, Jones)
A Young Pretty Girl Like You (Orbach, Haines)
I'll Never Fall in Love Again (O'Hara, Orbach)
Promises, Promises (Orbach)

PUMP BOYS AND DINETTES (October 1, 1981, Off Broadway, Colonnades Theatre Lab; transferred, February 4, 1982, Princess Theatre)

CBS Records 37790 stereo

Music, lyrics: John Foley, Mark Hardwick, Margaret LaMee, Debra Monk, Malcolm Ruhl, John Schimmel; musical direction: John Miller

Cast: John Foley, Mark Hardwick, Debra Monk, Cass Morgan, John Schimmel, Jim Wann

Songs: Highway 57 (company)
Taking It Slow (Foley, Hardwick, Schimmel, Wann)
Serve Yourself (Hardwick)
Menu Song (Morgan, Monk)
The Best Man (Monk)
Fisherman's Prayer (Foley, Hardwick, Schimmel, Wann)
Catfish (Foley, Hardwick, Schimmel, Wann)
Mamaw (Foley)
Be Good or Be Gone (Morgan)

Drinkin' Shoes (company)
Pump Boys (Foley, Hardwick, Schimmel, Wann)
Mona (Foley)
The Night Dolly Parton Was Almost Mine (Hardwick)
Tips (Morgan, Monk)
Sister (Morgan, Monk)
Vacation (Morgan, company)

No Holds Barred (company)
Farmer Tan (Hardwick, Morgan, Monk)
Closing Time (company)

PURLIE (March 15, 1970, Broadway Theatre)

Ampex Records A40101 stereo

Music: Gary Geld; lyrics: Peter Udell; based on the play Purlie Victorious by Ossie Davis; musical direction: Joyce Brown

Cast: C. David Colson, John Heffernan, Sherman Hemsley, Linda Hopkins, Cleavon Little, Melba Moore, Novella Nelson

Songs: Walk Him Up the Stairs (Hopkins, company)
New Fangled Preacher Man (Little)
Skinnin' a Cat (Hemsley, chorus)
Purlie (Moore)
The Harder They Fall (Little, Moore)
The Barrels of War (Colson)
The Unborn Love (Colson)
Big Fish, Little Fish (Heffernan, Colson)
God's Alive (Colson)
I Got Love (Moore)

Great White Father (male chorus)
Down Home (Little, Nelson)
First Thing Monday Mornin' (chorus)
He Can Do It (Nelson, Moore)
The World Is Comin' to a Start (Colson, company)
Walk Him Up the Stairs (reprise) (Little, company)

RAISIN (October 18, 1973, Forty-Sixth Street Theatre)

Columbia KS 32754 stereo

Music: Judd Woldin; lyrics: Robert Brittan; based on Lorraine Hansberry's A Raisin in the Sun; musical direction: Howard A. Roberts

Cast: Deborah Allen, Virginia Capers, Ralph Carter, Herb Downer, Ernestine Jackson, Robert Jackson, Helen Martin, Joe Morton, Marenda Perry

Songs: Prologue (orchestra)
Man Say (Morton, E. Jackson)
Whose Little Angry Man (E. Jackson)
Runnin' to Meet the Man (Morton, company)
A Whole Lotta Sunshine (Capers)
Alaiyo (R. Jackson, Allen)
Sweet Time (E. Jackson, Morton)
You Done Right (Morton, Capers)

He Come Down This Morning (Downer, Capers, Perry, Martin, E. Jackson, Carter, company)
It's a Deal (Morton)

Sidewalk Tree (Carter)
It's a Deal - coda (Morton)
Not Anymore (Morton, E. Jackson, Allen, Capers)
It's a Deal (reprise) (Morton, Capers, E. Jackson)
Measure the Valleys (Capers)
Finale (company)

REDHEAD (February 5, 1959, Forty-Sixth Street Theatre)

RCA LSO 1104 stereo

Music: Albert Hague; lyrics: Dorothy Fields; musical direction: Jay Blackton

Cast: Bob Dixon, Pat Ferrier, Richard Kiley, Cynthia Latham, Joy Nichols, Doris Rich, Leonard Stone, Gwen Verdon

Songs: Overture (orchestra)
The Simpson Sisters (ensemble)
The Right Finger of My Left Hand (Verdon)
Just for Once (Verdon, Kiley, Stone)
I Feel Merely Marvelous (Verdon)
The Uncle Sam Rag (Stone, ensemble)
Erbie Fitch's Twitch (Verdon)
She's Not Enough Woman for Me (Kiley, ensemble)
Behave Yourself (Verdon, Latham, Rich)

Look Who's in Love (Verdon, Kiley)
My Girl Is Just Enough Woman for Me (Kiley, ensemble)
Dream Dance (Essie's Vision) (orchestra)
Two Faces in the Dark (Dixon, ensemble)
I'm Back in Circulation (Kiley)
We Love Ya, Jimey (Nichols, Ferrier, ensemble)
Pick-Pocket Tango (orchestra)
I'll Try (Verdon, Kiley)
Chase and Finale (company)

REX (April 25, 1976, Lunt-Fontanne Theatre)

RCA ABL 1-1683 stereo

Music: Richard Rodgers; lyrics: Sheldon Harnick; musical direction: Jay Blackton

Cast: Tom Aldredge, Barbara Andres, Glenn Close, Ed Evanko, Penny Fuller, Merwin Goldsmith, Michael John, Nicol Williamson

Songs: Overture (orchestra)
Te Deum (chorus)
No Song More Pleasing (Evanko, Williamson)
At the Field of Cloth of Gold (company)
Where Is My Son? (Williamson)
As Once I Loved You (Andres)
The Chase (Aldredge, Goldsmith, Evanko, men)
Away from You (Williamson, Fuller)
Elizabeth (Evanko)

--- Why? (Williamson)
So Much You Loved Me (Fuller)
Christmas at Hampton Court (John, Close, Fuller)
The Wee Golden Warrior (Aldredge, chorus)
Christmas at Hampton Court (reprise) (chorus)
From Afar (Williamson)
In Time (Fuller)
Finale (Te Deum) (company)

THE RINK (February 9, 1984, Martin Beck Theatre)

Polydor Records 823 125-1 Y-1 stereo CD

Music: John Kander; lyrics: Fred Ebb; musical direction: Paul Gemignani

Cast: Jason Alexander, Ronn Carroll, Scott Ellis, Scott Holmes, Mel Johnson, Jr., Frank Mastrocola, Liza Minnelli, Chita Rivera

Songs: Colored Lights (Minnelli)
Chief Cook and Bottle Washer (Rivera)
Don't Ah Ma Me (Rivera, Minnelli)
Blue Crystal (Holmes)
Under the Rollercoaster (Minnelli)
Not Enough Magic (Holmes, Minnelli, Rivera, Ellis, Johnson, Mastrocola, Alexander, Carroll)
We Can Make It (Rivera)
After All These Years (men)
Angel's Rink and Social Center (Minnelli, men)
--- What Happened to the Old Days? (Rivera, Carroll, Johnson)
The Apple Doesn't Fall (Rivera, Minnelli)
Marry Me (Alexander)
Mrs. A (Rivera, Minnelli, Alexander, men)
The Rink (men)
Wallflower (Rivera, Minnelli)
All the Children in a Row (Minnelli, Ellis)
Finale (Rivera, Minnelli)

RIVERWIND (December 12, 1962, Off Broadway, Actors' Playhouse)

London AMS 78001 stereo

Music, lyrics: John Jennings; musical direction: Abba Bogin

Cast: Helen Blount, Lawrence Brooks, Martin J. Cassidy, Brooks Morton, Dawn Nickerson, Elizabeth Parrish, Lovelady Powell

Songs: Prelude (orchestra)
I Cannot Tell Her So (Cassidy)
I Want a Suprise (Nickerson)
Riverwind (Parrish)
American Family Plan (Morton, Powell)
Pardon Me While I Dance (Brooks, Nickerson)

--- Wishing Song (Brooks, Cassidy, Parrish, Nickerson)
Interlude (orchestra)
Sew the Buttons On (Blount, Nickerson)
Almost, but Not Quite (Morton, Powell)
A Woman Must Think of These Things (Parrish)
I Love Your Laughing Face (Caddisy)
A Woman Must Never Grow Old (Parrish, Blount)
I'd Forgotten How Beautiful She Could Be (Brooks, Nickerson)
Riverwind (company)

THE ROAR OF THE GREASEPAINT - THE SMELL OF THE CROWD (May 16, 1965, Shubert Theatre)

RCA LSO 1109 stereo

Music, lyrics: Leslie Bricusse, Anthony Newley; musical direction: Herbert Grossman

Cast: Joyce Jillson, Anthony Newley, Gilbert Price, Cyril Ritchard, Sally Smith

Songs: Overture (orchestra)
The Beautiful Land (chorus)
A Wonderful Day Like Today (Ritchard, chorus)
It Isn't Enough (Newley, chorus)
Things to Remember (Ritchard, chorus)
Put It in the Book (Smith, chorus)
With All Due Respect (Newley, chorus)
This Dream (Newley, chorus)
Where Would You Be Without Me? (Newley, Ritchard)
--- My First Love Song (Newley, Jillson)
Look at That Face (Ritchard, Smith, chorus)
The Joker (Newley)
Who Can I Turn To (When Nobody Needs Me) (Newley)
That's What It Is to Be Young (chorus)
What a Man! (Newley, Ritchard, chorus)
Feeling Good (Price, chorus)
Nothing Can Stop Me Now (Newley, chorus)
Things to Remember (reprise) (Ritchard)
My Way (Newley, Ritchard)
The Beautiful Land (reprise) (chorus)
Sweet Beginning (Newley, Ritchard, chorus)

THE ROBBER BRIDEGROOM (October 9, 1976, Biltmore Theatre)

Columbia Special Products P14589 stereo

Music: Robert Waldman; lyrics: Alfred Uhry; based upon the novella by Eudora Welty; musical direction: Tony Trischka

Cast: Barry Bostwick, Rhonda Coullet, Barbara Lang, Carolyn McCurry, Lawrence John Moss, Trip Plymale, Ernie Sabella, Stephen Vinovich, Dennis Warning, Tom Westerman

Songs: Once Upon the Natchez Trace (Bostwick, Coullet, Vinovich, Lang, Moss, Plymale, Sabella, company)

Suddenly the Day Looks Sunny (Bostwick)
Two Heads (Moss, Sabella, company)
Steal with Style (Bostwick, company)
Rosamund's Dream (Coullet, Bostwick)
The Pricklepear Bloom (Lang, company)
Nothin' Up (Coullet, company)
Deeper in the Woods (Westerman, Warning, company)

Riches (Vinovich, Bostwick, Lang, Coullet)
Little Pieces of Sugar Cane (Bostwick, Coullet, company)
Love Stolen (Bostwick, company)
Poor Tied Up Darlin' (Moss, Plymale, company)
Mean As a Snake (McCurry, company)
Goodbye Salome (Moss, Lang, company)
Sleepy Man (Coullet, company)
Where Oh Where Is My Baby Darlin'? (Bostwick, Vinovich, Coullet, company)
Pass Her Along (company)
Wedding Ceremony (Warning)
Finale (Bostwick, company)

THE ROCKY HORROR SHOW (March 10, 1975, Belasco Theatre)

Ode Records SP77026 stereo CD

Music, lyrics: Richard O'Brien; musical direction: D'Vaughn Preshing

Cast: Tim Curry, Jamie Donnelly, Boni Enten, Abigale Haness, Graham Jarvis, Meat Loaf, Bill Miller, Kim Milford, Bruce Scott

Songs: Science Fiction (Donnelly)
Double Feature (Donnelly)
Dammit Janet (Haness, Miller)
Over at the Frankenstein Place (Haness, Miller)
Sweet Transvestite (Curry)
Time Warp (Scott, Donnelly, Enten, Jarvis, company)
The Sword of Damoclese (Milford)
Charles Atlas Song (Curry)
What Ever Happened to Saturday Night (Meat Loaf)

Charles Atlas Song (reprise) (Curry)
Toucha, Toucha, Touch Me (Haness)
Once In Awhile (Haness, Miller)
Eddie's Teddy (Meat Loaf, company)
Planet Shmanet Janet (Curry, company)
Rose Tint My World (Curry, Enten, Haness, Milford, Miller)
I'm Going Home (Curry)
Super Heroes (Haness, Miller, company)

THE ROTHSCHILDS (October 19, 1970, Lunt-Fontanne Theatre)

Columbia S 30337 stereo

Music: Jerry Bock; lyrics: Sheldon Harnick; based on _The Rothschilds_ by Frederic Morton; musical direction: Milton Greene

Cast: Robby Benson, Kenneth Bridges, Jill Clayburgh, Keene Curtis, Lee Franklin, David Garfield, Allen Gruet, Timothy Jerome, Paul Hecht, Hal Linden, Michael Maitland, Leila Martin, Jon Peck, Chris Sarandon, Mitchell Spera, Paul Tracey, Thomas Trelfa

Songs: Overture (orchestra)
Pleasure and Privilege (Curtis, company)
One Room (Martin, Linden)
He Tossed a Coin (Linden, Trelfa, Bridges, Peck, ensemble)
Sons (Linden, Martin, Franklin, Benson, Maitland, Spera)
Everything (Hecht, Martin, Garfield, Gruet, Jerome, Sarandon, Peck)
Rothschild and Sons (Linden, Hecht, Garfield, Gruet, Jerome, Sarandon)

Allons (Curtis, men)
Rothschild and Sons (reprise) (Linden, Hecht, Garfield, Gruet, Jerome, Sarandon)
Sons (reprise) (Martin, Linden, Hecht, Garfield, Gruet, Jerome, Sarandon)
Give England Strength (Curtis, men)
This Amazing London Town (Hecht, men)
They Say (Tracey, men)
I'm in Love! I'm in Love! (Hecht)
I'm in Love! I'm in Love! (reprise)(Clayburgh, Hecht)
In My Own Lifetime (Linden)
Have You Ever Seen a Prettier Little Congress? (Curtis, company)
Stability (Curtis, company)
Bonds (Hecht, Garfield, Gruet, Jerome, Sarandon, Curtis, ensemble)
The Will (Finale) (Linden)

RUGANTINO (February 6, 1964, Mark Hellinger Theatre)

Warner Brothers Records HS 1528 stereo

Music: Armando Trovajoli; lyrics: Pietro Garinei, Sandro Giovannini; musical direction: Bruno Nicolai

Cast: Aldo Fabrizi*, Lando Fiorini, Nino Manfredi*, Bice Valori*, Ornella Vanoni*

Songs: Introduzione (orchestra)
Tirollallero (Fiorini, chorus)
La Morra (chorus)
Ballata di Rugantino (Manfredi, chorus)
Anvedi si che Paciocca (Vanoni, Fiorini, chorus)
E Bello Ave 'Na Donna Dentro Casa (Fabrizi)
La Berlina (chorus)
Roma Nun Fa La Stupida Stasera (Manfredi, Vanoni, Valori, Fabrizi, Fiorini, chorus)

Introduzione (orchestra)
Ciumachella de Trastevere (Fiorini, chorus)
'Na Botta E Via (Vanoni)
Sempre Boia E (Valori)

Saltarello (chorus)
Tira A Campa (Fabrizi, chorus)
E L'Omo Nio (Vanoni)
Stornelli E Finale (Valori, Vanoni, Manfredi, chorus)

Note: Rome cast recording, with some (*) who also appeared in New York production. First foreign language attraction to use subtitles on Broadway.

RUNAWAYS (May 13, 1978, Plymouth Theatre)

Columbia JS 35410 stereo

Music, lyrics: Elizabeth Swados; musical direction: Elizabeth Swados

Cast: Bernie Allison, Trini Alvarado, Leonard D. Brown, Mark Anthony Butler, Ray Contreras, Jossie De Guzman, Karen Evans, Judith Fleisher, Patience Higgins, Bruce Hlibok, Diane Lane, Evan H. Miranda, Nan-Lynn Nelson, Venustra K. Robinson, Randy Ruiz, David Schechter, John Schimmel

Songs: Where Do People Go (company)
Every Now and Then (Allison, company)
Minnesota Strip (Robinson)
Song of a Child Prostitute (Lane, De Guzman, Ruiz, Contreras)
Find Me a Hero (Schechter, company)
The Undiscovered Son (Miranda, Fleisher, Schimmel)
No Lullabies for Luis (De Guzman, Contreras, Higgins, company)
We Are Not Strangers (Miranda, company)
The Basketball Song (Brown, company)
Let Me Be a Kid (company)
Revenge Song (company)
Enterprise (Evans, Nelson, Butler, company)
Lullaby from Baby to Baby (Alvarado, Hlibok, Evans)
Sometimes (Robinson, Schechter, company)
Where Are Those People Who Did "Hair" (Schechter, Evans)
To the Dead of Family Wars (Evans)
Lonesome of the Road (Contreras, Allison, company)
Let Me Be a Kid (reprise) (company)

SAIL AWAY (October 3, 1961, Broadhurst Theatre)

Capitol SWAO 1643 stereo

Music, lyrics: Noel Coward; musical direction: Peter Matz

Cast: Charles Braswell, Grover Dale, Patricia Harty, James Hurst, Paul O'Keefe, Elaine Stritch

Songs: Come to Me (Stritch, men)
Sail Away (Hurst, company)
Where Shall I Find Him? (Harty)
Beatnik Love Affair (Dale)

Later Than Spring (Hurst)
The Passenger's Always Right (Braswell, men)
Useful Phrases (Stritch)
--- You're a Long, Long Way from America (Stritch, company)
The Customer's Always Right (Braswell, men)
Something Very Strange (Stritch)
Go Slow, Johnny (Hurst)
The Little Ones' ABC (Stritch, O'Keefe, children)
Don't Turn Away from Love (Hurst)
When You Want Me (Dale, Harty)
Why Do the Wrong People Travel? (Stritch)

ST. LOUIS WOMAN (March 30, 1946, Martin Beck Theatre)

Capitol 355 mono reissued: DW 2742

Music: Harold Arlen; lyrics: Johnny Mercer; based on the novel God Sends Sunday by Arna Bontemps; musical direction: Leon Leonardi

Cast: Pearl Bailey, June Hawkins, Ruby Hill, Harold Nicholas, Robert Pope

Songs: Li'l Augie Is a Natural Man (Pope)
Any Place I Hang My Hat Is Home (Hill, chorus)
I Had Myself a True Love (Hawkins)
Legalize My Name (Bailey)
Cakewalk Your Lady (chorus)
Come Rain or Come Shine (Hill, Nicholas)
--- Lullaby (Hill)
Sleep Peaceful (Mr. Used-to-Be) (Hawkins)
Leavin' Time (chorus)
It's a Woman's Prerogative (Bailey)
Ridin' on the Moon (Nicholas, chorus)

SALVATION (March 11, 1969, Off Broadway, Village Gate)

Capitol SO 337 stereo

Music, lyrics: Peter Link, C.C. Courtney; musical direction: Kirk Nurock

Cast: Yolande Bavan, C.C. Courtney, Boni Enten, Marta Heflin, Peter Link, Joe Morton, Annie Rachel, Chapman Roberts

Songs: Salvation (Courtney, Bavan, Rachel, Roberts, Morton, Heflin)
In Between (Heflin, Rachel, Bavan, Roberts)
1001 (Roberts)
Honest Confession Is Good for the Soul (Courtney, Enten, Link, company)
Ballin' (company)
Let the Moment Slip By (Rachel)
Gina (Morton, Link, company)
For Ever (Roberts, Morton, Heflin)
If You Let Me Make Love to You Then Why Can't I Touch

You (company)

There Ain't No Flies on Jesus (Roberts, Link, Morton, company)
Deadalus (Bavan)
Let's Get Lost in Now (Link, Morton, company)
Back to Genesis (company)
Tomorrow Is the First Day of the Rest of My Life (company)

THE SAP OF LIFE (October 2, 1961, Off Broadway, One Sheridan Square)

Blue Pear BP 1002 mono

Music: David Shire; lyrics: Richard Maltby, Jr.; musical direction: Julian Stein

Cast: Jack Bittner, Patricia Bruder, Jerry Dodge, Lilian Fields, Kenneth Nelson, Dina Paisner, Lee Powell

Songs: Saturday Morning (Nelson, Dodge)
Farewell, Family (Nelson, Bittner, Paisner)
Charmed Life (Nelson, Dodge)
Arrival in the City (Nelson, Dodge, Powell)
Fill Up Your Life with Sunshine (Bittner, Paisner)
Good Morning (Bruder, Nelson)
Watching the Big Parade Go By (Dodge)

The Love of Your Life (Nelson, Dodge, Bittner, Paisner)
Introduction, Act Two (orchestra)
A Hero's Love (Nelson, Bruder)
Children Have It Easy (Nelson, Fields)
She Loves Me Not (Dodge, Powell, Nelson)
Mind Over Matter (Bittner)
Time and Time Again (Bruder)
Finale (company)

SARATOGA (December 7, 1959, Winter Garden Theatre)

RCA LSO 1051 stereo

Music: Harold Arlen; lyrics: Johnny Mercer; based on the novel Saratoga Trunk by Edna Ferber; musical direction: Jerry Arlen

Cast: Carol Brice, Howard Keel, Carol Lawrence, Odette Myrtil

Songs: One Step, Two Step (chorus)
I'll Be Respectable (Lawrence)
Gettin' a Man (Brice, Myrtil)
Why Fight This? (Lawrence, Keel)
Petticoat High (chorus)
A Game of Poker (Keel, Lawrence)
Love Held Lightly (Myrtil)
A Game of Poker (reprise) (Lawrence, Keel)

Saratoga: Duet (Keel, Lawrence)
Countin' Our Chickens (Lawrence, Keel)

You or No One (Keel)
The Cure (chorus)
The Man in My Life (Lawrence)
The Men Who Run the Country (men)
Goose Never Be a Peacock (Brice)
Dog Eat Dog (men)
The Railroad Fight (orchestra)
Finale (company)

SAY, DARLING (April 3, 1958, ANTA Theatre)

RCA LOC 1045 mono

Music: Jule Styne; lyrics: Betty Comden, Adolph Green; musical direction: Sid Ramin

Cast: Vivian Blaine, Jerome Cowan, Johnny Desmond, Mitchell Gregg, David Wayne

Songs: Overture (orchestra)
Try to Love Me (Blaine)
It's Doom (Desmond)
The Husking Bee (Desmond, cast)
It's the Second Time You Meet That Matters (Desmond)
Let the Lower Lights Be Burning (Wayne, Cowan)
Chief of Love (Blaine)

Say, Darling (Desmond)
The Carnival Song (Wayne, Blaine)
Try to Love Me (Desmond)
Dance Only with Me (Blaine, Gregg)
Something's Always Happening on the River (Wayne, cast)
Finale (cast)

SCRAMBLED FEET (June 11, 1979, Off Broadway, Village Gate)

DRG Records 6105 stereo

Music, lyrics: John Driver, Jeffrey Haddow; musical direction: Jimmy Wisner

Cast: Evalyn Baron, John Driver, Jeffrey Haddow, Roger Neil

Songs: Haven't We Met? (ensemble)
Goin' to the Theatre (ensemble)
Makin' the Rounds (ensemble)
Agent Sketch (Haddow, Driver) spoken
Composer Tango (Neil, Baron)
British (Haddow, Baron, Driver)
Could Have Been (Driver, Baron)
Theatre-Party-Ladies (Driver, Haddow, Neil)

Guru (Haddow) spoken
Love in the Wings (Baron, Neil)
Good Connections (Driver, Haddow)
More Than Love (Neil)
Have You Ever Been on the Stage? (Baron)
Advice to Producers (ensemble)

Happy Family (ensemble)

THE SECRET LIFE OF WALTER MITTY (October 26, 1964, Off Broadway, Players Theatre)

Columbia OS 2720 stereo

Music: Leon Carr; lyrics: Earl Shuman; based on the story by James Thurber; musical direction: Joe Stecko

Cast: Cathryn Damon, Marc London, Rue McClanahan, Christopher Norris, Lette Rehnolds, Eugene Roche, Charles Rydell, Lorraine Serabian, Rudy Tronto

Songs: Prologue: The Secret Life (company)
The Walter Mitty March (London, company)
Walking with Peninnah (London, Norris)
Drip, Drop Tapoketa (London, company)
Aggie (London)
Don't Forget (London, Serabian, Norris)
Marriage is for Old Folks (Damon, London, Tronto, boys)
Willa (Rydell)
Confidence (Tronto, Damon, London, company)

Hello, I Love You, Goodbye (Roche, London, Tronto)
Fan the Flame (Damon, boys)
Two Little Pussycats (McClanahan, Rehnolds)
Now That I Am Forty (London, Damon, Tronto, company)
You're Not (London, Serabian, company)
Aggie (reprise) (Serabian)
Lonely Ones (London, Damon, Roche, Rydell)
The Walter Mitty March (reprise) (company)
Epilogue: The Secret Life (Damon, Serabian, company)

SEESAW (March 19, 1973, Uris Theatre)

Buddah BDS 95006-1 stereo reissued: Columbia CSP X 15563

Music: Cy Coleman; lyrics: Dorothy Fields; based on the play Two for the Seesaw by William Gibson; musical direction: Don Pippin

Cast: LaMonte DesFontaines, Giancarlo Esposito, Ken Howard, Michele Lee, Cecelia Norfleet, Tommy Tune

Songs: Seesaw (company)
My City (company)
Nobody Does It Like Me (Lee)
In Tune (Lee, Howard, company)
Spanglish (Esposito, Lee, Howard, company)
Welcome to Holiday Inn (Lee)
You're a Lovable Lunatic (Howard)
He's Good for Me (Lee)
Ride Out the Storm (DesFontaines, Norfleet, company)

Entr'acte (orchestra)
We've Got It (Howard)
Chapter 54, Number 1909 (Tune, Howard, Lee, company)

Seesaw Ballet (orchestra)
It's Not Where You Start (Tune, company)
I'm Way Ahead (Lee)
Seesaw (reprise) (Lee)
It's Not Where You Start (reprise) (company)

SEVENTEEN (June 21, 1951, Broadhurst Theatre)

RCA LOC 1003 mono reissued: CBM 1-2034

Music: Walter Kent; lyrics: Kim Gannon; based on the novel by Booth Tarkington; musical direction: Vincent Travers

Cast: Frank Albertson, Alonzo Bosan, Joan Bowman, Bonnie Brae, Carol Cole, Ann Crowley, Doris Dalton, Maurice Ellis, Dick Kallman, Ellen McCown, Sherry McCutcheon, Harrison Muller, Kenneth Nelson, Elizabeth Pacetti, Helen Wood

Songs: Weatherbee's Drug Store (chorus)
This Was Just Another Day(Crowley, Nelson)
Things Are Gonna Hum This Summer (chorus)
How Do You Do, Miss Pratt? (Nelson)
Summertime Is Summertime (chorus)
Reciprocity (Crowley, chorus)
Ode to Lola (McCown, Wood, Bowman, Brae, Cole, McCutcheon, Pacetti)

A Headache and a Heartache (Dalton, Albertson)
Ooh-Ooh-Ooh, What You Do to Me (Muller, chorus)
The Hoosier Way (Muller, chorus)
If We Only Could Stop the Old Town Clock (Crowley, Nelson, Muller)
I Could Get Married Today (Nelson, Ellis, Bosan)
After All, It's Spring (McCown, Kallman, chorus)

1776 (March 16, 1969, Forty-Sixth Street Theatre)

Columbia BOS 3310 stereo

Music, lyrics: Sherman Edwards; musical direction: Peter Howard

Cast: Betty Buckley, Clifford David, William Daniels, William Duell, Rex Everhart, Paul Hecht, Ronald Holgate, Ken Howard, Scott Jarvis, Henry LeClair, B.J. Slater, Virginia Vestoff, David Vosburgh

Songs: Overture (orchestra)
Sit Down, John (Daniels, company)
Fiddle, Twiddle and Resolve (Daniels)
Till Then (Daniels, Vestoff)
The Lees of Old Virginia (Holgate, Everhart, Daniels)
But, Mr. Adams (Daniels, Everhart, Howard, Vosburgh, LeClair)
Yours, Yours, Yours (Daniels, Vestoff)

He Plays the Violin (Buckley, Everhart, Daniels)

Cool, Cool, Considerate Men (Hecht, chorus)
Momma Look Sharp (Jarvis, Duell, Slater)
The Egg (Everhart, Daniels, Howard)
Molasses and Rum (David)
Is Anybody There? (Daniels)
Finale (company)

Note: Rex Everhart replaces Howard da Silva for this recording.

SEVENTH HEAVEN (May 26, 1955, ANTA Theatre)

Decca DL 9001 mono

Music: Victor Young; lyrics: Stella Unger; based upon the play by Austin Strong; musical direction: Max Meth

Cast: Robert Clary, Gloria DeHaven, Patricia Hammerlee, Ricardo Montalban, Gerrianne Raphael, Chita Rivera

Songs: Overture (orchestra)
C'est La Vie (Clary, chorus)
Where Is That Someone for Me (DeHaven, chorus)
Camille, Collette, Fifi (Rivera, Hammerlee, Raphael)
A Man with a Dream (Montalban, chorus)
Remarkable Fellow (Montalban, chorus)
If It's a Dream (DeHaven)
Happy Little Crook (Clary)
Sun at My Window, Love at My Door (DeHaven, Montalban, chorus)
A "Miss You" Kiss (Montalban, chorus)
White and Gold Ballet (orchestra)
Love, Love, Love (Raphael, Hammerlee, Rivera, men)
Love Sneaks Up on You (Clary, Hammerlee)
C'est La Vie (reprise) (Clary, chorus)

70, GIRLS, 70 (April 15, 1971, Broadhurst Theatre)

Columbia S 30589 stereo

Music: John Kander; lyrics: Fred Ebb; based upon the play Breath of Spring by Peter Coke; musical direction: Oscar Kosarin

Cast: Thomas Anderson, Tommy Breslin, Hans Conried, Joey Faye, Dorothea Freitag, Ruth Gillette, Lloyd Harris, Lillian Hayman, Henrietta Jacobson, Gil Lamb, Lucie Lancaster, Abby Lewis, Steve Mills, Mildred Natwick, Lillian Roth, Goldye Shaw, Beau Tilden, Bobbi Tremain, Jay Velie, Coley Worth

Songs: Old Folks (company)
Home (Natwick, Roth, Lancaster, Lamb, Conried, Hayman, Shaw)
Broadway My Street (Hayman, Shaw, Anderson, Faye, Harris, Jacobson, Tilden, Tremain, Velie, Worth)
The Caper (Conried)

Coffee in a Cardboard Cup (Hayman, Shaw)
You and I, Love (Mills, Lewis, Anderson, Gillette, Harris, Tremain, Velie, Worth)
Do We? (Lancaster, Lamb)
Hit It, Lorraine (Natwick, Conried, Roth, Lancaster, Freitag)

See the Light (Roth, Faye, Worth, Anderson, Velie)
Boom Ditty Boom (Natwick, Conried, Roth, Lamb, Hayman, Lancaster, Shaw)
Believe (Hayman, Natwick, Conried, Roth, Lamb, Lancaster, Shaw)
Go Visit (Breslin, Jacobson)
70, Girls, 70 (company)
The Elephant Song (Natwick, Hayman, Shaw)
Yes (Natwick, company)
Finale (company)

SHE LOVES ME (April 23, 1963, Eugene O'Neill Theatre)

MGM Records SE 4118OC-2 (two records) stereo reissued: Stet DS-2-15008

Music: Jerry Bock; lyrics: Sheldon Harnick; based on a play by Miklos Laszlo; musical direction: Harold Hastings

Cast: Trude Adams, Barbara Baxley, Marion Brash, Jack Cassidy, Gino Conforti, Barbara Cook, Ludwig Donath, Nathaniel Frey, Daniel Massey, Peg Murray, Wood Romoff, Joe Ross, Jo Wilder, Ralph Williams

Songs: Prelude (orchestra)
Good Morning, Good Day (Williams, Frey, Baxley, Cassidy, Massey)
Sounds While Selling (Massey, Frey, Cassidy, Brash, Murray, Adams)
Thank You, Madam (Frey, Massey, Cassidy, Baxley, Brash, Murray)
Days Gone By (Donath, Massey)
No More Candy (Cook)
Three Letters (Cook, Massey)
Tonight at Eight (Massey)
I Don't Know His Name (Cook, Baxley)
Perspective (Frey)

Good Bye, Georg (Baxley, Frey, Cassidy, Williams, chorus)
Will He Like Me? (Cook)
Ilona (Cassidy)
I Resolve (Baxley)
A Romantic Atmosphere (Romoff)
Tango Tragique (Massey, Cook, Romoff)
Dear Friend (Cook)

Overture to Act II (orchestra)
Try Me (Williams)
Where's My Shoe? (Cook, Massey)
Ice Cream (Cook)
She Loves Me (Massey)

A Trip to the Library (Baxley)
Grand Knowing You (Cassidy)
Twelve Days to Christmas (Conforti, Wilder, Ross, company)
Ice Cream (reprise) (Cook, Massey)

SHENANDOAH (January 7, 1975, Alvin Theatre)

RCA ARL 1-1019 stereo

Music: Gary Geld; lyrics: Peter Udell; based on an original screenplay by James Lee Barrett; musical direction: Lynn Crigler

Cast: Ted Agress, John Cullum, Chip Ford, Gordon Halliday, Gary Harger, Joel Higgins, Penelope Milford, Robert Rosen, David Russell, Joseph Shapiro, Jordan Suffin, Donna Theodore, Charles Welch

Songs: Raise the Flag of Dixie (ensemble)
I've Heard It All Before (Cullum)
Why Am I Me (Shapiro, Ford)
Next to Lovin' (I Like Fightin') (Suffin, Higgins, Rosen, Agress, Russell)
Over the Hill (Milford)
The Pickers Are Comin' (Cullum)
Meditation (Cullum)

We Make a Beautiful Pair (Theodore, Milford)
Violets and Silverbells (Milford, Halliday, Welch, ensemble)
It's a Boy (Cullum)
Papa's Gonna Make It Alright (Cullum)
Freedom (Theodore, Ford)
Violets and Silverbells (reprise) (Higgins, Theodore)
The Only Home I Know (Harger, ensemble)
Meditation (Cullum)
Pass the Cross to Me (ensemble)

SHOESTRING '57 (November 5, 1956, Off Broadway, Barbizon Plaza Theatre)

Offbeat Records O-4012 mono reissued: Painted Smiles PS 1362

Music: Bud McCreery, Shelley Mowell, Claibe Richardson, Harvey Schmidt, Charles Strouse, G. Wood; lyrics: Tom Jones, Bruce Kirby, Bud McCreery, Paul Rosner, Mike Stewart, G. Wood; musical direction: Dorothea Freitag

Cast: Beatrice Arthur, John Bartis, Danny Carroll, Fay DeWitt, Dody Goodman, Dorothy Greener, Bill McCutcheon, G. Wood

Songs: Dress Rehearsal (company)
Entire History of the World in Two Minutes and Thirty-Two Seconds (company) music: Mowell; lyrics: Stewart
What's a Show (Bartis) music: Mowell; lyrics: Stewart
Renoir, Degas and Toulouse (DeWitt) music, lyrics:

McCreery
Three Loves (Carroll) music: Strouse; lyrics: Stewart
Tennessee Williams' Notes from a Certain S.R.O. (Goodman) spoken
Gonna Be Rich (Wood) music, lyrics: Wood
Mink, Mink, Mink (Arthur, Goodman, Greener) music, lyrics: McCreery

---

Don't Say You Like Tchaikovsky (company) music: Richardson; lyrics: Rosner
WAbash 4-7473 (Carroll) music: Wood; lyrics: Kirby
Rochelle Hudson Tango (Goodman, Wood) music: Richardson, lyrics: Rosner
At Twenty-Two (Bartis) music: Schmidt; lyrics: Jones
Lament on Fifth Avenue (company) music: Richardson; lyrics: Rosner
Coffee (DeWitt, McCutcheon) spoken
Paducah (Bartis) music: Mowell; lyrics: Stewart
On a Shoestring (company) music, lyrics: Wood

Note: Recorded in 1959; selections and cast differ on original recording from the reissue; reissue listed above.

SHOESTRING REVUE (February 28, 1955, Off Broadway, President Theatre)

Offbeat Records O-4011 mono reissued: Painted Smiles PS 1360

Music: Leopold Anteime, David Baker, Ronny Graham, Sheldon Harnick, Jim Mahoney, Lloyd B. Norlin, Charles Strouse; lyrics: Lee Adams, Anthony Chalmers, Ronny Graham, Sheldon Harnick, Jim Mahoney, Mike Stewart; musical direction: Dorothea Freitag

Cast: Beatrice Arthur, Fay DeWitt, Dody Goodman, Dorothy Greener, Bill McCutcheon, G. Wood

Songs: Man's Inhumanity to Man (company) music: Strouse; lyrics: Stewart
Roller Derby (Greener) spoken
Someone Is Sending Me Flowers (Goodman) music: Baker; lyrics: Harnick
In Bed with the Reader's Digest (company) spoken
Garbage (Arthur) music, lyrics: Harnick
The Trouble with Miss Manderson (Goodman, Wood) spoken
The Sea Is All Around Us (McCutcheon) music: Baker; lyrics: Harnick
Family Trouble (Goodman, Wood) music: Anteime; lyrics: Chalmers

---

The Arts (Arthur, Greener, DeWitt) music: Strouse; lyrics: Adams
Grace Fogarty (Greener) spoken
Laddie (DeWitt) music, lyrics: Mahoney
Couldn't Be Happier (Arthur) spoken
Medea in Disneyland (Greener, company) music: Norlin; lyrics: Harnick
Fresh and Young (company) music, lyrics: Graham

Note: Recorded in 1959; selections and cast differ on original recording from the reissue; reissue listed above.

SHOW BOAT (Revival, May 19, 1932, Casino Theatre)

Columbia Special Products AC 55 mono

Music: Jerome Kern; lyrics: Oscar Hammerstein II, P.G. Wodehouse; based on Edna Ferber's novel; musical direction: Victor Young

Cast: Countess (Olga Medolago) Albani, James Melton, Helen Morgan, Frank Munn, Paul Robeson

Songs: Overture (orchestra)
Ol' Man River (Robeson)
Bill (Morgan) lyrics: Wodehouse
--- Can't Help Lovin' Dat Man (Morgan)
You Are Love (Melton)
Make Believe (Melton)
Why Do I Love You? (Munn, Albani)
Finale (chorus)

Note: Studio cast recording; Morgan and Robeson are the only stage cast members.

SHOW BOAT (Revival, January 5, 1946, Ziegfeld Theatre)

Columbia ML 4058 mono

Musical direction: Edwin McArthur

Cast: Carol Bruce, Jan Clayton, Helen Dowdy, Charles Fredericks, Colette Lyons, Kenneth Spencer

Songs: Overture (orchestra)
Cotton Blossom (chorus)
Only Make Believe (Clayton, Fredericks)
Ol' Man River (Spencer, chorus)
--- Can't Help Lovin' Dat Man (Bruce, Dowdy, Spencer, chorus)
Life Upon the Wicked Stage (Lyons, chorus)
You Are Love (Clayton, Fredericks, chorus)
Why Do I Love You? (Clayton, Fredericks, chorus)
Bill (Bruce) lyrics: Wodehouse
Nobody Else But Me (Clayton, chorus)

SHOW BOAT (Revival, July 19, 1966, New York State Theatre)

RCA LSO 1126 stereo

Musical direction: Franz Allers

Cast: Barbara Cook, Stephen Douglass, Rosetta Le Noire, Allyn Ann McLerie, Eddie Phillips, Constance Towers, William Warfield, David Wayne

Cotton Blossom (chorus)
Make Believe (Cook, Douglass)
Ol' Man River (William Warfield, chorus)
Can't Help Lovin' Dat Man (Towers, Le Noire, Warfield, chorus)
Life Upon the Wicked Stage (McLerie, chorus)
--- You Are Love (Cook, Douglass, chorus)
At the Chicago World's Fair (opening, Act II) (chorus)
Why Do I Love You? (Cook, Douglass, Wayne, chorus)
Bill (Towers) lyrics: Wodehouse
Good Bye My Lady Love (McLerie, Phillips) music, lyrics: Joe Howard
After the Ball (Cook, chorus) music, lyrics: Charles K. Harris
Finale: Ol' Man River (Warfield, chorus)

SHOW BOAT (Revival, April 24, 1983, Gershwin Theatre)

Painted Smiles PS 1379 (Jerome Kern Revisited, vol 3) stereo

Musical direction: Dennis Deal

Cast: Karla Burns, Lonette McKee

Songs: Mis'ry's Comin' Aroun' (McKee, Burns, chorus)
Hey, Feller! (Burns, chorus)

SHOW GIRL (January 12, 1961, Eugene O'Neill Theatre)

Roulette Records SR 80001 stereo

Music, lyrics: Charles Gaynor; musical direction: Robert Hunter

Cast: Carol Channing, Jules Munshin, les Quat' Jeudis

Songs: Overture (orchestra)
The Girl in the Show (Channing)
Calypso Pete (Channing)
The Girl Who Lived in Montparnasse (Munshin, les Quat' Jeudis)
Join Us in a Cup of Tea (Channing)
This Is a Darned Nice Funeral (Channing)
The Yahoo Step (Channing)
Switchblade Bess (Channing)
--- Mambo-Java (les Quat' Jeudis)
You Haven't Lived Until You've Played the Palace (Channing)
Somewhere There's a Little Bluebird (Channing)
The Story of Marie (Channing, les Quat' Jeudis)
My Kind of Love (Channing, Munshin)
The Inside Story (Channing)
The Girl in the Show (reprise) (Channing)

RCA CBL 2-1851 (two records) stereo

Music: Leonard Bernstein, Mary Rodgers, Richard Rodgers, Stephen Sondheim, Jule Styne; lyrics: Stephen Sondheim; Pianists/co-musical direction: Tim Higgs, Stuart Pedlar

Cast: Tim Higgs, David Kernan, Julie McKenzie, Millicent Martin, Stuart Pedlar, Ned Sherrin

Songs: Comedy Tonight (Martin, McKenzie)
Love Is in the Air (Kernan)
The Little Things You Do Together (McKenzie, Kernan)
You Must Meet My Wife (Martin, Kernan)
Getting Married Today (Martin, McKenzie, Kernan)
I Remember (Kernan)
Can That Boy Foxtrot (Martin, McKenzie)
--- Too Many Mornings (McKenzie, Kernan)
Company (Martin, McKenzie, Kernan)
Another Hundred People (McKenzie)
Barcelona (McKenzie, Kernan)
Being Alive (Kernan, Martin, McKenzie)
I Never Do Anything Twice (Martin)
Bring On the Girls (Kernan)
Ah, Paree! (Martin)
Buddy's Blues (Kernan, Martin, McKenzie)
Broadway Baby (McKenzie)
--- You Could Drive a Person Crazy (Martin, McKenzie, Kernan)
Everybody Says Don't (Martin, McKenzie, Kernan)
There Won't Be Trumpets (Martin, McKenzie, Kernan)
Anyone Can Whistle (Kernan)
Send in the Clowns (Martin)
Pretty Lady (Martin, McKenzie, Kernan)
We're Gonna Be All Right (Martin, Kernan) music: R. Rodgers
--- A Boy Like That (Martin, McKenzie) music: Bernstein
The Boy from ... (Martin) music: M. Rodgers
If Momma Was Married (Martin, McKenzie) music: Styne
Losing My Mind (McKenzie)
Could I Leave You? (Kernan)
I'm Still Here (Martin)
Side by Side by Side (Martin, McKenzie, Kernan, Higgs, Pedlar, Sherrin)

Note: London cast recording (1976) with same cast except for Higgs and Pedlar.

SILK STOCKINGS (February 24, 1955, Imperial Theatre)

RCA LOC 1016 mono reissued: LSO 1102(e)

Music, lyrics: Cole Porter; suggested by Ninotchka by Melchior Lengyel; musical direction: Herbert Greene

Cast: Don Ameche, Leon Belasco, Henry Lascoe, Hildegarde Neff, David Opatoshu, Gretchen Wyler

Songs: Overture (orchestra)
Too Bad (Lascoe, Belasco, Opatoshu, chorus)
Paris Loves Paris (Ameche, Neff)
Stereophonic Sound (Wyler, chorus)
It's a Chemical Reaction, That's All (Neff)
All of You (Ameche)
Satin and Silk (Wyler)
Without Love (Neff)

Hail Bibinski (Opatoshu, Lascoe, Belasco, chorus)
As on Through the Seasons We Sail (Ameche, Neff)
Josephine (Wyler, chorus)
Siberia (Lascoe, Belasco, Opatoshu)
Silk Stockings (Ameche)
The Red Blues (chorus)
Too Bad (reprise) (company)

SIMPLY HEAVENLY (August 20, 1957, Playhouse Theatre)

Columbia OL 5240 mono

Music: David Martin; lyrics: Langston Hughes; based on the 'Simple' stories of Mr. Hughes; musical direction: David Martin

Cast: Marilyn Berry, John Bouie, Anna English, Brownie McGhee, Claudia McNeil, Melvin Stewart, Duke Williams

Songs: Prelude (orchestra)
Simply Heavenly (Berry)
Let Me Take You for a Ride (English, Stewart)
Broken Strings (McGhee)
Flying Saucer Monologue (Stewart) spoken
Did You Ever Hear the Blues? (McNeil, Bouie)
I'm Gonna Be John Henry (Stewart)
When I'm in a Quiet Mood (McNeil, Bouie)

Look for the Morning Star (English)
Gatekeeper of My Castle (Berry, Stewart)
Let's Ball Awhile (English, ensemble)
Beat It Out, Mon (Williams, ensemble)
The Men in My Life (English)
Good Old Girl (McNeil)
Mississippi Monologue (Stewart) spoken
Look for the Morning Star (reprise) (company)

SING MUSE! (December 6, 1961, Off Broadway, Van Dam Theatre)

Blue Pear BP 1004 mono

Music: Joseph Raposo; lyrics: Erich Segal; musical direction: Jerry Goldberg

Cast: Brandon Maggart, Paul Michael, Karren Morrow, Bob Spencer, Ralph Stantley

Songs: Helen Quit Your Yellin' (Morrow, Stantley)
I Am a Travelling Poet (Spencer)

Out to Launch (Morrow)
O Pallas Athene (Spencer)
Your Name May Be Paris (Morrow, Spencer)
Sing Muse! (Morrow, Spencer)
You're in Love (Morrow, Spencer)
The Wrath of Achilles (Stantley, Maggart, Michael)
No Champagne (Spencer)
--- Please Let Me Read (Stantley, Maggart, Michael)
Business Is Bad (Stantley, Maggart)
In Our Little Salon (Morrow)
Fame! (Michael, Maggart, Stantley)
I'm to Blame (Maggart, Stantley)
We'll Find a Way (Morrow, Spencer)
A Day at the Sexmockena Mambo (Stantley, Michael, Maggart)
Tonight's the Flight (Morrow)
Finale (company)

SING OUT, SWEET LAND! (December 27, 1944, International Theatre)

Decca DL 8023 mono

Traditional folk music, with original music: John Mundy, Elie Siegmeister; original lyrics: Edward Eager; musical direction: Elie Siegmeister

Cast: Herk Armstrong, Alfred Drake, Juanita Hall, Burl Ives, Alma Kaye, Jack McCauley, Bibi Osterwald, Ted Tiller

Songs: As I Was Going Along (Drake, chorus)
Where (Drake)
Big Rock Candy Mountain (Ives)
Blue Tail Fly (Ives, chorus)
I'm Goin' Down the Road (Ives, McCauley)
Little Mohee (Drake, Kaye)
Wanderin' (drake)
--- I Have Been a Good Boy (McCauley)
Frankie and Johnny (Ives, Kaye, McCauley, Tiller)
The Roving Gambler (McCauley, Kaye, Osterwald)
Hammer Ring (Armstrong, ensemble)
Watermelon Cry (Hall)
Didn't My Lord Deliver Daniel (Armstrong, Hall, ensemble)
Trouble, Trouble (Hall, ensemble)
Basement Blues (Hall, ensemble)
Casey Jones (Osterwald, chorus)
More Than These (Drake, chorus)

SKYSCRAPER (November 13, 1965, Lunt-Fontanne Theatre)

Capitol SVAS 2422 stereo

Music: James Van Heusen; lyrics: Sammy Cahn; based on Dream Girl by Elmer Rice; musical direction: John Lesko

Cast: Rex Everhart, Julie Harris, Peter L. Marshall, Dick O'Neill, Charles Nelson Reilly

Songs: Overture (orchestra)
An Occasional Flight of Fancy (Harris, ensemble)
Run for Your Life (Marshall, O'Neill)
Local 403 (Everhart, chorus)
Opposites (Harris, Marshall)
Just the Crust (Reilly, O'Neill)

Everybody Has the Right to Be Wrong (Marshall, Harris)
Everybody Has the Right to Be Wrong (reprise) (Harris)
The Gaiety (chorus)
More Than One Way (Marshall, chorus)
Haute Couture (Everhart, chorus)
Don't Worry (Reilly, O'Neill)
I'll Only Miss Her When I Think of Her (Marshall)
Spare That Building (company)

SMILING THE BOY FELL DEAD (April 19, 1961, Off Broadway, Cherry Lane Theatre)

Sunbeam LB 549 mono

Music: David Baker; lyrics: Sheldon Harnick; musical direction: Julian Stein

Cast: Lucinda Abbey, Russell Bailey, Ted Beniades, Claiborne Cary, Gino Conforti, Dodo Denny, Charles Goff, Justine Johnston, Danny Meehan, Heinz Neumann, Louise Larabee, Phil Leeds, Joseph Macaulay, Geraine Richards, Joseph Schaeffer, Irene Siegfried, Warren Wade

Songs: Sons of Evergreen (company)
Let's Evolve (Meehan, boys)
The ABC's of Success (Meehan, Macaulay)
If I Felt Any Younger Today (Macaulay, Larabee, Goff, Abbey, Schaeffer, Richards, Neumann, Denny, Conforti, Siegfried)
More Than Ever Now (Cary)
I've Got a Wonderful Future (Meehan)
Small Town (Macaulay, Larabee, Johnston, Goff, Abbey, Schaeffer, Richards, Neumann, Denney, Conforti, Siegfried)
Heredity-Environment (Leeds)
The Gatsby Bridge March (Bailey, Johnston)

A World to Win (Cary, Meehan)
The Wonderful Machine (Meehan, company)
Temperance Polka (Beniades, Wade, chorus)
Daydreams (Meehan)
Daydreams (reprise) (Cary)
Me and Dorothea (Leeds)
Two by Two (Cary, Meehan)
Finale (Meehan, company)

SNOW WHITE AND THE SEVEN DWARFS (October 18, 1979, Radio City Music Hall)

Buena Vista Records 5009 stereo

Music: Frank Churchill; lyrics: Larry Morey; new music: Jay Blackton; new Lyrics: Joe Cook; musical direction: Donald Pippin

Cast: Richard Bowne, Mary Joe Salerno

Songs: Overture (orchestra)
Prelude (company) includes narration
Welcome to the Kingdom (company) music: Blackton; lyrics: Cook
Queen's Presentation (company) music: Blackton; lyrics: Cook
I'm Wishing (Salerno, ladies)
One Song (Bowne)
With a Smile and a Song (Salerno, chorus)
--- Whistle While You Work (Salerno)
Heigh-Ho (dwarfs)
Bluddle-Uddle-Um-Dum (The Washing Song) (Dwarfs)
Will I Ever See Her Again (Bowne) music: Blackton; Lyrics: Cook
The Dwarfs' Yodel Song (The Silly Song) (Salerno, dwarfs)
Some Day My Prince Will Come (Salerno)
One Song (reprise) (Bowne, company)
Some Day My Prince Will Come (reprise) (company)
Finale (Here's the Happy Ending) (company) music: Blackton; lyrics: Cook

SO LONG, 174th STREET (April 27, 1976, Harkness Theatre)

Original Cast Records OC 8131 stereo

Music, lyrics: Stan Daniels; based on Joseph Stein's comedy Enter Laughing; musical direction: Milton Rosenstock

Cast: Loni Ackerman*, Kaye Ballard, James Brennan*, Stan Daniels, George S. Irving*, Patti Karr, Barbara Lang*, Robert Morse*, Lawrence John Moss*, Arthur Rubin

Songs: Overture (orchestra)
David Kolowitz, the Actor (Morse, chorus)
It's Like (Morse, Ackerman)
I'm Undressing Girls with My Eyes (Morse, Moss, girl's chorus)
Bolero on Rye (Karr, Morse, Rubin)
Whoever You Are (Morse)
Say the Words (Irving, Morse, Lang, Brennan)
You (Lang, Morse, chorus)
My Son, the Druggist (Ballard)
--- He Touched Her (Morse, Moss, men's chorus)
Men (Ackerman, Brennan, girl's chorus)
Boy, Oh Boy (Morse, company)
The Butler's Song (Irving)
Being with You (Morse, Ackerman)
If You Want to Break Your Mother's Heart (Ballard, chorus)
Hot Cha Cha (Daniels)

So Long, 174th Street (Morse, company)

Note: Studio cast album, recorded in 1981, with some cast members (*) from the stage production.

SONG AND DANCE (September 18, 1985, Royale Theatre)

RCA HBC 1-7162 stereo CD

Music: Andrew Lloyd Webber; lyrics: Don Black; musical direction: John Mauceri

Cast: Bernadette Peters (Cynthia Onrubia: voice on telephone)

Songs: Overture (orchestra)
Take That Look Off Your Face (Peters)
Let Me Finish (Peters)
So Much to Do in New York (Peters)
First Letter Home (Peters)
English Girls (Peters)
Capped Teeth and Caesar Salad (Peters, Onrubia)
You Made Me Think You Were in Love (Peters)
Capped Teeth and Caesar Salad (reprise) (Peters)
So Much to Do in New York (II) (Peters)
Second Letter Home (Peters)
Unexpected Song (Peters)

Come Back with the Same Look in Your Eyes (Peters)
Take That Look Off Your Face (reprise) (Peters)
Tell Me on a Sunday (Peters)
I Love New York: So Much to Do in New York (III) (Peters)
Married Men (Peters)
Third Letter Home (Peters)
Nothing Like You've Ever Known (Peters)
Finale: Let Me Finish (Peters)
What Have I Done? (Peters)
Take That Look Off Your Face (reprise) (Peters)

SONG OF NORWAY (August 12, 1944, Imperial Theatre)

Decca DLP 8002 mono reissued: MCA 1524E

Music: Edvard Grieg; lyrics: Robert Wright, George Forrest; based on a play by Homer Curran; musical direction: Arthur Kay

Cast: Sig Arno, Helena Bliss, Lawrence Brooks, Kitty Carlisle, Kent Edwards, Gwen Jones, Walter Kingsford, Robert Shafer, Ivy Scott

Songs: Prelude (orchestra)
Legend (Shafer)
Hill of Dreams (Brooks, Bliss, Shafer)
Freddy and His Fiddle (Edwards, Jones, chorus)
Now (Carlisle, chorus)
Strange Music (Brooks, Bliss)
Midsummer's Eve (Bliss, Brooks, Carlisle, Shafer, chorus)

--- March of the Trollgers (chorus)
Hymn of Betrothal (Scott, chorus)
Now (reprise) (Carlisle, chorus)
Strange Music (reprise) (Brooks, Bliss, chorus)
Midsummer's Eve (reprise) (Shafer, Bliss, chorus)
Bon Vivant (Arno, Brooks, chorus)
Three Loves (Carlisle)
Down Your Tea (Carlisle, chorus)
Nordraak's Farewell (Shafer)
Three Loves (reprise) (Carlisle, Bliss, chorus)
I Love You (Bliss)
At Christmastime (Kingsford, Scott, Bliss, chorus)
Finale (Brooks, Bliss, Shafer, chorus) poem: Milton Lazarus

Note: Kitty Carlisle replaced Irra Petina for this recording, due to contractural problems. Petina recorded her own studio version for Columbia, recently available on JJA Records 19782.

SONG OF NORWAY (Revival, June 22, 1958, Off Broadway, Jones Beach Marine Theatre)

Columbia CS 8135 stereo

Musical direction: Lehman Engel

Cast: Perryne Anker, Sig Arno, Brenda Lewis, William Linton, William Olvis, Muriel O'Malley, John Reardon, Helena Scott

Songs: Prelude (orchestra)
The Legend (Olvis)
Hill of Dreams (Olvis, Reardon, Scott)
Freddy and His Fiddle (Linton, Anker, chorus)
Now (Lewis, chorus)
Strange Music (Reardon, Scott)
Hymn of Betrothal (O'Malley, Olvis, chorus)
Finale, Act I (Lewis, Reardon, Olvis, Scott, chorus)
--- Bon Vivant (Arno, Reardon, chorus)
Three Loves (Lewis, Reardon)
Nordraak's Farewell (Olvis)
Finaletto (Lewis, Scott, Reardon, chorus)
I Love You (Scott)
Concerto (Stan Freeman, piano, chorus)

SOPHISTICATED LADIES (March 1, 1981, Lunt-Fontanne Theatre)

RCA CBL 2-4053 (two records) stereo

Music, lyrics: Duke Ellington, and others; musical direction: Mercer Ellington

Cast: Priscilla Baskerville, Hinton Battle, P.J. Benjamin, Gregg Burge, Gremlinn T. Creole, Michael Scott Gregory, Gregory Hines, Phyllis Hyman, Terri Klausner, Judith Jamison, Michael Lichtefeld

Songs: Things Ain't What They Used to Be (orchestra) music: Mercer Ellington
Sophisticated Lady (orchestra)
Perdido (orchestra) music: Juan Tizol
I've Got to Be a Rug Cutter (Battle, Burge, Gregory, Lichtefeld)
Music Is a Woman (Hines, Jamison) lyrics: John Guare
The Mooche (orchestra) music: Duke Ellington, Irving Mills
Hit Me with a Hot Note and Watch Me Bounce (Klausner) lyrics: Don George
Love You Madly (Jamison)
Perdido (Battle, Creole) music: Juan Tizol; lyrics: Ervin Drake, Hans Lengsfelder
Fat and Forty (Benjamin) music, Lyrics: Skeets Tolbert
It Don't Mean a Thing (Hyman, men) lyrics: Irving Mills

Bli-Blip (Benjamin, Klausner) lyrics: Duke Ellington, Sid Kuller
Cotton Tail (orchestra)
Take the 'A' Train (Hyman, Hines) music, lyrics: Billy Strayhorn
Solitude (Baskerville) lyrics: Eddie de Lange, Irving Mills
Don't Get Around Much Any More (Hines) lyrics: Bob Russell
I Let a Song Go Out of My Heart (Jamison) lyrics: Henry Nemo, Irving Mills, John Redmond
Caravan (Burge, ensemble) music: Duke Ellington, Juan Tizol; lyrics: Irving Mills
Something to Live For (Hines) music, lyrics: Duke Ellington, Irving Mills, Billy Strayhorn
Rockin' in Rhythm (company) music: Duke Ellington, Irving Mills, Harry Carney

---

In a Sentimental Mood (Hyman) lyrics: Manny Kurtz, Irving Mills
I'm Beginning to See the Light (Jamison, Hines) music, lyrics: Duke Ellington, Don George, Johnnie Hodges, Harry James
Satin Doll (Benjamin) lyrics: Billy Strayhorn, Johnny Mercer
Just Squeeze Me (Klausner) lyrics: Lee Gaines
Dancer in Love (orchestra)
Drop Me Off in Harlem (Battle, Benjamin, Hines, Burge, Baskerville, ensemble) lyrics: Nick Kenny
Echoes of Harlem (orchestra)
I'm Just a Lucky So-and-So (Hines, men) lyrics: Hal David
Hey Baby (Benjamin)

Imagine My Frustration (Klausner) music, lyrics: Duke Ellington, Billy Strayhorn, Gerald Wilson
Kinda Dukish (Hines)
I'm Checking Out Goombye (Hyman) music, lyrics: Duke Ellington, Billy Strayhorn
Do Nothing 'Til You Hear from Me (Hines) lyrics: Bob Russell
I Got It Bad and That Ain't Good (Hyman) lyrics: Paul Francis Webster
Mood Indigo (Klausner) music, lyrics: Duke Ellington,

Irving Mills, Albany 'Barney' Bigard
Sophisticated Lady (Hines) lyrics: Mitchell Parish, Irving Mills
It Don't Mean a Thing (reprise) (Hines, company)

THE SOUND OF MUSIC (Novemner 16, 1959, Lunt-Fontanne Theatre)

Columbia KOS 2020 stereo CD

Music: Richard Rodgers; lyrics: Oscar Hammerstein II; suggested by The Trapp Family Singers by Maria Augusta Trapp; musical direction: Frederick Dvonch

Cast: Theodore Bikel, Brian Davies, Elizabeth Howell, Kurt Kasznar, Marion Marlowe, Mary Martin, Patricia Neway, Muriel O'Malley, Lauri Peters, Karen Shepard

Songs: Preludium (female chorus)
The Sound of Music (Martin)
Maria (Neway, O'Malley, Howell, Shepard)
My Favorite Things (Martin, Neway)
Do-Re-Mi (Martin, children)
Sixteen Going On Seventeen (Peters, Davies)
The Lonely Goatherd (Martin, children)
How Can Love Survive (Marlowe, Kasznar)

The Sound of Music (reprise) (Martin, Bikel, children)
Laendler (orchestra)
So Long, Farewell (children)
Climb Ev'ry Mountain (Neway)
No Way to Stop It (Bikel, Kasznar, Marlowe)
An Ordinary Couple (Martin, Bikel)
Processional (female chorus)
Sixteen Going On Seventeen (reprise) (Martin, Peters)
Edelweiss (Bikel)
Climb Ev'ry Mountain (company)

SOUTH PACIFIC (April 7, 1949, Majestic Theatre)

Columbia ML 4180 mono reissued: JS 32604E

Music: Richard Rodgers; lyrics: Oscar Hammerstein II; based on James A. Michener's Tales of the South Pacific; musical direction: Salvatore Dell'Isola

Cast: Juanita Hall, Barbara Luna, Mary Martin, Ezio Pinza, William Tabbert

Songs: Overture (orchestra)
Dites Moi (Luna)
A Cockeyed Optimist (Martin)
Twin Soliloquies (Martin, Pinza)
Some Enchanted Evening (Pinza)
Bloody Mary (men's chorus)
There Is Nothin' Like a Dame (men's chorus)
Bali Ha'i (Hall)

I'm Gonna Wash That Man Right Outa My Hair (Martin, girls' chorus)

A Wonderful Guy (Martin, girls' chorus)
Younger Than Springtime (Tabbert)
Happy Talk (Hall)
Honey Bun (Martin)
Carefully Taught (Tabbert)
This Nearly Was Mine (Pinza)
Finale (Martin, Pinza, Luna)

SOUTH PACIFIC (Revival, June 12, 1967, New York State Theatre)

Columbia OS 3100 stereo

Musical direction: Jonathan Anderson

Cast: Irene Byatt, Eleanor Calbes, David Doyle, Florence Henderson, Mickey Karm, Justin McDonough, Brad Sullivan, Giorgio Tozzi, Dana Shimizu, Keenan Shimizu

Songs: Overture (orchestra)
Dites-moi (D. Shimizu, J. Shimizu)
A Cockeyed Optimist (Henderson)
Twin Soliloquies (Henderson, Tozzi)
Bloody Mary (men's chorus)
Some Enchanted Evening (Tozzi)
There Is Nothing Like a Dame (Doyle, Sullivan, Karm, men's chorus)
Bali Ha'i (Byatt)
I'm Gonna Wash That Man Right Outa My Hair (Henderson, girls' chorus)

A Wonderful Guy (Henderson, girls' chorus)
Younger Than Springtime (McDonough)
Bali Ha'i (reprise) (Calbes)
Happy Talk (Byatt)
Honey Bun (Henderson, chorus)
You've Got to Be Carefully Taught (McDonough)
This Nearly Was Mine (Tozzi)
Finale (Henderson, Tozzi, D. Shimizu, K. Shimizu)

STARTING HERE, STARTING NOW (March 7, 1977, Off Broadway, Barbarann Theatre Restaurant)

RCA ABL 1-2360 stereo

Music: David Shire; lyrics: Richard Maltby, Jr.; musical direction: Robert W. Preston

Cast: Loni Ackerman, George Lee Andrews, Margery Cohen

Songs: The Word Is Love (company)
Starting Here, Starting Now (company)
A Little Bit Off (Cohen)
I Think I May Want to Remember Today (Ackerman, Cohen)
We Can Talk to Each Other (Andrews, Cohen)
Just Across the River (company)
Crossword Puzzle (Ackerman)
Autumn (Cohen)

I Don't Remember Christmas (Andrews)
I Don't Believe It (company)
Barbara (Andrews)
Pleased with Myself (company)

Flair (Andrews)
Travel (company)
Watching the Big Parade Go By (Cohen)
I Hear Bells (Andrews, company)
What About Today? (Ackerman) lyrics: Shire
One Step (company)
Song of Me (Cohen)
Today Is the First Day of the Rest of My Life (Ackerman, Cohen)
A New Life Coming (company)
Flair (reprise) (company)

STOP THE WORLD - I WANT TO GET OFF (October 3, 1962, Shubert Theatre)

London AMS 88001 stereo reissued: Polydor 820 261-1 Y-1 CD

Music, lyrics: Leslie Bricusse, Anthony Newley; musical direction: Milton Rosenstock

Cast: Jennifer Baker, Susan Baker, Anthony Newley, Anna Quayle

Songs: Overture (orchestra)
The A. B. C. Song (chorus)
I Wanna Be Rich (Newley)
Typically English (Quayle)
Lumbered (Newley)
Glorious Russian (Quayle)
Meilinki Meilchick (Newley, Quayle)
Gonna Build a Mountain (Newley)

Typische Deutsche (Quayle)
Family Fugue (J. Baker, S. Baker, Newley, Quayle)
Nag! Nag! Nag! (chorus)
Once In a Lifetime (Newley)
All American (Quayle)
Mumbo Jumbo (Newley)
Someone Nice Like You (Newley, Quayle)
What Kind of Fool Am I? (Newley)

STOP THE WORLD - I WANT TO GET OFF (Revival, August 3, 1978, New York State Theatre)

Warner Brothers Records HS 3214 stereo

Musical direction: George Rhodes

Cast: Shelly Burch, Sammy Davis, Jr., Marion Mercer

Songs: Overture (orchestra)
The A. B. C. Song (chorus)
I Wanna Be Rich (Davis, Mercer, chorus)
Typically English (Mercer, Davis, chorus)

Lumbered (Davis)
Gonna Build a Mountain (Davis, chorus)
Glorious Russian (Mercer, chorus)
Meilinki Meilchik (Mercer, Davis, chorus)
Typische Deutsche (Mercer, chorus)
Life Is a Woman (Davis)
All-American (Mercer, chorus)
Once In a Lifetime (Davis, Burch)
Mumbo Jumbo (Davis, chorus)
Someone Nice Like You (Davis, Mercer)
What Kind of Fool Am I (Davis)

STREET SCENE (January 9, 1947, Adelphi Theatre)

Columbia ML 4139 mono reissued: CSP COL 4139

Music: Kurt Weill; lyrics: Langston Hughes; from the book by Elmer Rice; musical direction: Maurice Abravanel

Cast: Helen Arden, Bennett Burrell, Hope Emerson, Juliana Gallagher, Peter Griffith, Beverly Janis, Anne Jeffreys, Remo Lota, Ellen Repp, Don Saxon, Wilson Smith, Polyna Stoska, Brian Sullivan, Creighton Thompson

Songs: Prelude (orchestra)
Ain't It Awful the Heat (Arden, Emerson, Repp, Sullivan, Smith, chorus)
I Got a Marble and a Star (Thompson)
Get a Load of That (Emerson, Arden, Repp)
When a Woman Has a Baby (Lota, Arden, Emerson, Stoska)
Somehow I Never Could Believe (Stoska)
Wrapped in a Ribbon and Tied in a Bow (Janis, chorus)
Lonely House (Sullivan)
Wouldn't You Like to Be on Broadway? (Saxon)
What Good Would the Moon Be? (Jeffreys)
Remember That I Care (Sullivan, Jeffreys)
Morning Music (orchestra)
Catch Me If You Can (Burrell, Gallagher, Griffith, children)
A Boy Like You (Stoska)
We'll Go Away Together (Sullivan, Jeffreys)
The Woman Who Lived Up There (ensemble)
Lullaby (nursemaids)
I Loved Her, Too (Griffith, Jeffreys, ensemble)
Don't Forget the Lilac Bush (Sullivan, Jeffreys)

SUBWAYS ARE FOR SLEEPING (December 27, 1961, St. James Theatre)

Columbia KOS 2130 stereo

Music: Jule Styne; lyrics: Betty Comden, Adolph Green; suggested by the book by Edmund G. Love; musical direction: Milton Rosenstock

Cast: Orson Bean, Sydney Chaplin, Bob Gorman, Carol Lawrence, Phyllis Newman, John Sharpe, Gene Varrone, Cy Young

Songs: Overture (orchestra)
Subways Are for Sleeping (Varrone, Young, Gorman, Sharpe)
Girls Like Me (Lawrence)
Subway Directions (Chaplin, Lawrence, chorus)
Ride Through the Night (Lawrence, chorus)
I'm Just Taking My Time (Chaplin, chorus)
I Was a Shoo-In (Newman, Bean)
Who Knows What Might Have Been? (Chaplin, Lawrence)
Strange Duet (Bean, Newman)

Swing Your Projects (Chaplin)
I Said It and I'm Glad (Lawrence)
Be a Santa (Chaplin, chorus)
How Can You Describe a Face? (Chaplin)
I Just Can't Wait (Bean)
Comes Once in a Lifetime (Chaplin, Lawrence)
What Is This Feeling in the Air? (Lawrence, company)
Finale (Chaplin, Lawrence, company)

SUGAR (April 9, 1972, Majestic Theatre)

United Artists UAS 9905 stereo

Music: Jule Styne; lyrics: Bob Merrill; based on the screen play Some Like It Hot by Billy Wilder, I.A.L. Diamond; musical direction: Elliot Lawrence

Cast: Elaine Joyce, Robert Morse, Cyril Ritchard, Tony Roberts, Sheila Smith

Songs: Overture (orchestra)
Penniless Bums (Morse, Roberts, men)
The Beauty That Drives Men Mad (Morse, Roberts)
We Could Be Close (Morse, Joyce)
Sun on My Face (Morse, Roberts, Joyce, ensemble)
November Song (Ritchard, men)

Sugar (Morse, Roberts)
Hey, Why Not! (Joyce, men)
Beautiful Through and Through (Ritchard, Morse)
What Do You Give to a Man Who's Had Everything? (Roberts, Joyce)
It's Always Love (Roberts)
When You Meet a Man in Chicago (Smith, ensemble)
Finale (company)

SUGAR BABIES (October 8, 1979, Mark Hellinger Theatre)

B'way Entertainment Records BE 8302 R (recorded 1983) stereo

Music: Jimmy McHugh; lyrics: Dorothy Fields, others; additional music, lyrics: Arthur Malvin; musical direction: Larry Blank

Cast: Jack Fletcher, Ann Miller, Mickey Rooney, Scot Stewart, Sid Stone, Jane Summerhays

Songs: Overture (orchestra)

A Good Old Burlesque Show (Rooney, chorus) lyrics: Malvin
Welcome to the Gaiety (Rooney, Fletcher) spoken
Let Me Be Your Sugar Baby (girlie chorus) music, lyrics: Malvin
Travelin': In Louisiana (chorus) lyrics: Malvin
I Feel a Song Comin' On (Miller)
Goin' Back to New Orleans (Miller, chorus) music, lyrics: Malvin
Sally (Stewart, chorus) lyrics: Malvin
Don't Blame Me (Miller)
Immigration Rose (Rooney, chorus)
Introduction (Fletcher) spoken
Down at the Gaiety Burlesque (Miller, girlie chorus) music, lyrics: Malvin
Mr. Banjo Man (Miller, girlie chorus) music, lyrics: Malvin

The Candy Butcher (Stone) spoken
Entr'acte (orchestra)
I'm Keeping Myself Available for You (Summerhays, girlie chorus) lyrics: Malvin
Exactly Like You (Summerhays, girlie chorus)
I'm in the Mood for Love (Miller)
I'm Just a Song and Dance Man (Rooney)
Warm and Willing (Summerhays)
McHugh Medley Introduction (Miller, Rooney)
I Can't Give You Anything but Love (Rooney)
I'm Shooting High (Miller)
When You and I Were Young Maggie Blues (Rooney, Miller)
On the Sunny Side of the Street (Miller, Rooney)
You Can't Blame Your Uncle Sammy (Miller, Rooney, chorus)

Note: "Additional musical material can be found on the Cassette version (BE-8302-C) which the show's producers deemed extraneous."

SUNDAY IN THE PARK WITH GEORGE (May 2, 1984, Booth Theatre)

RCA HBC 1-5042 stereo CD

Music, lyrics: Stephen Sondheim; musical direction: Paul Gemigani

Cast: Barbara Bryne, Mary D'Arcy, Cris Groenendaal, Dana Ivey, Charles Kimbrough, Kurt Knudson, Judith Moore, Nancy Opel, William Parry, Mandy Patinkin, Bernadette Peters, Robert Westenberg, Brent Spiner, Melanie Vaughan

Songs: Sunday in the Park with George (Peters, Patinkin)
No Life (Kimbrough, Ivey)
Color and Light (Patinkin, Peters)
Gossip (Vaughan,D'Arcy, Bryne, Moore, Parry)
The Day Off (Patinkin, Bryne, Moore, Opel, Spiner, Vaughan,D'Arcy, Westenberg, Parry)
Everybody Loves Louis (Peters)
Finishing the Hat (Patinkin)
We Do Not Belong Together (Patinkin, Peters)

Beautiful (Bryne, Patinkin)
Sunday (company)
It's Hot Up Here (company)
Chromolume #7 (orchestra)
Putting It Together (Moore, Groenendaal, Kimbrough, Parry, Opel, Westenberg, Ivey, Patinkin, Knudson, Bryne)
Children and Art (Peters, Patinkin)
Lesson #8 (Patinkin)
Move On (Patinkin, Peters)
Sunday (reprise) (company)

SWEENEY TODD THE DEMON BARBER OF FLEET STREET (March 1, 1979, Uris Theatre)

RCA CBL 2-3379 (two records) stereo CD ('highlights')

Music, lyrics: Stephen Sondheim; based on a version by Christopher Bond; musical direction: Paul Gemignani

Cast: Len Cariou, Carole Doscher, Cris Groenendaal, Victor Garber, Skip Harris, Ken Jennings, Betsy Joslyn, Frank Kopyc, Angela Lansbury, Craig Lucas, Edmund Lyndeck, Merle Louise, Robert Ousley, Richard Warren Pugh, Sarah Rice, Joaquin Romaguera, Jack Eric Williams

Songs: Prelude (orchestra)
The Ballad of Sweeney Todd - Attend the Tale of Sweeney Todd (Cariou, company)
No Place Like London (Garber, Cariou, Louise)
The Barber and His Wife (Cariou)
The Worst Pies in London (Lansbury)
Poor Thing (Lansbury)
My Friends (Cariou, Lansbury)
The Ballad of Sweeney Todd - Lift Your Razor High, Sweeney! (company)
Green Finch and Linnet Bird (Rice)
Ah, Miss (Garber, Rice, Louise)
Johanna (Garber)

Pirelli's Miracle Elixir (Jennings, Cariou, Lansbury, Romaguera, company)
The Contest (Romaguera)
The Ballad of Sweeney Todd - Sweeney Pondered and Sweeney Planned (company)
Wait (Lansbury)
The Ballad of Sweeney Todd - His Hands Were Quick, His Fingers Strong (Groenendaal, Kopyc, Pugh)
Johanna (reprise) (Lyndeck)
Kiss Me (Rice, Garber)
Ladies in Their Sensitivities (Williams, Lyndeck)

Pretty Women (Lyndeck, Cariou, Garber)
Epiphany (Cariou, Lansbury)
A Little Priest (Lansbury, Cariou)
God, That's Good (Jennings, Lansbury, Cariou, company)
Johanna (reprise) (Garber, Cariou, Louise, Rice)

By the Sea (Lansbury, Cariou)
Wigmaker Sequence (Cariou, Garber)

The Ballad of Sweeney Todd - Sweeney'd Waited Too Long Before (Doscher, Harris, Joslyn, Lucas, Ousley)
The Letter (Doscher, Harris, Joslyn, Lucas, Ousley, Cariou)
Not While I'm Around (Jennings, Lansbury)
Parlor Songs (Williams, Lansbury, Jennings)
Final Sequence (company)
The Ballad of Sweeney Todd - Attend the Tale of Sweeney Todd (company)

SWEET CHARITY (January 29, 1966, Palace Theatre)

Columbia KOS 2900 stereo CD

Music: Cy Coleman; lyrics: Dorothy Fields; based on an original screenplay by Federico Fellini, Tullio Pinelli, Ennio Flaiano; musical direction: Fred Werner

Cast: Michael Davis, Helen Gallagher, Eddie Gasper, James Luisi, John McMartin, Thelma Oliver, Harold Pierson, Arnold Soboloff, Gwen Verdon, John Wheeler

Songs: Overture (orchestra)
You Should See Yourself (Verdon)
Big Spender (Gallagher, Oliver, girls)
Charity's Soliloquy (Verdon)
Rich Man's Frug (orchestra)
If My Friends Could See Me Now (Verdon)
Too Many Tomorrows (Luisi)
There's Gotta Be Something Better Than This (Verdon, Gallagher, Oliver)

Charity's Theme (orchestra)
I'm the Bravest Individual (Verdon, McMartin)
The Rhythm of Life (Pierson, Gasper, Soboloff, chorus)
Baby Dream Your Dream (Gallagher, Oliver)
Sweet Charity (McMartin, chorus)
Where Am I Going? (Verdon)
I Love to Cry at Weddings (Wheeler, Davis, Gallagher, Oliver, chorus)
I'm a Brass Band (Verdon, men)
Finale (company)

SWEET CHARITY (Revival, April 27, 1986, Minskoff Theatre)

EMI America SV 17196 stereo

Musical direction: Fred Werner

Cast: Debbie Allen, Mark Jacoby, Irving Allen Lee, Tanis Michaels, Bebe Neuwirth, Stanley Wesley Perryman, Michael Ruppert, Tom Wierney, Lee Wilkof, Allison Williams

Songs: Overture (orchestra)
You Should See Yourself (Allen)
Big Spender (Neuwirth, Williams, girls)

Rich Man's Frug (orchestra)
If My Friends Could See Me Now (Allen)
Too Many Tomorrows (Jacoby)
There's Gotta Be Something Better Than This (Allen, Neuwirth, Williams)

I'm the Bravest Individual (Allen, Rupert)
The Rhythm of Life (Lee, Michaels, Perryman, chorus)
Baby Dream Your Dream (Neuwirth, Williams)
Sweet Charity (Rupert)
Where Am I Going? (Allen)
I'm a Brass Band (Allen, men)
I Love to Cry at Weddings (Wilkof, Wierney, Neuwirth, Williams, chorus)
And She Lived Happily Ever After (orchestra)
If My Friends Could See Me Now (reprise) (company)

Note: For this revival production, "Sweet Charity" and "I'm the Bravest Individual" have new melodies and some altered lyrics.

TAKE FIVE (October 10, 1957, Off Broadway, Downstairs at the Upstairs)

Offbeat Records O-4013 mono

Music: Michael Brown, Ronny Graham, Bart Howard, Stan Keen, Edward C. Redding, Philip Springer, Jonathan Tunick, Steven Vinaver; lyrics: Michael Brown, Ronny Graham, Bart Howard, Stan Keen, Carolyn Leigh, Edward C. Redding, Steven Vinaver; pianos: Gordon Connell, Stan Keen

Cast: Jean Arnold, Ceil Cabot, Ronny Graham, Ellen Hanley, Gerry Matthews

Songs: Julius Monk Presents (Julius Monk) spoken
Cast Call (company) music, lyrics: Keen
Upstairs at the Downstairs Waltz (company) music, lyrics: Howard
Roger, the Rabbit (Cabot) music, lyrics: Vinaver
Night Heat! (Graham, Matthews) spoken
Perfect Stranger (Hanley) music, lyrics: Howard
Gristedes (Arnold) music: Tunick; lyrics: Vinaver
Poet's Corner (company) spoken

Gossiping Grapevine (company) music, lyrics: Redding
Westport! (Arnold) music: Springer; lyrics: Leigh
Witchcraft! (Matthews) music, lyrics: Brown
The Pro Musica Antiqua (Hanley) music: Tunick; lyrics: Vinaver
Harry the Hipster (Graham) spoken
Doing the Psycho-Neurotique (company) music, lyrics: Graham

Note: A live recording.

TAKE ME ALONG (October 22, 1959, Shubert Theatre)

RCA LSO 1050 stereo

Music, lyrics: Robert Merrill; based on the play Ah, Wilderness by Eugene O'Neill; musical direction: Lehman Engel

Cast: Peter Conlow, Jackie Gleason, Eileen Herlie, Susan Luckey, Una Merkel, Robert Morse, Walter Pidgeon

Songs: Overture (orchestra)
The Parade (Pidgeon, chorus)
Oh, Please (Pidgeon, Herlie, Merkel, chorus)
I Would Die (Morse, Luckey)
Sid, Ol' Kid (Gleason, chorus)
Staying Young (Pidgeon)
I Get Embarrassed (Gleason, Herlie)

We're Home (Herlie)
Take Me Along (Gleason, Pidgeon)
Volunteer Firemen Picnic (Gleason, Pidgeon, chorus)
Wint's Song (Conlow)
That's How It Starts (Morse)
Promise Me a Rose (Herlie)
Staying Young (reprise) (Pidgeon)
Little Green Snake (Gleason)
Nine O'Clock (Morse)
But Yours (Gleason, Herlie)
Finale (Gleason, Herlie, chorus)

TAKING MY TURN (June 9, 1983, Off Broadway, Entermedia Theatre)

Broadway Limited BLR-1001-R stereo reissued: CSP BLR 1001

Music: Gary William Friedman; lyrics: Will Holt; musical direction: Barry Levitt

Cast: Mace Barrett, Victor Griffin, Tiger Haynes, Cissy Houston, Marni Nixon, Sheila Smith, Ted Thurston, Margaret Whiting

Songs: This Is My Song (company)
Somebody Else (company)
Fine for the Shape I'm In (Whiting, Nixon, Houston)
Two of Me (Smith)
Janet Get Up (company)
I Like It (company)
I Never Made Money from Music (Haynes)
Vivaldi (Nixon, company)
In April (Whiting)
Do You Remember? (Thurston, company)

Pick More Daisies (company)
Taking Our Turn (company)
Sweet Longings (Smith, company)
I Am Not Old (Houston)
Do You Remember? (reprise) (Thurston, company)
The Kite (Griffin)
Good Luck to You (Barrett, company)
In the House (Barrett)
It Still Isn't Over (Thurston, Whiting)

This Is My Song (reprise) (company)

TALLULAH (October 30, 1983, Off Broadway, Cheryl Crawford Theatre)

Painted Smiles PS 1348 stereo

Music: Arthur Siegel; lyrics: Mae Richard; musical direction: Bruce W. Coyle

Cast: Joel Craig, Helen Gallagher, Tom Hafner, Eric Johnson, Ken Lundie, Russell Nype, Patrick Parker, Clark Sterling

Songs: Darling (Hafner, Johnson, Lundie, Parker, Sterling, Gallagher)
Tallulah (Gallagher, Hafner, Johnson, Lundie, Parker, Sterling)
When Do I Dance for You (Gallagher, Nype)
Home Sweet Home (Gallagher, Hafner, Johnson, Lundie, Parker, Sterling)
I've Got to Try Everything Once (Gallagher, Craig)
You're You (Gallagher, Hafner, Johnson, Lundie, Parker, Sterling)
I Can See Him Clearly (Gallagher)
Tallulahbaloo (Hafner, Johnson, Lundie, Parker, Sterling)
The Party Is Where I Am (Gallagher, Hafner, Johnson, Lundie, Parker, Sterling)

Stay Awhie (Gallagher, Hafner, Johnson, Lundie, Parker, Sterling)
It's a Hit (Hafner, Johnson, Lundie, Parker, Sterling)
If Only He Were a Woman (Gallagher, Hafner, Johnson, Lundie, Parker, Sterling)
Tallulah (Nype)
Love Is on Its Knees (Gallagher, Craig, Hafner, Johnson, Lundie, Parker, Sterling)
Don't Ever Book a Trip on the IRT (Gallagher, Lundie, Hafner, Johnson, Parker, Sterling)
It's a Hit (reprise) (Gallagher, Hafner, Johnson, Lundie, Parker, Sterling)
You Need a Lift (Gallagher)
Tallulah Finale (Gallagher, Hafner, Johnson, Lundie, Parker, Sterling)
I'm the Woman You Wanted (Gallagher)

THE TAP DANCE KID (December 21, 1983, Broadhurst Theatre)

Polydor 820 210-1 Y-1 stereo CD

Music: Henry Krieger; lyrics: Robert Lorick; based on Nobody's Family Is Going to Change by Louise Fitzhugh; musical direction: Don Jones

Cast: Martine Allard, Hinton Battle, Jackie Lowe, Gail Nelson, Jimmy Tate, Alan Weeks, Samuel E. Wright

Songs: Overture (orchestra)

Another Day (Nelson, Allard, Tate)
Four Strikes Against Me (Allard)
Class Act (Nelson, Battle, Weeks)
They Never Hear What I Say (Allard, Tate)
Dancing Is Everything (Tate)
Fabulous Feet (Battle)
I Could Get Used to Him (Lowe)
Man in the Moon (Battle)

Like Him (Allard, Nelson)
My Luck Is Changing (Battle)
Someday (Allard, Tate)
I Remember How It Was (Nelson)
Tap Dance (Weeks)
Dance If It Makes You Happy (ensemble)
William's Song (Wright)
Class Act (reprise) finale (ensemble)

Note: Gail Nelson and Jimmy Tate replace Hattie Winston and Alfonso Ribeiro of the original cast.

TENDERLOIN (October 17, 1960, Forty-Sixth Street Theatre)

Capitol SWAO 1492 stereo

Music: Jerry Bock; lyrics: Sheldon Harnick; based on the novel by Samuel Hopkins Adams; musical direction: Hal Hastings

Cast: Charles Aschmann, Lee Becker, Raymond Bramley, Carvel Carter, Lanier Davis, Nancy Emes, Maurice Evans, Rex Everhart, Margery Gray, Stokley Gray, Ron Husmann, Irene Kane, Jack Leigh, Wynne Miller, Christine Norden, Eddie Phillips, Eileen Rodgers

Songs: Overture (orchestra)
Bless This Land (chorus)
Little Old New York (Rodgers, Becker, chorus)
Dr. Brock (Evans)
Artificial Flowers (Husmann, chorus)
What's in It for You? (Evans, Husmann)
Reform (Becker, Emes, Carter)
Tommy, Tommy (Miller)
The Picture of Happiness (Husmann, M. Gray, chorus)

Dear Friend (Evans, chorus)
The Army of the Just (Evans, Davis, Leigh, Aschmann, S. Gray)
How the Money Changes Hands (Evans, Rodgers, Norden, Phillips, Becker, chorus)
Good Clean Fun (Evans, chorus)
My Miss Mary (Husmann, Miller, chorus)
My Gentle Young Johnny (Rodgers, girls)
The Trial (Miller, Kane, Everhart, Bramley, chorus)
Reform (reprise) (girls)
Finale (Evans, company)

TEXAS, LI'L DARLIN' (November 25, 1949, Mark Hellinger Theatre)

Decca DL 5188 mono reissued: Columbia CSP X-14878

Music: Robert Emmett Dolan; lyrics: Johnny Mercer; musical direction: Will Irwin

Cast: Kenny Delmar, Mary Hatcher, Danny Scholl, Loring Smith, Fredd Wayne

Songs: Texas, Li'l Darlin' (Delmar, chorus)
The Yodel Blues (Delmar, Hatcher)
A Month of Sundays (Scholl, Hatcher)
Hootin' Owl Trail (School, chorus)
The Big Movie Show in the Sky (Scholl, chorus)
Politics (Delmar, Smith)
Affable, Balding Me (Hatcher, Wayne)
It's Great to Be Alive (chorus)
The Yodel Blues (reprise) (Hatcher, Delmar)
Hootin' Owl Trail (reprise) (orchestra)
Texas, Li'l Darlin' (company)
It's Great to Be Alive (reprise) (company)

THEY'RE PLAYING OUR SONG (February 11, 1979, Imperial Theatre)

Casablanca Records NBLP 7141 stereo

Music: Marvin Hamlisch; lyrics: Carole Bayer Sager; musical direction: Larry Blank

Cast: Lucie Arnaz, Robert Klein

Songs: Fallin' (Klein)
Workin' It Out (Klein, Arnaz, chorus)
If He Really Knew Me (Arnaz, Klein)
They're Playing My Song - His (Klein)
They're Playing My Song - Hers (Arnaz, Klein)
Right (Arnaz, Klein, chorus)
Just for Tonight (Arnaz)

Entre Acte (orchestra)
When You're in My Arms (Klein, Arnaz, chorus)
If He Really Knew Me (reprise) (Klein, Arnaz)
I Still Believe in Love (Arnaz)
Fill in the Words (Klein, chorus)
They're Playing Our Song (company)

THIS IS THE ARMY (July 4, 1942, Broadway Theatre)

Decca DL 5108 mono reissued: Columbia CSP X 14877

Music, lyrics: Irving Berlin; musical direction: Milton Rosenstock

Cast: Irving Berlin, Stuart Churchill, James 'Stump' Cross, Julie Oshins, Earl Oxford, Robert Shanley, Ezra Stone, Philip Truex

Songs: Overture (orchestra)
This Is the Army, Mr. Jones (chorus)
I'm Getting Tired So I Can Sleep (Churchill, octet)
I Left My Heart at the Stage Door Canteen (Oxford, chorus)
The Army's Made a Man Out of Me (Stone, Truex, Oshins)
What the Well Dressed Man in Harlem Will Wear (Cross)
How About a Cheer for the Navy (chorus)
American Eagles (chorus)
With My Head in the Clouds (Shanley, chorus)
Oh, How I Hate to Get Up in the Morning (Berlin, chorus)

THREE GUYS NAKED FROM THE WAIST DOWN (February 5, 1985, Off Broadway, Minetta Lane Theatre)

Polydor Records 820 244-1 Y-1 stereo CD

Music: Michael Rupert; lyrics: Jerry Colker; musical direction: Henry Aronson

Cast: Scott Bakula, Jerry Colker, John Kassir

Songs: Overture (orchestra)
Promise of Greatness (Bakula)
Angry Guy (Colker)
Lovely Day (Colker)
Don't Wanna Be No Superstar (Bakula, Colker)
Operator (Kassir)
Screaming Clocks (The Dummies Song) (cast)
The History of Stand-Up Comedy (cast)
Dreams of Heaven (Kassir)
Don't Wanna Be No Superstar (reprise) (cast)
Kamikaze Kabaret (cast)

The American Dream (cast)
What a Ride (cast)
The 'Hello Fellas' TV Special World Tour (cast)
A Father Now (Colker)
'Three Guys Naked from the Waist Down' Theme (cast)
Dreams of Heaven (reprise) (Kassir)
I Don't Believe in Heroes Anymore (Bakula)
Promise of Greatness (reprise) (Bakula)

THREE WISHES FOR JAMIE (March 21, 1952, Mark Hellinger Theatre)

Capitol S-317 mono reissued: Capitol L 8119 (Stet DS-15012)

Music, lyrics: Ralph Blane; based on the novel by Charles O'Neal; musical direction: Joseph Littau

Cast: Peter Conlow, Robert Halliday, Anne Jeffreys, Charlotte Rae, John Raitt, Bert Wheeler

Songs: Prologue (orchestra)
The Wake (ensemble)
The Girl That I Court in My Mind (Raitt)
My Home's a Highway (Jeffreys, chorus)

We're for Love (Wheeler, chorus)
My Heart's Darlin' (Jeffreys, Raitt)
Love Has Nothing to Do with Looks (Wheeler, Halliday, Rae, chorus)
Goin' on a Hayride (Jeffreys, Raitt, chorus)
My Heart's Darlin' (reprise) (Jeffreys, Raitt)
I'll Sing You a Song (Wheeler, Halliday, Rae, chorus)

It Must Be Spring (Jeffreys, chorus)
Wedding March (ensemble)
The Army Mule Song (Raitt, Wheeler, Conlow, chorus)
What Do I Know? (Jeffreys)
Love Has Nothing to Do with Looks (reprise) (Conlow, Rae)
It's a Wishing World (Jeffreys, Raitt)
Trottin' to the Fair (Raitt, Halliday, chorus)
April Face (Jeffreys, Raitt, Wheeler)
Kevin's Prayer (Wheeler)
Finale (ensemble)

THE THREEPENNY OPERA (Revival, March 10, 1954, Off Broadway, Theatre de Lys)

MGM Records E3121 mono reissued: Polydor 820 260-1 Y-1 CD

Music: Kurt Weill; lyrics: Bert Brecht (English translation by Marc Blitzstein); musical direction: Stanley Matlowsky

Cast: Beatrice Arthur, John Astin, Joseph Beruh, Bernard Bogin, Paul Dooley, William Duell, Lotte Lenya, Scott Merrill, Gerald Price, Charlotte Rae, Jo Sullivan, George Tyne, Martin Wolfson

Songs: Prologue (Price) spoken
Overture (orchestra)
The Ballad of Mack the Knife (Price)
Morning Anthem (Wolfson)
Instead-of-Song (Wolfson, Rae)
Wedding Song (Astin, Beruh, Bogin, Dooley)
Pirate Jenny (Lenya)
Army Song (Merrill, Tyne, Astin, Beruh, Bogin, Dooley)
Love Song (Merrill, Sullivan)
Ballad of Dependency (Rae)
Melodrama and Polly's Song (Merrill, Sullivan)
Ballad of the Easy Life (Merrill)
The World Is Mean (Sullivan, Wolfson, Rae)

Barbara Song (Arthur)
Tango-Ballad (Lenya, Merrill)
Jealousy Duet (Sullivan, Arthur)
How to Survive (Merrill, Rae, ensemble)
Useless Song (Wolfson)
Solomon Song (Lenya)
Call from the Grave (Merrill)
Death Message (Merrill)
Finale: The Mounted Messenger (Duell, ensemble)

THE THREEPENNY OPERA (Revival, May 1, 1976, Beaumont Theatre)

Columbia PS 34326 stereo

English translation by Ralph Manheim and John Willett;
musical direction: Stanley Silverman

Cast: C.K. Alexander, Tony Azito, Roy Brocksmith, Blair Brown, Ellen Greene, Raul Julia, Caroline Kava, Glenn Kezer, David Sabin, Robert Schlee, Jack Eric Williams, Elizabeth Wilson

Songs: Overture (orchestra)
Ballad of Mac the Knife (Brocksmith, Azito, Schlee, Williams)
Peachum's Morning Hymn (Alexander)
"No They Can't" Song (Alexander, Wilson)
Wedding Song for the Less Well-Off (chorus)
Cannon Song (Julia, Sabin, chorus)
Liebeslied (Kava, Julia)
Barbara Song (Kava)
First Threepenny Finale (Kava, Alexander, Wilson)
Polly's Lied (Kava, Julia)
Ballad of Sexual Obsession (Wilson)
Pirate Jenny (Greene)

Ballad of Immoral Earnings (Greene, Julia)
Ballad of Gracious Living (Julia)
Jealousy Duet (Brown, Kava)
Second Threepenny Finale (Julia, Greene, chorus)
Song of the Insufficiency of Human Endeavor (Alexander)
Solomon Song (Greene)
Call from the Grave (Julia)
Ballad in Which Macheath Begs All Men for Forgiveness (Julia)
Third Threepenny Finale (Sabin, Kezer, Brocksmith, Williams, Wilson, Alexander, Julia, Kava, Brown, Greene, chorus)
Ballad of Mac the Knife (reprise) (Brocksmith)

A TIME FOR SINGING (May 21, 1966, Broadway Theatre)

Warner Brothers Records HS 1639 stereo

Music: John Morris; lyrics: Gerald Freedman, John Morris; based on How Green Was My Valley by Richard Llewellyn; musical direction: Jay Blackton

Cast: Brian Avery, Ivor Emmanuel, Frank Griso, George Hearn, Elizabeth Hubbard, Laurence Naismith, Tessie O'Shea, Philip Proctor, Gene Rupert, Harry Theyard, Shani Wallis

Songs: Come You Men (male chorus)
How Green Was My Valley (Emmanuel, chorus)
Old Long John (male chorus)
What a Good Day Is Saturday (O'Shea, chorus)
Someone Must Try (Emmanuel, chorus)
Oh, How I Adore Your Name (Wallis)
That's What Young Ladies Do (Emmanuel)

When He Looks at Me (Wallis)
Far from Home (O'Shea, Naismith, Grisco, men)
I Wonder If (Rupert, Avery, Theyard, Proctor, Hearn)
A Time for Singing (O'Shea, chorus)

Let Me Love You (Wallis)
I've Nothing to Give (Emmanuel)
Let Me Love You (reprise) (Wallis)
Why Would Anyone Want to Get Married? (Griso, O'Shea, Naismith, men)
I'm Always Wrong (Wallis)
There Is Beautiful You Are (Emmanuel)
Three Ships (O'Shea, Hubbard, Avery, chorus)
Tell Her (Naismith, Grisco)
The Mountains Sing Back (Emmanuel)
Peace Come to Every Heart (company)
Gone in Sorrow (Hubbard, Grisco, company)
How Green Was My Valley (reprise) (company)

TINTYPES (October 23, 1980, John Golden Theatre)

DRG Records S2L 5196 (two records) stereo

A selection of popular songs between the Civil War and the Roaring Twenties; musical direction: Mel Marvin

Cast: Carolyn Mignini, Lynne Thigpen, Trey Wilson, Mary Catherine Wright, Jerry Zaks

Songs: Ragtime Nightingale (piano)
The Yankee Doodle Boy (Zaks, company)
Ta-Ra-Ra Boom-De-Ay! (company)
I Don't Care (company)
Come Take a Trip in My Airship (company)
Kentucky Babe (company)
A Hot Time in the Old Town Tonight (Thigpen, company)
Stars and Stripes Forever (company)
Electricity (company)
El Capitan (Wilson, company)
Pastime Rag (piano)
Meet Me in St. Louis (Mignini)
Waltz Me Around Again, Willie (Mignini, company)
Wabash Cannonball (company)
In My Merry Oldsmobile (company)

Wayfaring Stranger (Thigpen)
Sometimes I Feel Like a Motherless Child (Thigpen)
Aye, Lye, Lyu, Lye (Mignini)
I'll Take You Home Again, Kathleen (Wilson)
America the Beautiful (Thigpen, company)
Wait for the Wagon (company)
What It Takes to Make Me Love You - You've Got It (Wilson, Wright)
The Maiden with the Dreamy Eyes (company)
If I Were on the Stage - Kiss Me Again (Mignini)
Shortnin' Bread (company)
Nobody (Thigpen)

Elite Syncopations (piano)
I'm Going to Live Anyhow, 'Til I Die (Thigpen, company)

Entr'acte (piano)
The Ragtime Dance (Thigpen, company)
I Want What I Want When I Want It (Wilson)
It's Delightful to Be Married (Mignini)
Fifty-Fifty (Thigpen, Wright, Mignini)
Then I'd Be Satisfied with Life (Zaks)
Jonah Man (Wright)
When It's All Goin' Out and Nothin' Comin' In (Wilson, Mignini, company)
We Shall Not Be Moved (company)

Hello, Ma Baby (company)
Teddy Da Roose (Wilson)
Bill Bailey, Won't You Please Come Home? (Thigpen)
She's Getting More Like the White Folks Every Day (Zaks, company)
You're a Grand Old Flag (company)
The Yankee Doodle Boy (company)
Toyland (Mignini)
Smiles (Zaks, Wright, company)

Note: This recording contains a spoken narration by the cast members.

TO BROADWAY WITH LOVE (April 29, 1964, The New York World's Fair)

Columbia OS 2630 stereo

Original music: Jerry Bock; original lyrics: Sheldon Harnick; musical direction: Franz Allers

Cast: Miriam Burton, Bob Carroll, Patti Karr, Nancy Leighton, Don Liberto, Rod Perry, Guy Rotondo, Millie Slavin

Songs: To Broadway with Love (ensemble) music: Bock; lyrics: Harnick
Old Folks at Home (Perry)
Dixie (Perry, ensemble)
Yankee Doodle Boy (Liberto)
Mary's a Grand Old Name (Liberto)
Every Day Is Ladies' Day with Me (ensemble)
The 88 Rag (Liberto) music: Colin Romoff; lyrics: Martin Charnin
Till the Clouds Roll By (ensemble)
Over There (Slavin)
Three Wonderful Letters from Home (male quintet)
Would You Rather Be a Colonel (Karr, girls)
Rose of Washington Square (Slavin)
Beautiful Lady (Carroll, Rotondo, girls) music: Bock; lyrics: Harnick

---

Another Op'nin', Another Show (company)
There's No Business Like Show Business (company)
Carousel Waltz (orchestra)
Speak Low (Slavin)
Buckle Down, Winsocki (ensemble)
Bali Ha'i (Burton)
I Still Get Jelous (Leighton, Rotondo)

F.D.R. Jones (Perry, ensemble)
Mata Hari Mine (ensemble) music: Bock; lyrics: Harnick
Remember Radio (ensemble) music: Bock; lyrics: Harnick
Popsicles in Paris (company) music: Bock; lyrics: Harnick
Finale (company)

TOP BANANA (November 1, 1951, Winter Garden Theatre)

Capitol S 308 mono reissued: T-11650

Music, lyrics: Johnny Mercer; musical direction: Harold Hastings

Cast: Jack Albertson, Bill Callahan, Lindy Doherty, Herbie Faye, Joey Faye, Judy Lynn, Rose Marie, Phil Silvers

Songs: Overture (orchestra)
The Man of the Year This Week (chorus)
You're So Beautiful That - (Doherty, Silvers)
Top Banana (Silvers, Albertson, Doherty, J. Faye, H. Faye, chorus)
Elevator Song (Going Up) (chorus)
Only If You're in Love (Lynn, Doherty)
My Home Is in My Shoes (Callahan, chorus)
I Fought Every Step of the Way (Marie)

You're O.K. for T.V. (Silvers, Lynn, ensemble)
You Gotta Have a Slogan You Can Sell (Silvers, ensemble)
Meet Miss Blendo (Silvers, ensemble)
Sans Souci (Marie, chorus)
That's for Sure (Lynn, Doherty, chorus)
A Dog Is a Man's Best Friend (Silvers, ensemble)
A Word a Day (Silvers, Marie)
Top Banana (reprise) (company)

TOUCH (November 8, 1970, Off Broadway, Village Arena Theatre)

Ampex Records A 50102 stereo

Music: Kenn Long, Jim Crozier; lyrics: Kenn Long; musical direction: David Rodman

Cast: Barbara Ellis, Phyllis Gibbs, Norman Jacob, Kenn Long, Ava Rosenblum, Susan Rosenblum

Songs: Windchild (cast) music, lyrics: Gary Graham
Cities of Light (A. Rosenblum, cast)
I Don't Care (Gibbs, cast)
Goodbyes (Jacob)
Come to the Road (Long, A. Rosenblum, cast)
Reaching, Touching (Ellis, Jacob, cast)

Quiet Country (cast)
Susan's Song (A. Rosenblum)
Tripping (Long, S. Rosenblum, cast)
Garden Song (cast)
Watching (Gibbs)

The Hasseltown Memorial Squaredance (cast)
Confrontation Song (cast)
Alphagenesis (cast)

TOVARICH (March 18, 1963, Broadway Theatre)

Capitol STAO 1940 stereo

Music: Lee Pockriss; lyrics: Anne Croswell; based on the comedy by Jacques Deval; musical direction: Stanley Lebowsky

Cast: Jean Pierre Aumont, Margery Gray, George S. Irving, Michael Kermoyan, Louise Kirtland, Vivien Leigh, Rita Metzger, Paul Michael, Bryon Mitchell, Louise Troy, Gene Varrone

Songs: Overture (orchestra)
I Go to Bed (Aumont)
The Only One (Leigh)
Nitchevo (Aumont, Kermoyan, Varrone, Metzger, ensemble)
Stuck with Each Other (Gray, Mitchell)
Say You'll Stay (Kirtland, Irving)
You Love Me (Leigh, Aumont)
A Small Cartel (Kirtland, Irving, ensemble)

Wilkes-Barre, Pa. (Leigh, Mitchell)
No! No! No! (Gray, Aumont)
That Face (Troy)
Uh-Oh! (Gray, Mitchell)
I Know the Feeling (Leigh)
It Used to Be (Kermoyan, Varrone, Troy, Michael)
All for You (Leigh, Aumont)
Make a Friend (Leigh, Gray, Troy, Aumont, Mitchell, Kermoyan, Varrone, ensemble)

A TREE GROWS IN BROOKLYN (April 19, 1951, Alvin Theatre)

Columbia ML 4405 mono reissued: AML 4405

Music: Arthur Schwartz; lyrics: Dorothy Fields; based on Betty Smith's novel; musical direction: Max Goberman

Cast: Delbert Anderson, Shirley Booth, Nathaniel Frey, Johnny Johnston, Albert Linville, Nomi Mitty, Marcia Van Dyke

Songs: Overture (orchestra)
Payday (company)
Mine 'Til Monday (Johnston, company)
Make the Man Love Me (Van Dyke, Johnston)
I'm Like a New Broom (Johnston, company)
Look Who's Dancing (Van Dyke, Booth, company)
Love Is the Reason (Booth)
If You Haven't Got a Sweetheart (Anderson, company)
I'll Buy You a Star (Johnston, company)

That's How It Goes (company)
He Had Refinement (Booth)
Growing Pains (Johnston, Mitty)

Is That My Prince? (Booth, Linville)
Halloween Ballet (orchestra)
Don't Be Afraid (Johnston)
Finale (Van Dyke, Johnston, Booth, Frey)

TUSCALOOSA'S CALLING ME ... BUT I'M NOT GOING! (December 1, 1975, Off Broadway, Village Gate)

Vanguard VSD 79376 stereo

Music: Hank Beebe; lyrics: Bill Heyer; musical direction: Jeremy Harris

Cast: Len Gochman, Patti Perkins, Renny Temple

Songs: Only Right Here in New York City (cast)
The Out of Towner (Gochman, Temple) spoken
Everything You Hate Is Right Here (cast)
Delicatessen (Perkins, cast)
Tuscaloosa's Calling Me ... but I'm Not Going (cast)

Things Were Out (Perkins)
Fugue for a Menage a Trois (cast)
Singles Bar (Perkins) includes spoken scene with Temple
Astrology (Gochman)
New York from the Air (Perkins, cast)
Tuscaloosa Tag (cast)

Note: A live recording.

TWO BY TWO (November 10, 1970, Imperial Theatre)

Columbia S 30338 stereo

Music: Richard Rodgers; lyrics: Martin Charnin; based on The Flowering Peach by Clifford Odets; musical direction: Jay Blackton

Cast: Marilyn Cooper, Joan Copeland, Harry Goz, Madeline Kahn, Michael Karm, Danny Kaye, Tricia O'Neil, Walter Willison

Songs: Why Me? (Kaye)
Put Him Away (Kaye, Goz, Karm, Cooper)
Something, Somewhere (Willison, family)
You Have Got to Have a Rudder on the Ark (Kaye, Goz, Karm, Willison)
Something Doesn't Happen (O'Neil, Copeland)
An Old Man (Copeland)
Ninety Again! (Kaye)
Two by Two (Kaye, family)

I Do Not Know a Day I Did Not Love You (Willison)
When It Dries (Kaye, family)
You (Kaye)
The Golden Ram (Kahn)
Poppa Knows Best (Kaye, Willison, Goz, Karm)

I Do Not Know a Day I Did Not Love You (reprise) (O'Neil, Willison)
As Far As I'm Concerned (Goz, Cooper)
Hey, Girlie (Kaye)
The Covenant (Kaye)

TWO GENTLEMEN OF VERONA (July 27, 1971, Off Broadway, Delacourte Theatre; transferred, December 1, 1971, St. James Theatre)

ABC Records BCSY 1001 (two records) stereo

Music: Galt MacDermot; lyrics: John Guare; based on the play by William Shakespeare; musical direction: Harold Wheeler

Cast: Jonelle Allen, John Bottoms, Diana Davila, Clifton Davis, Alix Elias, Georgyn Geetlein, Sheila Gibbs, Raul Julia, Alvin Lum, Norman Matlock, Frank O'Brien, Jose Perez

Songs: Summer, Summer (I Love My Father) (chorus)
That's an Interesting Question (Davis, Julia, chorus)
I'd Like to Be a Rose (Davis, Julia, chorus)
Thou Hast Metamorphosed Me (Julia)
Symphony (Julia, chorus)
I Am Not Interested in Love (Davila)
Love Is That You? (O'Brien, Geetlein)
Thou Hast Metamorphosed Me (reprise) (Davila)
What Does a Lover Pack (Julia, Davila, chorus)
Pearls (Bottoms)
I Love My Father (Julia)

Two Gentlemen of Verona (Davila, Elias, chorus)
Follow the Rainbow (Davis, Julia, Davila, Elias, Bottoms, Perez)
Where's North (chorus)
Bring All the Boys Back Home (Matlock, chorus)
Love's Revenge (Davis)
To Whom It May Concern Me (Allen, Davis)
Night Letter (Allen, Davis)

Love's Revenge (reprise) (Davis)
Calla Lilly Lady (Julia)
Land of Betrayal (Elias)
Thurios Samba (O'Brien, Matlock, chorus)
Hot Lover (Perez, Bottoms)
What a Nice Idea (Davila)
Who Is Silvia? (Julia, chorus)
Love Me (Allen)

Eglamour (Lum, Allen)
The Lovers Have Been Sighted (Matlock, Julia, chorus)
Mansion (Davis)
What's a Nice Girl Like Her? (Julia)
Dragon Music (Land of Betrayal) (orchestra)
Don't Have the Baby (Elias, Perez, Davila, Bottoms)
Milkmaid (Gibbs, Bottoms)
Finale - Love Has Driven Me Sane (company)
Where's North (orchestra)

TWO ON THE AISLE (July 19, 1951, Mark Hellinger Theatre)

Decca DL 8040 mono

Music: Jule Styne; lyrics: Betty Comden, Adolph Green; musical direction: Herbert Greene

Cast: Fred Bryan, Dolores Gray, Bert Lahr, Kathryne Mylroie

Songs: Overture (orchestra)
Show Train (chorus)
Hold Me, Hold Me, Hold Me (Gray)
Here She Comes Now (chorus)
There Never Was a Baby Like My Baby (Gray)
Catch Our Act at the Met (Lahr, Gray, chorus)

Give a Little - Get a Little (Gray, chorus)
Everlasting (Mylroie, Bryan, chorus)
If You Hadn't But You Did (Gray)
The Clown (Lahr)
How Will He Know? (Gray)
Finale (chorus)

TWO'S COMPANY (December 15, 1952, Alvin Theatre)

RCA LOC 1009 mono reissued: CBM 1-2757

Music: Vernon Duke; lyrics: Ogden Nash, Sammy Cahn; musical direction: Milton Rosenstock

Cast: David Burns, Bette Davis, Ellen Hanley, Sue Hight, Peter Kelley, Deborah Remsen, Hiram Sherman

Songs: Overture (orchestra)
Theatre Is a Lady (Kelley, chorus)
Turn Me Loose on Broadway (Davis)
It Just Occured to Me (Kelley, Remsen, chorus)
A Man's Home (Sherman) music, lyrics: Sheldon Harnick
Roundabout (Hanley)

Roll Along, Sadie (Davis, Sherman, chorus)
Out of the Clear Blue Sky (Kelley, Hight)
Esther (Burns)
Haunted Hot Spot (Hanley)
Purple Rose (Davis, Sherman, chorus)
Just Like a Man (Davis)
Finale (Davis, company)

Note: Original issue lists vocalist on "Theatre Is a Lady" as Bill Callahan.

THE UNSINKABLE MOLLY BROWN (November 3, 1960, Winter Garden Theatre)

Capitol SWAO 1509 stereo

Music, lyrics: Meredith Willson; musical direction: Herbert Greene

Cast: Mony Dalmes, Mitchell Gregg, Tammy Grimes, Woody Hurst, Tom Larson, Harve Presnell, Joe Pronto, Joseph Sirola

Songs: Overture (orchestra)
I Ain't Down Yet (Grimes, men)
Belly Up to the Bar, Boys (Grimes, Sirola, men)
I've A'Ready Started In (Presnell, Sirola, Hurst, Larson, Pronto)
I'll Never Say No (Presnell)
My Own Brass Bed (Grimes)
The Denver Police (men)
Bea-u-ti-ful People of Denver (Grimes)
Are You Sure? (Grimes, chorus)

I Ain't Down Yet (reprise) (Grimes, Presnell)
Happy Birthday, Mrs. J.J. Brown (Dalmes, Gregg, chorus)
Bon Jour (The Language Song) (Grimes, chorus)
If I Knew (Presnell)
Chick-a-Pen (Presnell, chorus)
Keep-a-Hoppin' (Presnell, chorus)
Leadville Johnny Brown (Presnell)
Up Where the People Are (orchestra)
Dolce Far Niente (Gregg)
I May Never Fall in Love with You (Grimes)
I Ain't Down Yet (finale) (company)

UP IN CENTRAL PARK (January 27, 1945, Century Theatre)

Decca DL 8016 mono reissued: JJA 19782B

Music: Sigmund Romberg; lyrics: Dorothy Fields; musical direction: Max Meth

Cast: Betty Bruce, Wilbur Evans, Eileen Farrell, Celeste Holm

Songs: Currier and Ives (Bruce)
The Big Back Yard (Evans, chorus)
When You Walk in the Room (Evans)
Carousel in the Park (Farrell)
April Snow (Farrell)
The Fireman's Bride (Holm, chorus)
Close as Pages in a Book (Evans, Farrell)
It Doesn't Cost You Anything to Dream (Evans, Farrell)

Note: 'Currier and Ives' included only on JJA reissue; Eileen Farrell and Celeste Holm did not appear in the stage production.

UPSTAIRS AT O'NEALS' (OCTOBER 28, 1982, Off Broadway, O'Neals')

Painted Smiles PS 1344 stereo

Music, lyrics: Michael Abbott, Douglas Bernstein, Martin Charnin, John Forster, Seth Friedman, Michael Leeds, Denis Markell, Ronald Melrose, Charles Strouse, Sarah Weeks; additional music: Stephen Hoffman, Paul Trueblood; additional lyrics: David L. Crane, Murray Horwitz, Marta Kauffman, Michael

Mooney, Jim Morgan; pianos: David Krane, Paul Ford

Cast: Douglas Bernstein, Randall Edwards, Bebe Neuwirth, Michon Peacock, Richard Ryder, Sarah Weeks

Songs: Upstairs at O'Neals' (company) music, lyrics: Charnin
Stools (Neuwirth, Bernstein, Ryder) music, lyrics: Charnin)
Cancun (Ryder) music, lyrics: Forster, Leeds
Something (Bernstein) music, lyrics: Bernstein, Markell
I Furnished My One Room Apartment (Weeks) music: Hoffman; lyrics: Mooney
Little H and Little G (company) music, lyrics: Melrose
The Ballad of Cy and Beatrice (Edwards) music: Trueblood; lyrics: Morgan
Soap Operetta (company) music: Friedman; lyrics: Crane, Friedman, Kauffman
---
Signed, Peeled and Delivered (Ryder, company) music, lyrics: Melrose
The Feet (company) music: Friedman; lyrics: Crane, Friedman, Kauffman
The Soldier and the Washerworker (Neuwirth) music, lyrics: Melrose
Talkin' Morosco Blues (Ryder) lyrics: Horwitz
Mommas' Turn (Edwards, Neuwirth, Peacock, Weeks) music, lyrics: Bernstein, Markell
All I Can Do Is Cry (Weeks) music, lyrics: Weeks, Abbott
Cover Girls (Neuwirth, Edwards, Peacock, Bernstein) music: Friedman; lyrics: Crane, Friedman, Kauffman
Boy, Do We Need It Now (Peacock) music, lyrics: Strouse
Upstairs at O'Neals' (reprise) (company)

THE UTTER GLORY OF MORRISSEY HALL (May 13, 1979, Mark Hellinger Theatre)

Original Cast Records OC 7918 stereo

Music, lyrics: Clark Gesner; musical direction: John Gordon

Cast: Willard Beckham, Marilyn Caskey, Taina Elg, Laurie Franks, John Gallogly, Karen Gibson, Bonnie Hellman, Celeste Holm, Dawn Jeffory, Anne Kaye, Becky McSpadden, Mary Saunders, Lauren Shub

Songs: Overture (orchestra)
Promenade (company)
Proud, Erstwhile, Upright, Fair (Holm, Gibson, Caskey)
Elizabeth's Song (Caskey)
Way Back When (Holm, Gibson)
Morning (Elg, girls)

The Letter (McSpadden, Gallogly, company)
Give Me That Key (Holm, McSpadden, Caskey)
Duet (Caskey, Beckham, company)
Interlude and Gallop (orchestra)
Oh, Sun (Kaye, Hellman, McSpadden, Jeffory, Shub)

You Will Know When the Time Has Arrived (Franks, Saunders, girls)
See the Blue (Holm, girls)
You Would Say (McSpadden, Gallogly, girls)
Reflection (Holm)
With Grateful Hearts (Saunders, Kaye)
The Ending (company)

VERY GOOD EDDIE (Revival, December 21, 1975, Booth Theatre)

DRG Records 6100 stereo

Music: Jerome Kern; lyrics: Anne Caldwell, Frank Craven, Harry Graham, Schuyler Greene, Elsie Janis, Herbert Reynolds, Harry B. Smith, P.G. Wodehouse; musical direction: Lynn Crigler

Cast: David Christmas, Spring Fairbank, Travis Hudson, Charles Repole, Virginia Seidel, Hal Shane, Cynthia Wells, Nicholas Wyman

Songs: Overture (orchestra)
We're on Our Way (company) lyrics: Greene
Some Sort of Somebody (Wells, Christmas) lyrics: Janis
Thirteen Collar (Repole) lyrics: Greene
Bungalow in Quogue (Seidel, Wyman) lyrics: Wodehouse
Isn't It Great to Be Married (Seidel, Fairbank, Repole, Wyman) lyrics: Greene
Good Night Boat (company) lyrics: Caldwell, Craven
Left All Alone Again Blues (Seidel) lyrics: Caldwell
Hot Dog! (company) lyrics: Caldwell
If You're a Friend of Mine (Seidel, Repole) lyrics: Graham
Wedding Bells Are Calling Me (company) lyrics: Smith

Honeymoon Inn (Wells, company) lyrics: Wodehouse
I've Got to Dance (Shane, company) lyrics: Greene
Moon of Love (Hudson, company) lyrics: Caldwell
Old Boy Neutral (Wells, Christmas) lyrics: Greene
Babes in the Wood (Seidel, Repole) lyrics: Smith
Katy-Did (Hudson) lyrics: Smith
Nodding Roses (Wells, Christmas) lyrics: Greene, Reynolds
Finale (company)

WAIT A MINUM! (March 7, 1966, John Golden Theatre)

London Records AMS 88002 stereo

A program of African songs; musical arrangements, direction: Andrew Tracey

Cast: Sarah Atkinson, Kendrew Lascelles, Michel Martel, Nigel Pegram, Andrew Tracey, Paul Tracey, Dana Valery

Songs: Amasalela (company)
Ndinosara Nani? (A. Tracey, P. Tracey, Pegram, Martel, Valery)

Jikele Maweni (Valery, A. Tracey, P. Tracey, Pegram, Martel)
Black-White Calypso (Pegram)
I Know Where I'm Going (A. Tracey, P. Tracey, Atkinson)
I Gave My Love a Cherry (P. Tracey, Valery, A. Tracey, Pegram, Martel)
Chuzi Mama Gwabi Gwabi (Valery, A. Tracey, P. Tracey, Pegram, Martel)
Foyo (P. Tracey, A. Tracey, Pegram)
London Talking Blues (Pegram)
Ayama (Martel, A. Tracey, P. Tracey)
The Gumboot Dance (company)

Hammer Song (A. Tracey, P. Tracey, Pegram, Martel, Valery, Atkinson)
Table Bay (Valery, A. Tracey, P. Tracey, Pegram)
A Piece of Ground (Pegram, A. Tracey)
Dirty Old Town (Valery, A. Tracey, P. Tracey, Pegram)
Sir Oswald Sodde (A. Tracey, Atkinson, Pegram, P. Tracey, Martel)
Johnny Soldier (Valery, A. Tracey, P. Tracey, Martel, Lascelles, Pegram)
Skalo-Zwi (Valery, company)
Amasalela (company)

WALKING HAPPY (November 26, 1966, Lunt-Fontanne Theatre)

Capitol SVAS 2631 stereo

Music: James Van Heusen; lyrics: Sammy Cahn; based on the play Hobson's Choice by Harold Brighouse; musical direction: Herbert Grossman

Cast: Ed Bakey, Burt Bier, Chad Block, Sharon Dierking, Gordon Dilworth, Ian Garry, George Rose, Emma Trekman, Louise Troy, Gretchen Van Aken, Norman Wisdom

Songs: Overture (orchestra)
Think of Something Else (Rose, Bakey, Garry, chorus)
Where Was I? (Troy)
How D'Ya Talk to a Girl? (Wisdom, Dilworth)
If I Be Your Best Chance (Troy, Wisdom)
What Makes It Happen? (Troy, Wisdom)
Use Your Noggin (Troy, Dierking, Van Aken)

You're Right, You're Right (Rose, Wisdom, Troy)
I'll Make a Man of the Man (Troy, Wisdom, Trekman)
Walking Happy (Troy, Wisdom, ensemble)
I Don't Think I'm in Love (Wisdom, Troy)
Such a Sociable Sort (Rose, ensemble)
It Might As Well Be Her (Wisdom, Dilworth)
People Who Are Nice (Rose, Bier, Block)
You're Right, You're Right (reprise) (Rose, Wisdom, Troy)
Finale (Wisdom, Troy)

WEST SIDE STORY (September 26, 1957, Winter Garden Theatre)

Columbia OS 2001 stereo reissued: JS 32603 CD

Music: Leonard Bernstein; lyrics: Stephen Sondheim; musical direction: Max Goberman

Cast: Mickey Calin, Marilyn Cooper, Grover Dale, Reri Grist, Carmen Guiterrez, Larry Kert, Carol Lawrence, Chita Rivera, Eddie Roll, Elizabeth Taylor

Songs: Prologue (orchestra)
Jet Song (chorus)
Something's Coming (Kert)
The Dance at the Gym (orchestra)
Maria (Kert)
Tonight (Lawrence, Kert)
America (Rivera, Cooper, Grist, girls)
Cool (Calin, chorus)
One Hand, One Heart (Lawrence, Kert)

Tonight (reprise) (ensemble)
The Rumble (orchestra)
I Feel Pretty (Lawrence, Copper, Guiterrez, Taylor)
Somewhere (Grist, ensemble)
Gee, Officer Krupke! (Roll, Dale, chorus)
A Boy Like That (Lawrence, Rivera)
I Have a Love (Lawrence, Rivera)
Somewhere (reprise) (chorus)

WHAT MAKES SAMMY RUN? (February 27, 1964, Fifty-Fourth Street Theatre)

Columbia KOS 2440 stereo

Music, lyrics: Ervin Drake; based on the novel by Bud Schulberg; musical direction: Lehman Engel

Cast: Robert Alda, Sally Ann Howes, Steve Lawrence, Bernice Massi, Barry Newman

Songs: Overture (orchestra)
A New Pair of Shoes (Lawrence, Alda, chorus)
You Help Me (Lawrence, Alda)
A Tender Spot (Howes)
Lites-Camera-Platitude (Lawrence, Howes, Alda)
My Hometown (Lawrence)
I See Something (Massi, Lawrence)
Maybe Some Other Time (Alda, Howes)

You Can Trust Me (Lawrence)
A Room Without Windows (Lawrence, Howes)
Kiss Me No Kisses (Howes)
I Feel Humble (Lawrence, Newman, chorus)
Something to Live For (Howes)
You're No Good (Massi, Lawrence)
The Friendliest Thing (Massi)
Wedding of the Year (chorus)
Some Days Everything Goes Wrong (Lawrence)

WHOOP-UP (December 22, 1958, Shubert Theatre)

MGM Records SE 3745 stereo

Music: Moose Charlap; lyrics: Norman Gimbel; based on Stay Away, Joe by Dan Cushman; musical direction: Stanley Lebowsky

Cast: Asia, Tony Gardell, Susan Johnson, Michael Kermoyan, Robert Lenn, Julienne Marie, Danny Meehan, Tom Raskin, Bobby Shields, Sylvia Syms, Romo Vincent, Ralph Young

Songs: Overture (orchestra)
Glenda's Place (Johnson, ensemble)
When the Tall Man Talks (Johnson)
Nobody Throws Those Bull (Vincent, ensemble)
Chief Rocky Boy (Gardell, ensemble)
Love Eyes (Young)
Men (Johnson)
Never Before (Marie)
Flattery (Johnson, Young)

'Caress Me, Possess Me' Perfume (Shields, Asia)
The Girl in Your Arms (orchestra)
The Best of What This Country's Got (Was Taken from the Indians) (Meehan)
I Wash My Hands (Young, Marie, Kermoyan, Raskin)
Sorry for Myself? (Syms)
Quarrel-tet (Johnson, Young, Lenn, Raskin)
What I Mean to Say (Meeham)
Montana (Johnson)
'Till the Big Fat Moon Falls Down (ensemble)

Note: The 'Overture' included only on the mono recording.

WILDCAT (December 16, 1960, Alvin Theatre)

RCA LSO 1060 stereo

Music: Cy Coleman; lyrics: Carolyn Leigh; musical direction: John Morris

Cast: Keith Andes, Lucille Ball, Charles Braswell, Clifford David, Edith King, Al Lanti, Ray Mason, Paula Stewart, Swen Swenson, Don Tomkins, Bill Walker

Songs: Overture (orchestra)
Oil! (chorus)
Hey, Look Me Over! (Ball, Stewart)
Wildcat (Ball)
You've Come Home (Andes)
That's What I Want for Janie (Ball)
What Takes My Fancy (Ball, Tomkins)
You're a Liar! (Ball, Andes)

One Day We Dance (David, Stewart)
Give a Little Whistle (Ball, Andes, chorus)
Tall Hope (Walker, Swenson, Mason, Braswell, men)
Tippy, Tippy Toes (Ball, King)
El Sombrero (Ball, Lanti, Swenson, chorus)

Corduroy Road (Andes, company)
Finale (company)

WISH YOU WERE HERE (June 25, 1952, Imperial Theatre)

RCA LOC 1007 mono reissued: RCA LSO 1108(e)

Music, lyrics: Harold Rome; based on _Having Wonderful Time_ by Arthur Kober; musical direction: Jay Blackton

Cast: Sidney Armus, Sheila Bond, Jack Cassidy, Patricia Marand, Sammy Smith, Paul Valentine

Songs: Overture (orchestra)
Camp Kare-Free Song (Smith, ensemble)
Goodbye Love (Marand, Bond, girls)
Ballad of a Social Director (Armus, ensemble)
Shopping Around (Bond)
Mix and Mingle (Cassidy, men)
Could Be (Marand, girls)
Tripping the Light Fantastic (ensemble)
Where Did the Night Go (Cassidy, Marand, ensemble)

Certain Individuals (Bond, ensemble)
They Won't Know Me (Cassidy)
Summer Afternoon (Valentine)
Don Jose of Far Rockaway (Armus, ensemble)
Everybody Loves Everybody (Bond, ensemble)
Wish You Were Here (Cassidy, men)
Relax (Valentine, Marand)
Flattery (Marand, Bond, Armus)
Finale (company)

THE WIZ (January 5, 1975, Majestic Theatre)

Atlantic SD 18137 stereo

Music, lyrics: Charlie Smalls; the new musical version of _The Wonderful Wizard of Oz_; musical direction: Charles H. Coleman

Cast: Hinton Battle, Dee Dee Bridgewater, Andre De Shields, Tiger Haynes, Mabel King, Stephanie Mills, Ted Ross, Clarice Taylor, Tasha Thomas

Songs: Prologue (company)
The Feeling We Once Had (Thomas)
Tornado (orchestra)
He's the Wizard (Taylor, company)
Soon As I Get Home (Mills)
I Was Born on the Day Before Yesterday (Battle)
Ease on Down the Road (Mills, Battle, Haynes, Ross)
Slide Some Oil to Me (Haynes)
I'm a Mean Ole Lion (Ross)

Be a Lion (Mills, Ross)
So You Wanted to See the Wizard (De Shields)
What Would I Do If I Could Feel (Haynes)
Don't Nobody Bring Me No Bad News (King)

Everybody Rejoice (Mills, ensemble)
Y'All Got It! (De Shields, company)
If You Believe (Bridgewater)
Home - Finale (Mills)

WOMAN OF THE YEAR (March 29, 1981, Palace Theatre)

Arista Records AL 8303 stereo

Music: John Kander; lyrics: Fred Ebb; based on the MGM film by Ring Lardner, Jr. and Michael Kanin; musical direction: Donald Pippin

Cast: Lauren Bacall, Roderick Cook, Marilyn Cooper, (the voice of Fred Ebb), Rex Everhart, Harry Guardino, Eivind Harum, Grace Keagy, Daren Kelly

Songs: Overture (orchestra)
Woman of the Year (Bacall, women)
The Poker Game (Guardino, men)
See You in the Funny Papers (Guardino)
When You're Right, You're Right (Bacall, Guardino)
Shut Up, Gerald (Bacall, Guardino, Cook)
So What Else Is New? (Guardino, Ebb)
One of the Boys (Bacall, Everhart, men)

Table Talk (Bacall, Guardino)
It Isn't Working (Cook, Kelly, Keagy, chorus)
I Told You So (Cook, Keagy)
I Wrote the Book (Bacall, women)
Happy in the Morning (Harum, Bacall, chorus)
Sometimes a Day Goes By (Guardino, men)
The Grass Is Always Greener (Bacall, Cooper)
We're Gonna Work It Out (Guardino, Bacall)

WONDERFUL TOWN (February 26, 1953, Winter Garden Theatre)

Decca DL 9010 mono reissued: MCA 1528E

Music: Leonard Bernstein; lyrics: Betty Comden, Adolph Green; based upon the play My Sister Eileen by Joseph Fields and Jerome Chodorov; musical direction: Lehman Engel

Cast: Edith Adams, Cris Alexander, Delbert Anderson, Jordan Bentley, Dort Clark, Warren Galjour, George Gaynes, Albert Linville, Rosalind Russell

Songs: Christopher Street (Galjour, chorus)
Ohio (Russell, Adams)
One Hundred Easy Ways (Russell)
What a Waste (Gaynes, Galjour, Linville)
A Little Bit in Love (Adams)
Pass That Football (Bentley)
Conversation Piece (Russell, Adams, Alexander, Gaynes, Clark)

A Quiet Girl (Gaynes)
Conga! (Russell, men)

My Darlin' Eileen (Adams, Anderson, men)
Swing! (Russell, chorus)
It's Love (Adams, Gaynes, chorus)
Ballet at the Village Vortex (orchestra)
Wrong Note Rag (Russell, Adams, chorus)

WORKING (May 14, 1978, Forty-Sixth Street Theatre)

Columbia JS 35411 stereo reissued: CSP HAS 35411

Music, lyrics: Craig Carnelia, Micki Grant, Steven Schwartz, James Taylor; additional music: Mary Rodgers; additional lyrics: Susan Birkenhead, Graciela Daniele, Matt Landers; from the book by Studs Terkel; musical direction: Stephen Reinhardt

Cast: Susan Bigelow, Arny Freeman, Bob Gunton, David Patrick Kelly, Robin Lamont, Matt Landers, Bobo Lewis, Joe Mantegna, Matthew McGrath, Lenora Nemetz, David Langston Smyrl, Lynne Thigpen

Songs: All the Livelong Day (company) (I Hear America Singing, by Walt Whitman) music, additional lyrics: Schwartz
Lovin' Al (Smyrl, company) music, lyrics: Grant
The Mason (Kelly) music, lyrics: Carnelia
Neat to Be a Newsboy (McGrath, boys) music, lyrics: Schwartz
Nobody Tells Me How (Lewis) music: Rodgers; lyrics: Birkenhead
Un Mejor Dia Vendra (Mantegna, Landers, chorus) music: Taylor; Spanish lyrics: Daniele, Landers
Just a Housewife (Bigelow, women) music, lyrics: Carnelia
Millwork (Lamont) music, lyrics: Taylor

If I Could've Been (Kelly, Thigpen, company) music, lyrics: Grant
Joe (Freeman) music, lyrics: Carnelia
It's an Art (Nemetz, company) music, lyrics: Schwartz
Brother Trucker (Mantegna, company) music, lyrics: Taylor
Fathers and Sons (Gunton) music, lyrics: Schwartz
Cleanin' Women (Thigpen) music, lyrics: Grant
Something to Point To (company) music, lyrics: Carnelia

THE WORLD OF KURT WEILL (June 6, 1963, Off Broadway, One Sheridan Square)

MGM Records SE 4180 OC stereo ("A Kurt Weill Cabaret")

Music: Kurt Weill; lyrics: Maxwell Anderson, Marc Blitzstein, Bertolt Brecht, Jacques Deval, Ira Gershwin, Will Holt; musical direction: Abraham Stokman

Cast: Will Holt, Martha Schlamme

Songs: The Ballad of the Easy Life (orchestra)

Barbara Song (Schlamme) lyrics: Brecht
Mack the Knife (Holt) lyrics: Brecht/Blitzstein
Tango Ballade (Holt, Schlamme) lyrics: Brecht/Blitzstein
Pirate Jenny (Schlamme) lyrics: Brecht
Le Roi d'Aquitaine (Schlamme) lyrics: Deval
Caesar's Death (Holt) lyrics: Holt
Saga of Jenny (Schlamme, Holt) lyrics: Gershwin
September Song (Holt) lyrics: Anderson
Mandalay Song (Holt) lyrics: Brecht
Surabaya Johnny (Schlamme) lyrics: Brecht
Bilbao Song (Schlamme) lyrics: Brecht
Survival Song (Holt) lyrics: Brecht/Blitzstein
Lost in the Stars (Holt, Schlamme) lyrics: Anderson

Note: Contains spoken introductions.

YOUR ARMS TOO SHORT TO BOX WITH GOD (December 22, 1976, Lyceum Theatre)

ABC Records AB 1004 stereo

Music, lyrics: Alex Bradford, Micki Grant; conceived from the Book of Matthew; musical direction: Chapman Roberts

Cast: Salome Bey, Alex Bradford, Clinton Derricks-Carroll, Vinnette Carroll, Sheila Ellis, Michael Gray, Delores Hall, William Hardy, Jr., Bobby Hill

Songs: Beatitudes I (company)
Good Time (Derricks-Carroll, company)
Sermon (Derricks-Carroll)
Jesus the Stranger (Hardy, company)
We Are the Priests and Elders (Hardy, Derricks-Carroll, Hill, Gray)
Something Is Wrong in Jerusalem (Bey, company)
Be Careful Whom You Kiss (Bey, company)
The Trial (Ellis, company)
It's Too Late Judas (company)
Judas Dance (orchestra)
Your Arms Too Short to Box with God (Hall, company)
See How They Done My Lord (Bey, company)
Come On Down (Bradford, Carroll, Ellis, Derricks-Carroll)
Can't No Grave Hold My Body Down (Derricks-Carroll)
Beatitudes II (Hill, company)
Didn't I Tell You (Hardy, company)
As Long As I Live (Derricks-Carroll, company)
Everybody Has His Own Way (Derricks-Carroll, Gray)
I Love You So Much Jesus (Hall)
We're Gonna Have a Good Time (reprise) (Derricks-Carroll, company)

YOUR OWN THING (January 13, 1968, Off Broadway, Orpheum Theatre)

RCA LSO 1148 stereo

Music, lyrics: Hal Hester, Danny Apolinar; suggested by Twelfth Night; musical direction: Charles Schneider

Cast: Danny Apolinar, Igors Gavon, John Kuhner, Tom Ligon, Leland Palmer, Marcia Rodd, Rusty Thacker, Michael Valenti

Songs: Opening (Gavon)
No One's Perfect, Dear (Thacker, Palmer)
The Flowers (Gavon, Palmer)
I'm Not Afraid (Apolinar, Valenti, Kuhner)
I'm Me (Apolinar, Valenti, Kuhner)
Somethin's Happ'nin' (Baby, Baby!) (Palmer, Ligon, Apolinar, Valenti, Kuhner)
Come Away, Death (Thacker)
I'm On My Way to the Top (Thacker)
She Never Told Her Love (Palmer)
Be Gentle (Palmer, Ligon)

The Apocalypse Fugue (Ligon, Apolinar, Valenti, Kuhner)
What Do I Know? (Palmer, Apolinar, Valenti, Kuhner)
The Now Generation (Palmer, Apolinar, Valenti, Kuhner)
The Middle Years (Rodd)
Young and in Love (Ligon)
Hunca Munca (company)
The Middle Years (reprise) (Thacker)
Don't Leave Me (Rodd, Thacker)
Your Own Thing (Apolinar, Valenti, Kuhner)

YOU'RE A GOOD MAN, CHARLIE BROWN (March 7, 1967, Off Broadway, Theatre 80 St. Marks)

MGM Records S1E-9 OC stereo reissued: Polydor 820262-1 Y-1 CD

Music, lyrics: Clark Gesner; based on the comic strip Peanuts by Charles M. Schultz; musical direction: Joseph Raposo

Cast: Bob Balaban, Gary Burghoff, Bill Hinnant, Skip Hinnant, Reva Rose

Songs: You're a Good Man, Charlie Brown (company)
Schroeder (Moonlight Sonata) (Ross, S. Hinnant)
Snoopy (B. Hinnant, Burghoff, Rose)
My Blanket and Me (Balaban)
Kite (Burghoff)
Dr. Lucy (Rose, Burghoff)
Book Report (Burghoff, Rose, Balaban, S. Hinnant)

The Red Baron (B. Hinnant)
T-E-A-M (Baseball Game) (company)
Queen Lucy (Rose, Balaban)
Peanuts Potpourri (B. Hinnant, Balaban, Burghoff) spoken
Little Known Facts (Rose, Balaban, Burghoff)
Suppertime (B. Hinnant, Burghoff)
Happiness (company)

ZORBA (November 17, 1968, Imperial Theatre)

Capitol SO 118 stereo

Music: John Kander; lyrics: Fred Ebb; adapted from Zorba the Greek by Nikos Kazantzakis; musical direction: Harold Hastings

Cast: Carmen Alvarez, Herschel Bernardi, John Cunningham, Ali Hafid, Lee Hooper, Maria Karnilova, Jerry Sappir, Angelo Saridis, Lorraine Serabian

Songs: Life Is (Serabian, company)
The First Time (Bernardi)
The Top of the Hill (Serabian, chorus)
No Boom Boom (Karnilova, Bernardi, Cunningham, men)
The Butterfly (Alvarez, Serabian, Cunningham, chorus)
Goodbye, Canavaro (Karnilova, Bernardi, Cunningham)
Grandpapa - Zorba's Dance (Bernardi)

Only Love (Karnilova)
The Bend of the Road (Serabian, Alvarez, Cunningham, chorus)
Entr'acte (Sappir, Hafid, Saridis)
Y'Assou (Bernardi, Karnilova, Cunningham, Serabian, company)
Why Can't I Speak? (Alvarez, Cunningham, Hooper)
The Crow (Serabian, women)
Happy Birthday (Karnilova)
I Am Free (Bernardi)
Life Is (reprise) (company)

ZORBA (Revival, October 16, 1983, Broadway Theatre)

RCA ABL 1-4732 stereo CD

Musical direction: Paul Gemignani

Cast: Lila Kedrova, Taro Meyer, Anthony Quinn, Debbie Shapiro, Robert Westenberg

Songs: Life Is (Shapiro, company)
The First Time (Quinn)
The Top of the Hill (Shapiro, company)
No Boom Boom (Kedrova, Quinn, Westenberg, men)
Mine Song (company)
The Butterfly (Meyer, Westenberg, women)
Goodbye, Canavaro (Kedrova, Quinn, Cunningham)
Grandpapa (Quinn, Shapiro, company)

Only Love (Kedrova)
The Bend of the Road (Shapiro, company)
Only Love (reprise) (Shapiro)
Yassou (company)
Women (Quinn)
Why Can't I Speak? (Meyer)
That's a Beginning (Westenberg, Meyer, Shapiro)
The Crow (Shapiro, chorus)
Happy Birthday (Kedrova)

I Am Free (Quinn)
Finale: Life Is (reprise) (Shapiro)

THE ZULU AND THE ZAYDA (November 10, 1965, Cort Theatre)

Columbia KOS 2880 stereo

Music, lyrics: Harold Rome; musical direction: Meyer Kupferman

Cast: Ossie Davis, Peter De Anda, Louis Gossett, Menasha Skulnik, Christine Spencer

Songs: Prelude (orchestra)
Tkambuza (Davis)
It's Good to Be Alive (Skulnik, Gossett)
Crocodile Wife (Davis)
River of Tears (Skulnik)
The Water Wears Down the Stone (Davis)
Like the Breeze Blows (De Anda, Spencer, ensemble)
Olsgetzaichnet (Skulnik, ensemble)

Entr'acte (orchestra)
Some Things (ensemble)
Zulu Love Song (Gossett)
May Your Heart Stay Young (Skulnik, ensemble)
How Cold, Cold, Cold (Davis)
Eagle Soliloquy (Gossett)
Finale (Skulnik, cast)

ADDENDA

ARMS AND THE GIRL (February 2, 1950, 46th Street Theatre)

Decca DL 5200 mono reissued: Columbia CSP X 14879

Music: Morton Gould; lyrics: Dorothy Fields; musical direction: Frederick Dvonch

Cast: Florenz Ames, Pearl Bailey, Nanette Fabray, Georges Guetary

Songs: Curtain Music (orchestra)
A Girl with a Flame (Fabray)
That's What I Told Him Last Night (Ames, girls)
I Like It Here (Guetary)
That's My Fella (Fabray)
A Cow and a Plow and a Frau (Guetary)
Nothin' for Nothin' (Bailey)
He Will Tonight (Fabray, Guetary)
You Kissed Me (Fabray, Guetary)
There Must Be Somethin' Better than Love (Bailey)
Curtain Music (orchestra)

THE GOLDEN LAND (November 11, 1985, Off Broadway, Second Avenue Theatre)

Golden Land Records GL 001 stereo

Songs of the Jewish culture; English lyrics: Zalmen Mlotek, Moishe Rosenfeld, others; musical direction: Zalmen Mlotek

Cast: Bruce Adler, Phyllis Berk, Joanne Borts, Marc Krause, Neva Small, Stuart Zagnit

Songs: Amerike, Hurrah far Uncle Sem! (cast)
Lozt Arayn! (Let Us In) (Krause, cast)
Vatch Your Step! (cast)
Oy, I Like Him! (Borts)
Dem Peddlers Brivele (The Peddler's Letter) (Zagnit)
A Brivele der Mamen (A Letter to Mother) (Berk)
Sabbath Montage:
Lekha Doydi (cast)
Sabbath Queen (cast)
Fraytik Oyf der Nakht (cast)
Sabbath Zmires (cast)
Ballad of the Triangle Fire (Small)
Mamenyu! Elergy for the Triangle Fire Victims (Berk)
Bread and Roses (cast)
Arbeter Froyen (Working Women) (cast)
A Grus fun di Trenches (Greetings from the Trenches) (Adler, Krause)
Lebn Zol Columbus! (Borts, Berk)
Gebentsht Iz Amerike (Blessed Is America!) (cast)
Fonye Ganev (The Czar Is a Thief) (cast)
Amerike, Hurrah! (reprise) (cast)

A Khulem (A Dream) (Borts, Adler)
Fun Downtown, Uptown (cast)

Fifty-Fifty (Adler, Krause, Borts)
Show You Care! (Berk, Small)
Wevd (Adler)
Joe and Paul's (Krause)
Ikh Bin a Border Bay Mayn Vayb (I Am My Wife's Border) (Adler, Zagnit)
Mayn Yiddishe Meydele (My Jewish Girl) (Zagnit)
The Badkhn's Song and The Wedding Dance (Adler, orchestra)
Papirosn (Cigarettes) (Small)
Got Un Zayn Mishpet Iz Gerekht (God and His Judgment Are Right) (Krause)
Belz, Mayn Shtetele Belz (Belz, My Little Town Belz) (Berk)
Yidl Mitn Fidl (Yidl with His Fiddle) (Berk)
Vu Nemt Men Parnose (How Does One Find a Living?) (Small)
Brother, Can You Spare a Dime (Berk)
Rumania, Rumania (Adler)
Finale:
A Khulem (reprise) (cast)
Gebentsht Iz Amerike (reprise) (cast)

NUNSENSE (December 12, 1985, Off Broadway, Cherry Lane Theatre)

DRG Records SBL 12589 stereo

Music, lyrics: Dan Goggin; musical direction: Michael Rice

Cast: Christine Anderson, Semina De Laurentis, Marilyn Farina, Edwina Lewis, Suzi Winson

Songs: Nunsense Is Habit-Forming (cast)
A Difficult Transition (cast)
Benedicite (Winson, Lewis)
The Biggest Ain't the Best (Lewis, Winson)
Playing Second Fiddle (Anderson, Farina)
So You Want to Be a Nun (De Laurentis)
Turn Up the Spotlight (Farina)

Lilacs Bring Back Memories (cast)
Tackle That Temptation with a Time-Step (Lewis, cast)
Growing Up Catholic (Anderson, cast)
We've Got to Clean Out the Freezer (cast)
Just a Coupl'a Sisters (Farina, Lewis)
I Just Want to Be a Star (Anderson)
The Drive-In (cast)
I Could've Gone to Nashville (De Laurentis)
Holier than Thou (Lewis, cast)
Finale (cast)

Chronology of Productions

The musical shows included in this directory are here arranged chronologically, providing the opening date, the show title, the theatre, and the number of performances, when available. Revival and transfer productions are noted. Some shows are listed as continuing, as of February, 1987. OB indicates Off Broadway.

1931		
Jun 3	The Band Wagon	New Amsterdam (262)
1932		
May 19	Show Boat (rev)	Casino (181)
1937		
Jun 16	The Cradle Will Rock	Venice (19)
1938		
Jan 3	The Cradle Will Rock (rev)	Windsor (108)
1940		
Oct 25	Cabin in the Sky	Martin Beck (156)
Oct 30	Panama Hattie	46th Street (501)
1941		
Jan 5	No for an Answer	Mecca OB (3)
Jan 23	Lady in the Dark	Alvin (162)
1942		
Jan 22	Porgy and Bess (rev)	Majestic (286)
Jul 4	This Is the Army	Broadway (113)
1943		
Mar 31	Oklahoma!	St. James (2,248)
Oct 7	One Touch of Venus	Imperial (567)
Nov 17	A Connecticut Yankee (rev)	Martin Beck (135)
Dec 2	Carmen Jones	Broadway (502)
1944		
Jan 28	Mexican Hayride	Winter Garden (479)
Aug 12	Song of Norway	Imperial (860)
Oct 5	Bloomer Girl	Shubert (657)
Oct 7	The Merry Widow (rev)	City Center OB (32)
Dec 27	Sing Out, Sweet Land!	International (102)
Dec 28	On the Town	Adelphi (462)
1945		
Jan 27	Up in Central Park	Century (504)
Apr 19	Carousel	Majestic (890)
Oct 6	Polonaise	Alvin (113)
1946		
Jan 5	Show Boat (rev)	Ziegfeld (418)
Feb 6	Lute Song	Plymouth (142)
Mar 30	St. Louis Woman	Martin Beck (113)

Apr 18	Call Me Mister	National (734)
May 17	Annie Get Your Gun	Imperial (1,147)
1947		
Jan 9	Street Scene	Adelphi (148)
Jan 10	Finian's Rainbow	46th Street (725)
Mar 13	Brigadoon	Ziegfeld (581)
Oct 9	High Button Shoes	Century (727)
Oct 10	Allegro	Majestic (315)
1948		
Jan 29	Look Ma, I'm Dancin'!	Adelphi (188)
Apr 30	Inside USA	New Century (339)
Dec 30	Kiss Me, Kate	Century (1,077)
1949		
Apr 7	South Pacific	Majestic (1,925)
Jul 15	Miss Liberty	Imperial (308)
Oct 30	Lost in the Stars	Music Box (281)
Nov 25	Texas, Li'l Darlin'	Mark Hellinger (293)
Dec 8	Gentlemen Prefer Blondes	Ziegfeld (740)
1950		
Feb 2	Arms and the Girl	46th Street (134)
Apr 24	Peter Pan	Imperial (321)
Oct 12	Call Me Madam	Imperial (644)
Nov 24	Guys and Dolls	46th Street (1,194)
Dec 21	Out of This World	New Century (157)
1951		
Mar 29	The King and I	St. James (1,246)
Apr 18	Make a Wish	Winter Garden (102)
Apr 19	A Tree Grows in Brooklyn	Alvin (267)
May 14	Flahooley	Broadhurst (40)
Jun 21	Seventeen	Broadhurst (180)
Jul 19	Two on the Aisle	Mark Hellinger (279)
Nov 1	Top Banana	Winter Garden (350)
Nov 12	Paint Your Wagon	Shubert (289)
1952		
Jan 3	Pal Joey (rev)	Broadhurst (540)
Mar 4	Paris '90	Booth (87)
Mar 21	Three Wishes for Jamie	Mark Hellinger (91)
May 5	Of Thee I Sing (rev)	Ziegfeld (72)
May 16	New Faces of 1952	Royale (365)
Jun 25	Wish You Were Here	Imperial (598)
Jun 26	A Night in Venice	Jones Beach Marine OB
Dec 15	Two's Company	Alvin (90)
1953		
Feb 11	Hazel Flagg	Mark Hellinger (190)
Feb 26	Wonderful Town	Winter Garden (559)
May 7	Can-Can	Shubert (892)
May 28	Me and Juliet	Majestic (358)
Dec 3	Kismet	Ziegfeld (583)
1954		
Mar 5	The Girl in Pink Tights	Mark Hellinger (115)
Mar 10	The Threepenny Opera (rev)	Theatre de Lys OB (96)
Mar 11	The Golden Apple (transferred: see Apr 20)	Phoenix OB (46)
Apr 8	By the Beautiful Sea	Majestic (268)
Apr 20	The Golden Apple (trans)	Alvin (127)
May 13	The Pajama Game	St. James (1,061)
Jun 24	Arabian Nights	Jones Beach Marine OB
Sep 30	The Boy Friend	Royale (485)

Oct 11	On Your Toes (rev)	46th Street (64)
Oct 20	Peter Pan	Winter Garden (152)
Nov 4	Fanny	Majestic (888)
Dec 1	Mrs. Patterson	National (101)
Dec 30	House of Flowers	Alvin (165)
1955		
Jan 27	Plain and Fancy	Mark Hellinger (461)
Feb 24	Silk Stockings	Imperial (478)
Feb 28	Shoestring Revue	President OB (96)
Apr 18	Ankles Aweigh	Mark Hellinger (176)
May 5	Damn Yankees	46th Street (1,019)
May 26	Seventh Heaven	ANTA (44)
Sep 20	The Threepenny Opera (rev)	Theatre de Lys OB (2,611)
Nov 30	Pipe Dream	Shubert (246)
1956		
Mar 15	My Fair Lady	Mark Hellinger (2,717)
Mar 22	Mr. Wonderful	Broadway (383)
May 3	The Most Happy Fella	Imperial (676)
May 22	The Littlest Revue	Phoenix OB (32)
Jun 14	New Faces of 1956	Ethel Barrymore (220)
Nov 5	Shoestring '57	Barbizon OB (110)
Nov 15	Li'l Abner	St. James (693)
Nov 26	Cranks	Bijou (40)
Nov 29	Bells Are Ringing	Shubert (924)
Dec 1	Candide	Martin Beck (73)
Dec 6	Happy Hunting	Majestic (412)
1957		
May 14	New Girl in Town	46th Street (431)
Aug 20	Simply Heavenly	Playhouse (62)
Sep 10	Mask and Gown	John Golden (39)
Sept 26	West Side Story	Winter Garden (732)
Sep 29	The Best of Burlesque	Carnegie Hall Playhouse OB (520)
Oct 10	Take Five	Downstairs OB
Oct 31	Jamaica	Imperial (555)
Dec 19	The Music Man	Majestic (1,375)
1958		
Jan 23	The Body Beautiful	Broadway (60)
Feb 4	Oh Captain!	Alvin (192)
Mar 12	International Soiree	Bijou (21)
Apr 3	Say, Darling	ANTA (332)
Jun 22	Song of Norway (rev)	Jones Beach Marine OB
Oct 11	Demi-Dozen	Upstairs OB
Oct 11	Goldilocks	Lunt-Fontanne (161)
Dec 1	Flower Drum Song	St. James (600)
Dec 22	Whoop-Up	Shubert (56)
Dec 23	A Party with Comden and Green	John Golden (38)
1959		
Feb 5	Redhead	46th Street (452)
Mar 9	Juno	Winter Garden (16)
Mar 19	First Impressions	Alvin (92)
Apr 23	Destry Rides Again	Imperial (472)
May 11	Once Upon a Mattress (transferred: see Nov 25)	Phoenix OB (216)
May 12	The Nervous Set	Henry Miller (23)
May 21	Gypsy	Broadway (702)
May 25	Leave It to Jane (rev)	Sheridan Sq OB (928)

Jun 9	The Billy Barnes Revue	York OB (199)
Sep 24	Pieces of Eight	Upstairs OB
Oct 22	Take Me Along	Shubert (448)
Oct 31	The Kosher Widow	Anderson OB (87)
Nov 16	The Sound of Music	Lunt-Fontanne (1,443)
Nov 18	Little Mary Sunshine	Orpheum OB (1,143)
Nov 23	Fiorello!	Broadhurst (796)
Nov 25	Once Upon a Mattress (trans)	Alvin (244)
Dec 7	Saratoga	Winter Garden (80)
1960		
Jan 20	Parade	Players OB (95)
Jan 28	Four Below Strikes Back	Downstairs OB
Feb 15	The Crystal Heart	East 74th St OB (9)
Mar 8	Greenwillow	Alvin (97)
Apr 14	Bye Bye Birdie	Martin Beck (607)
Apr 16	Oh, Kay! (rev)	East 74th St OB (89)
Apr 27	Finian's Rainbow (rev) (transferred: see May 23)	City Center OB (15)
Apr 28	Christine	46th Street (12)
May 3	The Fantasticks	Sullivan OB (continuing)
May 4	Ernest in Love	Grammercy OB (111)
May 23	Finian's Rainbow (rev - trans)	46th Street (12)
Sep 28	Greenwich Village, USA	One Sheridan OB (87)
Sep 29	Dressed to the Nines	Upstairs OB
Sep 29	Irma La Douce	Plymouth (524)
Oct 12	Kittiwake Island	Martinique OB (7)
Oct 17	Tenderloin	46th Street (216)
Nov 3	The Unsinkable Molly Brown	Winter Garden (532)
Dec 3	Camelot	Majestic (873)
Dec 16	Wildcat	Alvin (171)
Dec 26	Do Re Mi	St. James (400)
1961		
Jan 12	Show Girl	Eugene O'Neill (100)
Apr 3	The Happiest Girl in the World	Martin Beck (96)
Apr 13	Carnival	Imperial (719)
Apr 19	Smiling the Boy Fell Dead	Cherry Lane OB (22)
May 18	Donnybrook!	46th Street (68)
Oct 2	The Sap of Life	One Sheridan OB (49)
Oct 3	Sail Away	Broadhurst (167)
Oct 10	Milk and Honey	Martin Beck (543)
Oct 12	Let It Ride!	Eugene O'Neill (68)
Oct 14	How to Succeed in Business...	46th Street (1,417)
Oct 21	Bei Mir Bistu Schoen	Anderson OB (88)
Oct 23	Kwamina	54th Street (32)
Nov 2	Kean	Broadway (92)
Nov 10	All in Love	Martinique OB (141)
Nov 18	The Gay Life	Shubert (113)
Dec 6	Sing Muse!	Van Dam OB (39)
Dec 27	Subways Are for Sleeping	St. James (205)
1962		
Jan 27	A Family Affair	Billy Rose (65)
Feb 5	Fly Blackbird	Mayfair OB (127)
Mar 15	No Strings	54th Street (580)
Mar 19	All American	Winter Garden (86)
Mar 22	I Can Get It for You Wholesale	Shubert (300)
Apr 6	Half-Past Wednesday	Orpheum OB (6)
May 8	A Funny Thing Happened...	Alvin (966)
May 15	Anything Goes (rev)	Orpheum OB (239)

May 19	Bravo Giovanni	Broadhurst (76)
Oct 3	Stop the World - I Want...	Shubert (556)
Oct 18	Dime a Dozen	Plaza 9 OB (728)
Oct 20	Mr. President	St. James (265)
Nov 17	Little Me	Lunt-Fontanne (257)
Dec 12	Riverwind	Actors OB (443)
1963		
Jan 6	Oliver!	Imperial (774)
Mar 18	Tovarich	Broadway (264)
Apr 2	Best Foot Forward (rev)	Stage 73 OB (224)
Apr 15	The Boys from Syracuse (rev)	Theatre Four OB (500)
Apr 23	She Loves Me	Eugene O'Neill (302)
Jun 6	The World of Kurt Weill	One Sheridan OB (228)
Oct 3	Here's Love	Shubert (334)
Oct 15	Ballad for Bimshire	Mayfair OB (72)
Oct 17	Jennie	Majestic (82)
Oct 24	110 in the Shade	Broadhurst (331)
Dec 8	The Girl Who Came to Supper	Broadway (112)
1964		
Jan 12	Jerico-Jim Crow	Sanctuary OB (32)
Jan 14	Athenian Touch	Jan Hus OB (1)
Jan 16	Hello, Dolly!	St. James (2,844)
Jan 21	Cabin in the Sky (rev)	Greenwich OB (47)
Feb 6	Rugantino	Mark Hellinger (28)
Feb 16	Foxy	Ziegfeld (72)
Feb 27	What Makes Sammy Run?	54th Street (540)
Mar 19	Cindy	Gate OB (318)
Mar 26	Funny Girl	Winter Garden (1,348)
Apr 4	Anyone Can Whistle	Majestic (9)
Apr 7	High Spirits	Alvin (376)
Apr 29	To Broadway with Love	World's Fair OB (97)
May 26	Fade Out Fade In	Mark Hellinger (271)
Jun 2	Folies Bergere	Broadway (191)
Jul 6	The King and I (rev)	New York State (40)
Aug 17	The Merry Widow (rev)	New York State (40)
Sept 22	Fiddler on the Roof	Imperial (3,242)
Sept 30	Oh What a Lovely War	Broadhurst (125)
Oct 6	Cambridge Circus	Plymouth (113)
Oct 20	Golden Boy	Majestic (569)
Oct 26	The Secret Life of Walter...	Players OB (96)
Oct 27	Ben Franklin in Paris	Lunt-Fontanne (215)
Nov 8	The Cradle Will Rock (rev)	Theatre Four OB (82)
Nov 23	Bajour	Shubert (232)
Dec 15	I Had a Ball	Martin Beck (199)
1965		
Feb 16	Baker Street	Broadway (313)
Mar 18	Do I Hear a Waltz?	46th Street (220)
Mar 30	The Decline and Fall...	Square East OB (273)
Apr 25	Half a Sixpence	Broadhurst (512)
May 11	Flora the Red Menace	Alvin (87)
May 16	The Roar of the Greasepaint...	Shubert (232)
Jun 22	Kismet (rev)	New York State (47)
Aug 10	Carousel (rev)	New York State (47)
Oct 4	Pickwick	46th Street (56)
Oct 10	Drat! The Cat!	Martin Beck (8)
Oct 17	On A Clear Day You Can See...	Mark Hellinger (273)
Nov 3	Just for Openers	Upstairs OB (395)
Nov 10	The Zulu and the Zayda	Cort (179)

Nov 13	Skyscraper	Lunt-Fontanne (241)
Nov 22	Man of La Mancha	ANTA OB (2,328)
Nov 29	Anya	Ziegfeld (16)
1966		
Jan 9	The Mad Show	New OB (871)
Jan 29	Sweet Charity	Palace (608)
Mar 7	Wait a Minum!	John Golden (457)
Mar 29	It's a Bird ...It's a Plane...	Alvin (129)
May 21	A Time for Singing	Broadway (41)
May 24	Mame	Winter Garden (1,508)
May 31	Annie Get Your Gun (rev) (transferred: see Sep 21)	New York State (47)
Jun 21	Below the Belt	Downstairs OB (186)
Jul 19	Show Boat (rev)	New York State (64)
Sep 21	Annie Get Your Gun (rev)	Broadway (77)
Oct 18	The Apple Tree	Shubert (463)
Oct 19	Mixed Doubles	Upstairs OB (428)
Nov 6	Man with a Load of Mischief	Jan Hus OB (240)
Nov 20	Cabaret	Broadhurst (1,166)
Nov 26	Walking Happy	Lunt-Fontanne (161)
Dec 5	I Do! I Do!	46th Street (584)
Dec 14	Breakfast at Tiffany's	Majestic (4 previews)
1967		
Jan 19	By Jupiter (rev)	Theatre Four OB (118)
Mar 7	You're a Good Man, Charlie...	Theatre 80 OB (1,597)
Apr 11	Illya Darling	Mark Hellinger (319)
Apr 26	Hallelujah, Baby!	Martin Beck (293)
Jun 12	South Pacific (rev)	New York State (104)
Sep 26	Now Is the Time for All...	Theatre de Lys OB (112)
Oct 17	Hair	Public OB (65)
Oct 23	Henry, Sweet Henry	Palace (80)
Nov 5	In Circles	Cherry Lane OB (222)
Nov 12	Hello, Dolly! (all Black cast)	St. James
Dec 7	How Now, Dow Jones	Lunt-Fontanne (221)
1968		
Jan 13	Your Own Thing	Orpheum OB (933)
Jan 18	The Happy Time	Broadway (286)
Jan 22	Jacques Brel Is Alive and...	Village Gate OB (1,847)
Jan 27	Darling of the Day	George Abbott (32)
Jan 28	House of Flowers (rev)	Theatre de Lys OB (57)
Feb 4	Golden Rainbow	Shubert (383)
Apr 10	George M!	Palace (433)
Apr 29	Hair (revised)	Biltmore (1,750)
May 2	New Faces of 1968	Booth (52)
May 9	The Believers	Garrick OB (300)
Oct 9	The Megilla of Itzik Manger	John Golden (78)
Oct 13	How to Steal an Election	Pocket OB (80)
Oct 20	Her First Roman	Lunt-Fontanne (17)
Oct 23	Maggie Flynn	ANTA (82)
Nov 1	Peace	Judson OB (192)
Nov 17	Zorba	Imperial (306)
Dec 1	Promises, Promises	Shubert (1,281)
Dec 20	Dames at Sea	Bouwerie OB (575)

1969		
Jan 22	Celebration	Ambassador (110)
Feb 3	Canterbury Tales	Eugene O'Neill (121)
Feb 6	Dear World	Mark Hellinger (132)
Mar 11	Salvation	Village Gate OB (239)
Mar 16	1776	46th Street (1,217)
Jun 4	Promenade	Promenade OB (259)
Jun 17	Oh! Calcutta!	Eden OB (1,314)
Oct 23	Jimmy	Winter Garden (84)
Dec 15	Gertrude Stein's First Reader	Astor Place OB (40)
Dec 18	Coco	Mark Hellinger (332)
1970		
Jan 26	The Last Sweet Days of Isaac	Eastside OB (485)
Jan 27	Joy	New OB (208)
Mar 2	Billy Noname	Truck OB (48)
Mar 15	Purlie	Broadway (690)
Mar 26	Minnie's Boys	Imperial (76)
Mar 28	Hello, Dolly! (Merman version)	St. James
Mar 30	Applause	Palace (896)
Apr 8	Cry for Us All	Broadhurst (9)
Apr 14	The Boy Friend (rev)	Ambassador (111)
Apr 26	Company	Alvin (706)
May 18	The Me Nobody Knows	Orpheum OB (587)
Oct 19	The Rothschilds	Lunt-Fontanne (505)
Nov 8	Touch	Village Arena OB (422)
Nov 10	Two by Two	Imperial (352)
1971		
Jan 19	No, No, Nanette (rev)	46th Street (861)
Apr 4	Follies	Winter Garden (522)
Apr 15	70, Girls, 70	Broadhurst (36)
May 5	Earl of Ruston	Billy Rose (5)
May 17	Godspell	Cherry Lane OB (1,270)
Jun 27	Two Gentlemen of Verona (transferred: see Dec 1)	Delacorte OB (20)
Oct 12	Jesus Christ Superstar	Mark Hellinger (720)
Oct 20	Ain't Supposed to Die a...	Ethel Barrymore (325)
Nov 2	The Grass Harp	Martin Beck (7)
Dec 1	Two Gentlemen of Verona (trans)	St. James (613)
Dec 19	Inner City	Ethel Barrymore (97)
1972		
Feb 14	Grease (transferred: see June 7)	Eden OB
Apr 9	Sugar	Majestic (505)
Apr 19	Don't Bother Me, I Can't Cope	Playhouse OB (914)
May 15	Hard Job Being God	Edison OB (6)
May 16	Don't Play Us Cheap	Ethel Barrymore (164)
Jun 7	Grease (trans)	Broadhurst (3,388)
Jun 19	Joan	Circle OB (64)
June 26	Mass	Metropolitan Opera
Oct 1	Berlin to Broadway...	Theatre de Lys OB (153)
Oct 4	Oh Coward!	New OB (294)
Oct 9	Dude, the Highway Life	Broadway (16)
Oct 23	Pippin	Imperial (669)
Nov 19	Ambassador	Lunt-Fontanne (8)
Nov 23	Doctor Selavy's Magic Theatre	Mercer OB (144)

Date	Show	Theatre (performances)
1973		
Feb 25	A Little Night Music	Shubert (527)
Mar 13	Irene (rev)	Minskoff (590)
Mar 19	Seesaw	Uris (296)
Apr 2	Karl Marx Play	American Place OB (31)
May 13	Cyrano	Palace (49)
Jun 18	The Faggot	Truck OB (182)
Oct 18	Raisin	46th Street (258)
Nov 13	Gigi	Uris (103)
Dec 18	Candide (rev)	Chelsea OB (48)
	(transferred: see Mar 5, 1974)	
1974		
Jan 8	Let My People Come	Village Gate OB (1,167)
Jan 27	Lorelei	Palace (320)
Mar 5	Candide (rev)	Broadway (740)
Mar 6	Over Here!	Shubert (341)
May 28	The Magic Show	Cort (1,859)
Oct 6	Mack and Mabel	Majestic (66)
1975		
Jan 3	Philemon	Portfolio OB (60)
Jan 5	The Wiz	Majestic (1,672)
Jan 7	Shenandoah	Alvin (1,050)
Jan 27	Lovers	Players OB (118)
Mar 3	Goodtime Charley	Palace (104)
Mar 10	The Rocky Horror Show	Belasco (45)
May 21	A Chorus Line	Public OB (101)
	(transferred: see Oct 19)	
Jun 1	Chicago	46th Street (947)
Sep 17	Boy Meets Boy	Actors OB (463)
Oct 14	Christy	Bert Wheeler OB (40)
Oct 19	A Chorus Line (trans)	Shubert (continuing)
Dec 1	Tuscaloosa's Calling Me...	Village Gate OB (205)
Dec 21	Very Good Eddie (rev)	Booth (307)
Dec 22	Downriver	St. Clements OB (14)
1976		
Jan 11	Pacific Overtures	Winter Garden (193)
Mar 2	Bubbling Brown Sugar	ANTA (766)
Mar 25	My Fair Lady (rev)	St. James (384)
Apr 25	Rex	Lunt-Fontanne (48)
Apr 27	So Long, 174th Street	Harkness (16)
May 1	The Threepenny Opera (rev)	Beaumont (307)
Jul 21	Guys and Dolls (rev)	Broadway (239)
Sept 25	Porgy and Bess (rev)	Uris (122)
Oct 5	Lovesong	Village Gate OB (23)
Oct 9	The Robber Bridegroom	Biltmore (145)
Dec 22	Your Arms Too Short...	Lyceum (427)
1977		
Feb 10	A Party with Comden...(rev)	Morosco (92)
Mar 7	Starting Here, Starting Now	Barbarann OB (120)
Apr 17	I Love My Wife	Ethel Barrymore (864)
Apr 18	Side by Side by Sondheim	Music Box (390)
Apr 21	Annie	Alvin (2,377)
May 2	The King and I (rev)	Uris (719)
Oct 29	The Act	Majestic (233)
1978		
Feb 19	On the Twentieth Century	St. James (460)
Apr 2	The Merry Widow (rev)	New York State (in repertory)

Apr 17 The Best Little Whorehouse... Entermedia OB
(transferred: see Jun 19)
May 9 Ain't Misbehavin' Longacre (1,604)
May 13 Runaways Plymouth (199)
May 14 Working 46th Street (25)
Jun 8 Piano Bar Westside OB (133)
Jun 14 I'm Getting My Act Together... Public OB (1,165)
Jun 19 The Best Little...(trans) 46th Street (1,639)
Aug 3 Stop the World...(rev) New York State (29)
Sep 20 Eubie! Ambassador (439)
Oct 22 King of Hearts Minskoff (48)
Dec 14 Ballroom Majestic (116)

1979

Jan 11 The Grand Tour Palace (61)
Feb 11 They're Playing Our Song Imperial (1,082)
Feb 21 In Trousers Playwrights OB (24)
Mar 1 Sweeney Todd... Uris (557)
Apr 8 Carmelina St. James (17)
May 13 The Utter Glory of Morrissey.. Mark Hellinger (1)
May 16 Festival City Center OB (7)
May 31 I Remember Mama Majestic (108)
Jun 11 Scrambled Feet Village Gate OB (831)
Sep 25 Evita Broadway (1,568)
Oct 8 Sugar Babies Mark Hellinger (1,208)
Oct 18 Snow White and the Seven... Radio City (103)
Oct 22 One Mo' Time Village Gate OB (1,372)
Dec 6 Five After Eight Cubiculo OB (10)
Dec 13 Oklahoma! (rev) Palace (301)

1980

Feb 17 The Housewives' Cantata Theatre Four OB (24)
Apr 30 Barnum St. James (854)
May 1 A Day in Hollywood... John Golden (588)
May 14 Musical Chairs Rialto (15)
May 29 Billy Bishop Goes to War Morosco (90)
Jul 15 The Pirates of Penzance (rev) Delacorte OB (35)
(transferred: see Jan 8, 1981)
Aug 25 42nd Street Winter Garden (continuing)
Oct 23 Tintypes John Golden (93)
Oct 25 One Night Stand Nederlander (8 previews)
Nov 20 Ka-Boom! Carter OB (70)
Dec 14 Onward Victoria Martin Beck (1)

1981

Jan 8 The Pirates of Penzance (trans) Uris (772)
Mar 1 Sophisticated Ladies Lunt-Fontanne (767)
Mar 5 Bring Back Birdie Martin Beck (4)
Mar 12 Marry Me a Little Actors OB (96)
Mar 29 Woman of the Year Palace (770)
Apr 1 March of the Falsettos Playwrights OB (170)
May 14 I Can't Keep Running in Place Westside OB (208)
Oct 1 Pump Boys and Dinettes Colonnades OB (573)
Oct 21 Cotton Patch Gospel Lambs OB (193)
Nov 10 Oh, Brother! ANTA (3)
Nov 16 Merrily We Roll Along Alvin (16)
Nov 18 Joseph and the Amazing... Entermedia OB (77)
(transferred: see Jan 27, 1982)

Dec 20	Dreamgirls	Imperial (1,522)
1982		
Jan 15	Forbidden Broadway	Palsson's OB (continuing)
Jan 27	Joseph and the Amazing (trans)	Royale (747)
Feb 3	Clues to a Life	Vineyard OB (20)
May 7	Is There Life After High...	Ethel Barrymore (12)
May 9	Nine	46th Street (739)
May 27	Do Black Patent Leather...	Alvin (5)
Jul 28	Little Shop of Horrors	Orpheum OB (continuing)
Aug 12	Charlotte Sweet	Cheryl Crawford OB (102)
Sept 23	A Doll's Life	Mark Hellinger (5)
Oct 7	Cats	Winter Garden (continuing)
Oct 13	Candide (rev)	New York State (in repertory)
Oct 28	Upstairs at O'Neals'	O'Neals' OB (308)
1983		
Mar 6	On Your Toes (rev)	Virginia (505)
Apr 24	Show Boat (rev)	Gershwin (73)
May 1	My One and Only	St. James (767)
May 9	The Cradle Will Rock (rev)	American Place OB (29)
Jun 9	Taking My Turn	Entermedia OB (245)
Aug 9	Preppies	Promenade (52)
Aug 21	La Cage aux Folles	Palace (continuing)
Aug 29	Nite Club Confidential (transferred: see May 11, 1984)	Riverwest OB (48)
Oct 16	Zorba (rev)	Broadway (362)
Oct 30	Tallulah	Cheryl Crawford OB (42)
Nov 21	Doonesbury	Biltmore (104)
Dec 4	Baby	Ethel Barrymore (241)
Dec 21	The Tap Dance Kid	Broadhurst (669)
1984		
Feb 9	The Rink	Martin Beck (204)
May 2	Sunday in the Park...	Booth (604)
May 11	Nite Club Confidential (trans)	Ballroom OB (156)
1985		
Feb 5	Three Guys Naked from the...	Minette OB (160)
Apr 8	Leader of the Pack	Ambassador (120)
Apr 16	Grind	Mark Hellinger (79)
Apr 25	Big River	Eugene O'Neill (continuing)
May 13	Mayor - The Musical	Village Gate (268)
Aug 21	The Mystery of Edwin Drood (transferred: see Dec 2)	Delacorte OB
Sept 18	Song and Dance	Royale (474)
Nov 11	The Golden Land	Second Ave OB (277)
Dec 2	The Mystery of Edwin (trans)	Imperial (continuing)
Dec 12	Nunsense	Cherry Land OB (continuing)
Dec 18	Jerry's Girls	St. James (139)
1986		
Jan 23	Jerome Kern Goes to Hollywood	Ritz (13)
Apr 27	Sweet Charity (rev)	Minskoff (continuing)
Aug 10	Me and My Girl	Marquis (continuing)

Performer Index

Dates following various titles indicate which of several productions featured the performer. (Br), (It) and other such abbreviations indicate the performer appeared only in the British, Italian or other foreign production.

ABBEY, LUCINDA
Smiling the Boy Fell Dead
ABEL, WILL B.
Coco
ABERLIN, BETTY
I'm Getting My Act...
Just for Openers
ACKERMAN, LONI (ZOE)
George M!
No, No, Nanette
Starting Here, Starting Now
So Long, 174th Street
ADAIR, JOHN
The Cradle Will Rock (1937)
ADAIR, YVONNE
Gentlemen Prefer Blondes
ADAM, NOELLE
No Strings
ADAMS, EDITH
Li'l Abner
Wonderful Town
ADAMS, EMILY
Joan
ADAMS, JOE
Jamaica
ADAMS, TRUDE
She Loves Me
ADIARTE, PAT
Flower Drum Song
ADLER, BRUCE
The Golden Land
The Kosher Widow
Oklahoma! (1979)
ADLER, JULIUS
The Kosher Widow
ADRIAN, MAX
Candide (1956)
AGRESS, TED
Shenandoah
AGRESTI, BEN
Ka-Boom!
AINSLEY, PAUL
Jesus Christ Superstar
AINSLIE, SCOTT
Cotton Patch Gospel
AKERS, KAREN
Nine
ALBANI, COUNTESS
Show Boat (1932)
ALBERGHETTI, ANNA MARIA
Carnival
ALBERT, DONNIE RAE
Porgy and Bess (1976)
ALBERT, EDDIE
Miss Liberty
ALBERT, MARGOT
Promenade
ALBERTSON, FRANK
Seventeen
ALBERTSON, JACK
Top Banana
ALBRIGHT, JESSICA
Bye Bye Birdie
ALDA, ALAN
The Apple Tree
ALDA, ROBERT
Guys and Dolls (1950)
What Makes Sammy Run?
ALDREDGE, TOM
The Nervous Set
Rex
ALESSANDRINI, GERARD
Forbidden Broadway

ALEXANDER, BARBARA
Anya
ALEXANDER, C.K.
The Threepenny Opera (1976)
ALEXANDER, CRIS
Wonderful Town
ALEXANDER, JASON
Merrily We Roll Along
The Rink
ALFORD, LAMAR
Godspell
ALLARD, MARTINE
The Tap Dance Kid
ALLEN, CLIFFORD
Hallelujah, Baby!
ALLEN, D.R.
How to Steal an Election
ALLEN, DEBORAH (DEBBIE)
Raisin
Sweet Charity (1986)
ALLEN, ELIZABETH
Do I Hear a Waltz?
The Gay Life
ALLEN, JEANNE
Leave It to Jane
ALLEN, JONELLE
George M!
Hair (1967)
Two Gentlemen of Verona
ALLEN, MARIANNA
Merrily We Roll Along
ALLEN, MICHAEL K.
New Faces of 1968
ALLEN, NORMAN
Half a Sixpence
ALLEN, RAE
Damn Yankees
ALLISON, BERNIE
Runaways
ALLMON, CLINT
The Best Little Whorehouse
ALLOWAY, JACKIE (JACQUELINE)
By Jupiter
George M!
ALPERT, ANITA
Kismet (1965)
ALPERT, LARRY
Let It Ride!
ALSTON, BARBARA
Ain't Supposed to Die...
ALTMAN, RUTH
The Boy Friend (1954)
ALVARDO, TRINI
Runaways
ALVAREZ, CARMEN
The Decline and Fall...
Irene
Li'l Abner
Zorba (1968)
AMECHE, DON
Goldilocks
Henry, Sweet Henry
Silk Stockings
AMES, FLORENZ
Arms and the Girl
Of Thee I Sing
AMICK, ALAN
The King and I (1977)
AMUNDSEN, MONTE
Juno
ANANIA, JOHN
Fly Blackbird
ANDERSON, CHRISTINE
Nunsense
ANDERSON, DEL (DELBERT)
Brigadoon
New Girl in Town
A Tree Grows in Brooklyn
Wonderful Town
ANDERSON, THOMAS
Don't Play Us Cheap
70, Girls, 70
ANDES, KEITH
Wildcat
ANDONIAN, LUCY
Kismet (1953)
ANDREAS, CHRISTINE
Clues to a Life
My Fair Lady (1976)
Oklahoma! (1979)
On Your Toes (1983)
ANDRES, BARBARA
The Boy Friend (1970)
Doonesbury
Rex
ANDREWS, GEORGE LEE
Starting Here, Starting Now
ANDREWS, JULIE
The Boy Friend (1954)
Camelot
My Fair Lady (1956)
ANDREWS, NANCY
Christine
The Cradle Will Rock (1964)
Juno
Little Me
Plain and Fancy
ANDREWS, MAXINE & PATTY
Over Here!
ANGELA, JUNE
The King and I (1977)
ANISTON, JOHN
Little Mary Sunshine
ANKER, PERRYNE
Song of Norway (1958)

ANSON, BARBARA
How to Steal an Election
ANTHONY, EUGENE J.
On Your Toes (1983)
ANTHONY, MICHAEL
Gertrude Stein's First...
ANZELL, HY
Little Shop of Horrors
APLON, BORIS
Anya
APOLINAR, DANNY
Your Own Thing
APTER, JEFFREY
Joan
Peace
ARDAO, DAVID
Joseph and the Amazing...
ARDEN, HELEN
Street Scene
ARKIN, JUKI
Milk and Honey
ARLEN, HAROLD
Bloomer Girl
ARLEN, STEVE
Cry for Us All
ARMBRUSTER, RICHARD
Goldilocks
ARMSTEAD, JOSHIE JO
Don't Play Us Cheap
ARMSTRONG, HERK
Sing Out, Sweet Land!
ARMUS, SIDNEY
Wish You Were Here
ARNAL, ISA
Kwamina
ARNAZ, LUCIE
They're Playing Our Song
ARNO, SIG
The Merry Widow (1964)
Song of Norway (1944, 1958)
ARNOLD, JEAN
Demi-Dozen
Take Five
ARONS, ELLYN
Jerry's Girls
ARRINGTON, DONALD
Downriver
ARTHUR, BEATRICE
Fiddler on the Roof
Mame
Shoestring '57
Showstring Revue
The Threepenny Opera (1954)
ASCHMANN, CHARLES
Tenderloin
ASHLEY, BARBARA
Out of This World
ASIA
Whoop-Up
ASKEY, DARRELL J.
Donneybrook!
ASTAIRE, FRED & ADELE
The Band Wagon
ASTAR, BEN
On Your Toes (1954)
ASTIN, JOHN
The Threepenny Opera (1954)
ASTOR, SUZANNE
New Faces of 1968
ATES, NEJLA
Fanny
ATKINS, CHOLLY
Gentlemen Prefer Blondes
ATKINS, TONY
The Body Beautiful
ATKINSON, DAVID
All in Love
The Girl in Pink Tights
ATKINSON, PEGGY
The Faggot
ATKINSON, SARAH
Wait a Minum!
ATTLES, JOSEPH
Bubbling Brown Sugar
Jerico-Jim Crow
Kwamina
AUBERJONOIS, RENE
Big River
Coco
AUER, MISCHA
The Merry Widow (1964)
AULL, DOROTHY
The Body Beautiful
AUMONT, JEAN PIERRE
Tovarich
AUSTIN, BETH
Onward Victoria
AUSTIN, IVY
Candide (1982)
AVERY, BRIAN
A Time for Singing
AYLER, ETHEL
Kwamina
AZITO, TONY
The Pirates of Penzance
The Threepenny Opera (1976)
BABATUNDE, OBBA
Dreamgirls
BABEL, SUE
Fiddler on the Roof
BACALL, LAUREN
Applause
Woman of the Year
BACIGALUPI, DENNIS
The Cradle Will...(1983-Br)
BADDELEY, HERMIONE
Canterbury Tales

BAGNERIS, VERNEL
One Mo' Time
BAILEY, DENNIS
Preppies
BAILEY, PEARL
Arms and the Man
Hello, Dolly! (1967)
House of Flowers (1954)
St. Louis Woman
BAILEY, ROBIN
Jennie
BAILEY, RUSSELL
Smiling the Boy Fell Dead
BAKER, JENNIFER & SUSAN
Stop the World (1962)
BAKER, KENNY
One Touch of Venus
BAKER, LENNY
I Love My Wife
BAKER, MARK
Candide (1973)
BAKER, RAYMOND
Is There Life After...
BAKEY, ED
Walking Happy
BAKULA, SCOTT
Three Guys Naked...
BAL, JEANNE
The Gay Life
BALABAN, BOB
You're a Good Man...
BALDWIN, BROOKS
The Cradle Will...(1983 - Br)
BALL, LUCILLE
Wildcat
BALLARD, BEVERLY
How to Steal an Election
BALLARD, KAYE
Carnival
The Decline and Fall...
The Golden Apple
So Long, 174th Street
BANE, PAULA
Call Me Mister
BANKE, RICHARD
Kismet (1965)
BANOME, NINO
Bravo Giovanni
BARBEAU, ADRIENNE
Grease
BARNES, CHERYL
The Magic Show
BARNES, MAE
By the Beautiful Sea
BARNES, THEO
In Circles
BARNETT, NATE
Don't Play Us Cheap
BARON, EVALYN
I Can't Keep Running...
Scrambled Feet
BARRETT, JOE
Boy Meets Boy
BARRETT, MACE
The Body Beautiful
Taking My Turn
BARRETT, RAINA
Oh, Calcutta!
BARRIE, BARBARA
Company
BARRY, BRENDAN
Pickwick (Br)
BARRY, GENE
La Cage aux Folles
BARTIS, JOHN
Shoestring '57
BARTLETT, D'JAMIN
Clues to a Life
A Little Night Music
BARTLETT, MICHAEL
Follies
BARTON, FRED
Forbidden Broadway
BARTON, JAMES
Paint Your Wagon
BASKERVILLE, PRISCILLA
Sophisticated Ladies
BASS, EMORY
By Jupiter
BASSETT, RALPH
Candide (1982)
BATES, LULU
New Girl in Town
BATSON, SUSAN
George M!
Hair (1968)
BATTEN, TOM
On the Twentieth Century
BATTLE, HINTON
The Tap Dance Kid
Sophisticated Ladies
The Wiz
BATTLES, JOHN
Allegro
BAUGHMAN, RENEE
A Chorus Line
BAVAAR, TONY
Paint Your Wagon
BAVAN, YOLANDE
Earl of Ruston
House of Flowers (1968)
Salvation
BAXLEY, BARBARA
She Loves Me
BAXTER, CONNIE
Carousel (1945)

BAYLIS, JOHN
The Crystal Heart
Her First Roman
BEACH, GARY
Doonsbury
BEAN, ORSON
Illya Darling
Subways Are for Sleeping
BEAN, REATHAL
Doonsbury
Lovers
Peace
BEATTY, ETHEL
Bubbling Brown Sugar
Eubie!
BEAUVAIS, JEANNE
The Boy Friend (1970)
BEAVERS, DICK
Pal Joey
BECKER, ED (EDWARD)
The Body Beautiful
Goodtime Charley
Jimmy
BECKER, LEE
Tenderloin
BECKERMAN, MARA
Charlotte Sweet
BECKHAM, WILLARD
The Utter Glory of...
BEECHMAN, LAURIE
Annie
Joseph and the Amazing...
BELASCO, LEON
Happy Hunting
Silk Stockings
BELL, MARION
Brigadoon
BELL, STEVEN
Jesus Christ Superstar
BELLINI, CAL
Her First Roman
BENIADES, TED
Smiling the Boy Fell Dead
BENJAMIN, P.J.
Sophisticated Ladies
BENSON, ROBBY
The Rothschilds
BENTLEY, JORDAN
Wonderful Town
BENZELL, MIMI
Milk and Honey
BERGEN, POLLY
First Impressions
BERGER, STEPHEN
Nite Club Confidential
BERK, PHYLLIS
The Golden Land
BERLIN, IRVING
This Is the Army
BERMAN, SHELLEY
A Family Affair
BERNARD, SUZANNE
New Faces of 1956
BERNARDI, HERSCHEL
Bajour
Zorba (1968)
BERNSTEIN, DOUGLAS
Mayor
Upstairs at O'Neals'
BERRY, ERIC
The Boy Friend (1954)
Pippin
BERRY, KEN
Billy Barnes Revue
BERRY, LEIGH
Cyrano
BERRY, MARILYN
Simply Heavenly
BERRY, MARY SUE
Camelot
BERUH, JOSEPH
The Threepenny Opera (1954)
BETTS, JACK
Greenwich Village, USA
BEVANS, PHILIPPA
My Fair Lady (1956)
BEWLEY, LOIS
First Impressions
BEY, SALOME
Dude
Your Arms Too Short to...
BHASKAR
Christine
BIBB, LEON
Annie Get Your Gun (1946)
BICHEL, KEN
I Love My Wife
BIER, BURT
Walking Happy
BIGELOW, SUSAN
Working
BIGGS, CASEY
The Cradle Will Rock (1983)
BIGLEY, ISABEL
Guys and Dolls (1950)
Me and Juliet
BIKEL, THEODORE
The Sound of Music
BILLINGS, JAMES
Candide (1982)
The Merry Widow (1978)
BINGHAM, BOB
Jesus Christ Superstar
BINOTTO, PAUL
One Night Stand

BIRD, HOWARD
The Cradle Will Rock (1937)
BISHOP, CAROLE (KELLY)
A Chorus Line
Piano Bar
BITTNER, JACK
The Sap of Life
BLACKMAN, EILEEN
Do Black Patent...
BLACKWELL, GEORGE
Candide (1956)
BLAINE, VIVIAN
Guy and Dolls (1950)
Say, Darling
BLAIR, PAMELA
A Chorus Line
King of Hearts
BLAIR, RICHARD
Below the Belt
Just for Openers
BLAYMORE, ENID
Musical Chairs
BLEEZARDE, GLORIA
New Faces of 1968
BLENDICK, JAMES
Cyrano
BLISS, HELENA
Song of Norway (1944)
BLOCK, CHAD
Coco
Walking Happy
BLOUT, HELEN
Fly, Blackbird
Musical Chairs
Riverwind
BLYDEN, LARRY
The Apple Tree
Flower Drum Song
Foxy
BOBBIE, WALTER
Grease
BOGARDUS, STEPHEN
March of the Falsettos
BOGGS, GAIL
Candide (1973)
BOGIN, BERNARD
The Threepenny Opera (1954)
BOLGER, RAY
All American
BOLIN, SHANON
Damn Yankees
Promenade
BOLYARD, LEWIS
Pal Joey
BOND, FRANCINE
I Can Get It for You...
BOND, RUDY
Illya Darling
BOND, SHEILA
Wish You Were Here
BONEY, ARMAND
The Body Beautiful
BOOTH, SHIRLEY
By the Beautiful Sea
Juno
A Tree Grows in Brooklyn
BORDEN, ESSIE
The Faggot
Joan
Peace
BORDEN, JOHNNY
Bye Bye Birdie
BORMAN, JOANNA
I Remember Mama
BORTS, JOANNE
The Golden Land
BOSAN, ALONZO
Seventeen
BOSLER, VIRGINIA
New Faces of 1952
BOSLEY, TOM
Fiorello!
BOSTWICK, BARRY
Grease
The Robber Bridegroom
BOTTOMS, JOHN
Two Gentlemen of Verona
BOUIE, JOHN
Simply Heavenly
BOVA, JOSEPH (JOE)
The Cradle Will Rock (1964)
42nd Street
Once Upon a Mattress
BOWAN, SYBIL
Donneybrook!
Maggie Flynn
BOWMAN, JOAN
Seventeen
BOWNE, RICHARD
Snow White and the...
BOZEMAN, BEVERLY
The Littlest Revue
BRADBURY, LANE
Gypsy
BRADFORD, ALBERTA
Don't Bother Me, I Can't...
BRADFORD, ALEX
Don't Bother Me, I Can't...
Your Arms Too Short to...
BRAE, BONNIE
Seventeen
BRAID, HILDA
Pickwick (Br)
BRAMLEY, RAYMOND
Tenderloin

BRYNNER, YUL
The King and I (1951, 1977)
BUCKLEY, BETTY
Cats
The Mystery of Edwin Drood
1776
BUCKLEY, HAL
The Cradle Will Rock (1964)
BUEHRLE, MARY
Do Black Patent...
BUFFERY, ANTHONY
Cambridge Circus
BULLOCK, LOU
The Faggot
BULOFF, JOSEPH
Oklahoma! (1943)
BUNNAGE, AVIS
Oh What a Lovely War (Br)
BURCH, SHELLY
Nine
Stop the World...(1978)
BURFORD, IAN
Pickwick (Br)
BURGE, GREGG
Sophisticated Ladies
BURGHOFF, GARY
You're a Good Man...
BURKHARDT, GERRY
The Best Little Whorehouse
BURKS, DONNIE (DONNY)
Billy Noname
Hair (1968)
BURLEY, TONI-SUE
Ambassador (Br)
BURNETT, CAROL
Fade Out, Fade In
Once Upon a Mattress
BURNS, DAVID
Do Re Mi
A Funny Thing Happened...
Hello, Dolly! (1964)
Out of This World
Two's Company
BURNS, KARLA
Show Boat (1983)
BURR, ROBERT
Bajour
BURRELL, BENNETT
Street Scene
BURRELL, DEBORAH (TERRY)
Dreamgirls
Eubie!
BURSKY, JAY
The Best Little Whorehouse
BURSTEIN, MIKE
The Megilla of Itzik...
BURSTEIN, PESACH
The Megilla of Itzik...
BURTON, KATE
Doonesbury
BURTON, MIRIAM
House of Flowers (1954)
To Broadway with Love
BURTON, RICHARD
Camelot
BUSH, THOMMIE
Billy Noname
BUTLER, MARK ANTHONY
Runaways
BUTLER, RHODA
Candide (1982)
Goodtime Charley
BYATT, IRENE
By Jupiter
South Pacific (1967)
BYBELL, PATRICIA
Allegro
BYRD, CAROLYN
Bubbling Brown Sugar
BYRNE, GAYLEA
All in Love
CABOT, CEIL
Demi-Dozen
Dressed to the Nines
Pieces of Eight
Take Five
CAESAR, SID
Little Me
CAFFEY, MARION J.
Mayor
CAIN, WILLIAM
Jerico-Jim Crow
CALBES, ELEANOR
South Pacific (1967)
CALIN, MICKEY
West Side Story
CALLAHAN, BILL
Call Me Mister
Top Banana
CALLAWAY, LIZ
Baby
CALLOWAY, CAB
Hello, Dolly! (1967)
CALLOWAY, CHRIS
Hello, Dolly! (1967)
CALLOWAY, NORTHERN J.
The Me Nobody Knows
CALVIN, HENRY
Kismet (1953, 1965)
CAMARA, LADJI
The Believers
CAMPBELL, CHARLES
Don't Bother Me, I Can't...
CAMPBELL, DEAN
Hazel Flagg
Make a Wish

COE, GEORGE
Company
Mame
On the Twentieth Century
COHEN, MARGERY
Berlin to Broadway
Starting Here, Starting Now
COHENOUR, PATTI
Big River
The Mystery of Edwin Drood
COLE, CAROL
Seventeen
COLE, KAY
Best Foot Forward
A Chorus Line
COLEMAN, HERBERT
Lost in the Stars
COLEMAN, MARILYN B.
Ain't Supposed to Die...
COLES, HONI
Gentlemen Prefer Blondes
My One and Only
COLKER, JERRY
Three Guys Naked...
COLLINS, BLANCHE
The Cradle Will Rock (1937)
COLLINS, CHARLES
The Last Sweet Days...
COLLINS, DOROTHY
Follies
COLLINS, JACK
Jimmy
COLSON, C. DAVID
The Last Sweet Days...
Purlie
COLTON, CHEVI
The Grand Tour
COLTON, JACQUE LYNN
In Circles
COLUMBUS, TOBIE
Let My People Come
COLYER, AUSTIN
Maggie Flynn
COMDEN, BETTY
On the Town
A Party with...(1958, 1977)
COMPTON, LINDA
Hair (1967)
CONFORTI, GINO
A Family Affair
Man of La Mancha
She Loves Me
Smiling the Boy Fell Dead
CONGDON, JAMES
Baby
42nd Street
CONLOW, PETER
Take Me Along
Three Wishes for Jamie
CONNELL, GORDON
Dressed to the Nines
Pieces of Eight
Take Five
CONNELL, JANE
Dear World
Demi-Dozen
Drat! The Cat!
Mame
Me and My Girl
New Faces of 1956
Pieces of Eight
CONNER, BARDELL
Guys and Dolls (1976)
CONRIED, HANS
Can-Can
70, Girls, 70
CONROY, ALLEN
New Faces of 1952
CONTE, CAROL
Jimmy
CONTRERAS, RAY
Runaways
CONVY, BURT
Billy Barnes Revue
Cabaret
Fiddler on the Roof
CONWAY, BURT
No for an Answer
CONWAY, CURT
No for an Answer
CONWAY, SHIRL
Plain and Fancy
COOK, BARBARA
Candide (1956)
Flahooley
The Gay Life
The Grass Harp
The Music Man
Plain and Fancy
She Loves Me
Show Boat (1966)
COOK, CAROLE
42nd Street
COOK, JILL
My One and Only
COOK, RODERICK
The Girl Who Came to Supper
Oh Coward!
Woman of the Year
COOKSON, PETER
Can-Can
COOPER, CHARLOTTE
Bei Mir Bistu Schoen
COOPER, MARILYN
Hallelujah, Baby!

I Can Get It for You...
Two by Two
West Side Story
Woman of the Year
COOPER, PEGGY
Goodtime Charley
COOPER, ROY
Canterbury Tales
COOPER, SARALOU
Greenwich Village, USA
COOTE, ROBERT
My Fair Lady (1956, 1976)
COPELAND, JOAN
Two by Two
COPPOLA, FRANK
The Faggot
CORBETT, MICHAEL
Downriver
COREY, IRWIN
Flahooley
CORCORAN, DANIEL
The Cradle Will Rock (1983)
CORTI, JIM
Candide (1973)
CORUM, PETE
Cotton Patch Gospel
COSDEN, ROBERT
The Athenian Touch
COTSIRILOS, STEPHANIE
Nine
COUDRAY, PEGGY
The Cradle Will Rock (1937)
COULLET, RHONDA
The Robber Bridegroom
COULTER, KAY
On Your Toes (1954)
COURTLAND, JEROME
Flahooley
COURTNEY, C.C.
Earl of Ruston
Salvation
COURTNEY, MARGARET
Ambassador (Br)
COURTNEY, RAGAN
Earl of Ruston
COWAN, EDIE
Annie
COWAN, JEROME
Say, Darling
COWLES, CHANDLER
Call Me Mister
COX, CATHERINE
Baby
One Night Stand
CRABTREE, DON
Destry Rides Again
CRAIG, DONALD
Annie
CRAIG, JOEL
Tallulah
CRAIN, STEPHEN
Oklahoma! (1979)
CREAN, JAN
Boy Meets Boy
CREIGHTON, PAT
Li'l Abner
CREOLE, GREMLINN T.
Sophisticated Ladies
CRESPI, LEE
In Circles
CRESSON, JAMES
Flora the Red Menace
CRISWELL, KIM
Baby
CROFOOT, GAYLE
The Act
CROFOOT, LEONARD JOHN
Barnum
CROSS, JAMES 'STUMP'
This Is the Army
CROWDER, JACK
Fly Blackbird
Hello, Dolly! (1967)
CROWLEY, ANN
Seventeen
CROWLEY, ED
How to Steal an Election
CRYER, DAVID
Mass
Now Is the Time for All...
CRYER, GRETCHEN
I'm Getting My Act...
Now Is the Time for All...
(as 'Sally Niven')
CUERVO, ALMA
Is There Life After High...
CULLUM, JOHN
Camelot
On a Clear Day You Can...
On the Twentieth Century
Shenandoah
CUMMINS, RONN
Damn Yankees
CUNNINGHAM, JOHN
Company
Zorba (1968)
CUNNINGHAM, RONNIE
By Jupiter
CURLEY, WILMA
I Can Get It for You...
CURRAN, KEITH
Mayor
CURRY, STEVE
Hair (1968)
CURRY, TIM
The Rocky Horror Show

CURTIS, DONNA
Now Is the Time for All...
CURTIS, KEENE
The Rothschilds
CUTLER, JESSE
Godspell
CYPHER, JON
Coco
DABDOUB, JACK
Coco
DALE, CLAMMA
Porgy and Bess (1976)
DALE, GROVER
Half a Sixpence
Sail Away
West Side Story
DALE, JIM
Barnum
DALEY, BOB
The Body Beautiful
DALMES, MONY
The Unsinkable Molly Brown
DALTON, DORIS
Seventeen
DAMON, CATHRYN
The Boys from Syracuse
Flora, the Red Menace
Foxy
The Secret Life of Walter...
DAMON, STUART
The Boys from Syracuse
Do I Hear a Waltz?
Irma la Douce
DANE, FAITH
Gypsy
DANGLER, ANITA
Cyrano
DANIELS, BILLY
Golden Boy
DANIELS, DAVID
Oh, Kay!
Plain and Fancy
DANIELS, STAN
So Long, 174th Street
DANIELS, WALKER
Hair (1967)
DANIELS, WILLIAM
On a Clear Day You Can See..
1776
D'ANTONAKIS, FLEURY
Do I Hear a Waltz?
DARBYSHIRE, MICHAEL
Pickwick
D'ARCY, MARY
Sunday in the Park
DARCY, PATTIE
Leader of the Pack
DARLING, JEAN
Carousel (1945)
DARLING, JENNIFER
Maggie Flynn
DARRIEUX, DANIELLE
Ambassador
DA SILVA, HOWARD
The Cradle Will Rock (1937)
Fiorello!
Oklahoma! (1943)
DATCHER, IRENE
Guys and Dolls (1976)
DAVID, CLIFFORD
The Boys from Syracuse
The Cradle Will Rock (1964)
On a Clear Day You Can...
1776
Wildcat
DAVID, KEITH
Clues to a Life
DAVIDSON, JOHN
Foxy
DAVIDSON, LORRAINE
Let My People Come
DAVIES, BRIAN
A Funny Thing...
The Sound of Music
DAVILA, DIANA
Two Gentlemen of Verona
DAVIS, BETTE
Two's Company
DAVIS, CHERRY
Damn Yankees
DAVIS, CLIFTON
How to Steal an Election
Two Gentlemen of Verona
DAVIS, FRED
Kiss Me, Kate
DAVIS, LANIER
Tenderloin
DAVIS, MARY
Hair (1968)
DAVIS, MICHAEL
All in Love
Promenade
Sweet Charity (1966)
DAVIS, OSSIE
Ballad for Bimshire
Jamaica
The Zulu and the Zayda
DAVIS, SAMMY, JR.
Golden Boy
Mr. Wonderful
Stop the World...(1978)
DAVIS, SHEILA KAY
Little Shop of Horrors
DAWSON, MARK
Ankles Aweigh
High Button Shoes

EVANS, JESSIE
Pickwick (Br)
EVANS, KAREN
Runaways
EVANS, MAURICE
Tenderloin
EVANS, REX
Gentlemen Prefer Blondes
EVANS, SUZANNAH
Hair (1967)
EVANS, WILBER
By the Beautiful Sea
The Merry Widow (1944)
Mexican Hayride
Up in Central Park
EVERETT, TANYA
Fiddler on the Roof
EVERHART, REX
1776
Skyscraper
Tenderloin
Woman of the Year
FABRAY, NANETTE
Arms and the Girl
High Button Shoes
Make a Wish
Mr. President
FABRIZI, ALDO
Rugantino
FAGAN, JOAN
Donnybrook!
FAIRBANK, SPRING
Very Good Eddie
FAIRBANKS, NOLA
A Night in Venice
FAIRCHILD, GEORGE
The Cradle Will Rock (1937)
FAIRMAN, BLAIN
Ambassador (Br)
FAISON, SANDY
Annie
Is There Life After...
FARINA, MARILYN
Nunsense
FARRELL, EILEEN
Up in Central Park
FARRELL, JIM
Dude
FAYE, HERBIE
Top Banana
FAYE, JOEY
Little Me
70, Girls, 70
Top Banana
FAYE, VINI
The Best of Burlesque
FEARL, CLIFFORD
Jimmy
FENHOLT, JEFF
Jesus Christ Superstar
FERGUSON, HELEN
Cabin in the Sky (1964)
FERNANDEZ, JOSE
The Me Nobody Knows
FERRER, JOSE
The Girl Who Came to Supper
FERRIER, PAT
Redhead
FIELDS, ALVIN
Downriver
FIELDS, JOE
Ain't Supposed to Die...
FIELDS, LILIAN
The Sap of Life
FINLEY, PAT
Greenwich Village, USA
FINNEY, MARY
Happy Hunting
FIORINI, LANDO
Rugantino (It)
FITCH, ROBERT (BOB)
Annie
Coco
The Crystal Heart
Half-Past Wednesday
Lorelei
FLAGG, FANNIE
Just for Openers
FLEISHER, JUDITH
Runaways
FLETCHER, JACK
Ben Franklin in Paris
Demi-Dozen
Dime a Dozen
Drat! The Cat!
Lorelei
Sugar Babies
FLETCHER, SUSANN
Do Black Patent Leather...
FLYNN, MARTHA
The Music Man
FOLEY, CHOTZI
Gypsy
FOLEY, JOHN
Pump Boys and Dinettes
FORAN, DICK
A Connecticut Yankee
FORBES, BRENDA
Darling of the Day
FORD, CHIP
Shenandoah
FORD, CLEBERT
Ain't Supposed to Die...
Ballad for Bimshire
FORD, RUTH
The Grass Harp

GRAHAM, WILLIAM
Little Mary Sunshine
GRANGER, FARLEY
First Impressions
GRANGER, MICHAEL
Fiddler on the Roof
GRANT, DOUGLAS
The Me Nobody Knows
GRANT, MICKI
The Cradle Will Rock (1964)
Don't Bother Me...
Jerico-Jim Crow
GRAUBART, JUDY
Below the Belt
Mixed Doubles
GRAY, DOLORES
Destry Rides Again
Two on the Aisle
GRAY, JOHN
Billy Bishop Goes to War
GRAY, MARGERY
Anything Goes
Tenderloin
Tovarich
GRAY, MICHAEL
Your Arms Too Short...
GRAY, OLIVER
Kean
GRAY, STOKLEY
Tenderloin
GRAY, TIMOTHY
High Spirits
GREEN, ADOLPH
On the Town
A Party with...(1958, 1977)
GREEN, H.F.
New Girl in Town
GREEN, JOANNA
In Trousers
GREEN, MARTYN
Canterbury Tales
GREEN, NORMA
No for an Answer
GREEN, TEDDY
Baker Street
Darling of the Day
Pickwick (Br)
GREENE, ELLEN
Little Shop of Horrors
The Threepenny Opera (1976)
GREENE, SAM
Ben Franklin in Paris
GREENER, DOROTHY
Leave It to Jane
Shoestring '57
Shoestring Revue
GREENHALGH, EDWARD
Foxy
GREENWICH, ELLIE
Leader of the Pack
GREENWOOD, CHARLOTTE
Out of This World
GREGG, JULIE
The Happy Time
GREGG, MITCHELL
No Strings
Say, Darling
The Unsinkable Molly Brown
GREGORY, MICHAEL SCOTT
Sophisticated Ladies
GREGORY, VIRGINIA
Philemon
GREY, JOEL
Cabaret
George M!
Goodtime Charley
The Grand Tour
The Littlest Revue
GRIFASI, JOE
The Mystery of Edwin Drood
GRIFFIES, ETHEL
Miss Liberty
GRIFFIN, VICTOR
Taking My Turn
GRIFFIS, WILLIAM
Cry for Us All
Jimmy
Over Here!
GRIFFITH, ANDY
Destry Rides Again
GRIFFITH, PETER
Street Scene
GRIGNON, MONICA
Boy Meets Boy
GRIMES, NICHOLS
The Cradle Will Rock (1964)
GRIMES, TAMMY
42nd Street
High Spirits
The Littlest Revue
The Unsinkable Molly Brown
GRISCO, FRANK
A Time for Singing
GRIST, RERI
West Side Story
GROENENDAAL, CRIS
Sweeney Todd
Sunday in the Park
GROENER, HARRY
Cats
Is There Life After High...
Oklahoma! (1979)
Oh, Brother!
GROUT, JAMES
Half a Sixpence

HANSEN, RONN
Athenian Touch
HARADA, ERNEST
Pacific Overtures
HARALDSON, MARION
The Merry Widow (1964)
HARDER, JAMES
Athenian Touch
HARDWICK, MARK
Pump Boys and Dinettes
HARDY, WILLIAM, JR.
Your Arms Too Short to...
HARGER, GARY
Shenandoah
HARISON, VICTOR
Kwamina
HARLEY, MARGOT
The Crystal Heart
Ernest in Love
HARMON, JOHNNY
Cindy
HARMON, MARY
By the Beautiful Sea
HARMON, PEGGY
Big River
HARNEY, BEN
Dreamgirls
HARPER, DOLORES
House of Flowers (1954)
HARPER, JESSICA
Doctor Selavy's Magic...
HARRINGTON, PAT
Call Me Madam
HARRINGTON, ROBERT
Peter Pan (1954)
HARRIS, BARBARA
The Apple Tree
On a Clear Day...
HARRIS, BRENDA
Greenwillow
HARRIS, JULIE
Skyscraper
HARRIS, LLOYD
70, Girls, 70
HARRIS, NIKI
A Day in Hollywood...
HARRIS, ROBERT H.
Foxy
HARRIS, SKIP
Sweeney Todd
HARRIS, TOM
Grease
HARRIS, WALTER
Hair (1968)
HARRISON, REX
My Fair Lady (1956)
HARROLD, JACK
Candide (1982)
HART, TONI
Bloomer Girl
HARTMAN, PAUL
Of Thee I Sing
HARTY, PATRICIA
Sail Away
HARUM, EIVIND
Woman of the Year
HARVEY, GEORGETTE
Porgy and Bess (1942)
HARVEY, JAMES
The King and I (1964)
HARWOOD, JAMES
Greenwich Village, USA
HASKELL, DAVID
Godspell
HASKELL, JACK
Mr. President
HATCH, DAVID
Cambridge Circus
HATCHER, MARY
Texas, Li'l Darlin'
HAVOC, JUNE
Mexican Hayride
HAWKINS, JUNE
Carmen Jones
St. Louis Woman
HAWORTH, JILL
Cabaret
HAYES, BILL
Me and Juliet
HAYES, BILLIE
New Faces of 1956
HAYES, RICHARD
The Nervous Set
HAYESON, JIMMY
Ain't Supposed to Die...
HAYMER, JOHNNY
New Faces of 1956
HAYMAN, LILLIAN
Hallelujah, Baby!
Kwamina
70, Girls, 70
HAYNES, TIGER (COLONEL)
Fade Out, Fade In
Finian's Rainbow (1960)
New Faces of 1956
Taking My Turn
The Wiz
HAYS, REX DAVID
King of Hearts
HAYWARD, THOMAS TIBBETT
A Night in Venice
HEARN, GEORGE
La Cage aux Folles
A Doll's Life
I Remember Mama
A Time for Singing

HEATH, LOUISE
The Last Sweet Days of...
HEATH, SIGRID
Lovesong
HECHT, PAUL
The Rothschilds
1776
HECKART, EILEEN
A Family Affair
HEFFERNAN, JOHN
Purlie
HEFLIN, MARTA
Earl of Ruston
Salvation
HELLMAN, BONNIE
The Utter Glory of...
HELMORE, TOM
House of Flowers (1968)
HEMPHILL, BARRY
The Believers
HEMSLEY, SHERMAN
Purlie
HEMSLEY, WINSTON DEWITT
Hallelujah, Baby!
Hello, Dolly! (1967)
HENDERSON, FLORENCE
Fanny
The Girl Who Came to Supper
South Pacific (1967)
HENDERSON, MARCIA
Peter Pan (1950)
HENDERSON, MELANIE
The Me Nobody Knows
HENDERSON, ROBERT
Candide (1973)
HENIG, ANDI
Big River
HENNING, DOUG
The Magic Show
HENRY, ANN
New Faces of 1956
HENRY, SUZANNE
Marry Me a Little
HENSON, JOHN
The Most Happy Fella
HEPBURN, KATHARINE
Coco
HERBERT, RALPH
Arabian Nights
HERLIE, EILEEN
All American
Take Me Along
HERMAN, JERRY
Jerry's Girls
HERNANDEZ, LUIS ROBERT
Flower Drum Song
HERRERA, JOHN
The Mystery of Edwin Drood
HEUCHLING, PETER
Do Black Patent Leather...
HEWER, JOHN
The Boy Friend (1954)
HEWETT, CHRISTOPHER
First Impressions
Kean
HEWETT, PEGGY
A Day in Hollywood...
HEYER, ROSEMARIE
By Jupiter
HIBBERT, GEOFFREY
The Boy Friend (1954)
HICKEY, WILLIAM
The Body Beautiful
The Decline and Fall of...
HICKMAN, JAMES
I Can Get It for You...
HIGGINS, JOEL
Shenandoah
HIGGINS, PATIENCE
Runaways
HIGGS, TIM
Side by Side by...(Br)
HIGHT, SUE
Two's Company
HIKEN, GERALD
Foxy
The Nervous Set
HILBRANDT, JAMES
In Circles
HILGENBERG, KATHERINE
Carousel (1965)
HILL, ANNABELLE
Kiss Me, Kate
HILL, BOBBY
Don't Bother Me, I Can't...
Your Arms Too Short to...
HILL, RUBY
St. Louis Woman
HILL, STEPHANIE
Flora, the Red Menace
HINES, GREGORY
Eubie!
Sophisticated Ladies
HINES, MAURICE
Eubie!
Bring Back Birdie
HINES, PATRICK
Cyrano
HINKLEY, DEL
How to Steal an Election
HINNANT, BILL
Dressed to the Nines
You're a Good Man, Charlie...
HINNANT, SKIP
You're a Good Man, Charlie...

HIRSCH, FLUFFER
Inner City
HLIBOK, BRUCE
Runaways
HODGES, ANN
No Strings
HODGES, EDDIE
The Music Man
HOFFMAN, PATTI
Do Black Patent Leather...
HOFFMAN, PHILIP
Baby
Is There Life After High...
HOLGATE, RON (RONALD)
A Funny Thing...
The Grand Tour
1776
HOLIDAY, BOB
Fiorello!
It's a Bird...
HOLIDAY, HOPE
Arabian Nights
Li'l Abner
HOLLIDAY, DAVID
Coco
HOLLIDAY, JENNIFER
Dreamgirls
HOLLIDAY, JUDY
Bells Are Ringing
HOLLIDAY, MARK
Athenian Touch
HOLLOWAY, STANLEY
My Fair Lady (1956)
HOLM, CELESTE
Bloomer Girl
Oklahoma! (1943)
Up in Central Park
The Utter Glory of...
HOLMES, MAYNARD
The Cradle Will Rock (1937)
HOLMES, SCOTT
The Rink
HOLT, WILL
The World of Kurt Weill
HONG, ARABELLA
Flower Drum Song
HOOKS, ROBERT
Hallelujah, Baby!
HOOPER, LEE
Kwamina
Mass
Zorba (1968)
HOPKINS, BRUCE
The Faggot
HOPKINS, LINDA
Inner City
Purlie
HORGAN, PATRICK
Baker Street
HORNE, LENA
Jamaica
HORTON, ROBERT
110 in the Shade
HORWITZ, DAVID
Candide (1973)
HOUSTON, CISSY
Taking My Turn
HOWARD, JOHN
Hazel Flagg
HOWARD, KEN
Seesaw
1776
HOWARD, LARRY
By the Beautiful Sea
HOWELL, ELIZABETH
The Sound of Music
HOWES, BOBBY
Finian's Rainbow (1960)
HOWES, SALLY ANN
I Remember Mama
Kwamina
What Makes Sammy Run?
HOWLAND, BETH
Company
Darling of the Day
HOYEM, ROBERT
Juno
HOYT, LON
Leader of the Pack
HUBBARD, ELIZABETH
A Time for Singing
HUBERT, JANET L.
Cats
HUDSON, TRAVIS
The Grand Tour
Very Good Eddie
HUEY, RICHARD
Bloomer Girl
HUGHES, RHETTA
Don't Play Us Cheap
HUMPHRIES, JULIA
Allegro
HUNTER, LESLYE
Christine
HURLEY, LAUREL
A Night in Venice
HURST, JAMES
Sail Away
HURST, WOODY
The Unsinkable Molly Brown
HUSMANN, RON
All American
Tenderloin

KALLMAN, DICK
Seventeen
KANE, IRENE
Tenderloin
KANSAS, JERI
42nd Street
KARATY, TOMMY
Cindy
KARIN, FIA
Parade
KARLOFF, BORIS
Peter Pan (1950)
KARLTON, SYLVIA
Allegro
KARM, MICHAEL (MICKEY)
South Pacific (1967)
Two by Two
KARNILOVA, MARIA
Bravo Giovanni
Bring Back Birdie
Fiddler on the Roof
Gigi
Gypsy
Zorba (1968)
KARR, PATTI
Musical Chairs
So Long, 174th Street
To Broadway with Love
KASSIR, JOHN
Three Guys Naked...
KASZNAR, KURT
The Sound of Music
KAVA, CAROLINE
The Threepenny Opera (1976)
KAYE, ALMA
Sing Out, Sweet Land!
KAYE, ANNE
Now Is the Time for All..
The Utter Glory of...
KAYE, DANNY
Two by Two
KAYE, JUDY
Oh, Brother!
KAYE, ROBERT (R.)
By Jupiter
Flora the Red Menace
Maggie Flynn
KAYE, STUBBY
Grind
Guys and Dolls (1950)
Li'l Abner
KAYS, ALAN
The Merry Widow (1978)
KEAGY, GRACE
Carmelina
Goodtime Charley
Woman of the Year
KEAN, BETTY & JANE
Ankles Aweigh
KEARNEY, LYNN
Christy
KEARNS, MARTHA T.
Christy
KEATON, DIANE
Hair (1968)
KEDROVA, LILA
Zorba (1983)
KEEL, HOWARD
Ambassador
Saratoga
KEELER, RUBY
No, No, Nanette
KELK, JACKIE
Me and Juliet
KELLAWAY, CECIL
Greenwillow
KELLER, JEFF(REY)
Charlotte Sweet
One Night Stand
KELLERMAN, SALLY
Breakfast at Tiffany's
KELLEY, PETER
Two's Company
KELLIN, MIKE
Pipe Dream
KELLOGG, LYNN
Hair (1968)
KELLY, DAREN
Woman of the Year
KELLY, DAVID PATRICK
Is There Life After High...
Working
KELLY, PATSY
Irene
No, No, Nanette
KELTON, PERT
Greenwillow
The Music Man
KEMBALL, COLIN
Oh What a Lovely War
KENDALL, JO
Cambridge Circus
KENNEY, ED
Flower Drum Song
KERCHEVAL, KEN
Berlin to Broadway...
KERMOYAN, KALEM (MICHAEL)
Anya
The Girl in Pink Tights
Tovarich
Whoop-Up
KERNAN, DAVID
Side by Side by Sondheim
Jerome Kern Goes to...(Br)

MC HUGH, BURKE
Greenwich Village, USA
MAC KAY, BRUCE
Donnybrook!
Greenwillow
Her First Roman
Oh Captain!
MC KECHNIE, DONNA
A Chorus Line
Company
Promises, Promises
MC KEE, LONETTE
Show Boat (1983)
MC KEEVER, JACQUELYN
Oh Captain!
MC KENZIE, JULIA
Side by Side by Sondheim
MAC KENZIE, WILL
Half a Sixpence
MC KIE, SHIRLEY
The Believers
MACKLIN, ALBERT
Doonesbury
MC LAIN, MARCIA
Downriver
MC LENNAN, ROD
My Fair Lady (1956)
MC LERIE, ALLYN ANN
Miss Liberty
Show Boat (1966)
MC MARTIN, JOHN
Follies
Little Mary Sunshine
Sweet Charity (1966)
MC NAIR, BARBARA
The Body Beautiful
MC NAMARA, MAUREEN
Festival
MC NAUGHTON, STEVE
Joseph and the Amazing...
MC NEELY, ANN
Cats
MC NEIL, CLAUDIA
Her First Roman
Simply Heavenly
MC NEIL, LONNIE
Eubie!
MC PHERSON, SAUNDRA
Hallelujah, Baby!
MC QUEEN, ARMELIA
Ain't Misbehavin'
MC QUEEN, BUTTERFLY
Athenian Touch
MC QUEEN, SIMON
The Boy Friend (1970)
MC QUEEN, STERLING
Guys and Dolls (1976)
MC SPADDEN, BECKY
Candide (1973)
The Utter Glory of...
MADDEN, DONALD
First Impressions
MAGGART, BRANDON
Applause
Musical Chairs
New Faces of 1968
Sing Muse!
MAGNUSEN, MICHAEL
Festival
MAITLAND, MICHAEL
The Rothschilds
MAKO
Pacific Overtures
MALLORY, VICTORIA
Follies
A Little Night Music
MANDAN, ROBERT
Applause
MANFREDI, NINO
Rugantino
MANGO, ANGELO
Leave It to Jane
MANN, SYLVIA
Cindy
MANN, TERRENCE V.
Cats
MANNING, JACK
Do I Hear a Waltz?
MANOFF, DINAH
Leader of the Pack
MANSUR, SUSAN
The Best Little Whorehouse
MANTEGNA, JOE
Working
MANZANO, SONIA
Godspell
MANZARI, ROBERT
Lovesong
MARAND, PATRICIA
It's a Bird...
Wish You Were Here
MARCY, GEORGE
The Littlest Revue
MARICLE, MARIJANE
Bye Bye Birdie
Hair (1967)
MARIE, JULIENNE
The Boys from Syracuse
Do I Hear a Waltz?
Foxy
Whoop-Up
MARIE, ROSE
Top Banana
MARK, MICHAEL
Cotton Patch Gospel
I Love My Wife

MATTSON, ERIC
Carousel (1945)
MAXWELL, ARTHUR
Me and Juliet
MAXWELL, ROSALIE
Kwamina
MAYRO, JACQUELINE
Cindy
Gypsy
MEADOWS, MICHAEL
Jesus Christ Superstar
MEAT LOAF
The Rocky Horror Show
MEDFORD, KAY
Funny Girl
MEEHAN, DANNY
Funny Girl
Smiling the Boy Fell Dead
Whoop-Up
MEERSMAN, PETER
The Cradle Will Rock (1964)
MEGNA, JOHN
Greenwillow
MELCHIOR, LAURITZ
Arabian Nights
MELL, RANDLE
The Cradle Will Rock (1983)
MELTON, JAMES
Show Boat (1932)
MENKEN, STEVE
Doctor Selavy's Magic...
MERCADO, HECTOR JAIME
Cats
MERCER, MARIAN
Promises, Promises
Stop the World...(1978)
MERCOURI, MELINA
Illya Darling
MEREDITH, MORLEY
Christine
MERKEL, UNA
Take Me Along
MERLIN, JOANNA
Fiddler on the Rood
MERMAN, ETHEL
Annie Get Your...(1946-1966)
Gypsy
Happy Hunting
Hello, Dolly! (1970)
Panama Hattie
MERRILL, DINA
On Your Toes (1983)
MERRILL, SCOTT
The Threepenny Opera (1954)
MERRITT, MYRA
Porgy and Bess (1976)
MESROBIAN, ROBERT
Candide (1956)
METZGER, RITA
Tovarich
MEYER, TARO
Zorba (1983)
MEYERS, MAIDA
The Housewives' Cantata
MEYERS, TIMOTHY
Grease
MICHAEL, PAUL
Sing Muse!
Tovarich
MICHAELS, FRANKIE
Mame
MICHAELS, TANIS
Sweet Charity (1986)
MICHELL, KEITH
Irma la Douce
MICHENER, DEAN
The Golden Apple
MIDDLETON, RAY
Annie Get Your Gun (1946)
Man of La Mancha
MIDDLETON, TONY
Cabin in the Sky (1964)
MIGENES, JULIA
Fiddler on the Roof
MIGNINI, CAROLYN
Tintypes
MILES, TERRIN
Golden Boy
MILFORD, KIM
The Rocky Horror Show
MILFORD, PENELOPE
Shenandoah
MILLER, ANN
Sugar Babies
MILLER, BILL
The Rocky Horror Show
MILLER, BUZZ
Bravo Giovanni
The Pajama Game
MILLER, JOHN
I Love My Wife
MILLER, WYNNE
Tenderloin
MILLS, ERIE
Candide (1982)
MILLS, STEPHANIE
The Wiz
MILLS, STEVE
70, Girls, 70
MINAMI, ROGER
The Act
MINEO, JOHN
Lorelei
MINNELLI, LIZA
The Act
Best Foot Forward

O'REILLY, JOHN
Hard Job Being God
O'REILLY, ROSEMARY
New Faces of 1952
ORMISTON, GEORGE
New Faces of 1968
O'SHEA, MILO
Dear World
O'SHEA, TESSIE
The Girl Who Came to...
A Time for Singing
OSHINS, JULIE
This Is the Army
OSLIN, KAY
Promises, Promises
OSTERWALD, BIBI
A Family Affair
The Golden Apple
Sing Out, Sweet Land!
O'SULLIVAN, MICHAEL
It's a Bird...
OUSLEY, ROBERT
Sweeney Todd
OWENS, PHILIP
The Faggot
OXFORD, EARL
This Is the Army
PACE, JEAN
Joy
PACETTI, ELIZABETH
Seventeen
PADILLA, SANDY
Joan
PAGE, CAROLANN
Candide (1973)
PAGE, EVELYN
Canterbury Tales
PAGE, KEN
Ain't Misbehavin'
Cats
Guys and Dolls (1976)
PAIGE, JANIS
Here's Love
The Pajama Game
PAISNER, DINA
The Sap of Life
PALMER, JONI
Billy Noname
PALMER, LELAND
Pippin
Your Own Thing
PALMER, PETER
Li'l Abner
Lorelei
PARIS, JUDITH
Ambassador (Br)
PARKER, LEONARD
Fly Blackbird
PARKER, LEW
Ankles Aweigh
PARKER, PATRICK
Tallulah
PARKER, ROXANN
Festival
PARRISH, ELIZABETH
La Cage aux Folles
Little Mary Sunshine
Riverwind
PARRY, WILLIAM
Sunday in the Park
PARSONS, ESTELLE
Pieces of Eight
The Pirates of Penzance
PATACHOU
Folies Bergere
International Soiree
PATINKIN, MANDY
Evita
Sunday in the Park
PATRICK, JULIAN
Juno
PATTERSON, DICK
Fade Out Fade In
PAUL, ALAN
Grease
PAULEE, MONA
The Most Happy Fella
PAULETTE, LARRY
Let My People Come
PAVEK, JANET
Christine
PEACHENA
Let My People Come
PEACOCK, MICHON
Upstairs at O'Neals'
PEARCE, ALICE
Gentlemen Prefer Blondes
PEARL, IRWIN
Minnie's Boys
PECK, JON
The Rothschilds
PEDLAR, STUART
Side by Side by...(Br)
PEGRAM, NIGEL
Wait a Minum!
PEN, POLLY
Charlotte Sweet
PENDLETON, AUSTIN
Fiddler on the Roof
The Last Sweet Days of...
PENN, GINA
Mass
PENN, ROBERT
Kean
Paint Your Wagon

RASH, PHILLIP
Oklahoma! (1979)
RASKIN, COBY
No for an Answer
RASKIN, TOM
The Body Beautiful
Whoop-Up
RATHBURN, ROGER
No, No, Nanette
RATKEVICH, PAUL
Boy Meets Boy
RAUCHER, GARY
Minnie's Boys
RAY, ANJE
The Believers
RAY, ROBERT
Oklahoma! (1979)
RAYMOND, HELEN
The Music Man
RAYSON, BENJAMIN
A Little Night Music
REAMS, LEE ROY
Applause
42nd Street
Lorelei
REARDON, JOHN
Do Re Mi
New Faces of 1956
Song of Norway (1958)
REDD, VERONICA
The Believers
REDDING, EARL
Brigadoon
REDFIELD, WILLIAM
Out of This World
REED, ALAINA
Eubie!
REED, ALYSON
Oh, Brother!
REED, BOBBY
Boy Meets Boy
REED, PAUL
Here's Love
How to Succeed...
The Music Man
Promises, Promises
REED, VIVIAN
Bubbling Brown Sugar
REEDER, GEORGE
Li'l Abner
REESE, LLOYD
Fanny
REEVE, SCOTT
Candide (1982)
REEVES, ROBERT
Allegro
REGAN, PATTI
Billy Barnes Revue
REHNOLDS, LETTE
The Secret Life of...
REILLY, CHARLES NELSON
Hello, Dolly! (1964)
How to Succeed...
Parade
Skyscraper
REILLY, WILLIAM
I Can Get It for You...
On a Clear Day You Can...
REINHARDT, STEVE
Godspell
REINKING, ANN
Goodtime Charley
REMICK, LEE
Anyone Can Whistle
REMSEN, DEBORAH
Two's Company
RENFROE, REBECCA
Bring Back Birdie
REPOLE, CHARLES
Very Good Eddie
REPP, ELLEN
Street Scene
REVILL, CLIVE
Irma la Douce
Oliver!
REXITE, SEYMOUR
Bei Mir Bistu Schoen
REYNOLDS, BILL
The Faggot
REYNOLDS, DEBBIE
Irene
RHODES, ERIK
Can-Can
RIBUCA, LINDA & YVONNE
Flower Drum Song
RICE, ADNIA
The Music Man
RICE, SARAH
Sweeney Todd
RICH, DORIS
Redhead
RICHARDS, BILL
The Body Beautiful
RICHARDS, DONALD
Finian's Rainbow (1947)
RICHARDS, GERAINE
Smiling the Boy Fell Dead
RICHARDS, JESS
Lovesong
Musical Chairs
RICHARDSON, IAN
My Fair Lady (1976)
RICHARDSON, RON
Big River
RICHERT, WANDA
42nd Street

TALIAFERRO, MABEL
Bloomer Girl
TALVA, GALINA
Call Me Madam
TARALLO, HARRY
Joseph and the Amazing...
TARLOW, FLORENCE
Inner City
Promenade
TATE, JIMMY
The Tap Dance Kid
TATUM, MARIANNE
Barnum
TAUBIN, AMY
Doctor Selavy's Magic...
TAYLOR, CLARICE
The Wiz
TAYLOR, ELIZABETH
West Side Story
TAYLOR, GINA
Leader of the Pack
TAYLOR, ROBIN
Festival
TAYLOR, RON
Little Shop of Horrors
TEAGUE, SCOOTER
110 in the Shade
TEETER, LARA
On Your Toes (1983)
TEIJELO, GERALD M.
On a Clear Day You Can...
TEMPLE, RENNY
Tuscaloosa's Calling Me...
TESTA, MARY
In Trousers
THACKER, RUSS (RUSTY)
Do Black Patent Leather...
The Grass Harp
Your Own Thing
THEODORE, DONNA
Shenandoah
THEYARD, HARRY
Man of La Mancha
A Time for Singing
THIGPEN, LYNNE
Tintypes
Working
THOMA, CARL
The Me Nobody Knows
THOMAS, DAVE
Paint Your Wagon
THOMAS, HUGH
The Fantasticks
THOMAS, TASHA
The Wiz
THOMAS, WILLIAM, JR.
La Cage aux Folles
THOMPSON, CREIGHTON
Street Scene
THOMPSON, EVAN
Jimmy
THOMPSON, JEFFERY V.
Eubie!
THOMPSON, JOHNNY V.R.
Miss Liberty
THOMPSON, SADA
Juno
THORNE, RAYMOND
Annie
Man with a Load of...
THORNTON, SANDRA
Gertrude Stein's First...
THURSTON, TED
Celebration
Let It Ride!
Taking My Turn
TICE, DAVID
In Circles
Peace
TILDEN, BEAU
70, Girls, 70
TILLER, TED
Sing Out, Sweet Land!
TIPTON, GEORGE
Kwamina
TITUS, ALAN
Mass
The Merry Widow (1978)
TOBEY, KENNETH
Golden Boy
TOBIA, RICARDO
Pacific Overtures
TOBIN, MATTHEW
The Boys from Syracuse
TOIGO, ALBERT
Kismet (1965)
TOM, LAUREN
Doonesbury
TOMKINS, DON
Wildcat
TOMLIN, LILY
Below the Belt
TONE, RICHARD
Parade
TONER, THOMAS
Me and My Girl
TORRES, ANDY
Billy Noname
TOWBIN, BERYL
A Family Affair
TOWERS, CONSTANCE
Anya
The King and I (1977)
Show Boat (1966)

TOWNSEND, K.C.
No, No, Nanette
TOZZI, GIORGIO
South Pacific (1967)
TRACEY, ANDREW & PAUL
Wait a Minum!
TRACEY, PAUL
The Rothschilds
TRAUBEL, HELEN
Pipe Dream
TRAVOLTA, JOHN
Over Here!
TREKMAN, EMMA
Walking Happy
TRELFKA, THOMAS
The Rothschilds
TREMAIN, BOBBI
70, Girls, 70
TRIBUSH, NANCY
Oh! Calcutta!
TRIKONIS, GUS
Bajour
TRONTO, RUDY
The Boys from Syracuse
Irma la Douce
The Secret Life of...
TROXELL, TOM
Hard Job Being God
TROY, LOUISE
High Spirits
Tovarich
Walking Happy
TRUEX, PHILIP
This Is the Army
TUCKER, JAN
Greenwillow
TUCKER, WAYNE
The Cradle Will Rock (1964)
TUDOR, RAY
Leave It to Jane
TUNE, TOMMY
My One and Only
Seesaw
TURENNE, LOUIS
Cyrano
TURGEON, PETER
Little Me
TURNER, CLYDE
Annie Get Your Gun (1946)
TURNER, PAT
I Can Get It for You...
TURQUE, MIMI
Man of La Mancha
TWIGGY
My One and Only
TYLER, JUDY
Pipe Dream
TYNE, GEORGE
The Threepenny Opera (1954)
TYRRELL, BRAD
Goodtime Charley
UGGAMS, LESLIE
Hallelujah, Baby!
Her First Roman
Jerry's Girls
UKENA, PAUL, JR.
The Best Little Whorehouse
ULLETT, NICK
Me and My Girl
ULMER, GEORGES
Folies Bergere
UMEKI, MIYOSHI
Flower Drum Song
URICH, TOM
Musical Chairs
URMSTON, KEN
Greenwich Village, USA
VACCARO, BRENDA
How Now, Dow Jones
VALENTI, MICHAEL
Your Own Thing
VALENTINE, JOE
Hard Job Being God
VALENTINE, PAUL
Oh Captain!
Wish You Were Here
VALERY, DANA
Wait a Minum!
VALLEE, RUDY
How to Succeed in Business
VALORI, BICE
Rugantino
VAN, BOBBY
No, No, Nanette
On Your Toes (1954)
VAN AKEN, GRETCHEN
Walking Happy
VAN DORP, GLORIA
Arabian Nights
VAN DYKE, DICK
Bye Bye Birdie
VAN DYKE, MARCIA
A Tree Grows in Brooklyn
VAN SCOTT, GLORY
Fly Blackbird
VAN WAY, NOLAN
Oh Captain!
VANDIS, TITOS
Illya Darling
On a Clear Day You Can...
VANLEER, JAY
Don't Play Us Cheap
VANONI, ORNELLA
Rugantino

VARNEY, AMELIA
Cindy
VARRONE, GENE
Bravo Giovanni
Drat! The Cat!
Goldilocks
The Grand Tour
A Little Night Music
Subways Are for Sleeping
Tovarich
VAUGHAN, MELANIE
Sunday in the Park
VAUGHN, DAVID
The Boy Friend (1970)
In Circles
Joan
Peace
VEJAR, RUDY
Kismet (1965)
The Merry Widow (1964)
VELIE, JAY
Call Me Madam
70, Girls, 70
VENORA, LEE
Kean
The King and I (1964)
Kismet (1965)
VENUTA, BENAY
Annie Get Your Gun (1966)
Hazel Flagg
VERA-ELLEN
A Connecticut Yankee
VERDON, GWEN
Can-Can
Chicago
Damn Yankees
New Girl in Town
Redhead
Sweet Charity (1966)
VEREA, LISETTE
The Merry Widow (1944)
VEREEN, BEN
Grind
Jesus Christ Superstar
Pippin
VERNON, GILBERT
Cranks
VERSO, EDWARD
I Can Get It for You...
VESTOFF, VIRGINIA
Baker Street
The Crystal Heart
Man with a Load of...
1776
VIDNOVIC, MARTIN
Baby
The King and I (1977)
Oklahoma! (1979)
VINCENT, ROMO
Whoop-Up
VINOVICH, STEPHEN
The Grand Tour
The Robber Bridegroom
VITA, MICHAEL
On Your Toes (1983)
VITI, GERALDINE
The Golden Apple
VOSBURGH, DAVID
A Doll's Life
1776
VYE, MURVYN
Carousel (1945)
WADE, WARREN
Smiling the Boy Fell Dead
WAKEFIELD, ANN
The Boy Friend (1954)
WALCHER, SUSIE
Hard Job Being God
WALDEN, GRANT
Best Foot Forward
WALDEN, STANLEY
Oh! Calcutta!
WALKEN, GLENN
Best Foot Forward
WALKEN, RONALD (CHRISTOPHER)
Best Foot Forward
WALKER, BARBARA
Five After Eight
WALKER, BILL
Wildcat
WALKER, JOSEPH A.
The Believers
WALKER, NANCY
Do Re Mi
Look Ma, I'm Dancin'!
On the Town
WALLACE, ART
Now Is the Time for All...
WALLACE, EMETT 'BABE'
Guys and Dolls (1976)
WALLACE, G.D.
Pipe Dream
WALLACE, GEORGE
Jennie
New Girl in Town
WALLACE, MERVIN
Porgy and Bess (1976)
WALLACE, PAUL
Gypsy
WALLIS, SHANI
A Time for Singing
WALSTON, RAY
Damn Yankees
WALTON, BOB
Preppies

WALTON, JIM
- Merrily We Roll Along

WANN, JIM
- Pump Boys and Dinettes

WARD, KEN
- Ka-Boom!

WARD, NANCEE
- The Best of Burlesque

WARDEN, JACK
- The Body Beautiful

WARFIELD, CHRIS
- The Cradle Will Rock (1964)

WARFIELD, WILLIAM
- Show Boat (1966)

WARNING, DENNIS
- Baby
- The Robber Bridegroom

WARREN, JEFF
- Brigadoon

WARREN, (JENNIFER) LEIGH
- Big River
- Little Shop of Horrors

WARREN, JULIE
- A Connecticut Yankee

WARREN, LESLEY (ANN)
- Drat! The Cat!
- 110 in the Shade

WARREN, VINCENT
- The Crystal Heart

WARRICK, RUTH
- Irene

WARRICK, NORMAN
- Pickwick (Br)

WASHBURN, JACK
- Mr. President

WASHINGTON, LAMONT
- Hair (1968)

WATANABE, GEDDE & LESLIE
- Pacific Overtures

WATERBURG, LAURA
- Onward Victoria

WATERS, ETHEL
- Cabin in the Sky (1940)

WATKINS, GORDON
- Kwamina

WATLING, DILYS
- Pickwick (Br)

WATSON, DOUGLASS
- Over Here!

WATSON, SUSAN
- Ben Franklin in Paris
- Bye Bye Birdie
- Carousel (1965)
- Celebration
- No, No, Nanette

WATTERS, HAL
- Berlin to Broadway

WATTS, ELIZABETH
- Destry Rides Again

WAYNE, DAVID
- Finian's Rainbow (1947)
- The Happy Time
- Say, Darling
- Show Boat (1966)

WAYNE, FREDD
- Texas, Li'l Darlin'

WAYNE, PAULA
- Best Foot Forward
- Golden Boy

WEAVER, FRITZ
- All American
- Baker Street

WEBB, ALYCE
- Ballad for Bimshire

WEBB, BARBARA
- Christine

WEBB, CHLOE
- Forbidden Broadway

WEBER, FREDRICKA
- Dime a Dozen
- The Last Sweet Days of...

WEBSTER, BYRON
- On a Clear Day You Can...

WEEDE, ROBERT
- Cry for Us All
- Milk and Honey
- The Most Happy Fella

WEEKS, ALAN
- Billy Noname
- The Body Beautiful
- Hallelujah, Baby!
- Oh, Brother!
- The Tap Dance Kid

WEEKS, SARAH
- Upstairs at O'Neals'

WEIL, ROBERT
- Once Upon a Mattress

WEINER, JOHN
- La Cage aux Folles

WEINRIB, LEN
- Billy Barnes Revue

WEISS, GORDON
- King of Hearts

WELBES, GEORGE
- Oh! Calcutta!

WELCH, CHARLES (C.)
- Darling of the Day
- Donnybrook!
- Shenandoah

WELCH, ELISABETH
- Jerome Kern Goes to...

WELDON, JOAN
- Kean
- The Merry Widow (1964)

WELLS, CYNTHIA
- Very Good Eddie

Technical Index

Key: M - Music
L - Lyrics
MuD - Musical Director
P - Piano

ABBOTT, MICHAEL
Upstairs at O'Neals' (M,L)
ABRAVANEL, MAURICE
One Touch of Venus (MuD)
Street Scene (MuD)
ACTMAN, IRVING
Guys and Dolls (MuD - 1950)
ADAMS, LEE
All American (L)
Applause (L)
Bring Back Birdie (L)
Bye Bye Birdie (L)
Golden Boy (L)
It's a Bird ... (L)
The Littlest Revue (L)
Shoestring Revue (L)
ADDISON, JOHN
Cranks (M)
ADLER, RICHARD
Damn Yankees (M,L)
Kwamina (M,L)
The Pajama Game (M,L)
ADRIAN, LOUIS
Kismet (MuD - 1953)
Peter Pan (MuD - 1954)
ALESSANDRINI, GERARD
Forbidden Broadway (M,L)
ALEXANDER, BROOKS
The Believers (MuD)
ALFORD, WILLIAM
Cry for Us All (L)
ALLERS, FRANZ
Annie Get Your..(MuD - 1966)
Brigadoon (MuD)
Camelot (MuD)
Carousel (MuD - 1965)
The King and I (MuD - 1964)
Kismet (MuD - 1965)
The Merry Widow (MuD - 1964)
My Fair Lady (MuD - 1956)
Paint Your Wagon (MuD)
Plain and Fancy (MuD)
Show Boat (MuD - 1966)
To Broadway with Love (MuD)
ANDERSON, JONATHAN
South Pacific (MuD - 1967)
ANDERSON, LEROY
Goldilocks (M)
ANDERSON, MAXWELL
Berlin to Broadway (L)
Lost in the Stars (L)
The World of Kurt Weill (L)
ANGELO, JUDY HART
Preppies (M,L)
ANKER, CHARLOTTE
Onward Victoria (L)
ANTEIME, LEOPOLD
Shoestring Revue (M)
APOLINAR, DANNY
Your Own Thing (M,L)
ARCHIBALD, WILLIAM
The Crystal Heart (L)
ARLEN, HAROLD
Bloomer Girl (M)
House of Flowers (M,L)
Jamaica (M)
St. Louis Woman (M)
Saratoga (M)
ARLEN, JERRY
House of Flowers (MuD-1954)
Saratoga (MuD)
ARONSON, HENRY
Three Guys Naked ... (MuD)
ASHMAN, HOWARD
Little Shop of Horrors (L)
AXELROD, DAVID
New Faces of 1968 (L)
BACH, J.S.
Mixed Doubles (M)
BACHARACH, BURT
Promises, Promises (M)

CHALMERS, ANTHONY
Shoestring Revue (L)
CHAPIN, HARRY
Cotton Patch Gospel (M,L)
CHAPIN, TOM
Cotton Patch Gospel (MuD)
CHAPLIN, CLIVE
Jerome Kern Goes...(MuD)
CHAPLIN, SAUL
A Party with Comden...(M)
CHARLAP, MARK (MOOSE)
Peter Pan (M - 1954)
Whoop-Up (M)
CHARLES, RAY
Finian's Rainbow (MuD - 1947)
CHARNIN, MARTIN
Annie (L)
I Remember Mama (L)
Pieces of Eight (L)
To Broadway with Love (L)
Two by Two (L)
Upstairs at O'Neals' (M,L)
CHOPIN, FREDERIC
Polonaise (M)
CHURCHILL, FRANK
Snow White and the...(M)
CLEMENTS, OTIS
Irene (L)
CLIFTON, JOHN
Man with a Load of...(M,L)
CLUGSTON, GLEN
Athenian Touch (MuD)
COGHILL, NEVILL
Canterbury Tales (L)
COHAN, GEORGE M.
George M! (M,L)
COHEN, MICHAEL
Below the Belt (MuD)
Just for Openers (MuD)
Mixed Doubles (M, MuD)
New Faces of 1968 (M)
COLBY, MICHAEL
Charlotte Sweet (L)
COLBY, ROBERT
Half-Past Wednesday (M,L)
COLEMAN, CHARLES H.
The Wiz (MuD)
COLEMAN, CY
Barnum (M)
Demi-Dozen (M)
I Love My Wife (M)
Little Me (M)
On the Twentieth Century (M)
A Party with Comden...(M)
Seesaw (M)
Sweet Charity (M)
Wildcat (M)
COLEMAN, SHEPARD
Hello, Dolly! (MuD - 1964)
Henry, Sweet Henry (MuD)
COLKER, JERRY
Three Guys Naked...(L)
COLLINS, KEN
Philemon (MuD)
COLSTON, ROBERT
Dime a Dozen (P)
Four Below Strikes Back (P)
COMDEN, BETTY
Bells Are Ringing (L)
Do Re Mi (L)
A Doll's Life (L)
Fade Out Fade In (L)
Hallelujah, Baby! (L)
Lorelei (L)
On the Town (L)
On the Twentieth Century (L)
A Party with Comden...(L)
Peter Pan (L - 1954)
Say, Darling (L)
Subways Are for Sleeping (L)
Two on the Aisle (L)
Wonderful Town (L)
CONNELL, GORDON
Demi-Dozen (P)
Take Five (P)
COOK, JOE
Snow White and the...(L)
COPPOLA, ANTON
The Boy Friend (MuD - 1954)
Bravo Giovanni (MuD)
New Faces of 1952 (MuD)
COREY, HERB
Greenwich Village, USA (L)
COSTA, BILL
Greenwich Village, USA (MuD)
COUGHLIN, BRUCE
Is There Life After...(MuD)
COURTNEY, C.C. & RAGAN
Earl of Ruston (M,L)
Salvation (M,L - C.C. only)
COWARD, NOEL
The Girl Who Came to...(M,L)
Oh Coward! (M,L)
Sail Away (M,L)
COYLE, BRUCE W.
Tallulah (MuD)
CRANE, DAVID L.
Upstairs at O'Neals' (L)
CRANKS, JOHN
Cranks (L)
CRAVEN, FRANK
Very Good Eddie (L)
CREATORE, LUIGI
Maggie Flynn (M,L)

CRIGLER, LYNN
Shenandoah (MuD)
Very Good Eddie (MuD)
CROSWELL, ANNE
Ernest in Love (L)
Tovarich (L)
CROZIER, JIM
Touch (M)
CRYER, GRETCHEN
I'm Getting My Act...(L)
The Last Sweet Days...(L)
Now Is the Time for All...(L)
CUNNINGHAM, BILLY
Let My People Come (MuD)
DANIELE, GRACIELA
Working (L)
DANIELS, STAN
So Long, 174th Street (M,L)
DARION, JOE
Illya Darling (L)
Man of La Mancha (L)
The Megilla of Itzik...(L)
DAVENPORT, DAVE
Pieces of Eight (M)
DAVENPORT, PEMBROKE
Arabian Nights (MuD)
Hazel Flagg (MuD)
I Had a Ball (MuD)
Kean (MuD)
Kiss Me, Kate (MuD)
Look Ma, I'm Dancin'! (MuD)
Out of This World (MuD)
DAVID, HAL
Promises, Promises (L)
DAVIES, GARETH
Ambassador (MuD)
DAVIS, BUSTER
Best Foot Forward (MuD)
Darling of the Day (MuD)
Hallelujah, Baby! (MuD)
No, No, Nanette (MuD)
DAVISON, LESLEY
Dime a Dozen (M,L)
DEAL, DENNIS
Nite Club Confidential (M,L)
DeCORMIER, ROBERT
The Happiest Girl in...(MuD)
DELL'ISOLA, SALVATORE
Allegro (MuD)
Ankles Aweigh (MuD)
Flower Drum Song (MuD)
Me and Juliet (MuD)
On Your Toes (MuD - 1954)
Pipe Dream (MuD)
South Pacific (MuD - 1949)
DELMET, PAUL
Paris '90 (M)
DEL VALLE, PETER
Lovers (L)
DeMAIN, JOHN
Porgy and Bess (MuD - 1976)
DENNIS, ROBERT
Oh! Calcutta! (M,L)
DePAUL, GENE
Li'l Abner (M)
DEREFINKO, ROD
Celebration (MuD)
DEVAL, JACQUES
Berlin to Broadway (L)
The World of Kurt Weill (L)
DeVRIES, PETER
New Faces of 1952 (L)
DIETZ, HOWARD
The Band Wagon (L)
The Gay Life (L)
Inside USA (L)
Jennie (L)
DINROE, DOROTHY
The Believers (M,L)
DODDS, MARCUS
Pickwick (MuD)
DOLAN, ROBERT EMMETT
Coco (MuD)
Foxy (M)
Juno (MuD)
Texas, Li'l Darlin' (M)
DOUGALL, BERNARD
Jerome Kern Goes to...(L)
DOWNS, STEPHEN
Festival (M,L)
DRAKE, ERVIN
Her First Roman (M,L)
What Makes Sammy Run? (M,L)
DRIVER, DONALD
Oh, Brother! (L)
DRIVER, JOHN
Scrambled Feet (M,L)
DUBEY, MATT
Happy Hunting (L)
New Faces of 1956 (L)
DUBIN, AL
42nd Street (L)
DUKE, VERNON
Cabin in the Sky (M)
The Littlest Revue (M)
Two's Company (M)
DVONCH, FREDERICK
Arms and the Girl (MuD)
Do I Hear a Waltz? (MuD)
First Impressions (MuD)
The King and I (MuD - 1951)
The Sound of Music (MuD)
EAGER, EDWARD
Sing Out, Sweet Land! (L)

EBB, FRED
The Act (L)
Cabaret (L)
Chicago (L)
Flora the Red Menace (L)
The Happy Time (L)
The Rink (L)
70, Girls, 70 (L)
Woman of the Year (L)
Zorba (L)
EDDY, DAVID
Athenian Touch (L)
EDENS, ROGER
A Party with Comden...(M)
EDWARDS, SHERMAN
1776 (M,L)
ELIOT, T.S.
Cats (L)
ELLINGTON, DUKE
Bubbling Brown Sugar (M)
Sophisticated Ladies (M,L)
ELLINGTON, MERCER
Sophisticated Ladies (MuD)
ELLIOTT, WILLIAM
The Pirates of Penzance (MuD)
ELMSLIE, KENWARD
The Grass Harp (L)
The Littlest Revue (L)
ENGEL, LEHMAN
Bajour (MuD)
Call Me Mister (MuD)
Destry Rides Again (MuD)
Do Re Mi (MuD)
Fanny (MuD)
Goldilocks (MuD)
I Can Get It for You...(MuD)
Jamaica (MuD)
Li'l Abner (MuD)
Song of Norway (MuD - 1958)
Take Me Along (MuD)
What Makes Sammy Run? (MuD)
Wonderful Town (MuD)
ENGVICK, WILLIAM
Clues to a Life (L)
ERCOLE, JOE
Ka-Boom! (M)
EUROPE, JIM
Eubie! (L)
EVANS, ALBERT
Nite Club Confidential (M,L,MuD)
EVANS, RAY
Let It Ride! (M,L)
Oh Captain! (M,L)
EYEN, TOM
Dreamgirls (L)
FAIN, SAMMY
Ankles Aweigh (M)
Christine (M)
Flahooley (M)
FANUELE, VINCENT
Nine (MuD)
FARJEAN, HERBERT
New Faces of 1952 (L)
FEINGOLD, MICHAEL
Berlin to Broadway (L)
FIELDS, DOROTHY
Arms and the Girl (L)
By the Beautiful Sea (L)
Jerome Kern Goes to...(L)
Redhead (L)
Seesaw (L)
Sugar Babies (L)
Sweet Charity (L)
A Tree Grows in...(L)
Up in Central Park (L)
FINN, WILLIAM
In Trousers (M,L)
March of the Falsettos (M,L)
FITZHUGH, ELLEN
Grind (L)
FOLEY, JOHN
Pump Boys and Dinettes (M,L)
FOOTE, JAY
Dime a Dozen (M)
FORD, JOAN
Goldilocks (L)
FORD, NANCY
I'm Getting My Act...(M)
The Last Sweet Days...(M)
Now Is the Time for...(M)
FORD, PAUL
Upstairs at O'Neals' (P)
FORNES, MARIE IRENE
Promenade (L)
FORREST, GEORGE
Anya (L)
Kean (L)
Kismet (L)
Song of Norway (L)
FORSTER, JOHN
Upstairs at O'Neals' (M,L)
FREEDMAN, GERALD
A Time for Singing (L)
FREEMAN, STAN
I Had a Ball (M,L)
FREITAG, DOROTHEA
Mask and Gown (M,L, MuD)
Oh, Kay! (MuD)
Shoestring '57 (MuD)
Shoestring Revue (MuD)
FREMONT, ROB
Piano Bar (M)
FRIBERG, CARL
New Faces of 1968 (M)

FRIEDMAN, ALAN
Pieces of Eight (M)
FRIEDMAN, DAVID
Boy Meets Boy (MuD)
Joseph and the...(MuD)
FRIEDMAN, GARY WILLIAM
The Me Nobody Knows (M)
Taking My Turn (M)
FRIEDMAN, SETH
Upstairs at O'Neals' (M,L)
FULLER, DEAN
New Faces of 1956 (M)
FULLUM, CLAY
Inner City (MuD)
The Last Sweet Days...(MuD)
FURBER, DOUGLAS
Me and My Girl (L)
GANNON, KIM
Seventeen (L)
GARDNER, HERB
One Night Stand (L)
GARINEI, PIETRO
Rugantino (L)
GAY, NOEL
Me and My Girl (M)
GAYNOR, CHARLES
Irene (L)
Show Girl (M,L)
GEHRECKE, FRANK
Greenwich Village, USA (L)
GEISS, GENE (TONY)
Mixed Doubles (L)
New Faces of 1968 (L)
GELD, GARY
Purlie (M)
Shenandoah (M)
GELLER, BRUCE
All in Love (L)
GEMIGNANI, PAUL
A Doll's Life (MuD)
Grind (MuD)
Merrily We Roll Along (MuD)
On the Twentieth Century (MuD)
Pacific Overtures (MuD)
The Rink (MuD)
Sunday in the Park...(MuD)
Sweeney Todd (MuD)
Zorba (MuD - 1983)
GERSHWIN, GEORGE
My One and Only (M)
Of Thee I Sing (M)
Oh, Kay! (M)
Porgy and Bess (M)
GERSHWIN, IRA
Berlin to Broadway (L)
Jerome Kern Goes to...(L)
Lady in the Dark (L)
My One and Only (L)
Of Thee I Sing (L)
Oh, Kay! (L)
Porgy and Bess (L)
The World of Kurt Weill (L)
GESNER, CLARK
New Faces of 1968 (M,L)
The Utter Glory of...(M,L)
You're a Good Man...(M,L)
GILBERT, W.S.
The Pirates of Penzance (L)
GIMBEL, NORMAN
Whoop-Up (L)
GLAZENER, JANET
Jerry's Girls (MuD)
GOBERMAN, MAX
Milk and Honey (MuD)
A Tree Grows in... (MuD)
West Side Story (MuD)
GOGGIN, DAN
Nunsense (M,L)
GOHMAN, DON
Ambassador (M)
GOLDBERG, JERRY
The Boy Friend (MuD - 1970)
Sing Muse! (MuD)
GOLDENBERG, BILLY
Ballroom (M)
GOLDMAN, JAMES
A Family Affair (M,L)
GOLDMAN, ROBERT
First Impressions (M,L)
GOLDMAN, WILLIAM
A Family Affair (M,L)
GOLDSTONE, BOB
The Housewives' Cantata (MuD)
GOODMAN, AL
Polonaise (MuD)
GOODMAN, BENNY
Bubbling Brown Sugar (M)
GORDON, BARRY
Musical Chairs (MuD)
GORDON, JOHN
The Utter Glory of...(MuD)
GOULD, MORTON
Arms and the Girl (M)
GRAHAM, GARY
Touch! (M,L)
GRAHAM, HARRY
Very Good Eddie (L)
GRAHAM, RONNY
Bravo Giovanni (L)
Four Below Strikes Back (M,L)
Mask and Gown (M,L)
New Faces of 1952 (M,L)
New Faces of 1956 (M,L)
New Faces of 1968 (M,L)
Shoestring Revue (M,L)
Take Five (M,L)

GRAND, MURRAY
New Faces of 1952 (M)
New Faces of 1956 (M,L)
New Faces of 1968 (M,L)
GRANT, MICKI
Don't Bother Me...(M,L)
Eubie! (L)
Working (M,L)
Your Arms Too Short...(M,L)
GRAY, JOHN
Billy Bishop Goes...(M,L,P)
GRAY, TIMOTHY
High Spirits (M,L)
GREEN, ADOLPH
Bells Are Ringing (L)
Do Re Mi (L)
A Doll's Life (L)
Fade Out Fade In (L)
Hallelujah, Baby! (L)
Lorelei (L)
On the Town (L)
On the Twentieth Century (L)
A Party with Comden...(L)
Peter Pan (L - 1954)
Say, Darling (L)
Subways Are for Sleeping (L)
Two on the Aisle (L)
Wonderful Town (L)
GREEN, PAUL
Berlin to Broadway (L)
GREENE, HERBERT
Anyone Can Whistle (MuD)
The Gay Life (MuD)
The Most Happy Fella (MuD)
The Music Man (MuD)
Silk Stockings (MuD)
Two on the Aisle (MuD)
The Unsinkable Molly...(MuD)
GREENE, MILTON
The Body Beautiful (MuD)
Fiddler on the Roof (MuD)
The Rothschilds (MuD)
GREENE, SCHUYLER
Very Good Eddie (L)
GREENWICH, ELLIE
Leader of the Pack (M,L)
GRIEG, EDVARD
Song of Norway (M)
GROSSMAN, HERBERT
Cry for Us All (MuD)
Drat! The Cat! (MuD)
The Roar of the Grease...(MuD)
Walking Happy (MuD)
GROSSMAN, LARRY
A Doll's Life (M)
Goodtime Charley (M)
Grind (M)
Minnie's Boys (M)
GRUDEFF, MARION
Baker Street (M,L)
GUARE, JOHN
Two Gentlemen of Verona (L)
GUILBERT, YVETTE
Paris '90 (M)
GUSTAFSON, KAREN
Illya Darling (MuD)
HACKADY, HAL
Ambassador (L)
Goodtime Charley (L)
Minnie's Boys (L)
New Faces of 1968 (L)
HADDOW, JEFFREY
Scrambled Feet (M,L)
HADJIDAKAS, MANOS
Illya Darling (M)
HAGUE, ALBERT
Plain and Fancy (M)
Redhead (M)
HAIMSOHN, GEORGE
Dames at Sea (L)
HALL, CAROL
The Best Little...(M,L)
HAMLISCH, MARVIN
A Chorus Line (M)
They're Playing Our Song (M)
HAMMERSTEIN, OSCAR II
Allegro (L)
Carmen Jones (L)
Carousel (L)
Flower Drum Song (L)
Jerome Kern Goes to...(L)
The King and I (L)
Me and Juliet (L)
Oklahoma! (L)
Pipe Dream (L)
Show Boat (L)
The Sound of Music (L)
South Pacific (L)
HANIGHEN, BERNARD
Lute Song (L)
HARBACH, OTTO
Jerome Kern Goes to...(L)
No, No, Nanette (L)
HARBURG, E.Y.
Bloomer Girl (L)
Darling of the Day (L)
Finian's Rainbow (L)
Flahooley (L)
The Happiest Girl...(L)
Jamaica (L)
HARDWICK, MARK
Pump Boys and Dinettes (M,L)
HARNICK, SHELDON
The Apple Tree (L)
The Body Beautiful (L)
Fiddler on the Roof (L)

Fiorello! (L)
The Littlest Revue (M,L)
The Merry Widow (L - 1978)
New Faces of 1952 (M,L)
Rex (L)
The Rothschilds (L)
She Loves Me (L)
Shoestring Revue (M,L)
Smiling the Boy Fell Dead (L)
Tenderloin (L)
To Broadway with Love (L)
Two's Company (M,L)
HARPER, WALLY
A Day in Hollywood...(MuD)
The Grand Tour (MuD)
HARRIS, HERB
The Best of Burlesque (MuD)
HARRIS, JEREMY
Tuscaloosa's Calling...(MuD)
HART, LORENZ
The Boys from Syracuse (L)
By Jupiter (L)
A Connecticut Yankee (L)
On Your Toes (L)
Pal Joey
HASTINGS, HAROLD (HAL)
Anya (MuD)
Baker Street (MuD)
Cabaret (MuD)
Company (MuD)
Damn Yankees (MuD)
Fiorello! (MuD)
Flora the Red Menace (MuD)
Follies (MuD)
A Funny Thing...(MuD)
It's a Bird...(MuD)
A Little Night Music (MuD)
New Girl in Town (MuD)
Once Upon a Mattress (MuD)
The Pajama Game (MuD)
She Loves Me (MuD)
Tenderloin (MuD)
Top Banana (MuD)
Zorba (MuD - 1968)
HATCH, JAMES
Fly Blackbird (L)
HAWKINS, JOHN
Canterbury Tales (M)
HELLERMAN, FRED
New Faces of 1968 (M)
HENDERSON, LUTHER
Ain't Misbehavin' (MuD)
HENDRY, TOM
Doctor Selavy's Magic...(L)
HENEKER, DAVID
Half a Sixpence (M,L)
Irma la Douce (L)
HERMAN, JERRY
La Cage aux Folles (M,L)
A Day in Hollywood...(M,L)
Dear World (M,L)
The Grand Tour (M,L)
Hello, Dolly! (M,L)
Jerry's Girls (M,L)
Mack and Mabel (M,L)
Mame (M,L)
Milk and Honey (M,L)
Parade (M,L)
HERRMANN, KEITH
Onward Victoria (M)
HERZOG, ARTHUR
Bubbling Brown Sugar (M)
HESTER, HAL
Your Own Thing (M,L)
HEYER, BILL
Tuscaloosa's Calling...(L)
HIGGINS, BILLY
Bubbling Brown Sugar (L)
HIGGS, TIM
Side by Side by...(MuD)
HILL, RICHARD
Canterbury Tales (M)
HILLIARD, BOB
Hazel Flagg (L)
HINES, EARL 'FATHA'
Bubbling Brown Sugar (M,L)
HIRSCHHORN, ROBERT
I Can't Keep Running...(MuD)
HIRST, GEORGE
A Connecticut Yankee (MuD)
HOCHMAN, LARRY
Do Black Patent...(MuD)
HOFFMAN, STEPHEN
Upstairs at O'Neals' (M)
HOLGATE, DANNY
Bubbling Brown Sugar (M,L,MuD)
Don't Bother Me...(MuD)
HOLIDAY, BILLIE
Bubbling Brown Sugar (L)
HOLMES, JACK
Dime a Dozen (M,L)
Dressed to the Nines (M,L)
HOLMES, RUPERT
The Mystery of Edwin...(M,L)
HOLOFCENER, LARRY
Mr. Wonderful (M,L)
HOLT, WILL
The Me Nobody Knows (L)
Taking My Turn (L)
The World of Kurt Weill (L)
HORWITT, ARNOLD B.
Plain and Fancy (L)
HORWITZ, MURRAY
Upstairs at O'Neals' (L)

LEVISTER, ALONZO
New Faces of 1968 (M)
LEVITT, BARRY
Taking My Turn (MuD)
LEWIS, MICHAEL J.
Cyrano (M)
LINK, PETER
Earl of Ruston (M,L)
King of Hearts (M, MuD)
Salvation (M,L)
LITTAU, JOSEPH
Carmen Jones (MuD)
Carousel (MuD - 1945)
Three Wishes for Jamie (MuD)
LIVINGSTON, JAY
Let It Ride! (M,L)
Oh Captain! (M,L)
LODIN, JEFF
Preppies (MuD)
LOEB, JOHN JACOB
Arabian Nights (M,L)
LOESSER, FRANK
Greenwillow (M,L)
Guys and Dolls (M,L)
How to Succeed in...(M,L)
The Most Happy Fella (M,L)
LOEWE, FREDERICK
Brigadoon (M)
Camelot (M)
Gigi (M)
My Fair Lady (M)
Paint Your Wagon (M)
LOMBARDO, CARMEN
Arabian Nights (M,L)
LONG, KENN
Touch (M,L)
LOPEZ, LILLIAN
Bubbling Brown Sugar (M,L)
LORICK, ROBERT
The Tap Dance Kid (L)
McARTHUR, EDWIN
Show Boat (MuD - 1946)
McCARTHY, JOSEPH
Irene (L)
McCREERY, BUD
Demi-Dozen (M,L)
Dime a Dozen (M,L)
Four Below Strikes Back (M,L)
The Littlest Revue (M,L)
Pieces of Eight (M,L)
Shoestring '57 (M,L)
MacDERMOT, GALT
Dude (M)
Hair (M, MuD - 1968)
Karl Marx Play (M,MuD)
Two Gentlemen of Verona (M)
MacDONALD, HUGH
Cambridge Circus (M, MuD)
McGLOHON, LOONIS
Clues to a Life (L)
McGREGOR, DION
Dressed to the Nines (L)
McHUGH, JIMMY
Jerome Kern Goes to...(L)
Sugar Babies (M)
McWHINNEY, MICHAEL
Below the Belt (L)
Dressed to the Nines (L)
Just for Openers (L)
Mixed Doubles (L)
New Faces of 1968 (L)
MAHONEY, JIM
Shoestring Revue (M)
MALTBY, RICHARD, JR.
Ain't Misbehavin' (L)
Baby (L)
The Sap of Life (L)
Starting Here...(L)
MALVIN, ARTHUR
Sugar Babies (M,L)
MANHEIM, RALPH
The Threepenny Opera (L-'76)
MARKELL, DENNIS
Upstairs at O'Neals' (M,L)
MARKOE, GERALD JAY
Charlotte Sweet (M)
MARKS, DENNIS
Pieces of Eight (L)
MARKS, WALTER
Bajour (M,L)
Four Below Strikes Back (M,L
MARTEL, TOM
Hard Job Being God (M,L)
MARTIN, DAVID
Simply Heavenly (M,MuD)
MARTIN, HUGH
Best Foot Forward (M,L)
High Spirits (M,L)
Look Ma, I'm Dancin'! (M,L)
Make a Wish (M,L)
MARTIN, RANDAL
Festival (L)
MARTIN, RUTH
A Night in Venice (L)
MARTIN, THOMAS
A Night in Venice (L,MuD)
MARVIN, MEL
Tintypes (MuD)
MATLOWSKY, SAMUEL
The Threepenny...(MuD-1954)
MATZ, PETER
No Strings (MuD)
Sail Away (MuD)
MAUCERI, JOHN
Candide (MuD - 1974/1982)
On Your Toes (MuD - 1983)
Song and Dance (MuD)

About the Compiler

RICHARD CHIGLEY LYNCH is Assistant Curator of the Billy Rose Theatre Collection of the New York Public Library. He compiled *Musicals! A Directory of Musical Properties Available for Production* and is a regular contributor to *Show Music*. His articles have also appeared in *Kastlemusick Monthly Bulletin*, *Record Collectors Journal*, and other periodicals in the music and recording field.